EBURY PRESS AND BLUE SALT
ESCAPED

Danish Khan is a journalist and historian living in London. He has been covering the UK and Europe for Times Now, ET Now and *Mumbai Mirror* for a decade. Prior to that, he worked as a journalist in Mumbai. Danish was awarded the Martin Senior scholarship and the Amersi Foundation scholarship at the University of Oxford, where he is also involved in the Global History of Capitalism Project. He has taught history at the University of Oxford and Stanford University.

Ruhi Khan is a London-based independent journalist. She has written on extradition cases for the Wire. She has worked with NDTV and *Mumbai Mirror* in India and been a curator at Twitter UK. Ruhi was a Jefferson Fellow at the East West Center, US, and a recipient of the Mary Morgan Hewitt Award for Women in Journalism. She is an Economic and Social Research Council (ESRC) scholar at the London School of Economics and Political Science and she also edits the Media@LSE Blog.

S. HUSSAIN ZAIDI PRESENTS

TRUE STORIES OF INDIAN
FUGITIVES IN LONDON

ESCAPED

DANISH KHAN & RUHI KHAN

BLUE
SALT

EBURY
PRESS

An imprint of Penguin Random House

EBURY PRESS

USA | Canada | UK | Ireland | Australia
New Zealand | India | South Africa | China

Ebury Press is part of the Penguin Random House group of companies
whose addresses can be found at global.penguinrandomhouse.com

Published by Penguin Random House India Pvt. Ltd.
4th Floor, Capital Tower 1, MG Road,
Gurugram 122 002, Haryana, India

First published in Ebury Press and Blue Salt by Penguin Random House India 2021

Copyright © Danish Khan and Ruhi Khan 2021

All rights reserved

10 9 8 7 6 5 4 3 2

The views and opinions expressed in this book are the authors' own and the
facts are as reported by them which have been verified to the extent possible,
and the publishers are not in any way liable for the same.

ISBN 9780143446095

Typeset in Adobe Caslon Pro by Manipal Technologies Limited, Manipal
Printed at Replika Press Pvt. Ltd, India

This book is sold subject to the condition that it shall not, by way of trade
or otherwise, be lent, resold, hired out, or otherwise circulated without the
publisher's prior consent in any form of binding or cover other than that in
which it is published and without a similar condition including this condition
being imposed on the subsequent purchaser.

www.penguin.co.in

To Ather Khan, for all the love,
and Mobin Khan, for all the strength

CONTENTS

INTRODUCTION

Mumbai, 25 May 2019. The flight was packed. It was a Saturday after all. The seatbelt signs were on. The stewardess, in her iconic beige suit, cream scarf cascading from her bright red hat with a matching berry red smile, was requesting everyone to put their phones and laptops on flight mode.

Last selfies were clicked. Quick goodbye texts were typed. Important emails were sent. Facebook and Instagram were updated. Seat belts were secured. Prayers were whispered.

The Mumbai–Dubai flight would take less than three hours. Many would then take another flight to complete their journey to their destinations with a layover at Dubai airport, often a delight for both shoppers and those simply looking to stretch their legs. On that Saturday, while seasoned fliers were making themselves comfortable, new ones nervously held on to their seats with much anticipation. Everyone was looking forward to a good start to their journey.

The pilot had begun taxiing the aircraft. EK 507 was now on the runway. An instruction video was being played. Passengers were bracing themselves for the take off. Quick prayers were muttered and little hands were held tight in strong palms. Yet the plane, instead of picking up speed, slowly turned and headed back. The perplexed passengers looked out of the window, murmuring their disbelief when the doors abruptly opened. Men walked in and politely escorted an elderly couple from the first class. After this brief interruption, with barely an explanation given for the delay, the crew resumed its routine tasks and the plane took off—all on board but two.

The couple who deboarded was no stranger to travelling. The two were bound for a country they visited often and from where they had returned just a few weeks ago. Yet, the Indian immigration officials had panicked when they were informed that the owner of the troubled debt-ridden airlines Jet Airways, Naresh Goyal and his wife Anita, had checked-in on a London-bound Emirates flight even as news of Jet Airways' financial woes was making headlines. They quickly sprang into action to ensure that the Goyals never left Indian shores.

Goyal's is a rags-to-riches story of a Patiala boy setting out to paint his name in the international skies. Jet Airways was born on 5 May 1993 and over the years grew to own 120 aircraft flying to destinations across the globe. But the man who was considered the king of India's open skies was now unequivocally being blamed for the downfall of India's premier airline as it had accumulated Rs 8000 crore in debt to a consortium of Indian banks led by the State Bank of India (SBI). It had its fleet of aeroplanes grounded and payments to pilots and suppliers were left pending.

While Naresh Goyal had resigned from the company's board in March and left for the UK only to return a few days later, a lookout notice had been issued against him to prevent him from leaving the country again, which the Goyals only discovered when they were deplaned. They challenged this in the Delhi High Court arguing that as no criminal complaint had been registered against them, there should have been no lookout notice against them too. Naresh Goyal expressed his intent to travel to the UK and sought the court's permission to do so. Justice Suresh Kait not just refused to grant him any interim relief but also asked the couple to deposit Rs 18,000 crore as a guarantee if they wished to travel abroad, thus effectively trapping the Goyals in India until Jet Airways cleared all its debts. Now, two years later, the couple have still not managed to set foot outside India.

Not too distant memories of another business tycoon who boarded a flight to London with '300 bags', as claimed by Enforcement Directorate (ED) officials in a Mumbai court, when his airline went bust, were enough to make the authorities spring into pre-emptive action. The public had been outraged with the Bharatiya Janata Party-led government for letting Vijay Mallya escape with the taxpayers' Rs 9000 crore in March 2016. The newly re-elected government of Narendra Modi did not want to take a chance with the Goyals escaping just two days after returning to power with a thumping majority. Jet Airways had shut operations as it was hard-pressed to find a buyer and was in unsurmountable debt after the talks with Etihad crashed. Jet had gone bust. In such a scenario, the Goyals travelling to London had rung alarm bells.

London was the panic button.

London was the escape route.

London was the long tedious court battle.

London was the new refuge.

London was freedom.

London was calling.

In the last few years, the idea that Britain is a haven for those who want to escape the Indian judicial system has firmly entrenched itself in the minds of most. However, it's not a recent trend and as this book explores, many fugitives from India have looked at London as a refuge. Since the early 1990s, which saw fugitive gangster Iqbal Mirchi and musician Nadeem Saifi fight extradition, to the current Vijay Mallya and Nirav Modi extradition cases in the UK courts, India's abysmal record in getting fugitives back from London has caused much consternation in the power corridors of New Delhi.

These high-profile cases which caught the imagination of the larger public helped dislodge the idea of Gulf states as the most favoured destination for those on the run. The UAE and Saudi Arabia have extradited the highest number of fugitives. In 2018, the government declared that India had made over 150 extradition requests with various foreign countries. Between 2002 and 2020, India put forth more than thirty extradition requests to the UK.

In contrast, India has managed to get just two people extradited from the UK since the signing of the extradition treaty between both the countries in 1993. Samirbhai Vinubhai Patel himself consented to his extradition, which means that his case did not come under the scrutiny of the UK's judicial system. Patel was alleged to be involved in the Godhra riots of 2002 and charged with murder, rioting and being a member of an unlawful assembly. He had escaped India when out on bail and moved to the UK. With his consent, he was extradited on 18 October 2016 to face trial in India.

More recently, the successful extradition of bookie Sanjeev Chawla, whose case this book explores in some detail, saw the UK-based businessman sent to India to face charges of match-fixing in the Indo-South Africa series in 2000, which brought into public glare several cricketers from both countries for allegedly manipulating the game of cricket for monetary considerations. Interestingly, no other cricketer, except the late Hansie Cronje, was mentioned as an accused alongside Chawla in the charge sheet by the Indian police. Chawla's case was decided first in his favour in the lower court, then turned around for India in the high court, making it one of the most interesting cases to understand how extradition, just like the game of cricket, is unpredictable until the final ball is bowled and the last man crosses the line.

From the signing of the extradition treaty in 1993 till now, India has made requests for the extradition of over forty individuals, but the sorry figure of just two successes until 2020 is testimony to both India's shoddy paperwork and the susceptibility of the UK to the financial charms of high-net-worth individuals. The series of failures may make it difficult to imagine that in the past, India has managed to effect some dramatic extraditions of very powerful and well-connected individuals before this extradition treaty was signed. However, with bookie Sanjeev Chawla's removal, could India's luck with extradition from the UK have finally taken a positive turn?

This book takes a close look at twelve extradition cases that are intimately tied up with the contours of India's transition as a free country. These twelve cases and the charges that they faced are symptomatic of some of the challenges the country faced as it moved from the Nehruvian era to coalition politics, followed by the country's liberalization to Modinomics.

The last ten years of the Tory government, while witnessing a rhetoric of reducing immigration, did not stop them from devising ingenious means to give citizenship to those ready to park huge funds in the UK. This route is very popular with Russians oligarchs, Chinese nouveau riche and the Gulf Sheikhs, to which can now be added a steady stream of Indian billionaires.

We begin this book with the most (in)famous case of extradition in current times: Vijay Mallya. The comprehensive December 2018 judgment by Westminster Magistrates' Court agreeing to Vijay Mallya's extradition was an emphatic win for India. But it was short-lived. Despite some minor roadblocks for Mallya, the high court allowed his appeal against the district judge's decision. And in doing so, the two-judge bench raised a question mark over the sustainability of the determination of a prima-facie case against Mallya reached by the district court. This euphoria, where Mallya declared that the UK High Court sort of 'vindicated' him, was also short-lived.

In May 2020, the high court upheld the decision of the district magistrate and dismissed Mallya's appeal. Yet, even with a much-sought win through the UK judicial system, India has been unable to take Mallya back to Mumbai. A desperate Mallya has now made a 'confidential' case to the UK Home Office and a decision on that is awaited. An earlier extradition request by India in the case of Surat blast accused Hanif Patel, approved by the courts, has seen the file lying with the Home Office for years. It is now confirmed that Patel will continue to remain in the UK.

But unlike the others, Mallya faces multiple legal battles in the UK courts filed by Indian and foreign banks, Diageo, and other companies whom he has dealt with in the past, either personally or as chairman of United Breweries. Mallya's extradition proceedings have been closely followed by both the Indian and the UK media.

Mallya never failed to turn up for his proceedings accompanied by his partner, the seemingly quiet and impeccably dressed Pinky Lalwani, whom he often looked to for strength during the long-troubled court hearings. His son Siddharth was also by his side on those crucial hearing dates, and Sid never disappointed the shutterbugs. From the angry outburst on the first day of the (main) extradition hearing at Westminster Magistrates' Court to the smug outpour of relief the day the high court read its interim judgment on giving the case a full hearing, Mallya's extradition is nothing but a rich kaleidoscope of arguments that is a study in itself and perhaps a template for future extradition cases.

No doubt, after playing a catch-me-if-you-can game throughout the globe, it was in London that the wanted diamantaire Nirav Modi chose to fight his imminent extradition. **Chapter two** explores the ultra-luxe lifestyle of Modi and his perfect escape plan gone awry as he languishes in a British prison from which no amount of gold can seem to secure his release. His 'billionaire diamantaire' persona has even led inmates to violently attack him in prison, demanding extortion. Yet attempt after attempt to secure bail has only dug him further into suspicion of the courts that he is not just a flight risk but also yields a mafia-esque persona to do harm to those who speak up against him.

Much to the shock of the petite jeweller, he has been subjected to a much harsher judicial diktat since day one in court. The main hearings in Modi's case took place in 2020 and closing arguments in the beginning of January 2021 with a decision expected on 25 February, but going by the timeline in Vijay Mallya's case, it might easily be another couple of years for us to hear the last in his case.

Sanjeev Chawla aka Sanjay, the only successful extradition after a lengthy court battle in recent years, is an important cog in the global syndicate of cricket match-fixing that has already consumed the careers of several top cricketers as its casualties. The district judge found prima-facie evidence against the bookie in the case of fixing the India-South Africa series of March 2000 involving South African skipper Hansie Cronje. Yet, the judge ordered his discharge on the grounds that the Tihar jail in New Delhi where he would be lodged during trial would breach his human rights. UK's Extradition Act 2003 demands that a person in judicial custody anywhere in the world meet with the European Convention on Human Rights' (ECHR) article 3 that demands that 'no one shall be subject to torture or to inhuman degrading treatment or punishment'. Tihar jail was found wanting in ensuring Chawla's human rights.

India submitted further assurances in the appeal in the high court regarding Chawla's accommodation in prison, following which the high court directed the district magistrate to order Chawla's extradition to India. After the home secretary signed that order, Chawla approached the high court to appeal against this judgment. The high court refused to grant him permission to appeal, thus conclusively sealing his fate with a return to India. In **chapter three**, we explore the murky world of cricket match-fixing, Cronje's testimony in South Africa that implicated him and the battle that ensued in UK courts that got India its first huge victory in recent decades, as all attempts by Chawla to remain in the UK proved futile.

The cases of Sanjeev Chawla, Iqbal Mirchi **(chapter 4)**, Nadeem Saifi **(chapter 5)** signify the crude and deep penetration of organized crime—match-fixing, drug cartels, underworld—in the very fabric of India. All three settled in the UK, but except Chawla, Nadeem and Mirchi (who died in 2013) comprehensively frustrated India's effort to get them extradited.

By the late 1970s and early 1980s, the underworld was no longer happy with just photo-ops and behind the scenes involvement in Bollywood. They had adopted a larger-than-life persona, carrying out bloodbath on the streets of Mumbai and thwarting attempts by the police to rein them in.

Iqbal Mirchi, allegedly a close confidante and leading drug lord of the dreaded mafia king Dawood Ibrahim, escaped to the UK when the cops were tightening their noose around him. Mirchi dodged UK laws, even though the US had put him on a list of international kingpins of the illicit drug trade. London provided him with the base to look after the empire of the Dawood gang, though he and his family deny any involvement with the underworld. His sons move between Dubai, London and Mumbai on the groundwork done by Mirchi whose stay in the UK was facilitated largely by the lethargic paperwork lodged by India for his extradition. It seems that Mirchi's success opened the floodgates to a string of failures for India.

The blood-soaked corpse of Gulshan Kumar outside a temple in Mumbai's suburb became the picture of the underworld's ascendancy. Successful music director Nadeem Saifi smartly stayed put in London after the Mumbai Police, perhaps a bit too early, named him an accused in the cassette king's brutal murder. Unlike Mirchi, Nadeem's case ran through the full course of the British judiciary, showing India had developed a better grasp of the requirements of extradition. Yet, Nadeem's trial brought to the attention of lawmakers in the UK how Indian police could fabricate documents to pin murder charges on a seemingly innocent man. Nadeem won substantial legal costs, though he still can't return to India.

In **chapter six**, we look at the case of terror accused Hanif 'Tiger' Patel; his extradition got the green signal from the judiciary, but his file got stuck in the Home Office based on representations that he would not get a fair trial in India and will be subject to inhuman treatment in the jails. Patel is accused of exploding two bombs in Surat in January and April 1993. He jumped bail and escaped to the UK in 1996 where he started life anew as a grocer.

He was arrested in February 2010 from Bolton on India's request, but a decade later, and despite defeat in the courts, Patel remains a free man in the UK. Since April 2014, successive home secretaries did not sign on the removal papers, despite the high court ruling against him in April 2013. Patel, like Chawla, was funded by the British taxpayers in the legal fight against extradition mounted by India. Yet both Chawla and Patel's cases moved through the gambit of the British judicial system for many years. The British taxpayers have footed more than Rs 2 crore in legal bills for Patel, causing outrage in the British tabloids. For the longest time, Patel's case seemed far from meeting its conclusion due to complications with his status as a political refugee and other more specific concerns regarding the case in India. The Home Office, based on fresh evidence, has decided to bar Patel's extradition.

Investigative agencies have continued to make blunders with subsequent cases that came up in the UK. One such huge blunder led to the soft acquittal of Raymond Varley, an accused in a massive child abuse scandal in Goa. Varley, a British national, who changed names and appearances to mask his identity and deeds, wriggled out of his extradition case, claiming to suffer from dementia. UK courts could not in good conscience send a man who was so ill to stand trial in India. India lost the case as the Crown Prosecution Service (CPS) did not make an application to get Varley examined independently, thus letting his assertions go (medically) unchallenged.

One had to see the passion and determination of activists in India and the UK who followed Varley's case to understand the enormity of his crimes. The scourge of child sex tourism in India and particularly in Goa was the by-product of the rampant poverty and increased international connectivity. In **chapter seven**, we look at how Varley, who was convicted in Britain for child sexual offences even before he was charged with a similar offence in India, managed to escape the long arm of the law by citing an illness that went unchallenged. Though India filed an appeal later, seeking to have Varley examined by an independent medical expert, the high court, while agreeing that he had a valid case to answer, refused by saying it was too late, thus setting Varley free.

Varley was not the only one who set out to exploit India's children. The case of Arti Dhir and Kaval Raijada is a prime example of the depth of depravity to which a seemingly normal couple can leap, driven by greed and easy money. They face charges of adopting an orphan in Gujarat only to get him killed in order to pocket the insurance money. The cruelty of intention and the brutality of the murder—that the police investigations unravel—are disguised by the poker face that Dhir showcases during the hearings and the outrage her beau displays on being confronted by the press. As the spotlight shines on the high profile cases of corruption and national security that India is pursuing extradition for, this case has relatively escaped the full glare of the Indian media. In **chapter eight,** we bring every detail into light.

No questions were asked of the authorities when a delayed assurance was solely responsible for letting the duo escape the law. The assurance required from New Delhi to re-examine a crucial law in Gujarat affecting those accused of double murder reached the Westminster Magistrates' Court the same day as the judge was to pronounce her judgment and was therefore not taken into consideration.

India challenged their discharge in the high court but failed to secure their extradition. Delays on India's part to provide the requisite assurances by the Gujarat government regarding consideration of parole for the duo meant that the high court was left with no alternative but to set the alleged murderers free. Interestingly, the senior district judge in her ruling remarked that the Scotland Yard could also possibly proceed against the couple as the planning and the transfer of money to carry out the murder was done from England.

A sharp indictment of India's poor and incomplete paperwork came in the sensational case of naval war room leak accused Ravi Shankaran. A former naval officer, Shankaran allegedly used an alias, Vic Branson, to leak sensitive and crucial security information to seal commercial contracts for his business that dealt with procuring naval supplies. The playboy middleman escaped to the UK even as the investigating officers were unravelling the plethora of disclosures the top-secret documents contained.

The case, as **chapter nine** shows, shook the fabric of the Indian armed forces and put a spotlight on the lucrative business of defence contracts and the dangerous extent one would go to secure them. Though India won in the trial court, Sir Brian Levenson, who delivered the leading judgment, upon appeal in the high court, was uncharacteristically sharp in his observations of the Central Bureau of Investigation's (CBI) lack of efforts. The court was aware of the seriousness of the allegations against Shankaran, but in the end, the man who risked India's security had the last laugh.

The next three cases we explore in this book took place before the 1993 India–UK extradition treaty was ratified. All three cases in the three decades following India's Independence uniquely intertwine the colonial legacy with the coming-of-age of the young Indian judiciary and law enforcement agencies as India pursued the extradition cases in the UK courts.

In **chapter ten**, we bring a much-used Bollywood script into the courtrooms of London. Our next fugitive, Manu Narang, not just has his name quite synonymous with Bollywood baddies, but he was also in Bollywood films, albeit only those financed by him. Manu Narang and his two brothers, Om and Rama, completed the Narang trio who owned Bombay's iconic Ambassador Hotel on the Marine Drive seafront with gorgeous views of the glistening shore and blue expansive waters. Their family bungalow in Bandra had a shimmering swimming pool with glass flooring providing an unhindered view from the room under it, an envy of most Bombay socialites who often partied at their suburban abode.

The Narang brothers were alleged to be top smugglers of their time with an unparalleled, well-oiled network that ensured a steady supply of exquisite idols and antiques in the lucrative art markets of New York, London and Paris. Manu and Om were arrested in 1976 after the Scotland Yard recovered two ancient sandstone pillars from a warehouse in London. The most famous *moorti chors* (idol thieves) were also successfully extradited despite their last-minute attempt to give their Delhi flight a miss. It is interesting that the next generation of Narangs have managed to rechristen themselves as successful hoteliers and are now a toast of page 3 parties.

Dharma Jayanti Teja might be a forgotten name today but in the 1960s, he emerged as the face of young, energetic, self-made capitalists without the backing of rich parents. The suave and well-educated Teja made the most of the surprising flexibility offered to him by Nehruvian socialism. The holes of corruption, fraud and misappropriation of funds that sunk his shipping empire exposed the political elites.

Extradition proceedings were launched against Teja, first in the US from where he again escaped, and then in the UK, where he was arrested at Heathrow airport. In **chapter eleven**, we show how his case had an international echo, as he had a Costa Rican diplomatic passport and no less than the President of Costa Rica intervened on his behalf, but deft handling by India and efficient follow-ups by the Indian High Commission in London tilted the case against him. One wonders if Teja lent his name to the sophisticated and well-groomed villain of Bollywood, essayed most memorably by Ajit. Teja's extradition is no less dramatic than a gripping Bollywood flick.

In **chapter twelve**, we look at the case of Mubarak Ali Ahmed, a Hyderabadi industrialist, impeccably dressed in rich suits in the finest cashmere, who ran away to Pakistan in 1950 to escape multiple cases of fraud and cheating filed against him in Bombay. Picked up by the Scotland Yard from a posh London hotel at the request of India, he was brought back in 1952 after an intense legal battle amidst stout opposition from Pakistan. Ahmed's extradition was not only a statement of the respect British courts had towards India's legal system but was also a major public relations coup for New Delhi.

While every chapter details the alleged crime and the drama that took place in the British courts, it is important to briefly understand how the process of extradition unfolds when India makes an extradition request to the UK.

The Extradition Act 2003 provides the legal basis for all extradition proceedings from the UK. India belongs to category 2, type B countries. The UK has a bilateral extradition agreement and an anti money laundering agreement with India. The process begins with India making an extradition request to the United Kingdom Central Authority (UKCA) at the Home Office. A valid request made by an appropriate authority on behalf of the Indian government will show the purpose of prosecuting the requested person on the basis of an allegation or conviction of an offence in India. If the basic criteria are satisfactory, the request is certified by the secretary of state and forwarded to the judiciary.

The Westminster Magistrates' Court then issues a warrant after which the requested person is arrested and produced in court. This warrant mandates a quick arrest and extradition of suspects wanted by the requesting state. The conditions that the requesting state has to meet at this stage are fairly basic, and mutual trust serves as the most important criteria to trigger a degree of automatic judicial proceedings without any political interference. The requested person is then produced at Westminster Magistrates' Court in London, where all extradition proceedings in England and Wales are conducted. The Extradition Unit, as part of the International Justice and Organised Crime Division (IJOCD) in the CPS, represents India in the UK courts. It is funded by UK taxpayers.

A decision of the Westminster Court can be challenged in the Royal Courts of Justice in London. This is where the high court decides whether to give permission to appeal against the district judge's decision. Extradition cases from India have never made it to the UK Supreme Court as the rare cases that go to the apex court need to show the widest public interest or constitutional importance. As it is an appeals court, it cannot hear a case until a relevant order of appeal has been made in the high court.

This process is explored in some detail in the twelve cases we discuss in this book. The last chapter ties the legal manoeuvres, hurdles and observations together with the highlights and outcomes of some other extradition cases, including those of south India's takeover tycoon Palaniappan Rajarathinam, the kidnapping

Kapoor siblings Rajesh and Seema, and the alleged bank fraudsters turned shopkeepers husband–wife duo, Jatinder and Asha Rani Angurala.

The last chapter also gives a short overview of the laws and treaties that have guided extradition between India and the UK since Independence. To better understand the process of extradition, which has gained a lot of traction in recent years, we have studied in much detail many extradition cases, have had long interviews with experts and pored over case laws and reports to understand the principles underlying the process. What was the background to the signing up of the extradition treaty between India and UK in 1992? Could the string of current failures to effect extradition from the UK be related to the now outdated objective that the 1993 treaty set to achieve? How will the successful extradition of Sanjeev Chawla impact other extradition cases? Is this the much-needed turning point for the India–UK extradition relationship?

This book hopes to thus serve as a crucial text to better understand the outcomes and the various stages through which the cases passed during their extradition proceedings. Several of the recent cases have been covered by us in our role as journalists, offering us a much closer look and the opportunity to attend the court proceedings and interact with a cross-section of solicitors and barristers, the accused, witnesses and experts. Many of these cases are live and their fate may change over time.

We have studied extradition cases of other countries and in other jurisdictions to compare and contrast the process, which has also provided valuable insights. These twelve cases were chosen as much for the significance of the allegations against them as for the interesting arguments raised during their hearings and the observations made in their judgments that we believe are crucial to understanding why they chose England to escape to and the process of extradition from the UK.

We have included a historical view from the days of a young independent India slowly emerging from its colonial past and working to convince the Queen's country to trust and respect its young judiciary during those early extradition requests to a more confident India using its sovereign assurances to override the concerns of the UK courts. Observations made by magistrates in courtroom and in their judgments throw light on these fragile bonds between the two nations and their interesting yet emerging relationship.

This book has gained immensely from the records accessed at the National Archives, UK, British Library, London Metropolitan Archives, House of Lord reports, Hansard, ProQuest newspapers, several books and news articles. It has also been enriched with the many useful and thought-provoking insights provided through many chats with expert witnesses, solicitors and barristers in courtrooms and chambers of London.

Our deepest gratitude to Anand Doobay for indulging our many queries throughout the writing of this book and giving us his invaluable guidance in understanding the finer points of law. This was, of course, done on the condition that we do not discuss the cases he is currently representing. We extend our thanks to Edward Fitzgerald QC, Mark Summers QC, and Toby Cadman for all their help.

For all the wit, humour and camaraderie during the tediously long court proceedings, we must thank our merry band of court reporters: Aditi Khanna, Gagan Sabarwal, Jonathan Gilbert, Karma Wangdi, Loveena Tandon, Mandy Clark, Nabanita Sircar, Naomi Canton, Poonam Joshi, Prasun Sonwalkar, Radhika Iyer, Rupanjana Dutta, Sanjay Suri and Vidya Ram.

We thank S. Hussain Zaidi, who has been instrumental in germinating the idea behind this book and has been a constant source of motivation, and Milee Ashwarya, editor-in-chief, Ebury Publishing, Penguin Random House India, for this wonderful opportunity and for many delightful chats. To our wonderful team of editors—Saksham Garg, Saloni Mital and Chanpreet Khurana—who have edited this book with an hawk's eye, and have patiently worked with us as we updated the cases until the very end. We owe them much. We are much thankful to Akangksha Sarmah for designing the cover of this book and to Sonjuhi Negi and Shruti Katoch, for introducing this book to its reader in interesting and innovative ways.

Some of these cases often became breaking news on the Times Network—Times Now, ET Now and Mirror Now—and for this we are grateful to Rahul Shivshankar, Hector Kenneth, Akash Goswami and Ashwin Raj. We also thank Sidharth Bhatia and Anuj Srivas of the Wire for carrying detailed news reports on some of these extradition cases. Special thanks to Meenal Baghel for creating space in *Mumbai Mirror* for the daily coverage of extradition cases, even though the copies, after a full day's hearing, could only reach the copy editors precariously close to the press deadline. Meenal has been a dear mentor, and we have learnt much from her. It was in the *Mumbai Mirror* newsroom that our first collaborative work began in the mid-2000s and we have never looked back.

Since this book is an extension of our passion for journalism, we must make a special mention of the late Vijay Dutt, former resident editor, *Hindustan Times* in London and Sachin Kalbag, executive editor at *Hindustan Times*, Mumbai, for giving our first breaks in journalism. We also thank Naved Masood for sharing his insights and providing a deeper contextual background to some of the cases we have explored.

The support of our family—from our parents to our little girls, who have given us the space and time to undertake this mammoth project—has been invaluable. Lastly, this project would not have been possible without the many long discussions and intense deliberations that became a continuous feature during our writing of this book. This book is an attempt to make the complex extradition cases in the UK courts accessible to wider demographics. As we delved deeper into our research, we realized what a Herculean task this is, and have made every effort possible to do justice to this project.

1

KING OF BAD DEBTS

On 18 December 2015, the sky in Goa erupted with a million sparkles. Did the New Year celebrations come early in the party capital of India? Of course not.

The King of Good Times, liquor baron Vijay Mallya, was celebrating his sixtieth birthday. Four hundred guests comprising the rich and famous, the super-rich and the infamous, politicians and actors, sport stars and fashionistas, singers and entrepreneurs and, of course, top models, flocked to the palatial Kingfisher villa on Candolim beach, often compared to Elvis Presley's Graceland or Hugh Hefner's Playboy Mansion.

'It's bigger than most hotels. It's cooler than any house. It's James Bond, it's Playboy Mansion, it's the land of plenty in white concrete and glass,' described cricketer Chris Gayle in his biography *Six Machine: I Don't Like Cricket . . . I Love It.* The 12,350 square feet villa hosted a majority of the guests for his birthday bash with the rest staying at the ultra-luxe Taj Holiday Village Resort & Spa, from where one could walk along a beautiful private stretch of the sun-kissed beach to get to Mallya's abode. Star performers for the evening included hugely expensive pop sensation Enrique Iglesias who was flown in especially to take everyone's breath away with his vocals and Bollywood's Sonu Nigam who sang the ever-popular Hindi birthday song: *Tum jiyo hazaaron saal . . . saal ke din ho pachaas hazaar* (May you live for thousands of years . . . and every year have 50,000 days).

The bash cost Mallya a whopping $2 million or Rs 14 crore. This even when he had avoided paying the employees of his defunct Kingfisher Airlines their salaries and dues for many months citing financial troubles. The irony of this was not lost. 'We are still not able to understand what you meant when you said "I don't have money to pay your salaries",' the disgruntled employees wrote to their boss.

In fact, Mallya was consistently warned to avoid pomp and banter in India and perhaps have a slightly muted celebration outside the country. But Mallya being Mallya had to live his life king-size. Perhaps he knew it was his final celebration in India and wanted to go out with a bang or he simply couldn't resist doing what he does best—throwing a grand party. Whatever Mallya's reasons for hosting the extravagant party, it backfired and earned him public ire. 'If you flaunt your birthday bashes even while owing the system a lot of money, it does seem to suggest to the public that you don't care. I think that is the wrong message to send,' Raghuram Rajan, the governor of the Reserve Bank of India (RBI), said.

Mallya was in trouble. His prized Kingfisher Airlines that he had launched with much fanfare when his son Siddharth turned eighteen was defunct since 2012. He owed the banks Rs 9000 crore and had been declared a wilful defaulter. The taxpayers were getting angry. The politicians were feeling the pressure. The press had few nice things to say about him.

But for those three days in December, Mallya was determined not to let anything upset him as he laughed and danced with his guests. 'My biggest assets are my friends and they are all here tonight,' said a beaming Mallya to the crowd wishing him a happy birthday.

As Mallya rose to success, so did his circle of friends. He was hardly ever found alone, always flanked by celebrities and gorgeous models. Mallya had a larger-than-life persona and an even larger appetite to have fun. The plethora of models who thronged Mallya often featured in the annual Kingfisher swimsuit calendar, shot by the ace photographer Atul Kasbekar in some of the most exotic locations in the world. Being featured in the Kingfisher calendar is a huge accomplishment for any model, young and old; Indian or international.

The calendar had been a regular feature since its inception in 2003. The 2020 calendar, shot in South Africa, featured top models including Pooja Chopra, Aditi Arya, Aishwarya Sushmita and Zoya Afroz. Bollywood superstars like Deepika Padukone, Katrina Kaif, Nargis Fakhri, Lisa Haydon, Esha Gupta, Yana Gupta, Tena Desae, Preeti Desai and Saiyami Kher have at one time or another been on the Kingfisher calendar. Even as the world was grappling with the COVID-19 pandemic and most global cities were under some form of lockdown, Kasbekar admitted that the UB Group was keen to continue its eighteen-year-old legacy in 2021 and was looking for a location with no quarantine or flight issues. They settled to shoot the 2021 Kingfisher calendar in Kerala. Popularly called 'God's own country', it provided some stunning backdrops of the meandering backwaters, emerald vegetation and golden skies.

Many remember the 2007 calendar, shot in the French Riviera on Mallya's swanky private yacht, his latest acquisition from the Emir of Qatar for $110 million. Formerly known as *Al Mirab*, the yacht boasted a state-of-the-art satellite navigation system and radar communication and came with sixteen cabins spread over three floors, a helipad and a garage for two Mercedes.

Mallya christened it the *Indian Empress* and lived like a king on it. His cabin came with not just a private deck that provided the most gorgeous view of the seas but also a jacuzzi and a masseur on hand. His enormous bedroom and sitting space along with the main entertaining rooms on the yacht were decorated with the finest artwork including a Husain, Renoir and Chagall.

Prior to this, he owned the 181-foot yacht *Indian Princess*, which he sold when he purchased the *Empress*. He also owned the 165-foot *Indian Achiever*, often docked in the Upper New York Bay, his pad to entertain his American contacts. In late 1995, Mallya bought a World War-weary yacht built in 1906 and gifted by Welsh actor Richard Burton to his wife Elizabeth Taylor, a very popular British-American actor, in 1967. The two met and fell in love on the sets of the 1963 film *Cleopatra*. The yacht made headlines when Burton presented his gorgeous wife a giant 69.4 carat Cartier diamond to express his deepest love. The couple called the yacht the *Kalizma* after their kids Kate, Liza and Maria. The *Kalizma* had seen everything from war to eternal love, but had yet more to experience.

It became the hottest party venue when it changed hands once again. The flamboyant Mallya spent $3 million to restore it in Edwardian style and deck it up ostentatiously with artwork from Pablo Picasso to Salvador Dali and from M.F. Husain to Anjolie Ela Menon. When he is not on board, all his yachts are available for hire which helps with their upkeep. While Mallya's love for yachts cannot be disputed, he admits the *Empress* was his favourite.

For almost a month in 2006, Mallya, along with his top bikini models whom he liked to call 'The Kingfisher Girls', enjoyed the glorious sun and shutterbugs from Cannes to Monte Carlo on the *Indian Empress*. 'When Kingfisher operates, it operates in style and we all know it,' said Mallya, in a cherry red Kingfisher vest, white shorts and a bright yellow logo cap, flanked by three models, in a video about the making of the calendar. 'Shooting the calendar is an event in itself. Not many calendars are shot with so much fun,' said the party king, shaking a leg on the beach at St Tropez.

When the Indian Premier League (IPL) was launched combining two of India's greatest obsessions—cricket and Bollywood, Mallya, knowing the effect of this potent mix, jumped right in. So when the influential Board of Control for Cricket in India (BCCI) announced its decision to launch franchise-based teams that would compete in Twenty20 cricket annually, Mallya was quick to bid in the inaugural auction of the IPL in January 2008. Thus, the Royal Challengers Bangalore (RCB) was purchased for $111.6 million (Rs 476 crore) by Mallya's United Spirits Limited. Mallya's personal fortune was around $1.2 billion in 2008, so buying the most expensive IPL franchise of the inaugural edition was not too steep for the seventh richest man in India.

Rahul Dravid was the captain of RCB which included cricketing legends like Anil Kumble, Zaheer Khan, Jacques Kallis, Mark Boucher, Cameron White, Misbah-ul-Haq and Virat Kohli. 'Dravid asked me if I wanted a performing team or a glamorous team, and I opted for the first,' Mallya confessed. He, however, added the glam quotient by hiring the White Mischief girls from the famous Washington Redskins cheerleading team. Soon the girls had their own fan following in India and became the most sought-after cheering squad during IPL matches.

Many of the IPL franchise owners were celebrities and Bollywood superstars like Shah Rukh Khan and Juhi Chawla via husband Jay Mehta for Kolkata Knight Riders; the bubbly actor Preity Zinta along with businessman and ex-boyfriend Ness Wadia for Punjab Kings IX; the winner of *Celebrity Big Brother* and Bollywood diva Shilpa Shetty, along with her UK-based industrialist husband Raj Kundra for Rajasthan Royals and the equally popular Nita Ambani, celebrity wife of the richest man in India, Mukesh Ambani for Mumbai Indians. Vijay Mallya fit right in with his Royal Challengers and his flamboyant array of pretty faces—both actors and models—who accompanied him to these matches and after-parties. While the ownership of some IPL teams has changed over the years, these celebrities still remain as icons in IPL ownership history.

When Mallya bought English cricketer Kevin Pietersen at the IPL auction in 2009 for $1.55 million, the British newspaper *The Telegraph* (6 February 2009) found them a perfect match: 'With a bloodstock farm and a fleet of vintage cars, Mallya knows how to spend his money and the parties he hosts on his yacht, the Indian Empress, are legendary in India. KP should fit right in to the Mallya world.'

Around this time, there were rumours abound that the gorgeous Bollywood newbie Deepika Padukone was dating Mallya's son Siddharth, often called Sid, while she was brand ambassador for RCB. Deepika's first film *Om Shanti Om* had paired her opposite Shah Rukh Khan and she was an instant success and the paparazzi followed her everywhere. Sid and Deepika became the talk of tinsel town when they were spotted in red and gold RCB jerseys cheering at every IPL match and dancing at every party Mallya hosted. RCB was the team to watch as much for what happened on the pitch as it was for what took place in the stands. The mystery surrounding Sid and Deepika ensured that the newspapers were kept busy and Sid became a star, albeit briefly, and was no longer just a star kid.

In 2018, Deepika married her Bollywood sweetheart Ranveer Singh at a private ceremony at Lake Como in Italy. Siddharth lives in Los Angeles and is trying his hand at acting, making his film debut in *Brahman Naman*, an adult comedy by Qaushiq Mukherjee, released on Netflix worldwide in 2016, and has launched his own production company. He was rumoured to be dating *Slumdog Millionaire* actress Freida Pinto though Pinto said they were just 'good friends'. Just like his father, Sid enjoys being spotted with pretty faces, often those that are easily recognizable in a crowd.

Vijay Mallya's passion for fast cars often led him to racing circuits across the world. He has been a long-time sponsor of Formula One teams like the Benetton F1 team and has invested heavily towards the establishment of the McDowell Grand Prix in India. In 2007, Mallya sponsored the Toyota team at the Monaco Grand Prix and used the occasion to flaunt his newly acquired yacht *Indian Empress* by hosting a massive gala onboard that included in its guest list the then CEO of Formula One, Bernie Ecclestone, Tadashi Yamashina of the Toyota Racing Formula One team and Flavio Briatore of Renault Formula One. They were joined by American rapper Jay-Z and Irish singer-musician Bono.

Over some of the finest and most expensive spirits and daintily elegant canapés, Ecclestone told Mallya that the small racing team Spyker was in trouble and looking for a buyer. Mallya jumped at the opportunity and after some intense negotiations, a consortium consisting of Mallya (with 75 per cent shares) and Spyker F1 shareholder Michiel Mol bought the team for $129 million. Mallya was now the owner of his very own Formula One racing team. 'I feel proud that an Indian has put its flag on the F1 circuit,' said

Mallya, who called his racing team 'Force India' and displayed the saffron, white and green of the Indian tricolour in the team's logo.

He soon roped in Shah Rukh Khan as a brand ambassador to get the Indian crowd hooked on to F1 racing. 'India has arrived,' the Bollywood superstar declared to the F1 fans, motivating them to be the 'force behind Force India'. Mallya unveiled the team's new Ferrari car called VJM01 (Vijay Mallya One) at the iconic Gateway of India at a star-studded event that was attended by Bollywood actors Shilpa Shetty and her sister Shamita Shetty, Lara Dutta and Sameera Reddy. A picture of him flanked by two of these gorgeous women on either side made all the newspapers the next day.

But Vijay Mallya's true moment to shine came when his team won second place in the 2009 Belgium Grand Prix and Mallya accompanied his winning driver, the Italian Giancarlo Fisichella who stood on the podium to take the silver medal. An ecstatic Mallya told his fans that Force India had delivered on its promise to bag a medal a year ahead of the deadline, making this the 'most memorable day of his Formula One career'.

The following year, Fisichella left Force India and joined his dream team Ferrari, but was full of gratitude to Mallya. 'It is true that it has always been an ambition to do this, and for Vijay to have allowed it to become a reality is very generous,' said an emotional Fisichella. Thus Mallya became a boss who was much loved on the F1 circuit.

He, in turn, deeply loved Force India. In 2011, mounting losses forced Mallya to let Sahara Group chairman Subrata Roy buy a 42.5 per cent share in the company for $100 million. But Force India could not survive long with over 450 creditors demanding a return of a total of $37.4 million with a mere $3,15,000 left in its bank. A heartbroken Mallya resigned from being the director in May 2018 and his son stepped in that position. A few months later, just before the Hungarian Grand Prix, his much-loved racing team went into administration. A consortium led by Canadian billionaire Lawrence Stroll, father of racing driver Lance Stroll,

now owns Force India but they have changed its name to Racing
Point.

Since Mallya bought the team in 2008, its performance steadily
improved with the team finishing sixth in 2017, six points higher
than a decade ago. Yet mounting costs during this period sent its
finances on a downward spiral and with it the hope of every member
on the team. Force India is no more. VJM11 was its last car.

* * *

Mallya's origins and growth and subsequently his downfall are
intrinsically linked to the fortunes of his companies. To understand
the many layers of Vijay Mallya's personality, it is imperative to
understand the history and the philosophy of the UB Group.

UBL was born in the mid-nineteenth century when Castle
Brewery was established in south India to supply the Nilgiri Hill
Country plantations. By 1885, Bangalore Brewery company was
set up to supply to British troops based in Bangalore, and was
followed by the British Brewery company in Madras in 1902.
A Scotsman Thomas Leishman consolidated these companies and
United Brewery Limited (UBL) was born. During colonial rule,
the English troops drank beer that was imported from England
but the long voyage meant that the beer was often not the best in
taste and texture. Leishman began supplying barrels of beer to the
English troops after a hot day and it soon became their favourite.
Thus the fortunes of UBL began to grow.

Meanwhile, in the east Indian town of Dhaka in 1924,
Lieutenant Colonel Bantwal Ganpati Mallya (BG Mallya) was
celebrating the birth of his third child whom he fondly named
Vittal. The affluent parents sent their children to prestigious
educational institutes like The Doon School in Dehradun followed
by Presidency College in Kolkata, where Vittal followed his father's
penchant for science and completed his graduation. He then took
what could now be constituted as a 'gap year', to travel to Latin
America where new structuralist ideas on economic theory and

development were taking root. Armed with more knowledge and understanding of the real world, Vittal joined UBL in Kolkata in 1952 but eventually moved to Bangalore a few years later.

Vittal married Lalitha and had a son Vijay. He wanted his son to someday take over UBL, but also instilled in him a discipline for hard work and taught him that there were no free lunches. At eleven, Vijay returned to Kolkata with his mother Lalitha and joined La Martiniere for Boys school followed by St Xavier's College. He got a degree in commerce followed by a master's in business administration (MBA). He then began working at UBL's sales and marketing division in Bihar and Uttar Pradesh. After that, he moved to the United States in 1977 to work for a UBL subsidiary company called American Hoechst and then to the United Kingdom to work for Berger Jenson & Nicholson. He returned to India in 1980 to join his father.

His first successful suggestion was to relaunch the Kingfisher lager brand, established in 1857, with a colourful logo and a fun lifestyle image. And thus was born the new and improved Kingfisher brand: *'The legacy of brewing, excitement, serious, fun and frolic, the camaraderie of youthful flamboyance—that's what it takes to be the king of good times—Kingfisher'.*

In 1983, when he took over as the chairman of UB Group after his father's sudden demise, many thought that with him at the helm, this would be the end of the century-old company. A decade later, he had increased sales almost ten times and taken the group to the number four position globally.

In 1988, he bought Berger paints and sold it for a profit a few years later. In 2005, he acquired the liquor manufacturer Shaw Wallace for $300 million and two years later, he bought Scottish whiskey giant Whyte and Mackay for $1.2 billion. Mallya took UB Group to heights few had anticipated, thus earning him a place as a successful case study in management books and an honorary doctorate of philosophy (PhD) in business administration by the California Southern University in Irvine. He was also nominated as a Global Leader for Tomorrow by the World Economic Forum and has been awarded the 'Legion of Honor', the highest civilian award of France.

Shaw Wallace's owner Manu Chhabria, who was also the founder of Dubai-based Jumbo Group, had rebuffed the young UB Group leader on several occasions, making him a tough challenge for Mallya. After Chhabria's death, his widow did not hesitate to sell the company to Mallya, which took the UB Group to the position of the third-largest spirit company in the world. The cherry on top was Chhabria's Wallace House headquarters, which once belonged to the family of the Mysore king Tipu Sultan, and now belonged to Mallya.

A huge fan of the 'Tiger of Mysore', Mallya spent $2 million to buy Tipu's sword and other armour at Sotheby's auctions in London. Mallya claimed that he wanted to open a museum in Bangalore dedicated to the fierce ruler of south India. He even brandished the historical sword in the Karnataka assembly in 2004 when he led the Janata Party into elections. He lost all seats. In 2016, he admitted that he gave the sword away as it brought him bad luck. He refuses to give any more details.

In 2009, Mallya also spent $1.8 million to get Mahatma Gandhi's personal items including his iconic round-rimmed spectacles, leather sandals, silver pocket-watch, and brass plate and bowl at an auction in New York. Tony Bedi, who was bidding on Mallya's behalf until the hammer fell at sixty times the original estimate of £30,000, grandly announced that Mallya 'was bidding for the country' after India unsuccessfully tried to stop that auction and repatriate Gandhi's items to his homeland. Mallya was hailed a patriotic hero.

Mallya met Samira Tyabjee, an air hostess on an Air India flight. They were attracted to each other instantly, exchanged contacts and dated a little before they got married in 1986. A month later, they moved to London to look after the UB Group's business interests in Europe. Their son Siddharth was born in 1987, and five years later, the two got divorced. Siddharth grew up in London.

In 1993, Mallya married his Bangalore neighbour Rekha and they have two daughters, Leana and Tanya, who live with their mother in San Francisco. Mallya has also adopted Laila, Rekha's daughter from her earlier marriage, who is now married and runs her own business. Mallya and Rekha separated a few years later. Sid was inducted into the UB Group board at the age of eighteen.

Today Pinky Lalwani, a former Kingfisher air hostess, and Mallya's partner for many years, is his only constant companion in London. The demure Lalwani lost her cool just once when a male reporter tried to indulge in some friendly banter. She prefers to remain away from the media glare but has never failed to accompany Mallya to his hearings. Rumour has it that the two got married in 2019, though they refuse to confirm it. But anyone who has seen the couple together would not fail to spot the love and devotion they share. Lalwani has, no doubt, been the strongest pillar of support to Mallya during these most trying times.

* * *

'We are not entering the business of transportation, but we are going to be in the aviation hospitality business,' Vijay Mallya announced in the boardroom as he laid the plans for Project Thunder to launch his airline, Kingfisher.

Project Thunder was intended to shake the world into recognizing India's Richard Branson. It was Mallya's most ambitious gamble. From spirits and sports to airlines, few understand what prompted Mallya to take such a huge risk. Mallya, however, was always confident. 'We are going to create a great airline brand,' he would say as he handpicked his own crew.

Kingfisher Airlines (KFA) was going to represent Mallya in every way. It was glamorous and luxurious. His crew wore bright red miniskirts with matching high heels as uniforms; they were gorgeous models, young and polite. His planes were shiny new, spacious, served meals, had in-flight entertainment and even offered first class. While no liquor could be served on the flight,

Mallya offered a free supply in his first class lounges. Of course, as a member of the Rajya Sabha (upper house) in Parliament and on the standing committee for civil aviation, Mallya was lobbying to get that rule changed.

Upgrade vouchers were used to lure loyal passengers of other airlines to fly Kingfisher. It was all about 'Fly the Good Times'. In fact, the very first announcement in the aircraft would be of Mallya on the mini screens saying: 'I have instructed my staff to treat you as a guest in my own home. If you miss anything, contact me personally.'

The airline was launched on 7 May 2005. The Air India hangar in Mumbai was lit up with Bollywood stars and other glitterati on the red carpet but not even the laser show was as bright as Mallya's grin. He grandly announced to one and all that he would be creating India's largest airline. This before even the first Mumbai to Bangalore flight took off.

At the 2005 Paris Air Show, Mallya put up a $3 billion shopping list to Airbus that included five A380 super-jumbos along with five each of A330s and A350s. Two years later, he added another $7 billion for fifty more aircraft. KFA also became the official partner of the Toyota F1 racing team.

KFA won several awards and was valued by Grant Thornton at Rs 4100 crore in 2012-13, which later was criticized for over-valuing the brand and was probed by the Serious Fraud Investigation Office. When Mallya entered the aviation industry, there was only Captain G.R. Gopinath's Air Deccan as a low-cost airline. SpiceJet, Go Air, IndiGo, Indus Air and Air One were planning to enter the airspace soon after. The aviation ministry predicted that the number of air passengers would rise to 50 million in the next five years. Mallya wanted to capitalize on this as fast as possible. Instead of waiting for the mandatory five years for any airline to begin international air travel, Mallya decided to bid for Air Sahara in 2006 but lost to Jet Airways that then rebranded it as Jet Lite. The following year, Mallya bought Gopinath's bleeding Air Deccan—and Kingfisher Red was born.

Another lavish party was thrown in the Air India hangar, several celebrities and business heads attended, and the promise to become the largest airline was repeated. With Air Deccan's acquisition, Mallya could now fly international. So as soon as the permit was secured, Mallya launched Kingfisher's first international flight from Bengaluru to London in September 2008. Domestically, KFA was carrying 10.9 million passengers every year through 412 flights daily with a fleet of seventy-seven aircraft. KFA received several awards including the 5-Star Airline status by Skytrax.

In 2009, KFA had a market share of 22.9 per cent with over 11 million passengers and was no doubt the largest passenger carrier in India. The airline had reached its zenith—and could only now fall. Shareholders of KFA were getting impatient as they were yet to receive their first dividend. The balance sheet showed continued losses even in 2010. In the first year, the losses were over $40 million but KFA had captured 9 per cent of the aviation market. The recession had hit the world in 2008 and affected air travel numbers, airport charges and fuel costs.

Mallya, who also owned a small fleet of his own private jets including a Hawker, a Gulfstream, an Airbus A310 and a Boeing 727, blamed it on over-taxation of fuel and the government's undue demand to buy fuel from them at a higher price than commercial sellers. Mallya also invested heavily in state-of-the-art technology like Autoland systems capable of executing take-offs and landing in heavy fog thus making KFA flights the first flights in India to operate in low-visibility conditions. Mallya had also contemplated floating an initial public offering (IPO) in 2006 and raising finances through the public but then decided not to go ahead with it. By 2010, it was too late without a restructuring of its debt.

So in November-December 2010, KFA worked with a consortium of banks led by the SBI to restructure its debt. The Rs 8000 crore debt restructure included converting Rs 1355 crore of lenders' debt and promoters' debt into preferential shares which would be converted into equity at a 61.6 per cent premium to the market price of KFA's stock. This led to an infusion of Rs 1158 crore into KFA in 2011. Mallya had planned to list the company on the Luxembourg Stock Exchange within six months to raise $200-300 million through global depository receipts (GDR).

The banks also stretched the repayment of loans to nine years and slashed the interest rates to 11 per cent, thus saving KFA over Rs 500 crore in annual interest costs. It also sanctioned KFA a fresh cash loan of Rs 800 crore. The banks took from Mallya as collateral two properties in Mumbai and Goa, his helicopters and yachts, shares of United Spirits and Mangalore Chemicals & Fertilizers, a corporate guarantee from United Beverages Holdings Ltd and a personal guarantee from Mallya and of course, the Kingfisher brand valued at Rs 3000 crore by Grant Thornton.

But even in 2011, KFA had major issues with cash flows and was struggling to pay its vendors and employees. Mallya borrowed from his other companies by pledging his own shares and pumping his personal money into KFA. One solution could have been a foreign investor but the Indian government did not allow foreign airlines to invest in India then. Even as a member of Parliament (MP), Mallya could not successfully lobby the government to open up the aviation sector to foreign investors.

In September 2011, KFA announced that it would be shutting down Kingfisher Red, KFA's low-cost carrier. Soon after, Neeraj Monga, head of research at Toronto-based Veritas Investment Research Corp., alerted the public that KFA was 'teetering on the verge of bankruptcy'. Monga was doubtful that KFA would manage to reach the targeted Rs 2000 crore, even though according to him KFA needed double that amount to be a viable airline. Mallya rubbished these claims and said the closure of Kingfisher Red was because the margins and yields were better in Kingfisher Class than Kingfisher Red and so the company was pursuing a more profitable path.

Lack of funding disrupted operations and cancellations were commonplace. Disgruntled employees affected service. In 2012, the SBI declared KFA a non-performing asset. On 1 April 2012,

KFA's international operations were suspended and by mid-2012, KFA had been forced to exit the low-cost carrier market. KFA was grounded in October and its licence was cancelled in December. Mallya spent his birthday that year at the shrine of Venkateswara in Tirupati and offered the Hindu deity 3 kg of gold worth about Rs 1 crore.

Mallya spent the next three years looking for ways and means to resurrect his airlines but to no avail. When he started KFA, Mallya was confident it would one day be UB Group's biggest revenue source. In seven short years, KFA met a sad demise. And with it began the end of the good times for its founder and his UB Group.

* * *

The request for Vijay Mallya's extradition was made by India on 9 February 2017 and certified by the UK's secretary of state eight days later. His arrest warrant was issued on 28 March. Mallya was arrested on 18 April, more than a year after he arrived in the United Kingdom in March 2016. He was granted bail the same day and continues to remain on bail. This arrest marked the beginning of the extradition process. On 25 September, India put forth additional charges against Mallya and so he was re-arrested in October and bailed once again.

Mallya's case was heard in the courtroom of the chief magistrate, who is the leader of over 300 district judges and deputy district judges in magistrates' courts across England and Wales and presides over the most complex and sensitive cases in magistrates' courts. Emma Arbuthnot, or Lady Arbuthnot of Edrom, who holds the position of chief magistrate, is the wife of a Conservative politician James Arbuthnot, Baron of Edrom, and has presided over the controversial extradition case of WikiLeaks' founder Julian Assange.

From 4 December 2017, extensive written statements and corroborative evidence were produced in this case by both parties,

several witnesses were called and cross-examined through five days
of oral evidence in December and almost three weeks in total until
the final hearing submissions made on 12 September 2018. The
judgment of the district court was given on 10 December 2018.

Mallya's arrest and the lengthy trial at Westminster Magistrates'
Court on charges of financial crime, provided a departure from the
prominent cases that preceded his case by at least a decade. Unlike
Nadeem Saifi and Iqbal Mirchi who were accused of murder,
underworld links and drug trafficking, Mallya's case signified
that a major industrialist like him too could face the ignominy
of standing in the dock. In terms of stature and wealth, the only
person who comes somewhat close to Mallya is Dharma Jayanti
Teja. Mallya's case represents the most extraordinary attempt
India has made to extradite its own national who was also a
lawmaker and a household name. Mallya and his supporters insist
that a political conspiracy has made him a convenient poster boy
of rogue capitalism, liable for punishment to satisfy the collective
consciousness of the middle class.

* * *

The first stop for all extradition cases in the UK is Westminster
Magistrates' Court situated at Marylebone Road in the heart of
London. Built in 2011, this modern four-storey building comprising
ten courtrooms replaced the more famous courts at Bow Street and
Horseferry Road. A public forecourt is where all the action takes
place; from reporters doing live interviews to cameramen waiting
patiently armed with their lens and tripods; from celebrities and
notorious criminals sneaking in quickly to avoid cameras to those
like Mallya who engage in a chat with eager reporters during a
lunch-time cigarette break.

As with any important case, there was speculation over who
would represent Mallya. 'Clare Montgomery, she is a big name,'
said the court staff manning the enquiry counter, a few days after
Mallya was brought to the court. Montgomery's reputation was

such that the usually busy and aloof court staff could not help but indulge in the British custom of small talk, as he pointed out that she was a legal heavyweight. Clare Montgomery QC had represented Augusto Pinochet in the House of Lords, defended several Russian oligarchs, and advised the prime minister of Thailand. She was assisted by Ben Watson, who specializes in complex extradition cases.

During the preliminary hearing, Mallya would be accompanied by the unassuming Anand Doobay, whose calm demeanour hides the fact that he is among the sharpest legal brains, for those looking for succour in extradition cases. In October 2010, he was one of the three independent lawyers appointed by the British government to review the country's extradition arrangements. They came up with a nearly 500-page report after a year of exhaustive study. He also prepared a report for the European Parliament on the European Arrest Warrant (EAW), which facilitates the arrest and transfer of a suspect within the European Union. Doobay got interested in law after watching *L.A. Law*, an American legal drama television series, a huge part of which perhaps he now experiences in his working life, minus any histrionics and in a calm manner even under immense pressure.

Representing the CPS were Mark Summers QC and Aaron Watkins. Summers came to command enormous respect from the Indian investigators for the way he countered the defence's witnesses on points that hit the government the most: be it the aspersions cast on the CBI or the allegations of a political witch hunt against Mallya. Summers was a counsel in the 9/11 attacks, Madrid train bombings and the spot-fixing in Pakistani cricket. The last prominent case in which Summers and Montgomery were on opposing sides was the Julian Assange trial. Summers was in Assange's defence team while Montgomery led the charge against the WikiLeaks founder.

On 2 October 2017, Mallya was arrested again as India added money laundering charges to the warrant. He was taken to Westminster Magistrates' Court and released on bail on the same conditions. Adding the charge of money laundering to fraud, seemed like an effort to tie together the various loose threads in this case. 'The money laundering is concerned with the destination of those funds (obtained through fraud)', Summers told the court. The prosecution's case was that Mallya laundered money through different banks to the Force India F1 team and tax havens. This was a new charge, and as is the procedure, Mallya was asked whether he consented to extradition. After a series of preliminary hearings and pre-trial reviews, the dates for the full extradition hearing were set for December 2017.

* * *

On Monday, 4 December 2017, the first day of the trial, Mallya arrived in a navy blue suit and a sky blue and white pin dot tie, and seemed less inclined to speak to the media. Perhaps he was looking forward to the action in the courtroom. However, as fate had it, just minutes before the court could commence at 10 a.m., the entire building had to be evacuated due to an alarm. Mallya had nowhere to go and had to come face-to-face with the journalists, some of whom were flown in by media organizations from India, outside the court. Montgomery watched in dismay while Mallya was hounded by reporters, every gesture and quote of his beamed live on TV news channels.

Back in the courtroom, at 11.10 a.m., Mallya stood up to confirm his name, marking the start of the trial. Right at the beginning of the proceedings, the judge seemed miffed over the issue of paginations in the documents submitted by India. Twenty minutes into Summers's submission, at 11.30 a.m., Montgomery interrupted, 'Mr Gupta was not involved in the process.' Gupta was one of the bank employees repeatedly cited by Summers when setting out the chronology of the loan from IDBI and discussing the manner in which the loan was given. At 11.52 a.m., she again stood to register another counterpoint. But it was Summers's day!

The court heard that Kingfisher in its loan application to the bank provided a rosy picture of the airline, whereas internal communications within the company painted a gloomy picture of the real position. Summers emphasized that Mallya had fraudulently acquired the loan which he never intended to pay back. The issue of Kingfisher's brand valuation, in the application for a loan from IDBI, was also taken up. It was alleged that Mallya relied on a higher brand valuation from one company rather than a lower one given by another company. Summers told the court that the loan amount was used to make interest payments to various banks; transfers to accounts in Axis Bank and Bank of Baroda; huge cash withdrawals in Goa; and funds transferred in twenty chunks to HSBC London.

On the second day, 5 December 2017, Mallya came to the court in his signature blue suit and a bright yellow tie. It was Montgomery's turn to make her opening arguments. 'In October 2019, Dr Mallya himself directly invested Rs 1,652 crore in Kingfisher,' she told the court. Seeking to take on the allegations made by Summers on the first day, Montgomery claimed that the collapse of Kingfisher was a business failure and went on to give a lowdown of the characteristics of the aviation industry in India. Financial experts Paul Rex and Dr Barry Humphreys threw more light on the aviation sector and discussed in somewhat great detail the reliance of the sector on government policies. Airlines in India could not bet on the fuel as state-owned companies had a monopoly on the oil sector. The restrictive clause of not allowing foreign collaboration was also cited as one of the factors that affected the profitability and viability of airlines in India.

There was a hint that the government was tilted towards Mallya's closest competitor Jet Airways and references were made to how, after the collapse of Kingfisher Airlines, Jet had the grounds open to enter into a joint venture with foreign airlines. The closure of Jet Airways, in 2019, is now being cited by Mallya on Twitter and during his interaction with journalists outside court to make the point that running an airline company in India is a tricky business. 'Look at what happened to Jet. Who would have

thought this would be possible few years ago.' At Westminster
Magistrates' Court, there were references to IndiGo and SpiceJet
to reinforce that Mallya's Kingfisher Airlines had missed the bus as
the period after the closure of Kingfisher was more lucrative as it
coincided with changed market realities and government support.

The most contentious part of Mallya's defence was raising
the plea of possible discrimination and harassment that he feared
would be meted out to him in India due to petty politics. This
involved even dragging the judiciary right up to the Supreme
Court. A study was cited to show that even the Supreme Court—
the highest judicial authority in India—was subject to corruption,
at worst, or at best, to incompetence. The role of the CBI and
the Directorate of Enforcement, popularly called Enforcement
Directorate (ED), also came under sharp arguments. 'Bear in mind
that Mr Asthana is in the court,' said Montgomery to the witness
before he started his evidence. The power play within the CBI's
top hierarchy gave enough ammunition to Mallya's defence team,
and notwithstanding the presence of the CBI's special director
Rakesh Asthana in the court, his name cropped up several times.

The most damning witness statement talking about the 'rot'
in the CBI came from Prof. Lawrence Saez. He mentioned a
news report in the *Indian Express* that spoke about Asthana's
appointment in the CBI being 'illegal, arbitrary and mala fide',
as pointed by a social organization in a petition. With this, Saez
was arguing that Asthana was close to the ruling party. The
next day, Saez was confronted by Summers. 'Serious allegations
have been made without giving any evidence. I hope you realize
that there is a difference between second-hand information and
primary research. You have relied on Wikipedia and press reports
that are not conclusive or definitive to run down the image of very
senior officers,' said Summers. As would be the case in most of
the extradition trials, fear of political victimization and partiality of
investigating agencies are common defences to mount in a bid to
prevent extradition. Asthana, however had the last laugh, when the
arguments maligning him held no water in the UK court.

Prison conditions is the other most effective tool that is deployed to delay and prevent extradition. However, it was a bit ironic that Mallya's grandfather Dr B.G. Mallya was, in fact, a senior prison official during the British rule in India whose primary task was to keep the standards in the prisons good enough for the inmates. He was a medical doctor and was posted in jails across British India. Perhaps Vijay Mallya's insistence that his honorary title 'Dr' be used to address him in British courts is a way to connect to his grandfather's legacy or simply to gain more credibility. But there is little doubt that the base for Vijay Mallya's Anglo lifestyle was made by his grandfather who was a regular at high table dinners at the mansions of governors and other high-ranking British officials. B.G. Mallya had spent much of his working life in Bengal. More than eighty years later, B.G. Mallya's grandson was highlighting in British courts how the same jails were not good enough to uphold his human rights. In fact, B.G. Mallya's promotions were dependent on how well the jail was administered.

The defence was pressing upon the need to have an expert visit the prison to which the court did not give its assent. As the case progressed, the issue of prison conditions continued to figure prominently. After much deliberation, it was decided that the court should be given a video recording of the cell in Arthur Road prison where Mallya was to be kept. Ultimately, the court accepted the video proof as credible enough to establish that Mallya will get the treatment, facilities and comfort in line with the ECHR requirements. However, it must be added that the defence never agreed with the prosecution on the issue of prison conditions.

The other constant theme all through the case was the contention that Mallya's case was politically motivated. Much to the consternation of the prosecution, the defence team also maintained that India had failed to establish a prima facie case against Mallya. In the wake of Summers's assertion that there was enough evidence to establish a prima facie case, Montgomery maintained that there was 'zero' evidence to support a case of fraud. During the trial, it emerged that the CPS would focus less on the charge of money laundering for which Mallya was arrested in October 2017. Instead, the prosecution would dwell on proving a prima facie case of fraud.

Financial expert Paul Rex and aviation sector pundit Dr Barry Humphreys appeared in court as defence witnesses. Rex, who was a banker by profession, appeared on day three of the trial and had appeared as a witness in a case involving the SBI and the BCCI around two decades ago. Montgomery went through Rex's witness statements where he referred to the SBI asking the RBI in February 2012 to categorize the Kingfisher loans from 'substandard' to 'standard'. Describing the SBI as a reputable entity, Rex sought to underline that an encouraging assessment by the SBI was likely to lead other banks to extend credit to Kingfisher.

The evidence from Rex was also used to dissect the conduct of the banks after the loans had turned bad. Particular attention was paid to Mallya's offer in March and April 2016 to repay 80 per cent of the Rs 5000 crore liability, which was not accepted by the consortium of banks. Rex described it as an 'attractive option' and, in a direct question from Montgomery on whether there could be other reasons behind the decision of the banks to decline the offer, said: 'They (state-owned banks) tend to be more susceptible to political pressures.' The import of Rex's statement was that this was not a straightforward case of fraud as it was made out to be by India. That banks could make decisions not consistent with their stated objective of recovering loans, under pressure from the political class.

Rex's witness statements were preceded by those of Humphreys who was the first witness. Humphreys weighed in on how the demise of Kingfisher Airlines was not intentional but a by-product of a range of issues outside the control of the airline's management. Both, Rex and Humphreys, were cross-examined by Summers. The clear hint of political pressure defining the conduct of the banks was necessary to be countered. Summers told the court that there could be valid reasons for the banks to not accept the terms under which Mallya offered to make repayments. According to the assessment made by the banks, they could not be faulted to assume that Mallya could pay more than what he was offering. Alluding to the £2 million (almost Rs 14 crore) birthday bash, Summers said that the banks' decision might have been influenced by it, making them believe that Mallya could be short-changing them.

It was also during the cross-examination of Rex that Summers had pointed out the 'washing machine activity' that involved sums of around £10–15 million being transferred between UB Group companies to put up the pretence of equity infusion into Kingfisher Airlines.

While Mallya's extradition trial was on, the high court was seized of the application filed by Indian banks seeking to freeze Mallya's global assets. The high court granted an extension to Mallya after the application was made that his legal team was busy in the extradition trial. The seeking of the freezing order opened the floodgates to multiple cases as other creditors joined the scramble to register their interest and establish their position in the pecking order if Mallya's assets were to be dispersed.

Two others—Margaret Sweeney, a Force India employee, and legal expert Martin Lau—also gave evidence on behalf of the defence. Sweeney, chief financial officer, Force India Formula 1 team, denied the prosecution's case that Mallya benefitted from Kingfisher Airlines' sponsorship of Force India. The CPS had claimed that two payments worth $9 million by Kingfisher Airlines to Force India were transferred to Mallya for his personal use. She told the court that the sponsorship money was used to pay Mercedes-Benz and McLaren Engineering for their services to Force India. The prosecution had referred to Kingfisher Airlines making payments in excess of the stipulated sponsorship deal, which pointed to Mallya benefitting out of it.

Sweeney, however, had an explanation for that. She told the court that the sponsors for F1 teams routinely made extra payments that accounted for the hospitality that they enjoyed during the racing season at venues across the world. She also countered the allegations that Airbus Industries and European Aeronautic

Defence and Space Company (EADS) had made several payments to Force India which illegally benefitted Mallya. The court was told that both the companies had their logos on the Force India car, which explained the payments made by them. At one point during the evidence being recorded by Sweeney, Montgomery and Summers entered into a verbal duel. In her cross-examination, Summers asked Sweeney whether Force India, which generally received sponsorship money from Kingfisher Airlines through Bank of Baroda, received ($2 million) through HSBC London.

This amount was transferred to HSBC London from Axis Bank, pointed out Summers to emphasize that the money was routed in a different way to ultimately reach and benefit Mallya. Montgomery told the court that it was a genuine marketing cost, and hence, Axis Bank was instructed to transfer the money to HSBC London for payment to Force India. The court was regularly reminded that all accounts at Force India were audited. Sweeney, Humphreys and Rex gave evidence that was largely technical, and concerned with very specific sectors. It was, however, the evidence of Prof. Martin Lau that generated the most heat.

Just like the other witnesses, Lau, too, stuck to his field of expertise as professor of South Asian law at the School of Oriental and African Studies (SOAS), University of London. But his comments about the Supreme Court and judiciary in India attracted a sharper and intense cross-examination by Summers. 'I hold the Supreme Court of India in the highest respect but at times some doubts are voiced about particular patterns. That does not mean it is a corrupt institution. At times it rules in favour of the government, especially when judges are close to retirement and angling for government posts.' He also spoke about the trial by media which meant, according to him, that Mallya would not get a fair trial in India. 'The use of panel discussions on TV channels and the emergence of quite powerful TV commentators who are liable to influence.'

Prof. Lau had cited a study to back the aspersions cast on the working of the Supreme Court. This made headlines and was flashed across news channels in India and social media. The next morning, the court was told by Summers of an unsolicited email received from one of the authors whose study was cited by Prof. Lau. The author, a professor in a UK university, said that they hold the Supreme Court in the highest esteem and were dismayed that their study was being used to malign or discredit the highest court of the land.

Summers also cited how a variety of studies and research has been done on courts across the world. In particular, he brought to the court's notice how a study done on the Supreme Court in Israel suggested that the verdict delivered by judges could be affected by whether they had eaten breakfast or not. 'There are all kinds of studies done on the courts and judiciary systems all around the world,' said Summers, even as those assembled burst into laughter. Countering the assertion of a media trial, Summers said that the courts in India would take into consideration all the factors and that the criminal justice system across jurisdictions was now faced with the issue of trial by media. 'This is a major case of fraud involving a substantial sum of money in a developing country and hence it is understandable that the media is interested in this case,' said Summers, keeping in mind Prof. Lau's observation that reporters and camerapersons had crowded Westminster Magistrates' Court to cover Mallya's trial.

On day 6 of the trial, the court heard evidence from Alan Mitchell, a prison expert who has been cited in several extradition cases. Dr Mitchell gave evidence in the Sanjeev Chawla and Nirav Modi cases, among others. He was chair of the Independent Prison Monitoring Advisory Group, Scotland, and a member of the Scottish Human Rights Commission. It was natural that the state of Arthur Road Jail and special arrangements made for Mallya thus came under intense scrutiny. But what took everyone by surprise was the dramatic account of the Chennai Six who were kept in Chennai jail.

Dr Mitchell told the court that he spoke to one member of the Chennai Six who confided the harsh realities of the prison conditions. His identity was not disclosed but Montgomery made the larger point on how (in)effective can the assurance of foreign governments be that the jail conditions do not violate the human rights of inmates. In the case of the Chennai Six, David Cameron, the then prime minister in 2014 had said that he had personally raised the matter with New Delhi, yet when the consular staff visited them, they were told that dental and other health concerns were not taken care of. Summers was clearly caught off-guard.

He told the court that these were hearsay conversations. 'The Indian government needs to be prepared. I am not being obstructive but this is a delicate issue.' 'The idea is to know what happens on ground despite assurances,' said Montgomery. At this moment, the court took a break for ten minutes to allow time to the defence to deliberate whether they would disclose the identity of the member of the Chennai Six whose prison ordeals were being discussed. When the court met at 11.58 a.m., Dr Mitchell continued his deposition and said that he would identify the Chennai Six member as 'A'. The horror story continued. 'A used a larger exercise area and was referred to a psychiatrist in hospital for excessive walking. Around fifteen guards came and grabbed him. In the hospital, he was gagged, beaten and forcibly injected medicines.' A staff member from the British High Commission forwarded his complaint to the ministry of home affairs, but he was advised by the High Commission to withdraw his complaint.

Painting a rather negative picture of the prison life in Chennai, Dr Mitchell continued: 'He (A) told me there would be frequent shortage of water', and that prisoners would drink water from an open well due to which A was 'diagnosed with hepatitis A'. The court heard, as the prosecution squirmed, that the Chennai Six were not provided the facility to make international calls for one year despite requests being made by the British High Commission. 'Despite formal requests, prison authorities gave no response,' said Dr Mitchell.

Montgomery then took Dr Mitchell through Mallya's case, asking him about the proposals at Arthur Road Jail for Mallya. 'I know the government of India has said that there are four doctors . . . but how many doctors are on duty during a particular time is not clear. It will be challenging for any prisoner to access healthcare.' Before asking Dr Mitchell about Arthur Road Jail, Montgomery stressed that Mallya suffers from coronary artery disease and diabetes. The alleged treatment of the Chennai Six, the highlighting of Mallya's own health condition, and the unreliability of assurances had now forced the CPS on the back foot.

When Summers stood at 12.38 p.m. to examine Dr Mitchell, he started with questions that did not need any confabulations or verification from India. Dr Mitchell is a veteran at giving evidence and rather sought-after for his expert take on prison conditions, but questions by Summers were calculated enough to take the sting away from the life-on-edge experience of the Chennai Six. It was now of utmost importance to strike at the very source.

Summers shot a volley of questions at Dr Mitchell. Did they (members of the Chennai Six) make unsolicited contact? Did you give evidence after taking notes? Did A confirm that it is a correct recording? Did A take a doctor's appointment? Did you speak with the British government? The final question in the series was whether it was possible that A could be using Dr Mitchell as a platform for a compensation claim.

Summers then sought to differentiate between the condition of Tihar jail and the facility in Arthur Road Jail where Mallya was sought to be kept. Dr Mitchell did not agree with Summers's characterization of the Government of India's (GoI) communication on barrack number 12 in Arthur Road Jail where Mallya was to be kept as detailed. 'There is no public information about barrack number 12 . . . I am unable to offer any comment. There is no reference as to how much drinking water will be available.' Just the mention of 'adequate' water was not good for Dr Mitchell who shot back with 'adequate? In the eyes of who?'

After lunch, the *jugalbandi* between Dr Mitchell and Summers continued. The defence had raised the question about the pictures of the rooms in barrack 12 being empty in a bid to discredit the submission by the GoI. Summers began by pointing out that when the pictures were taken, there were only three inmates in barrack 12, and hence it looked empty. Barrack 12 has a capacity for six people and past inmates included leader of the Nationalist Congress Party Chhagan Bhujbal and media baron Peter Mukerjea. 'The Maharashtra state assures Mallya minimum 3 square metres in barrack 12,' said Summers, adding that 'mattress, pillow, blanket, adequate ventilation and light' will be provided.

The horrid conditions faced by the Chennai Six and notwithstanding the submissions by Summers of a somewhat welcoming Arthur Road Jail for Mallya, the Day 6 proceedings were a reminder of how precariously Mallya was placed and how far removed he was from his days of pomp and splendour. Did it ever cross his mind how his grandfather would react to this battle of narratives on the state of Indian prisons?

* * *

'Don't waste my time on the kerbside,' was Mallya's annoyed response to reporters thrusting their microphones at his face. Despite the multiple court visits, neither the media nor Mallya seemed to have got over each other. Multiple pairs of eyes would scan the busy road in the quest to locate his car. As soon as he was spotted, reporters would surround him; his gait would now be determined by how newsy the proceedings of the court were the previous day, and how provocative they were expected to be on that day—for that would decide the intensity at which the journalists would besiege him and accordingly delay his entry to the court building.

There is no doubt that Mallya loved to bask in the spotlight and looked forward to his interactions with the press. But so great many were his appearances that the Q&A session would degenerate into uncharted territories. There were occasions when Mallya would get irritated, but that annoyance would reflect in a harmless change to his face, a mild shaking of his head, or the deliberate use of a friendly yet sarcastic tone. Perhaps he always kept in mind that the real battle was what happened inside, and not outside, the court.

A selected sample of interactions between reporters and Mallya outside Westminster Magistrates' Court on 27 April 2018:

Reporter 1: What about charges of money laundering?

Mallya: Figure it out, it's all public document.

Reporter 2: Would that be the final oral hearing?

Mallya: I hope so.

Reporter 3: Is your team still sticking that the evidence submitted (by CPS) is not admissible?

Mallya (looks a bit irritated, after a brief pause, speaks in a changed tone): You have heard it all yet you are asking me?

Reporter 3: You had an extended word with your lawyer just now . . .

Mallya: I may have had an extended word with my lawyer; does that mean I am obliged to share it all with you?

Reporter 3: Not obliged, I am just asking . . .

Mallya: I am not obliged to answer you either. Whatever is discussed between lawyers and me, ultimately gets submitted in the court. You are sitting in the court, you are hearing everything. I have nothing more to add.

Reporter 3: Today the judge in some ways sounded satisfied on the admissibility of evidence . . .

Mallya: The judge will decide what the judge wants to decide. All right. I am not going to speculate. You want to speculate, go ahead. Why are you wasting my time? Why are you wasting my time on the kerbside?

Reporter 3: Am just asking a question . . .

Mallya: Now you are asking me to speculate, so I can answer your question.

Reporter 4: So see you on the 11th (July, the next hearing) . . .

Mallya: Absolutely.

Reporter 4: And until then, you are enjoying the summer. Any plans?

Mallya: Any plans, such as . . .?

Reporter 4: I don't know, are we going to see you somewhere . . .?

Mallya: I don't know where you go . . . (everybody guffaws)

Mallya's interaction with the media turned serious as the case progressed. Bits from the assortment of new facts, arguments and counter-arguments made in the courtroom were regurgitated by reporters, as he went in and came out of the court building. He became more guarded and circumspect at answering them. Frankly, there was not much he could add, neither did he seem interested in doing that.

What would most likely elicit a full response was any indication that he was seeking to delay the proceedings or had run away from India to the safe sanctuary of the UK. These questions would be met by very firm and confident rebuttals. But over time, he had stopped reacting to such assertions by reporters eager to get a statement from him. Initially, he used to be a bit guarded but eventually started saying, with no reservations, that no matter what, the media in India will say what they want to say.

At times, safely ensconced inside the court building, and aware that there were no cameras around and no recording could be done, he would speak or show some news items on his phone. This would usually be during the short walk from the courtroom to the room allotted to defendants to discuss privately with their lawyers. Piping hot pizzas would be waiting for his team for lunch, after which he would step out for his mandatory smoke.

* * *

On 27 April, the Westminster Court ruled that the evidence submitted by the CBI against Mallya was admissible, bringing an end to the anxiety that had gripped the prosecution. Montgomery had regularly spoken about the lack of prima facie evidence, but now the magistrate's ruling had set the record straight. This was a good turnaround for the CBI and ED as, during a hearing in June 2017, the judge had not taken kindly to the delay in the serving of evidence against Mallya. 'Are Indians normally very prompt in their responses? They have taken six months so far and we haven't got any further forward in the past six weeks,' Arbuthnot had asked Aaron Watkins on 13 June 2017.

This remark along with the constant 'no prima facie evidence' riposte by Montgomery in subsequent hearings had cast a shadow over the Indian investigations. The hearing on 27 April 2018 was a source of immense relief for the prosecution. The court having settled the issue of admissibility of evidence, the defence's sole focus was on the conditions in the Arthur Road prison. Based on the photographs of barrack 12 of the Arthur Road Jail where Mallya was to be kept after extradition, Summers assured the court on 31 July 2018 that Mallya would not face overcrowding, and would have access to toilet facilities, beddings and mattresses, natural air and light. But in the wake of the evidence by Dr Mitchell and Montgomery's description of barrack 12 as 'impenetrable to natural light', the judge asked for a video of barrack 12 shot during mid-day with no artificial light.

At the next hearing on 12 September 2018, Arbuthnot said that she had watched the video thrice, but that the most important point for her to consider was whether there was a prima facie case against Mallya or not. Montgomery did not raise any question over the authenticity of the video, just as she had done over the pictures of barrack 12 at the previous hearing. But she struck at the CBI and repeated that the case against Mallya was ill-founded. 'This is a matter in which CBI has been forced to file charges,' she said and reiterated that the prosecution had failed to make out a case against Mallya. At one point, she told the court that Rakesh Asthana went to heads of banks with reprisals to file cases against Mallya. It was the last day before the judgment came on 12 December 2018, and was also the day when Mallya caused the Jaitley storm.

'I met him (Arun Jaitley) in the Parliament and told him I am going to London,' claimed Mallya at the end of the court proceedings, when he was besieged by cameras. His statement took the focus away from the nearly four hours of courtroom battle. Although Jaitley, the finance minister, was quick to release a statement saying the meeting with Mallya was unscheduled and he advised him to meet the banks, Mallya's utterances turned the focus of the case. It raised a larger question that if a senior cabinet minister knew that Mallya was going to fly away to London, could the government have done more to keep him in the country?

This was also the day when the banks served or tried to serve him, in a rather dramatic fashion, notice for the bankruptcy petition. As he slowly made his way to his car and just before he opened the door, a man attempted to hand him a white envelope. Mallya did not take it and it fell. The man picked it up and tried unsuccessfully to hand it to Mallya again. He then threw it inside the car and, on the second attempt, the envelope fell near Mallya's feet, who was in the front seat. All this was happening while reporters continued to ask Mallya questions. Mallya picked it and held it just long enough to read what was written on the envelope, before flicking it out of the car.

That envelope contained a notice of a bankruptcy petition filed on behalf of Indian banks by TLT solicitors. It sought to inform Mallya to be present or have a representative at the Northampton County Court. Giving reference to the Worldwide Freezing Order (WFO), it showed Mallya to be in debt of Rs 1,05,37,55,18,936.05! As per the rules in England, a debtor has to be served the notice of bankruptcy petition, and one way of prolonging the matter is by not accepting the notice and then feigning ignorance when the court summons. In all likelihood, after attempts to serve the notice through the post were unsuccessful, the bailiff tried to deliver it outside Westminster Magistrates' Court.

* * *

On 10 December 2018, the day of the judgment at Westminster Magistrates' Court, Mallya entered the courtroom with Pinky Lalwani; they sat next to each other in the public gallery as his case was deferred. Both were visibly tense and seemed to be seeking comfort from each other. As has been the routine, Lalwani was carrying a bottle of water for Mallya. When Chief Magistrate Emma Arbuthnot took her chair in court number 1, it took her less than a minute to make it clear that she was convinced Vijay Mallya can be extradited to India. The next twenty-five minutes were music to the ears of Indian ED and CBI teams who were present along with officials from the Indian High Commission. Judge Arbuthnot did not agree with any objection raised by the defence that could have barred Mallya's extradition.

Arbuthnot, in an unusually lengthy judgment, ruled that there was a prima facie case against Vijay Mallya on three charges. These were: making false representations to make a gain, conspiracy to defraud, and money laundering. She also accepted the assurances by the GoI that prison facilities were good enough to ensure that they did not violate Mallya's human rights and met the article 3 requirements of the ECHR.

Asthana had made fifteen trips to London to attend the proceedings, but was not present on the day of the judgment due to the unprecedented fallout within the CBI. Television channels went into celebratory mode breaking the news of Mallya's extradition and his return to India soon. Times Now that had carried Mallya's interview claiming innocence hours before the verdict was jubilantly flashing 'Great Day for India, NDA brings him to book' as it interviewed Finance Minister Jaitley for a reaction. India Today, NDTV, CNN-IBN (now CNN-News18) and Republic TV ran lengthy programmes talking about how this was a significant victory for India and perhaps served as a warning to those wanting to commit crimes and escape to the UK.

While *Hindustan Times* reminded its readers that Mallya's extradition had hinged on conditions in Mumbai's Arthur Road prison and that the court had found 'no ground to believe Mallya faces any risk to human rights', *Bloomberg Quint* had an image of Mallya behind bars with an article that asked 'what happens next' after the court approved his extradition. *The Hindu* cautioned that 'a lengthy appeal process is likely'.

Mallya's extradition made headlines across the world that read: 'UK court orders Indian tycoon Mallya to be extradited on fraud charges' (*Reuters*); 'UK court says beer baron Vijay Mallya should be extradited to India' (CNN); 'Vijay Mallya India's "King of Good Times" should be extradited to India, U.K. Court says' (the *New York Times*); 'In a big win for Modi government, British court rules to extradite Vijay Mallya to India' (*Forbes*); and the BBC wrote a long feature on 'Vijay Mallya: India's most controversial businessman'.

Another round of cheers went up in the press when Home Secretary Sajid Javid signed Mallya's extradition in February 2019 and when the high court dismissed his appeal on paper but scheduled an oral hearing instead on 2 July.

* * *

On 2 July 2019, Vijay Mallya entered court three of the high court at the Royal Courts of Justice building, where his application for leave to appeal was to be heard by a two-judge bench. This was a renewed oral application by Mallya, as Justice William Davis had rejected the first 'on paper' application in April 2019. Four hours were granted to the defence led by Clare Montgomery to make their oral submissions. Mallya came with his full entourage—his son Sid, partner Pinky Lalwani, friends and personal staff.

Mallya's team pointed out to the judges the 'very serious errors' in Arbuthnot's decision and that those errors were 'both of fact and law'. It was clear that the defence was rankled by Arbuthnot's reference to Mallya as 'glamorous, flashy, famous, bejewelled, bodyguarded, ostensibly billionaire playboy.' In a rather cheeky way, Mallya's counsel Montgomery, at the very beginning, brought this description of Mallya to the notice of the judges: 'And regardless of whether that pen portrait was fair or necessary, it is unlikely to increase this court's appetite to review kindly whether the SDJ (senior district judge) fell into error.'

Mallya sought to appeal, both, the decision of the Westminster Magistrates' Court, and the decision of the secretary of state to order his extradition. The appeal against the magistrates' court's decision was sought on five grounds—prima facie case, extraneous condition, prison conditions and on two grounds under fair trial. The appeal against the secretary of state's decision to order his extradition was filed with the plea that proper consideration was not given to protect Mallya's specialty rights in India. In extradition cases, the principle of specialty is a device to ensure that the requested person will not be tried for offences other than for what he is sought to be extradited. Mallya contended that he faced over forty ongoing criminal cases in India, and it was likely that his extradition would not bring a halt to them, thus breaching the specialty condition.

As Justice George Leggatt and Justice Andrew Popplewell heard Montgomery, the extraordinarily large windows made the cramped courtroom prone to the periodic but rapid change in the intensity of the sunlight, adding a rather dramatic flair to the proceedings.

Montgomery began her arguments from where she left off at Westminster Magistrates' Court. She is a reporters' delight; her loud voice and clear diction make it easier to take notes, compensating for her polite but unapproachable demeanour to journalists. Seated behind her were her junior Ben Watson and solicitor Anand Doobay, the bespectacled and unassuming legal eagle who has mastered the extraordinary feat of shunning the limelight while taking up celebrity cases.

As it turned out, the judges rejected all the grounds for appeal against Arbuthnot's decision, but agreed that the objections raised on the finding that a prima facie case was made out against Mallya met the threshold to allow an appeal. Among the defence's plea was, what they claimed, a seminal issue of extradition law 'never been grappled with in the senior courts in the UK'. This was whether a UK court could construe a case, on its own, to answer which was different to the case advanced by the requesting state. This meant that the senior district judge based her decision to establish that a prima facie case had been made against Mallya on charges for which he was not being prosecuted in India.

It was claimed that India changed the case from a conspiracy to defraud, to committing fraud by false representation by Mallya and others. The fraud by false representation case was advanced at a much later stage without explicitly laying out or identifying that it was Mallya himself who made these (allegedly) false representations and not others at Kingfisher Airlines. Most importantly, this shifting of the case was not consistent with the working of the extradition law. The courts were constrained to adjudicate the merits of the application by a requesting state by focusing on the conduct as described in the request. And as per the original request from India, claimed the defence, the district judge was entitled only to decide whether Mallya and others had conspired to defraud IDBI along with senior bankers and not raise the bar from conspiracy to false representation.

India's victory was, however, short-lived when the high court agreed that Mallya could appeal against the district judge's decision on the prima facie case against him. This, Mallya told us, the authors, as we left the court, is the biggest declaration from the high court that perhaps there may not be a case against him to warrant his extradition and he felt 'vindicated'.

Mallya knew that if he was successful in making a strong case in the high court against the decision of the district judge, he may not only secure himself a huge victory but also prove that he 'rightly deserves vindication'. This is perhaps one of the most important wishes Mallya has, as is evident from the many conversations he has had with us over the years—his desperation to prove to the world that he is just a businessman whose business went bust and he has always endeavoured to pay back his debts. With this, he perhaps hopes to get back his lost life.

* * *

On 11 February 2020, the hearings for the appeal against the district judge's decision to order Mallya's extradition began in courtroom three of the iconic Royal Courts of Justice, presided by Lord Justice Stephen Irwin and Mrs Justice Elisabeth Laing.

The court was hearing arguments on the only surviving ground of appeal (of the six made by Mallya) that the district judge's decision—that there was a case for Mallya to answer (prima facie case requirement), based on her assessment of the evidence presented by the government and the appellant—was wrong. The CBI and ED team had flown in from India and representatives of the High Commission of India were also present in the courtroom.

The central argument by Mallya's team was that the district judge had strayed away from the GoI's case that Mallya never intended to repay the loan and had instead selectively used the evidence to conclude that there was a prima facie case against Mallya. Using words like 'travesty', 'misrepresentation', 'quite hard to understand' to describe the December 2018 judgment by Emma Arbuthnot, Montgomery constantly referred to the government not providing the entirety of documents so as to make the case against Mallya appear stronger. She also went on to argue that the district judge herself said that she would not be considering all the evidence. 'There is a vast amount of evidence and I am limiting myself,' Arbuthnot had said.

Montgomery used the economic downturn in the aviation sector as a key defence for Mallya defaulting on the loans. Her four-point attack on the lower court's decision rested on four arguments: lower court found a case which is not in fact being prosecuted in India, and it was impermissible to do so; it applied the wrong test when considering whether there was a prima facie case for Mallya to answer; it was wrong to conclude that a prima facie case had been demonstrated in relation to conspiracy to defraud, fraud by false representation and/or money laundering and finally; the lower court was wrong to admit some of the government's evidence.

Montgomery went on to cite a list of evidence that she believed was not considered and the documents that were presented in parts, reports and figures not considered or misrepresented. At one point, the judge had to interrupt her: 'You lived and breathed this . . . you have to slow down.'

Even though Mallya did not raise this point in court, Summers went on to add that the fraud alleged in Mallya's extradition proceedings represented but a part of a broader fraud upon numerous Indian banks under criminal investigation in India, adding that this conduct had already spawned a raft of criminal and civil litigation within and outside of India. Summers advised the court to be 'alert' and treat Mallya's appeal with 'considerable caution' as Mallya had, during the proceedings in the lower court, included 'his own one-sided narrative and commentary' and 'over-complication and artificially elaborate analysis'.

The day was taken up largely with Montgomery going through witness statements and raising issues with their admissibility and lack of corroborative evidence. At one point, she raised the issue of corruption and political motivation in the investigating agencies involved in Mallya's case.

> *Montgomery: To examine the question of admissibility of evidence, the court can look at fresh evidence . . . Mr Asthana (CBI lead on Mallya's case) has acted corruptly in relation to investigation in . . .*
> *Judge: Was there any judgment involving Asthana?*
> *Montgomery: No, but the court in India did not accept his strike out application.*

The next day, the court began by stressing on the importance of creating a chronology of events that both parties agreed on. 'We will not be giving extempore ruling and will require to agree on a chronology,' said Lord Justice Irwin suggesting a deadline of 4 p.m. on 17 February, to which both parties agreed.

The morning was spent largely with Montgomery going through emails between Mallya and the bank, valuation reports and IDBI's own internal documents relating to the loan given to Mallya, telling the court that Arbuthnot was 'simply wrong to conclude what she did . . . we did not know she would make the assumption she did about the misrepresentation'.

Montgomery: We submit all the relevant figures were publicly announced and most certainly known to IDBI and were not false but can be shown to be accurate. Our primary case is that the figures were known then and so the idea, that misrepresentation was done to commit fraud, does not stand.

Lord Justice Irwin: Suppose there were two groups of lenders and one group did not know that. There are conspirators supposedly located at the level of chairman and executive committee and at the level of the large commercial group. But at each of those levels there are non-conspirators who are taking part. As per the bank's internal communication everyone knows, as brought out by the minutes of the credit committee meeting.

Montgomery: The case has been made that this was a conspiracy that Kingfisher was not eligible for loan . . . and one of the things that might have saved KFA was Etihad coming in . . . as it did pick up stake in Jet. In airline business so much is out of the control of its management . . .

After lunch, Montgomery very briefly discussed the viability of the KFA business. 'Several parties including IDBI, SBI, RBI, Grant Thornton agreed that it was a viable business, so people and groups outside KFA believed in its future,' she told the court.

At 2.35 p.m., Summers stood to argue for the GoI. He explained that establishing a prima facie case does not involve 'proof of guilt', or even the production of a 'strong' case. He told the court that the GoI's contention from the onset was that the evidence in the case could conveniently demonstrate that Mallya indulged in: lying and misrepresentation to induce the grant of loans from IDBI; the knowing misapplication of funds contrary to the purpose for which they were lent by the bank; and finally, incriminating conduct following the dispersal of the funds which speaks to the intention from the start not to repay the loans as required.

'There is enough in the 32,000 pages of overall evidence' to ensure that the GoI's case meets the obligations of the extradition treaty and 'not just a prima facie case but overwhelming evidence of dishonesty', Summers said. 'It is not just a prima facie case but an overwhelming case. There is nothing marginal or borderline in this case. Her (Arbuthnot's) judgment runs,' Summers argued.

The CPS maintained that Mallya obtained substantial funds from IDBI, and the motivation to do so was Kingfisher Airlines' grave financial position. But once received, the loan funds were immediately applied for purposes other than the ones they were granted for. It was also alleged that Mallya 'ultimately, deliberately defaulted on their repayment despite possessing the ability to repay them'. Summers told the court that while Mallya 'may have hoped to save his ailing business, he also knew and intended that, if he did not, he could and would dishonestly default on these loans'.

Thus the 'unchanging core of the government's case is that the loans were obtained dishonestly through fraud'. Summers agreed with the district judge's decision to call out 'rank dishonesty perpetrated by a person in a position of rare wealth, and therefore power and influence, and who ultimately used that position to commit a substantial fraud against a publicly owned bank'.

On the final day of the hearing, Summers discussed the emails and said they provided a 'rare window' on what went on. He told the court that KFA knew they had lost ground to other carriers and were not performing as the rest of the market was performing because of their high operating leverage. Summers contended that knowing the airline was making huge losses, the company made 'knowing misrepresentations' to secure the loan.

Summers: Bank trusts what it's being told, takes those representations and relies on it. There were no checks made by anybody on these figures and we say those were actions made by an insider banker.

Lord Justice Irwin: Is that person identified and said to be a co-conspirator?

Summers: Yes, Mr Sridhar. Mrs Kabra, a junior officer, gave evidence to the Indian government against Sridhar. She said 'I was just told what to do, what the end result is going to be' and 'he told, we have to positively recommend the proposal because the company was having support of UB Group and Mr Mallya'.

Summers then explained that the creditors were listed by the SBI and the Rs 950 crore loan was needed to pay them off. Of which SBI put in Rs 500 crore and the other banks the remaining. Seven days later, they needed Rs 150 crore urgently. '150 of 950?' asked the judge, to which Summers replied that 'we believe it was outside the 950'. 'Would an infusion of equity not alter the trading losses?', the judge asked, but Summers was adamant that KFA knew it was not going to get any money from investors. 'Looking at the emails, is it so surprising that the equity promised never came?' Summers went on to talk about projections and tax in the KFA accounts, but was interrupted by Montgomery.

Montgomery: Mark Summers's theory that the differed tax was left out is completely false!
Lord Justice Irwin: Maybe it's best for him to develop his arguments first.
Montgomery: My Lord, I am sorry!

Summers argued that Mallya still had the ability to pay creditors—either from his personal wealth or from UB Group. But what did he do? As far as the corporate guarantee was concerned, United Breweries Holdings Limited (UBHL) gradually set about diluting its assets/shareholdings in UB Group companies over a period of time, without informing the bank. Mallya sold United Spirits, but banks were not notified. Banks are of the view that this was done to siphon off the funds. Mallya had personally obtained $40 million as the result of a deed of disengagement following the sale of United Spirits to Diageo—that money fell squarely in the personal guarantee, but instead of handing it to the banks, he siphoned it off to trusts for his children.

> *Summers: It speaks in volumes to dishonesty. He had the ability to pay, he chose instead to go down a different path. Would it be an irrational or a perverse jury that concluded that that was his intention from the beginning?'*
>
> *Lord Justice Irwin: It may be a bad character reference (CR), it is bad CR. But on what basis does the evidence show that it was intended right from the beginning?*
>
> *Summers: Dishonest intention to avoid security. Therefore it serves as bad CR under the 2003 (Criminal) Justice Act.*
>
> *Lord Justice Irwin: What I don't see is that it shows that was his intention from earlier . . . .*
>
> *Summers: When you set it against what happened with misrepresentation then it's possible for the jury to conclude that this was something he planned all along.*
>
> *Lord Justice Irwin: What have the banks got back?*
>
> *Summers: Nothing. The answer is nothing has been realized.*
>
> *Justice Elisabeth Laing: What is HPCL–BG?*
>
> *Summers (looks clueless): ?*
>
> *(Mallya's defence team sniggers. Anand Doobay tries hard to hide his smirk.)*
>
> *Montgomery (standing up and looking smug): Oil company. Bank guarantee.*

Summers continued to argue that Mallya routed the KFA funds to other companies, to freight companies for funding corporate jets for his personal use. The evidence shows Rs 10 million (Rs 1 crore) was used to settle a bill of Rs 9.87 million for renting a jet, payments to a C. Jameson which A. Raghunathan, former chief financial officer, Kingfisher Airlines, confirms were for the corporate jet used exclusively by Mallya. There are also cash withdrawals. 'Evidence from the controller of Mumbai airport says what the jet was used for—all for Dr Mallya!'

Summers did not discount the corruption at the banks. The GoI's primary case is that what went on inside the bank was 'so bizarre and so very far from what one would expect from officers of a public institution that a jury could conclude that they knew what the appellant was up to . . . especially if one takes into account meetings that were unaccounted for and the diaries that have been misplaced', following which junior officers have been asked to recommend loans to sanction before due diligence is done. CPS had argued in the district court evidence that multiple unrecorded secret meetings around the relevant time took place between Mallya and Ragunathan (for KFA) and senior bank officials, and that the 2009 diary for those meetings appears to have disappeared.

Concluding his arguments, Summers told the judges that the evidence 'as a whole' establishes a clear case of fraud for Mallya to answer before the Indian courts and requested them to dismiss Mallya's appeal.

Mallya in his dark blue suit and a lighter shade of azure tie sat beside Pinky Lalwani who was dressed in a bright yellow and orange shirt with brown trousers and a brown fur gilet. Both looked grim.

At 3 p.m., Montgomery stood up to make her final arguments. She was definitely irritated and had already lost her cool with Summers earlier in the day when the judges took a short break, much to Summers's chagrin and the astonishment of all those present in the court.

Montgomery handed the judges the audit certificate of 2009 and simply said 'GoI chose not to include this in evidence. This shows that the differed tax was not disavowed.' On email exchanges in September, she said that there were emails that GoI had failed to produce. 'It's wrong for GoI to say that the absence of emails implies that nothing was sent.' Referring to a document by Dr Humphreys, Mallya's counsel said that there were significant operational problems in 2009. '"Lies," says Mr Summers,' mocked Montgomery, much to the amusement of the entire court.

A litany of charges was once again refuted by Mallya's defence as part of the closing statement. The basic submission being there was no concealment or dishonesty in the relationship between the banks and KFA. 'At its core, our complaint is the judge reached a tipping point because of a misunderstanding. There are problems at every turn'.

> *Montgomery: This is (a) very dense case . . .*
> *Lord Justice Irwin: I'm not sure you have to tell us this at the end of the third day.*
> *Montgomery: Thank you for your patience.*

* * *

On 20 April 2020, the London High Court dismissed the appeal of Vijay Mallya against the Westminster Magistrates' Court's decision to extradite him to India, thus upholding the 10 December 2018 judgment of District Judge Emma Arbuthnot who had found there was a prima facie case for Mallya to be sent to the secretary of state to sign on the extradition order.

Mallya had approached the high court against this decision of the senior district judge, Arbuthnot, on grounds that alleged that the senior district judge had delivered the judgment beyond the scope of the original case made by India and erred in law in its approach. The high court found that 'this submission is quite untenable. It is clear beyond any doubt that the district judge directed herself properly'. Lord Justice Irwin and Mrs Justice Elisabeth Laing found that 'the evidence, taken as a whole, was such that a reasonable jury, on one possible view of the facts, could draw a safe inference that there was a conspiracy'. They described the December 2018 judgment by Westminster Magistrates' Court as an 'impressive, well-structured and thoroughly judicial approach'.

Montgomery had told the high court that the lower court erred in its approach to the admissibility of the evidence provided by India. The court accepted Montgomery's submission that 'section 161 statements dealing with events that their makers had not seen were inadmissible' and should be given 'no weight on those matters'. However, they concluded that there was no reason why the points witnesses made on the documents could not be taken into account 'as informed explanations of or commentary on the documents, rather than as evidence of relevant events'.

Mallya had also raised questions on the senior district judge's decision that a prima facie case of fraud by false representation and money laundering was made out. India had argued that Mallya took the loan with no intent to pay back and made submission in the district court that showed Mallya had directed Kingfisher Airlines loan funds into his personal and non-KFA accounts. Montgomery had argued that the evidence supplied by India did not show that Mallya intentionally made any false representations.

The high court found that the evidence showed 'at least to some extent, that the loan had not been used for paying the creditors . . . and that it had been used contrary to the undertaking imposed by condition'. This, they believe, was sufficient for Arbuthnot to find that there was a prima facie case of fraud by false representation.

On money laundering, the court noted that neither side made any substantive oral submissions about this part of the case and had agreed that if a prima facie case of misrepresentation or of conspiracy to defraud was established, it would be conceded that Mallya's use of the KFA funds would amount to money laundering.

The high court concluded that it did not matter if Arbuthnot 'went further than she needed to, or, indeed, if her approach was wrong. We have held there is a prima facie case both of misrepresentation and of conspiracy, and thus there is also a prima facie case of money laundering'.

The forty-six-page judgment noted that the magistrate 'did not misdirect herself in law in her approach to finding a prima facie case'. One of the objections raised by Mallya that the district judge did not consider all the evidence, 'represents a seizing upon a phrase in the judgment, and is barren of merit.'

While the court noted that 'the scope of the prima facie case found by SDJ (Westminster Court) is in some respects wider than that alleged by the Respondent in India' may offer some consolation to Mallya, the judges have been emphatic in spelling out that Mallya must go to India.

This final leg in the Vijay Mallya extradition battle in the high court was a lonely affair. With London under lockdown, the judgment was handed down remotely. Neither Mallya nor any legal representatives were present; the media too stayed away from the courtroom. Yet, the significance of this judgment lies not just in Mallya losing his appeal but also how India, after mounting losses in extradition cases, has now turned the tide with this huge victory.

The next recourse for Mallya was appealing to the Supreme Court for which he would need to get permission from the high court. The permission to appeal in the Supreme Court was to be filed within fourteen days of this verdict. However, the apex court only hears cases with significant public interest or those affecting laws and legislations. Mallya quickly appealed for permission but the high court on 14 May 2020 refused his application to appeal to the Supreme Court, thus paving the way for his extradition to India.

The decision, delivered remotely, marks the end of an extraordinarily long and bitter legal battle between India and the liquor baron, who has been in the UK ever since he came to London in March 2016. The decision meant that Mallya could be sent to India in the following twenty-eight days.

But Mallya's legal team found another loophole to exploit. A confidential appeal to the UK Home Department has ensured that Mallya's extradition file remains closed as his other matter is dealt with. Looking at a similar situation of Hanif Tiger Patel (that we explore in a separate chapter), it seems anybody's guess when Mallya will be extradited, if ever.

As a last measure, Mallya can also approach the European Court of Human Rights (ECtHR) based in Strasbourg, France, on the grounds that his extradition impairs his human rights, further delaying his extraction from the UK. An interim ruling by the ECtHR could also halt his extradition process.

* * *

Overlooking the Regent's Park and located close to Madame Tussauds in the heart of London lies 18-19 Cornwall Terrace; it was from this urban pad that Mallya travelled to Westminster Magistrates' Court which is a five-minute drive. At one stage, it looked like his London townhouse would be taken over by the Swiss bank UBS; Mallya's desperate attempts to save it were glaringly visible.

Along with the extradition proceedings and other commercial disputes, Mallya was engaged in a bitter legal battle with UBS in the Business and Property Courts. Unlike the other cases, this case had his son Siddharth and mother Lalitha as defendants alongside Vijay Mallya.

In October 2005, Rose Capital Ventures Limited had purchased 18 and 19 Cornwall Terrace, formerly used as offices, to be converted into a residential property. The buildings were constructed in the 1820s and had suffered substantial damages during World War II. In 2007, Rose Capital, the British Virgin Islands registered company, was purchased by Gladco Properties Inc, which is owned by the Sileta Trust. This Sileta Trust, in turn, belongs to the Mallya family trust, thus effectively making Vijay Mallya the owner of the property.

In March 2012, Rose Capital took a £20.4 million loan from UBS secured by a mortgage over the residential premises. The loan was on an interest-only basis; in other words, the monthly payment covers only the interest component on the loan, without diminishing the principal borrowed. This hints that Mallya had a cash crunch, especially as the property had undergone massive repairs and upgrade. It was lying vacant since 2003, and was previously used by the Dairy Council as its administrative offices. But if you are imagining a dowdy set of offices, you could not be far from the truth. This property was attractively big enough for the local council to get a proposal to open it as a posh private school. Mallya's London home could have easily been a busy school with 245 pupils and a staff of forty!

Planning permission to convert the property from office space to residential use was granted in 2008, but it was only in 2012 that the house became habitable. For two years, building works were carried out by Kier Construction Ltd, a century-old leading UK construction behemoth. In February 2011, the repair works were taken over by Quad Contracts, which went on till late 2012. Cornwall Terrace was to be a 'high class home for Dr Vijay Mallya and his family members and United Breweries Group's corporate guests'. This entailed excavation of new basement, a garage at rear ground, new rooflights, use of roof as terrace, sunken roof garden, installation of a lift (big enough to have a wheelchair) serving all floors, new bathrooms and kitchen, among several other major work heads.

Negotiating the strict council rules to keep the character of the area intact and ensure preservation, the house when it was finally completed, had more than 35 rooms. It was spread over five floors – lower ground, ground floor, first floor, second floor and the third floor. At the rear of the house, lie an assortment of super cars including Bentleys, Rolls-Royces, Ferraris and his signature Maybach 62 with the VJM1 number plate. Just like Mallya, his London home is flamboyant and ostentatiously decorated, oozing wealth and grandeur.

Yet, non-payment of dues and disagreements over the tenure of the loan led to litigation. UBS initiated legal proceedings in March 2016, the same month when Mallya came to London from India. Starting from the county court, the case escalated to the high court and in March 2018, the bank sought possession of the property over non-payment of the £20.4 million loan. After successful applications to strike out several of Mallya's grounds, UBS had an upper hand as the case moved to the final stages. In November 2018, Mallya was directed to pay £88,000 in interim legal costs after the high court ruled that most of the grounds put forward by Mallya were 'bound to fail', adding to Mallya's precarious financial situation.

But Mallya once again proved that his negotiation skills and business acumen could seal many a deal. In May 2019, he convinced UBS to agree on a consent term, which set 30 April 2020 as the deadline to pay the mortgage and other expenses amounting to over Rs 200 crore. Till then, Mallya and his family—partner Pinky Lalwani, son Sid and mother Lalitha—could continue to stay there. This allowed Mallya some leeway to concentrate on the other cases without the constant worry about losing his London home.

The Cornwall Terrace property was crucial to access the expensive and posh clubs in central London of which he is a member, and hold discussions with his legal team and business associates. Besides, being landlocked in the UK, London's fine dining and shopping offered some consolation to Mallya who was benched from globetrotting.

On 20 March 2020, Vijay Mallya got two judgments from the high court—one pertaining to his London property and the other rescinding the sale of the super yacht Force India.

Justice Nigel Teare presided over both the hearings with the counsels arguing over the telephone. The coronavirus lockdown was just imposed, and central London had become a ghost town. The usually buzzing Rolls Building was deserted, and when Justice Teare sat in court number 8, apart from the court officials, there was no one else, except us, the authors. Mallya, the bank and their counsels joined the hearing through phone lines.

In the morning session, Justice Teare set aside his own January 2020 order for the sale of Force India pursuant to Qatar Bank's unpaid mortgage for which the yacht was a security. This was because Qatar Bank itself had sought the sale to be set aside, as a third party had in effect paid the sum secured by the mortgage.

Neil Henderson, the counsel for Indian banks, sought, and got, an undertaking that Force India would not be removed from

the jurisdiction as they had a WFO against Mallya. Yet Mallya's
victory in the case was enough for the banks to up their ante.

Henderson's intervention was much more intense during
the case pertaining to Mallya's London property. By virtue of
the WFO, Mallya had to seek the court's approval on his plans
to refinance the property to pay UBS and save Cornwall Terrace.
That application was also listed before Justice Teare. UBS, not
surprisingly, had no objection, but Henderson put forth a stout
opposition to the proposal by Rose Capital.

To repay UBS by the 30 April 2020 deadline, Rose Capital
sought the approval of Justice Teare to enter into a new loan and
mortgage agreement with Birchwood Hills Inc, which was registered
in the Bahamas and wholly owned by a Mallya family investment
entity. The counsel for Rose Capital pointed out that the new loan
was for the repayment of a loan to a completely independent party
and that, as Cornwall Terrace is listed in the WFO, it wouldn't be
possible to get a refinance from an unconnected party.

Over the phone put on speaker, Henderson pointed out the
'concern about the conduct of Dr Mallya', and how there was no
evidence of all the entities that Rose Capital had approached for
a loan. 'Rose Capital is subject to the worldwide freezing order,'
said Henderson and added that the Indian banks feared a possible
leakage of equity.

This did not work to sway Justice Teare who responded:
'Mr Henderson, if the transaction is necessary to pay UBS and
prevent possession being taken by UBS . . . it doesn't matter if Rose
Capital is using Dr Mallya's own resources.'

The arguments continued for over two hours, at the end of
which Justice Teare approved the refinancing. While the WFO is
taken out to protect the interest of the creditors, it does not bar the
use of assets in the ordinary and proper course of business, which is
how the refinancing proposal was characterized by the court.

'The purpose of the WFO is not to punish Dr Mallya,' observed
Justice Teare. After a volley of failures and disappointments,
20 March 2020 became the day Mallya registered a resounding

success. He had managed to save two of his prized possessions—his treasured house and his beloved yacht.

The more famous pad of the Mallyas is the palatial country house in Tewin village, Hertfordshire, 20 miles north of London. The quintessential English village dates back to the Anglo-Saxon times, boasts of a picturesque countryside rich in flora and fauna and has a population of barely 2000. Mallya's property Ladywalk was previously owned and occupied by Anthony Hamilton, father of F1 champion Lewis Hamilton, and hence has always been the cynosure of all eyes in the sleepy village.

Though not much is visible from the main entrance, a public footpath runs around the property, providing an unrestricted view of the enormous spread that includes the main house Ladywalk and a lodge called Bramble Lodge with plenty of land for Mallya's five dogs—Bichon lapdogs Elsa and Daisy, golden retrievers Luna and Bella and a St Bernard called Spirit—to play chase.

Security at Ladywalk is a priority and several CCTV cameras are in operation 24x7 at various entry and exit points along the periphery of the extensive property. Guards, dressed in black and armed with iPads and binoculars, are ever vigilant, and more so for snoopy scribes. The large modern house sits on 30 acres of land and boasts of swimming pools, tennis courts and several outhouses. The two-year renovation of the property saw a continuous flow of architects, landscape artists, builders and gardeners. But what the locals most look forward to is the plethora of supercars that take to the narrow roads leading to Queen Hoo Lane. A sure sign that the party king is at home!

The story begins on 11 June 2014. This property was already on the market through estate agents Savills and Knight Frank with at least one prospective buyer lined up. Mallya paid Hamilton a visit, instantly fell in love with the property and immediately made an offer. An offer that Anthony Hamilton could not refuse.

So desperate was Mallya to make this his new home that a written agreement between the two was signed that day, thus sealing the fate of this property. Interestingly, this agreement specified the 'Buyer' as: 'Dr Vijay Mallya and/or, Miss Leena Vijay Mallya, Miss Tanya Vijay Mallya, Mr Siddhartha Vijay Mallya OR to his/their order'. Mallya's Cornwall Terrace address in London was listed as the residential address. The deal was signed for a whopping £13 million and strangely no deposit was taken by Hamilton on that day.

On 11 June 2014, Anthony Hamilton signed as the 'seller', witnessed by Force India's Deputy Head Robert Fernley, and Mallya signed the agreement under his own name as a 'buyer', witnessed by his chartered accountant Dr Lakshmi Kanthan. The only signature on the preliminary agreement under the 'buyer' was that of Mallya. None of his children had accompanied him to view the property and there is no evidence to suggest that they were aware that they were put as buyers then or had authorized Mallya to purchase the property on their behalf.

This property has all the hallmarks of being owned and occupied by Mallya. A fleet of supercars making their way down the drive, hordes of people descending to party all night long and a constant delivery of goods and services. Yet when we dig deeper into the ownership, Vijay Mallya is a phantom lurking everywhere yet really nowhere.

Ladywalk is propped up on a complex structure of ownership that defines the existence of many such marquee properties in the UK. Mallya has never disputed claims that he bought his new family home with the intention of securing it for his son and two daughters. Though he has often nonchalantly challenged reporters to prove that the Ladywalk property was bought by him through ill-gotten money. If one can lawfully hide the real ownership and flow of funds, why wouldn't billionaires exercise the option and bask in the security this provides them?

Here is how the complex network of newly created trusts, registered in far-off tax havens, operated through a discreet Swiss financial firm, secured for Mallya his most prized home in the UK: On 29 January 2015, Ladywalk LLP was established under the Limited Liability Partnerships Act 2000, 'to carry on the business of investing in, owning and letting residential property' (clause 3) and the net profits of the business were to be distributed between limited partners (99.9 per cent) and the general partner (0.1 per cent). There were two limited partners: 1: Continental Administrative Services Limited (CASL) as trustee of Welwyn Property Trust and 2: CASL as trustee of Tewin Property Trust. The general partner was CASL as trustee of Sileta Trust.

Sileta Trust, established on 21 July 2007, has Lalitha Mallya as the settlor and Vijay Mallya as the protector, for a 100-year 'Trust Period'. As a protector, Vijay Mallya then added his children— Leena, Tanya and Siddharth—as beneficiaries of the Sileta Trust by a resolution dated 1 May 2016. Both the Welwyn Property Trust and Tewin Property Trust were established on 25 January 2015, just four days before the agreement was entered into. The two trusts established in the British Virgin Islands (BVI) bear names derived from the location of the property: Queen Hoo Lane, Tewin, Welwyn, Hertfordshire, AL6 0LT. Ladywalk LLP was also established in the BVI. This was also the registered address for Ladywalk LLP.

CASL is a Switzerland-based, corporate trustee company run by one Andrea Rishaal Vallabh, who executed the Ladywalk property deal on behalf of three separate trusts. On 3 July 2015, Andrea Vallabh signed a declaration stating that he held his interest in Ladywalk LLP as a nominee and trustee of CASL, as a trustee of Sileta Trust. But Andrea is kin to Jayprakash Vallabh, who resigned from the position of director of McDowell & Co. (Scotland) in July 2015. McDowell & Co. (Scotland) was set up in July 1993 with Vijay Mallya as its founding director.

Interestingly, Jayprakash along with his wife Susanna held a 10 per cent stake in Kingfisher Airlines. He also held a significant stake in Watson Ltd based in Mauritius that owned a 21 per cent stake in UBHL. Jayprakash and Susanna were also directors of CAS Nominees, registered in the Isle of Man, that serves as the principal trustee of the Golden Eagle Trust, a Mallya family trust established by the patriarch Vittal in the 1980s.

The bond between the Mallyas and the Vallabhs dates back many decades, and to many offshore companies that have been linked to Mallya's flagship businesses. It is, therefore, not surprising to see the Vallabhs once again take centre stage in securing the Ladywalk property for Mallya. It also comes as no surprise that CASL was constituted under the laws of St Kitts and Nevis, perhaps the most secretive tax haven today.

Ladywalk properties were split into two entities: Ladywalk for £1,14,99,999 and Bramble Lodge for £15,00,000. On 4 June 2015, Mallya confirmed paying a deposit of £1.3 million and promised to pay £4.5 million split into £1.5 million on completion of the sale of Bramble Lodge and £3 million on completion of this agreement, and the remaining £7.2 million on the exchange of deeds on 15 July 2015. This agreement was signed by Vijay Mallya under 'For & On Behalf Of Buyer(s)' and Anthony Hamilton. There were no witness signatures.

On 17 July 2015, Ladywalk LLP purchased the Ladywalk and Bramble Lodge properties. There is no direct evidence of the person who paid the remaining funds. But accounts of Ladywalk LLP between 3 July 2015 and 31 July 2016 reveal a more complicated web of financial transactions that could have been used to make the final payment towards these properties. Another company, Ladywalk Investments, was created in the BVI that managed to secure funds through the financial company Edmond de Rothschild (Suisse) S.A. against the Ladywalk and Bramble Lodge properties, put up as collateral by Ladywalk LLP for a credit facility term of ten years. The amount credited into Ladywalk LLP accounts was £7.2 million.

In the eyes of the law, the legal owner of the palatial Ladywalk and Bramble Lodge properties is Ladywalk LLP, though the economic ownership of the properties would be enjoyed by Mallya's daughters as they would likely stand to gain or lose by an increase or decrease in the value of the properties.

Years of renovations and several hundred thousand pounds spent, created for Mallya his perfect refuge when he left India a year later, perhaps safe in the knowledge that his possession of this property is secured. Vijay Mallya, who proudly flaunts Ladywalk as his UK home, legally holds no ownership of the property.

It comes as little surprise that Mallya is adept at using an intricate and secretive web of companies in such offshore locations like Nevis and the BVI to own properties and conduct financial transactions. While many tax havens have seen their laws diluted due to the constant pressure by countries to curb money laundering, Nevis, with a population of less than 12,000, has redoubled its pledge to secrecy. Once a British colony, St Kitts and Nevis achieved independence in 1983. The federal constitution gives Nevis autonomy that the island has maximized to the fullest. A year later, on the advice of an American lawyer, the first premier Simeon Daniel passed the Nevis Business Corporation Ordinance Act 1984 that opened Nevis to offshore investors and it has never looked back.

With its premiers being financial consultants, they are adamant to ensure that this tiny volcanic island remains the most lucrative destination for those looking to create highly anonymized corporations for the explicit purposes of money laundering and tax evasion. After all, Nevis makes $5–6 million annually in just renewal fees from the companies registered on its shores. Even though tens of thousands of companies registered in St Kitts and Nevis were mentioned in the Paradise Papers and Panama Papers leaks, tracing their ownership has proved almost impossible.

The Swiss Leaks in 2015 showed how the HSBC Private Bank in Switzerland helped its customers set up companies registered in the BVI to circuit through tax laws. In 2016, it was found through the Panama Papers leak that the (now defunct) law firm and corporate services provider, Mossack Fonseca, though based in Panama, had used the BVI to register over 1.13 lakh companies for its clients, making this island—an overseas territory of the UK, located near Puerto Rico—their most favoured tax haven destination. The International Consortium of Investigative Journalists' recent Financial Crimes Enforcement Network (FinCEN) Files showed that one in every five suspicious activity reports filed by banks contained a client with an address in the BVI.

For the Tewin villagers, VJ, as he is fondly called, is a celebrity owner of Ladywalk, their most interesting landmark. Mistaking curious (Indian) journalists to be Mallya's acquaintances/guests, the staff at local pubs spoke glowingly about VJ. But that was in March 2016, which was when Mallya had left India. As the visits became more frequent, revealing the true purpose, the staff's indulgence turned into indifference and locals became circumspect.

Tewin may have been thrust into bad press due to its notorious resident, but one, they say, who has a heart of gold. It is believed that Mallya donated a Christmas tree to the village when the local fir tree was uprooted in an accident. While few have interacted with him, they know that Mallya attended a barn dance at the nearby hamlet of Bull's Green and Pinky Lalwani also expressed interest in joining the local walking group. Largely, the couple have kept to themselves, more so after the news of his trial made headlines and reporters swooped down on the quiet village.

Mallya remains constrained with the cap on his monthly expenses and the multitude of court cases that he faces. There have been occasions where two or even three cases relating to him have been listed in the high court on the same day. Apart from the Indian banks led by SBI, other creditors have approached courts to exact their dues. Indian banks succeeded in getting the Bangalore debt recovery tribunal's order certified in the UK by approaching the high court. This put in motion a WFO, and a situation where Mallya and his family members have to ration their expenses.

From the weekly cap of £18,000 set by the court to come down to monthly expenses of £22,500 is no mean feat for the former 'King of Good Times'. These figures are away above the average household expenses, but for a man known for his lavish lifestyle, the very notion of having a budgetary limit can be revolting. Indian banks have succeeded in pushing him into a corner, but so far he has managed to thwart their endeavours to get him declared bankrupt.

It is quite difficult to ascertain the true picture of Mallya's situation. What is certain is that he is in a financial squeeze, with the banks forcing him to declare the major items of his household expenses—he told the court he spends £1000 a week on groceries, £250 on petrol and £1159 for a high-speed internet connection that is required for Mallya to undertake his 'consultancy services'. At the same time, he is a member of exclusive private clubs including Annabel's, dines out at fancy restaurants, rides a Silver Maybach with a VJM1 number plate among a fleet of fancy cars and is in occupation of two massive properties in England.

* * *

To understand what Mallya continues to miss will require going back to 18 April 2017 when he was first brought to Westminster Magistrates' Court. Mallya was bailed on a £650,000 bond, debarred from travelling outside England, and from applying for travel documents. Mallya may have access to all the comforts and riches, but with his wings clipped and movement curtailed, he is just a shadow of his former self. He would have liked to attend F1 races across the world, but now the only option he has is the British Grand Prix at Silverstone. The cricket matches he attended and the odd public appearances he made in London could provide him with neither comfort nor pleasure. This was a case of fame coming back to haunt him across the seven seas.

During the ICC Cricket World Cup in June 2019, as India took on Australia at the Oval in London, the media had expected cricket-crazy Mallya to make an appearance. And so, it seems, had many Indian cricket fans. Dressed in a light blue suit with an open-collared white and blue striped shirt, Mallya accompanied his beau, Pinky Lalwani, looking splendid in a hot pink jacket trimmed with fur and sporting dark shades, and his aged mother Lalitha to the VIP entrance gate at the Oval. He often wears blue suits at the matches, which he says is his way of showing support to the Men in Blue.

No sooner had they got out of their car, than the crowd chanting 'Chor! Chor!' (thief, thief) and 'Paise de!' (give our money back) began heckling him and his family. A defiant Mallya took out his phone and began recording selfies with the hostile crowd.

He later tweeted a picture with his son inside the stadium with the caption: 'Great to watch cricket with my son and even sweeter to see India's emphatic victory over Australia'. A similar incident happened in January 2017 during the ICC Champions Trophy when Mallya had gone to watch the match between South Africa and West Indies at the Oval.

Though Mallya tries to have a nonchalant attitude towards people calling him names, in his less guarded moments, the hurt and pain this causes him is obvious to see. On less stressful days at the court, Mallya is happy to indulge in light banter about cricket with journalists outside the court.

Public appearances have never been easy for Mallya since his escape to London. In June 2016, Mallya made an appearance at the launch of Suhel Seth's book at the London School of Economics and Political Science (LSE) where the high commissioner of India, Navtej Sarna, was a panellist along with UK cabinet minister Jo Johnson, brother of Boris Johnson. Journalist Rishi Majumdar, who was at the LSE event, remembers seeing Sarna quickly make an excuse and leave after spotting Mallya in the audience. Mallya, who was sitting at the back near the exit, came into the room just after the event started. Many like Majumdar found it quite ironic that an event on best practices by CEOs was attended by a man who was believed to have done the exact opposite.

To have an Indian diplomat and a (un)popular offender in the same room was a blunder that sent the ministry of external affairs into a frenzy. Statements were quickly issued that the event had two segments—first, a book launch event where the invitees were determined by LSE, and the second was a reception by the High Commission for a select few guests. 'Mallya was certainly not an invitee to the reception at the High Commission for which the invitations were issued by the High Commission, and was not present,' the MEA statement said. LSE also clarified that Mallya was not on its list of invitees.

Mallya was extremely upset with all the fuss created by his simple presence at what was a public event as each organizer denied ever inviting him. He took to Twitter to hit back: 'Never gate-crashed in my life . . . I am not a gatecrasher and would never be one; I went for my friend—the author. Sat quietly with my daughter and listened. Headline news and unfounded speculation followed; No evidence, No charge sheet. Before claiming all this should I not be given a chance to pursue my legal remedies? Most unfair.'

With the media turning hostile, Mallya has embraced Twitter as his new best friend. And while he gets trolled ruthlessly, he also has many who support him and, of course, the media is always paying attention to what he says, even when they don't react. He has taken to Twitter to argue his innocence, make offers of debt repayment, plead his victimhood from a ruthless administration and always show the unfairness of the circumstances of his life today. He is one fugitive who confronts the media head-on, boldly faces the angst of the public, and stands strong against all those who take pleasure in his downfall.

On 18 December 2020, Mallya spent his birthday attending court proceedings in his bankruptcy case, albeit virtually, requesting the judge to release funds from assets frozen by the courts. His counsel told the court that, failing this influx of funds, there was a good chance that Mallya would go unrepresented in the next hearing. The court then agreed to release £240,000 (plus 20 per cent of the value added tax on that amount), a sum that only covered his legal costs until December 2020. Mallya was back in the court in January 2021, requesting further funds. He claimed he had lost his income from the consultancy services that he had provided in recent years. With his life's earnings frozen by the authorities, he claims he was now facing penury.

There was no sign of Mallya's return to India when this book went into print in early February 2021. But what is clearly evident is that a man whose life was much celebrated just five short years ago, is now a mere shadow of his larger-than-life persona. There is no doubt that the party king has disappeared from public celebrations just like the fireworks that once lit up the skies, soon melt into the darkness.

2

COUNT OF MONTE CORRUPTION

In 1815, a nineteen-year-old sailor Edmond Dantès docked at the port in Marseilles, France. He was as handsome as he was intelligent, rich in character and in material possessions and soon to be the captain of his ship. His fiancée, a beautiful Catalan girl called Mercedes, awaited his return with dreams of a happily ever after.

Alas, even well-planned lives throw shocks that one can never fathom; for Dantès was arrested on his wedding day, declared a traitor to Napoleon Bonaparte and imprisoned. His rivals made sure he was put away for a long, long time.

For fourteen endless years, Dantès was put behind bars in the notorious prison Château d'If. But one day he escaped and made his way to an island called Monte Cristo, where he was the king with vast treasures. But his life was irrevocably altered by his experiences in prison and the rage and vehemence he felt for those responsible had completely consumed him. He pledged revenge and set out to wreck the lives of those who took the peace from his world. Adopting many aliases and disguises, his life's mission was to destroy all those who destroyed his carefully planned life. The once humble and ethical Dantès was now truly turned over to the dark side.

When Alexandre Dumas wrote *The Count of Monte Cristo* in 1844, little did he realize that the protagonist Edmond Dantès would become an alias for a twenty-first-century fugitive, diamantaire Nirav Modi.

A petite jeweller with giant ambitions, Nirav Modi launched his NIRAV MODI brand with the aim of making it synonymous with the aesthetic beauty and glamour of the diamonds that adorned the bodies of A-list celebrities across the world. The fifty-year-old diamond trader, who founded Firestar Diamond that claimed $2 billion in jewellery sales in 2015, made his international foray with his first flagship store in the glittering New York City, thus fulfilling his aspiration of selling to the elusive high-profile clientele and fitting in snugly with the global glitterati.

Modi is a stark contrast to his grandfather, Keshavlal Modi, who built the diamond business by importing gems from Europe to the tax-free Puducherry, a union territory on the west coast of India and a former colony of the French and the Portuguese. The Ebenezer Scrooge of his times, Keshavlal avoided fanfare of any kind, which meant he never spent a dime more than required, sometimes not even that. But unlike Charles Dickens's immortalized character from *A Christmas Carol*, Keshavlal never looked for redemption. A true miser to his last days, Keshavlal, even when he moved to Singapore, strongly believed in being stingy and trusting only members of the close-knit Palanpuri Jains of the Gujarati community who were deeply intertwined in business and family.

Keshavlal arranged the marriage of his eldest son Deepak to another Palanpuri jeweller Chinubhai Choksi's eldest daughter Gita in 1966. Choksi had a well-established gems and jewellery business empire extending to London, New York, Hong Kong and Antwerp and the famous Gitanjali Gems is an amalgamation of the names of Choksi's two daughters Gita and Anjali.

A married Deepak settled in Antwerp and began trading in rough diamonds. He became an important supply partner to the global diamond company De Beers and climbed the ranks to be one of the wealthiest Indians in Belgium. In those days in Antwerp, 'blood diamonds' were easily available and several traders made huge profits on the back of this shady African trade.

Unlike Keshavlal, Deepak loved to flaunt his wealth. His love
for luxury brands and high-end outfits stood out against his father's
frugal lifestyle. Nirav, Deepak and Gita's eldest son, was born in
1971 followed by a sister Purvi and brother Nehal. While Nirav
grew up with his parents in the posh neighbourhood of Edegem in
Antwerp, Nehal was sent to New York to live with their aunt Nina
Choksi, who was divorced then and had no children of her own.

When Nirav was eight, his mother met with a tragic accident
and lost her life (it has now emerged through leaked medical
records that she had died by suicide). His father remarried
within months of losing his wife—to an interior designer called
Pragna Dave, not of the Palanpuri community. Soon they had a
son, Neeshal.

Deepak still runs a diamond business in Antwerp. Nirav Modi
wanted to be a Wall Street trader and was keen to study finance
and learn Japanese. However, he did not complete his studies and
soon dropped out of The Wharton School of the University of
Pennsylvania when he was nineteen. Rumour has it that his father
took a huge fall on the stock exchange and could no longer support
Modi's fancy lifestyle in the US. Another rumour says that Modi's
romance with the stock market crashed along with his family's
fortunes and so he decided to return to India to learn the ropes of
the diamond trade from his uncle Mehul Choksi.

Mehul and his brother Chetan took over their father's business
while they were still studying at HR College of Commerce and
Economics in south Mumbai. Chinubhai was losing his vision due
to glaucoma and, after having lost the support of his brothers when
they separated to create their own empires, could only rely on his
sons to run his business. Mehul Choksi, who was often bullied for
being overweight and called 'Pappu', grabbed this opportunity to
prove himself. He knew success in business could win him many
friends and those that didn't come to him, were lured with luxurious
parties and expensive gifts. Choksi was a neoliberal entrepreneur.
He invested crores in marketing and promotions, hiring some big
names in Bollywood like Aishwarya Rai-Bachchan, Bipasha Basu

and Kareena Kapoor, and expanding his platter of jewellery to suit a range of budgets thus including India's aspirational middle-class into its customer base, reaching a market capital of over Rs 5000 crore at one point.

Nirav Modi idolized his uncle, who soon took him under his wing, sharing not just office space at Prasad Chambers at Opera House, which the family owned since the 1960s, but teaching him everything he knew. Choksi was often a man without a plan, letting his gut rule his head, often dipping in and out of business ventures on a mere whim and accumulating debts in the process. As the debts mounted, Choksi began staying away from the spotlight.

After a decade under Choksi's tutelage, Modi established his own company, Firestar Diamond, in 1999 which was involved in sorting diamonds. He later moved into gems trading and then into manufacturing jewellery. In 2010, Modi decided to expand into the luxury jewellery market with the Christie's auction brochure in Hong Kong featuring the ostentatious Golconda Lotus necklace that centred a rare 12.29-carat Indian diamond surrounded by pink diamonds from the famous Anglo-Australian Rio Tinto's Argyle mine and cost a whopping $3.75 million or Rs 16.3 crore. Thus began Modi's non-stop foray into the global ultra-luxe diamond market.

This fame wasn't based on a lucky chance, but something that came out of months of studying Christie's and Sotheby's catalogues to analyse buyer behaviour and trends in the market. In 2010, after the Wall Street crash, the prices of large diamonds had plummeted, and Modi zapped up large diamonds wherever he could. This included a large stock of the rare pink ones used in the Golconda Lotus necklace, some blue stones and another large cache of yellow and colourless ones that together cost almost $60 million. All these stones appreciated in value at least two–three times over the next five years.

The Christie's auction had put Modi on the global map of luxe jewellery. His Orchid Ainra necklace, with two pear-shaped diamonds weighing 10.02 carats and 2.66 carats respectively, interspaced with a burgundy hexagonal-shaped diamond, sold at a 2015 Christie's auction in Hong Kong for Rs 13 crore. As Modi's popularity began growing in the press in India, many started referring to him as NiMo, so as not to confuse (but also rhyme) with the Prime Minister of India Narendra Modi who is called NaMo. Nirav Modi was so enthralled by this nickname that he got cufflinks made for himself that represented the clownfish Nemo and proudly wore them to important events.

To Modi, business success was not enough; he had an insatiable thirst to be in the spotlight of the rich and the famous, though he spoke little and often shied away from taking centre stage. At the grand opening of the NIRAV MODI boutique in New York in 2015, the brand's first store in the US, located on the highly sought-after 'Gold Coast' Madison Avenue, the short-statured diamantaire from Palanpur in Gujarat was flanked by lanky Hollywood beauties Naomi Watts and Deborra-Lee Furness as he posed in a soft oyster shirt opened at his neck and a bright-blue suit with a blood-red satin pocket square.

Models Coco Rocha, Nimrat Kaur and Lisa Haydon also smiled for the shutterbugs with the petite man who owns a plethora of rare gems and diamonds in some of the most exquisite jewellery collections on display. Donald Trump Jr and his wife Vanessa also dropped in. Modi then invited the celebrities, socialites and influencers to join him at a private dinner where they were entertained by none other than the celebrity DJ power couple Hannah Bronfman and Brendan Fallis on the rooftop of Rockefeller Center.

Modi may be new on the designer circuit, but he was definitely chased by established models. The former Miss World and model Lisa Haydon confessed that she had approached Modi through a friend to express her desire to wear the exquisite jewellery in a commercial for him. Modi gladly took her on board. She soon signed on to be one of the main NIRAV MODI brand ambassadors, featuring on several billboards and in print advertisements globally and becoming the face of the launch of its flagship store in New York.

A commercial shot in Paris, shows Haydon showcasing the Majestic Mogok Ruby Suite and Constellation necklace and showstopper jewellery from the Luminance and Sakura collections. In a chat with Haydon, the clip of which was released by Modi's company before the advertisement went on air, the jeweller explains the exquisiteness of this collection. 'The finest rubies in the world come from . . . Burma's Mogok valley. To find one ruby is rare . . . it took five years for us to find an entire suite of Mogok rubies, twenty-seven rubies of this red colour, transparency and character and it's extremely rare'. Modi took immense pride in his collections, especially as he has often said he himself designed many of the more exquisite pieces.

His New York store's window display boasted the breathtaking and highly sought-after Maharani diamond necklace (worth $1.65 million) and the store's interior had hand-crafted paper art window frieze reflecting his iconic signature jewellery, including the Jasmine necklace with 65 carats of briolette and jasmine cut diamonds from the Fluire collection, the Mughal collection and the much-admired Embrace bangles and rings.

To Modi, the boutique was a place to enthral and enchant his customers. 'The sophisticated American woman will recognize, as soon as she enters the boutique, that the entire experience is designed to pay tribute to her beauty, and to reflect and reveal her inner radiance,' said Modi.

Flanked on either side by luxury brands like Vacheron Constantin, the Swiss watch manufacturer founded in 1755, and Kwiat, the veteran diamond house known for its engagement rings since 1907, and with Tiffany's, Graff, De Beers, Hueb and Buccellati yonder, Modi felt as tall as the nearby Trump Tower.

Modi was desperate to stand out and shine and he sure did as the opening of the store made it to newsprint across the world. Nirav Modi had arrived in the West.

His designs graced the skin of celebrities around the world, including Kate Winslet who wore over 100 carats of diamonds in a bracelet and earrings from the Luminance collection along with a classic ring on the red carpet to the 88th Academy Awards in February 2016 for her supporting role nomination in the film *Steve Jobs*. At the 2017 Academy Awards, *Hidden Figures* actor Taraji P. Henson, nominated in the Best Actress category, dazzled everyone with a 103-carat diamond necklace and an emerald ring. At the Vanity Fair Oscar Party, models Kate Upton and Stella Maxwell and actor Olivia Munn also wore Nirav Modi jewellery, while brand ambassador Rosie Huntington-Whiteley sported the emerald-cut diamond drop earrings from the Celestial collection that perfectly paired with her shimmering silver Versace gown.

Supermodel Karlie Kloss walked the red carpet in a Mughal choker paired with studs that Modi takes credit for designing himself. She also posed with Modi at the Halloween charity event in New York in October 2017. In early 2018, Dakota Johnson of *Fifty Shades of Grey* fame, wore the designer on the Golden Globes red carpet, while Amy Adams donned the Luminance ring along with Jasmine rings, paired with Luminance earrings at the Annual Critics' Choice Awards. NIRAV MODI was soon turning into a jewellery brand that was a regular feature on the red carpet, sprinting the Indian jeweller into the class of A-list global designers.

In early 2017, Bollywood actor Priyanka Chopra served as a global ambassador for the NIRAV MODI collection and shot several commercials, including one with actor Sidharth Malhotra. She also graced the December 2017 cover of *Hello!* magazine wearing NIRAV MODI Dew Drop earrings. Calling her association with Modi 'a meeting of minds in many ways', Chopra had then told the press that 'we are both fiercely proud of our heritage and are united by the idea of bringing a modern India to the global forefront. His jewels are one of a kind and effortless, with an understated elegance'.

NIRAV MODI flagship stores, which opened in Defence Colony in New Delhi in 2014 and Kala Ghoda in south Mumbai in 2015, were designed by the famous Spanish interior designer Jaime Hayon, who is known for an installation called Carousel, made up of 15 million crystals, in the Swarovski theme park in the Tyrol mountains. To get Hayon to design his store was a fashion coup that few could pull.

Bollywood divas flaunted NIRAV MODI jewellery on many occasions. From Aishwarya Rai-Bachchan who wore the diamond flowers at a *Stardust* event to Kareena Kapoor Khan who dazzled in Fluire earrings at the Times of India Film Awards (TOIFA); from Jacqueline Fernandez displaying the Luminance ring and earrings at the Filmfare Glamour and Style Awards to Kajol showcasing the Luminance earrings and ring at the HT India's Most Stylish Awards; from Shraddha Kapoor who wore the Lotus earrings at the Navbharat Times Awards to Anushka Sharma who posed in the Celestial earrings and Brocade ring at the Lux Golden Rose Awards; from Nimrat Kaur sparkling in the Entremblant earrings and Orchestra ring at the Readers Travel Awards to Priyanka Chopra walking the red carpet in a Celestial necklace at the Toronto International Film Festival; Bollywood celebrities were much in love with NIRAV MODI jewellery and loved to be seen in it at events and parties.

Nirav Modi got Maharaja Gaj Singh II to host a private reception at the Taj group's Umaid Bhawan Palace in Jodhpur to mark the brand's fifth anniversary in 2016. The guest list comprising the rich in their designer suits and sparkling jewellery were his perfect clientele. The palace lawns saw an extravagant luncheon with flowing champagne and wine as the models walked the ramp in gowns made with exquisite fresh flowers. Roses, orchids, lilies and chrysanthemums in a variety of colours were crafted on to the outfits from 2 a.m. so they did not wilt before the fashion show, and the models exhibited some of Modi's exclusive floral-inspired jewellery collections including a necklace that was worth Rs 12 crore!

The outdoor dinner saw a grand Rajasthani thali made with recipes from the Maharaja's kitchen accompanied by Sufi music and followed by dancing to the tunes of the Indian band

The Bartender. The guests left with a gift bag of jewellery and the purchases they made from the exquisite collections on display at the Palace.

Nirav Modi's generous nature often eclipses his shrewd business acumen. After Lisa Haydon delivered a baby boy, Modi hosted a party for her at the Grand Palais in Paris in September 2017 where the new mum dazzled in a Pear Emerald Suite, making it to the cover of several luxury publications. Modi had also flown Shahid Kapoor and his wife Mira to an event in Jaipur and bore all the expenses for their stay at Umaid Bhawan Palace, with the intention that their celebrity status would get headlines and make him the talk of the elite party circuits in India. Earlier, during their wedding reception in Mumbai in 2015, Mira Rajput had worn cascade earrings, a bracelet and ring from the Luminance collection over a Manish Malhotra lehenga and her look was the talk of the town for weeks.

In November 2017, Modi held a lavish and exclusive dinner party at Mumbai's Four Seasons hotel, roping in three-star Michelin chef, the Italian Massimo Bottura, whose restaurant Osteria Francescana in Modena, Italy, ranked among the top five in the World's 50 Best Restaurants Awards since 2010 and has long waiting queues that stretch for months. Bottura prepared a special seven-course meal for Modi's invitees that included fashion diva and Bollywood actor Sonam Kapoor. The Bollywood fashionista had attended the NIRAV MODI jewellery preview at One&Only The Palm Dubai in 2011, wearing a stunning diamond necklace. 'Nirav's jewellery is very clean and beautiful. It is like wearing a piece of art,' she had said.

Another significant moment in the brand's expansion came in October 2016 when Modi opened his jewellery boutique in London's famous Old Bond Street near the exclusive Mayfair. British Indian industrialists like Aditya Mittal, son of Lakshmi Mittal, and president of ArcelorMittal; Dheeraj Hinduja, younger son of Gopichand of the Hinduja Brothers, and chairman of Ashok Leyland; and Siddhartha Lal, son of Vikram Lal, and director of Eicher Motors, were among the billionaires on Modi's guest list.

Actress and model Rosie Huntington-Whiteley was the face of the NIRAV MODI brand in the UK as she posed with Modi for the shutterbugs. In a campaign shot by renowned photographer Patrick Demarchelier, Priyanka Chopra and Huntington-Whitely are in black and white, wearing exquisite jewellery shown in colour, which symbolizes the 'coming together of classic and contemporary and echoes the essence of a woman and brings out her strength and beauty', Modi said.

Atelier Marika Chaumet, the French luxury interior designer, was engaged to create a feminine, ethereal and luxurious feel to the 2300 square feet, two-storey boutique with over 1200 square feet earmarked for its retail operations and a dedicated client area situated upstairs. Mother-of-pearl finishes, frosted glass and brushed metal created the opulence that could feather the exquisite jewels and also light up their sparkle with glass top bars and crystal chandeliers.

His jewellery collections, costing hundreds of thousands of pounds, soon became a hit with the celebrities, Arab royalty and Russian oligarchs who frequent the Queen's capital for shopping expeditions. He used models and actors popular globally and yet with the right local flavour to market his brand in the region and on an international platform. For his Hong Kong store, he picked Chinese actor Zhang Ziyi, who is not just an icon to the Chinese population, but also known worldwide for her role in the popular *Crouching Tiger, Hidden Dragon* movie.

With a net worth of $1.8 billion, he was ranked eighty-fifth on *Forbes*'s 2017 annual list of India's wealthiest people and 1234 globally. In 2016, he was ranked forty-sixth in India and 1067th among the world's billionaires.

Modi was also the first Indian jeweller to have graced the cover of Sotheby's and Christie's catalogues. NIRAV MODI was not just a brand synonymous with glamour but the man himself was also enjoying a stardom afforded to few Indian designers. As a regular in the party circuit in London, Paris, Dubai, Hong Kong and New York, Modi was much written about in fashion and luxury magazines and his jewellery collections were most sought after.

Ami Javeri, a citizen of the US, who met Nirav Modi during her MBA in Wharton, and soon became his wife, acted as the trustee of the Nirav Modi Foundation and oversaw the Scholarship for Excellence, which helps 250 students annually. Her friendship with socialite Elina Meswani, wife of Nikhil Meswani, director of Reliance Industries, helped her foray into Mumbai's elite society that emulated the New York social scene. Ami used her social skills to expand the jewellery brand among the rich and the famous in India.

Nirav Modi once told the press that they would never see his wife and their three kids, Rohin, Apasha and Ananya, with him in any frame. The couple claimed to speak Gujarati with their children at home and not pamper them with treasures bought from the family wealth. A tradition in the Modi household is to host birthday parties at home and the children are allowed to only keep three presents of their choosing; the rest is given away.

Modi is also a very hands-on jewellery designer. Though he is not much of an artist with a pencil, he is one with a vision and eye for detail to create exclusive designs that are often one of a kind and draw inspiration from the activities of everyday life. One such idea was born when he observed his girls putting their scrunchies on their wrists as pretend bangles. He transformed this into a 1600-diamond bangle that moulded to the shape of one's wrist due to its 800 locks, and his Embrace bangle collection was born. It was graded by the Gemological Institute of America and only high colour and high clarity diamonds were used to appeal to Western sensibilities. Modi loves to tell everyone that the Embrace bangle caught the imagination of the American filmmaker Steven Spielberg who simply couldn't resist trying it on.

Modi is among the top echelons of Indian society, both individually and through familial links. His brother Nehal ran the Modi business in the US. His half-brother Neeshal, who graduated from City, University of London, headed Modi's Europe division, while his sister Purvi managed the jewellery designs as a consultant from Hong Kong. Purvi is married to Mayank Mehta, who is brother to the Rosy Blue group's Russell Mehta's wife Mona. Mona and Mayank's first cousin Preeti was married to Mehul Choksi. Choksi's daughter Priyanka married Akash Mehta, a diamond merchant based in Antwerp. She was managing a company Nirav had invested in called A Jaffe.

Russell and Mona's daughter Shloka married India's richest man Mukesh Ambani's son Akash in 2019, in a wedding attended by politicians, businessmen, actors, sport stars and other celebrities from India and across the globe. Neeshal Modi is married to Isheta Salgaocar, daughter of Goa's mining baron Dattaraj Salgaocar and Dipti Ambani, sister to the Ambani brothers Mukesh and Anil. Vipul Ambani, who was the Reliance patriarch Dhirubhai's younger brother Nathubhai's son, was made the CFO of Modi's Firestar India. Vipul Ambani was managing the finances and expansion of the business in India. Firestar International's finances were handled by Modi's cousin, Mihir Bhansali along with his wife Rakhi in New York. Both Ambani and Bhansali were Nirav's close confidants and knew his business inside out.

While most people in Nirav's extended family tree are socialites and public figures, he has managed to keep his wife and children away from the media glare. His children went to Dhirubhai Ambani International School in posh Bandra, Mumbai, where the kids of Bollywood stars go, and his son later moved to Charterhouse, a 250-acre exclusive private boarding school founded in 1611 near London whose yearly fees are over £40,000. Its distinguished alumni includes socialites, politicians, celebrity journalists, scientists and global businessmen.

His son was sent to this school to help him cultivate the rich and famous of British society where elitism opens doors and close bonds formed during school and college seem to curry favour in professional lives years later, like the Etonians in the UK Parliament and judiciary and the Bullingdon Club boys in the

Tory party. In India, Modi had joined the billionaire club called
The Young Presidents' Organization (now YPO) that includes
business leaders, top officials in the banking and financial world
and those from old elite families of erstwhile Bombay. Thus
Modi was well aware of the benefits that belonging to a powerful
fraternity brought into his personal life and business.

Modi strived hard to portray himself not just as a hugely
successful entrepreneur, but also a connoisseur of contemporary
art, patron of upcoming artists and a philanthropist. He created
connections with socialites and elites by offering them lucrative
positions within his organization. Arundhati De, Shobha De's
daughter, and Aparna Chudasama, Mumbai's former mayor Nana
Chudasama's daughter-in-law and Bharatiya Janata Party (BJP)
leader Shaina N.C.'s sister-in-law, were hired by the firm to look
after sales. Aparna's husband Akshay is a corporate lawyer.

Modi's familial connections and the vast circuit of socialites
and celebrities roving around him made him a young global Indian
businessman that few could ignore. He left no stone unturned
to build contacts and establish relationships with those that he
perceived could be beneficial to him. This meteoric rise to fame
was largely attributed to the company he cultivated and the
relationships he forged.

Modi was a people-pleaser and courted the press in his
signature ostentatious style. Veteran business journalist Pavan C.
Lall recalls that in January 2017, even as Modi's offices were being
raided by the income-tax authorities, he was not shying away from
the press. Five days after the raid, Modi sent his vintage burgundy
Bentley limousine to Lall's office to get him to his Kala Ghoda
store for an interview when the scribe cited parking concerns in
that area. The Bentley boasted a licence plate that read 'DAF',
short for 'Diamonds Are Forever'.

Lall recalls Modi wearing a huge blood-red 4-carat diamond
on a platinum band, its light creating an 'almost other-worldly
glow around the wearer'. When Lall enquired whether it was a
Burmese ruby, promptly came Modi's reply: 'Six million dollars.'

After regaling Lall with tales of a princess from Oman purchasing jewellery worth Rs 1.8 crore from that very store, Modi confessed that his business was raided by the income-tax department and that they were looking for Rs 120 crore!

He, however, did not seem too perturbed to Lall, though the always immaculately dressed and clean-shaven Modi was now a tired-looking man sporting a week-old beard and attire that seemed to have not been changed for a couple of days, signalling that perhaps all was not well.

Yet, the tenacious Modi soon bounced back. So it comes as no surprise that as a special invitee to the British high commissioner's residence in New Delhi in November 2017, Modi also met Prince Charles and Camilla, Duchess of Cornwall, when they attended, as part of the India–UK Year of Culture, the Elephant Parade event which was supported by Nirav Modi's jewellery brand. In a *bandhgala* black suit sporting his signature blood-red satin pocket square, Modi could be seen posing with the charming prince and his wife.

Modi's penchant for posing for photographs with the political elite got him in the same frame as the Indian prime minister on his visit to the Davos 2018 Summit. This was just days before NiMo disappeared as the news of his audacious fraud erupted in India. The opposition Congress party and the others had a field day linking the swindler to the government.

'Guide to looting India by Nirav Modi—1. Hug PM Modi 2. Be seen with him in DAVOS. Use that clout to: A. Steal 12,000 crore B. Slip out of the country like Mallya, while the government looks the other way,' Congress President Rahul Gandhi wrote on Twitter with the hashtag #From1Modi2another.

Calling it an impromptu photo-op, the ministry of external affairs' spokesperson Ravish Kumar said that Nirav Modi was 'neither a part of the official delegation' nor was there a 'meeting with the PM and this gentleman'. Nevertheless, the picture circulated widely in the press and social media raising many questions over how yet another alleged scamster who moved in high political circles managed to flee the country before his scam erupted in public discourse.

* * *

On Valentine's Day 2018, at three minutes past 9 a.m., as the Indian stock markets opened trading, Punjab National Bank (PNB) informed the exchanges that it had detected a $1.8 billion fraud, plunging its shares by 9.81 per cent with the effect snowballing into dropping share prices of other state-owned lenders and affecting the Sensex, Bombay Stock Exchange's benchmark.

The CBI and ED probing the fraud found two unscrupulous employees of India's second-largest lending bank PNB's Brady House branch in south Mumbai were in cahoots with Modi to pull off what is now termed as one of the biggest banking frauds. Gokulnath Shetty, a deputy manager in its foreign exchange department, now retired, and Manoj Kharat, who operated the financial messaging system SWIFT, were arrested by the CBI.

The bank officers issued over a hundred letters of undertakings (LoUs) or letters of credit which were basically unauthorized bank guarantees to Modi and his uncle without any requisite collateral or documents for import. Once the LoUs were issued, Modi and Choksi would present them to overseas branches of Indian banks like Allahabad Bank, Axis Bank, Canara Bank and the SBI in Antwerp, Bahrain, Frankfurt, Hong Kong and Mauritius and get money in local currency to pay their 'suppliers'. Effectively what this meant was that Modi and Choksi would avail of bank credit without any security. This was not a normal loan transaction, but under the mirage of paying foreign suppliers, the Indian banks were happy to extend credit to a globally renowned diamond merchant, whom they wrongly assumed was already vetted by PNB for trade finance guarantees.

While huge funds were transferred through this mechanism over several years, the top brass of PNB remained ignorant of these transactions as these unsecured guarantees were not recorded in the core banking system. Hence, the top management was unaware of the obligations mounting in the bank's name by extending credit to Modi without any securities.

However in mid-January 2018, when an employee from Modi's company made a visit to the bank to ask them for further credit in a similar fashion, he was met by a new bank employee who was rather taken aback by such a request. When the official insisted that the bank had done a similar thing on several occasions in the past and should do so once again, the bank employee began probing into past transactions and thus uncovered the biggest banking fraud in the history of independent India amounting to $1.8 billion.

The biggest fraudsters according to the bank's complaint to the CBI were Nirav Modi and his uncle Mehul Choksi, with the bank losing over Rs 13,700 crore. Both, however, had left the country in early January, long before any warrant was issued in their name. The authorities believe that of the total fraud money, Modi channelled Rs 560 crore to his account, Rs 220 crore to wife Ami's account and another Rs 174 crore to his father Deepak's account. Apart from foreign accounts, funds were also transferred to Pacific Diamonds, his new firm and other companies floated for the purpose of money laundering.

The CBI arrested over twenty people, including directors and senior management, accountants and auditors associated with Modi/Choksi businesses. They raided Modi's boutiques in India, seized the jewellery and gems, froze his Indian bank accounts and attached a property lien that states that the creditor is owed money, so until the debt is repaid, the title will be unclear. The CBI also impounded his art collection and luxury cars that included a Porsche and Rolls-Royce.

From his luxury sea-facing apartment in Samudra Mahal in Worli, Mumbai, the authorities recovered antique jewellery worth over Rs 15 crore which included a lone diamond ring valued at Rs 10 crore, luxury watches costing Rs 1.4 crore and paintings by Amrita Sher-Gil, M.F. Husain and K.K. Hebbar valued at

Rs 10 crore. Besides these, Modi also had artwork by F.N. Souza, V.S. Gaitonde, S.H. Raza and Akbar Padamsee. He also collected Chinese artwork and masterpieces by Zeng Xiaojun and Xu Lei and sculptures from Italy and the United States.

The ED conducted 251 country-wide searches and the value of the total seized assets was Rs 7664 crore, of which the twenty-one immovable properties were worth Rs 524 crore and included a farmhouse in Alibaug, a solar power plant, 135 acres of land in Ahmednagar, and residential and office properties in Mumbai and Pune.

The agency had also attached the diamantaire's two apartments at New York's iconic Central Park valued at $29.99 million (Rs 217 crore). The investigators released photographs of his apartments which ooze luxury. The properties were bought in the name of The Ithaca Trust for $25 million and $4.99 million.

In London, the ED seized a property in the heart of the bustling metropolis valued at £6.25 million or Rs 57 crore. Flat number 103, Marathon House on 200 Marylebone Road, was owned by Purvi (Modi's sister) and was bought in 2017 in the name of Belvedere Holdings Group Limited which is managed by Trident Trust in Singapore, which has been established by Monte Cristo Trust and has Purvi Modi as settlor and beneficiary.

The diamantaire's eleven properties in Dubai worth over Rs 56 crore were also attached by ED. In Hong Kong, after the Union Bank of India filed a writ at the high court in September 2018 demanding Modi pay more than $5.49 million plus interest, after his firms allegedly defaulted on repayments, the ED, in October, attached Modi's properties in Hong Kong worth Rs 255 crore. In total, the ED has attached Nirav Modi's properties in four countries worth over Rs 637 crore.

A special Prevention of Money Laundering Act (PMLA) court had on 20 March 2019 allowed the CBI to sell 173 paintings and the luxury vehicles owned by Modi to raise funds to pay those he owed money to. The art collection was sold at a professional auction through an auction house, Saffronart, the first for India's premier investigating agency. The CBI put up sixty-eight pieces of art and the bidding lasted over two hours with eight agents frantically working over phone bids and some more over online bids that came from the United States, Canada and Belgium.

Camelot Enterprises, a firm owned by Modi, had sent a legal notice through its law firm India Law Alliance to the department in a bid to stop the auction, terming it unlawful as 'only 19 of the artworks from the 68 belongs to the company'. Nevertheless, the auction went through. The tax department had found the paintings in a climate-controlled room on Modi's property and had linked it to Camelot and other companies of Modi to recover tax of Rs 95.91 crore. The department recovered a net of Rs 54.84 crore, after taking away the commission to the auction house and the buyers' premium.

V.S. Gaitonde's untitled abstract artwork fetched Rs 25.24 crore, making it the most expensive bid for artwork from India. A phone bid of Rs 16.1 crore secured Raja Ravi Varma's 1881 artwork depicting the 'Maharaja of Travancore and his brother welcoming Richard Temple-Grenville, 3rd duke of Birmingham and Chandos, Governor-General of Madras (1875-80) on his official visit to Trivandrum in 1880'. F.N. Souza's 'Cityscape' and 'Golly-wog' went for over Rs 1 crore each, while Akbar Padamsee's 'Grey Nude' fetched Rs 1.72 crore.

Modi's fleet of thirteen luxury cars was sold through an online auction in April 2019 conducted by the Metal Scrap Trade Corporation (MSTC). The Rolls-Royce Ghost, Modi's most expensive car, rumoured to ferry his three lap dogs, still had the steering wheel wrapped in plastic and the driver's seat pushed behind. While his car was parked in his duplex home in south Mumbai, nine other cars were at Samudra Mahal, a luxury residential tower in Worli, Mumbai. Interested parties were allowed a look at the cars from 21–23 April, but there were no car keys provided to check out the interior of the car or test-drive it. Yet, this did not deter enthusiasts from picking up a luxury ride at the auctions.

The Ghost pegged at Rs 1.33 crore sold for Rs 10,000 more. The Porsche Panamera sold for Rs 54.6 lakh, while his Mercedes-Benz 4Matic GL 350 CDI pegged at Rs 37.8 lakh sold for Rs 53.76 lakh. Modi's Mercedes-Benz CLS 350 and Honda CR-V went under the hammer for Rs 16 lakh and Rs 10.26 lakh, while the highest bids for Choksi's BMW X1 and Toyota Innova Crysta were Rs 11.75 lakh and Rs 18.06 lakh, respectively. In total, the ED raised Rs 3.29 crore, 9 per cent higher than the total base price set at Rs 3.01 crore.

During this time, reports of how Modi and Choksi cheated many also emerged. Paul Alfonso, a Canadian businessman, had met Modi at the Beverly Hills hotel during its centennial celebrations in 2012. The duo then ran into each other at events and clubs in Malibu and New York where Modi, the older of the two, seems to not just have shared a drink or two with the young Alfonso but also imparted wisdom to the moon-eyed entrepreneur. An impressed Alfonso stayed in touch with Modi and when he decided to pop the question to his girlfriend, it was Modi he first thought of to make for him the perfect engagement ring.

Unaware that Modi was a wanted man in India, Alfonso discussed in detail the design he wanted for the $100,000 engagement ring he had in mind. Modi offered him the 'perfect' 3.2-carat diamond at the wholesale rate of $120,000. But Alfonso's girlfriend hinted she liked another ring featured in a magazine and so the enamoured beau contacted Modi to get that ring which included a 2.5-carat diamond for $80,000. Alfonso wired $200K to a Hong Kong account of the jeweller and received the delivery of the rings a fortnight later in Vancouver but without the authenticity certificates.

When the promised certificates failed to come even after Modi repeatedly assured him that he would send them, Alfonso's suspicions grew. The couple took the rings to a valuer to get them insured, only to discover that they were fake. The stress of this tore the couple apart. The jilted fiancé has sued Modi for forgery and emotional distress to the tune of $4.2 million in a court in California.

Diamond experts like Hardik Hundiya and former employees like Santosh Srivastava, who was the managing director in Choksi's company, too revealed how Modi and his uncle sold substandard diamonds and issued fake certificates.

But it wasn't just jewellery that turned out to be fake. Modi's famous art collection was also found to include many fakes and investigators are also probing if Modi was involved in proliferating the art market with fakes as he often gifted his international clients and the crème-de-la-crème of Indian society paintings done by famous artists. Nirav Modi wanted to create an impression that he was a connoisseur of art with an eye to spot priceless artwork and upcoming talent. He was photographed often with several contemporary paintings donning the walls of his offices and homes. Like his paintings, he too was what met the eye.

* * *

A huge underground vault runs below Modi's four-storeyed property on 31 Old Bond Street in London. This is where the NIRAV MODI showroom is situated and where the fugitive diamantaire was suspected to be hiding in a flat above the shop. Modi had got this property on a fifteen-year lease from a company called Sure Honest Ltd registered in the British Virgin Islands. This company had bought the land and the property for £36 million (Rs 350 crore). While the lease expires in 2031, the store underwent massive renovations to house exquisite diamonds. The massive vault underneath had hidden many treasures and many secrets of the mysterious jewellery designer.

Modi pays a rent of £17,000 a month for his £8 million three-bedroom apartment at Centre Point in New Oxford Street. The thirty-three-storey tower has eighty-two luxury apartments that range from £1.8 million for a small one-bedroom flat to £55 million for the two-storey five-bedroom penthouse. Modi's modest flat still boasts of high-end luxury with gorgeous views of the central London skyline.

The resurrected business—a wholesale trader and retailer of jewellery and watches—incorporated in May 2018 runs from a townhouse situated in Soho and has Centre Point as its official address. Modi, who also holds a national insurance number, a requisite for those who earn money from employment in the UK, draws a salary of £250,000 a year from this business.

In the US, three shell companies floated by Modi were involved in the purchase of two swanky apartments in New York City. These companies—Firestar Diamond Inc. (FDI), A Jaffe Inc. and Fantasy Inc.—filed for Chapter 11 bankruptcy in a New York court just before news of the scam broke. An examiner was appointed by the court to look into their transactions. The examiner's reports shed light on the complexities of ownership of these properties and the suspicion that they were bought with Indian taxpayers' money taken through ill-gotten means.

One of the properties was in the name of Central Park Real Estate LLC (CPRE), an affiliate of Nirav Modi's Firestar Group, bought in 2007 for $5 million with a $3 million mortgage through HSBC bank. The mortgage was slowly paid over the years but when the bank started asking for more details to re-mortgage, Modi's business associates suggested he pay off the loan in a lump sum. The HSBC mortgage of about $3 million was paid through foreign direct investment funds and the title was transferred on 29 December 2017 to The Ithaca Trust whose beneficiaries were his wife Ami and their children while his sister Purvi was a settler. According to the examiner's report, $6 million was transferred to the Commonwealth Trust Company on 2 January 2018 by Purvi Modi's account at the Bank of Singapore. On the same day, The Ithaca Trust wired $6 million to Firestar Group Inc.'s HSBC account for the purchase of CPRE.

In a similar fashion, a second property was purchased on 7 September 2017 in the Ritz-Carlton Residences at 50 Central

Park South by another shell company called Central Park South Properties owned by The Ithaca Trust for '$25 million in cash'. A complex web of transactions ensured that it was sufficiently difficult to trace the money to its source and was handled by lawyers from India. According to the examiner, another $1 million was moved to The Ithaca Trust which then transferred it to Central Park South Properties LLC for unknown reasons.

It is widely believed that Modi has signed divorce papers to shield his wife and children living in the US, and is providing a generous settlement and exorbitant trust funds for his children. It is believed that Ami has reverted to her maiden name Javeri and the kids, too, no longer use Modi as their surname. His son, studying in the UK, has returned to his mother in New York.

* * *

Nirav Modi was spotted at Davos in Switzerland in January 2018 in the photograph with Prime Minister Narendra Modi. That photograph came in handy for the media when the scam broke. 'Nimo becomes Namo's baby', read a headline in the *Telegraph* on 16 February 2018. He never returned to India and disappeared off the map, leading the investigating officers on a wild goose chase across the globe. A Red Notice was issued against Modi and Choksi and their passports were revoked. Yet, the investigators believed that Modi travelled across many countries, leaving them perplexed and assuming that he carried more than one passport. Finding NiMo became a priority.

The investigating agencies first suspected NiMo had moved to Dubai. Their suspicion grew as Modi's legal team reached the United Arab Emirates (UAE) and the authorities believed this was to consult Modi on the next course of action. However, the investigating officers met with no luck in Dubai.

In early April 2018, Indian authorities submitted a request to Hong Kong's Department of Justice for Modi's arrest as they suspected he was hiding in Hong Kong. Modi had opened his first boutique in Hong Kong in 2015 at the Elements shopping centre in West Kowloon. Two years later, he opened others at IFC Mall and Tsim Sha Tsui shopping arcade. In early February 2018, the agencies had noticed the company carrying out extensive trade in Hong Kong and suspected it was to move assets to the beleaguered businessman.

In late April, NDTV flashed a story that Nirav Modi was spotted in New York. According to them, Modi was staying in a suite in JW Marriott Essex House New York, a block away from his flagship store on Madison Ave. It was reported that JW Marriott staff saw Nirav Modi once and his wife Ami Modi several times in the building.

In June 2018, at a social gathering, an official from the UK High Commission in London let it slip that they believed Modi had escaped to Belgium after India started putting pressure on the UK to get him arrested as he was suspected to be living in a posh central London neighbourhood. The authorities seemed to be quite baffled how Modi could travel between countries even with his passport revoked and an Interpol notice against him. While all this was just conjecture, it pointed out that the Indian authorities were quite clueless on Modi's whereabouts and clearly had no plan to apprehend him anytime soon.

It comes as no surprise that Modi was finally tracked down by a dedicated team of reporters from the UK's *Telegraph* newspaper in March 2019. Journalists Mick Brown and Robert Mendick along with video producer Emma Mills found him living in an ultra-luxe apartment in the heart of London, not too far from his now shut flagship store in Old Bond Street. His new office is situated a few blocks away and the fugitive businessman was found to often walk there with his little canine friend.

When he was interrupted by Brown, though caught completely off guard, Modi still had a smile pasted on his face and responded with a nonchalant 'no comment' to the plethora of questions posed to him.

This ease with which he confidently walked on London's street while making taxpayers lose millions angered many in India and the government was forced to pull all diplomatic strings to get him arrested. They had no excuse. *Telegraph* had tracked him down, shown the world how the fugitive still wore a luxurious Ostrich skin jacket, carried a pricey puppy and had once again opened shop.

Finally, in March 2019, UK Home Secretary Sajid Javid certified India's extradition request for Nirav Modi that was made in August the previous year, following which Westminster Magistrates' Court issued his arrest warrant.

This sent reporters to Modi's Centre Point residence and they managed to track him down during one of his regular walks. Again the barrage of questions was met with an off-hand 'no comments' and 'stop stalking me' from Modi, although his smile had disappeared, replaced by clear annoyance.

Modi hired the finest legal firm in the UK for extradition cases, Boutique Law helmed by Anand Doobay, who had worked out an 'arrest by arrangement' with the extradition unit of Scotland Yard. The date of arrest was set for 25 March. His lawyers had no doubt that they would secure bail when he was produced in Westminster Magistrates' Court. This is a fairly easy task in cases of financial fraud and Modi would then return to his business and live his luxurious lifestyle while the case crawled in the UK courts.

Nirav Modi had found freedom in the United Kingdom. Whether it was walking his dog on Oxford Street or resurrecting his business under a new name in a new location, Modi almost had his life back to normal in the bustling English capital. And the 'arrest by arrangement', he believed, ensured he could continue doing so, even while on bail.

Modi felt secure in this knowledge, confident that nothing in his plans could go awry, so it came as a rather rude shock to him and his team when he was arrested in the most unlikely of places, but perhaps also fitting perfectly to the crime he allegedly perpetrated.

Modi had walked into the Holborn branch of UK-based Metro Bank to open a new account, with his documents supporting his identity and residence proof. According to bank procedures, these documents would then be run through several software checks to ascertain the credibility of the customer. But one of the officials at the bank recognized Modi's name linking him to bank fraud and intimated the police. The cops then decided to arrest him immediately.

* * *

On 19 March 2019, the beleaguered businessman, dressed in a crisp white shirt and trousers, sat in the dock in Westminster Magistrates' Court room 1 when his case was heard close to noon. He was asked whether he consented to his extradition. 'I do not consent,' said Modi, clearly and boldly, confident that he would head home soon.

Modi's counsel George Hepburne Scott, a barrister known for his shrewd acumen with the extradition law and his uncanny knack for securing bail for his clients, told the court that Modi was forthcoming and always in regular contact with Scotland Yard even before India issued his extradition request. The court was informed that Modi had lived in the UK since January 2018 when he came here to pursue 'an imminent IPO (initial public offering) in London, stressing that he was in London much 'before the criminal complaint was filed' in India. Modi had offered to pay the court £5,00,000 as surety on an income of £20,000 a month. Hepburne Scott also tried to show the court that Modi had familial ties to the UK as his son studied in London

Jonathan Swain of the CPS, representing India, argued that Modi had not returned to India as he was deliberately evading justice and as this was a high value and sophisticated fraud, Modi had access to considerable means that could aid his escape. The bespectacled Swain was relentless in arguing against Modi's bail, adding that though 'various entities were involved' in the alleged £1.2 billion bank fraud, they 'were controlled by Nirav Modi who was a partner in all the firms'.

After a tension-filled short break, the judge, Marie Mallon, returned to announce that she had substantial grounds to refuse bail as she feared Modi would fail to surrender to the court if bail were to be granted as he had access to large resources due to the high-value amount of the alleged fraud.

A clearly baffled Modi kept glancing at his solicitor even as the judge spoke to him directly and told him her decision. He slowly nodded his head, accepting that he would now spend the next ten days in Her Majesty's Prison Wandsworth. The billionaire would be languishing behind bars in one of UK's largest prisons, a far cry from the comfort and luxury afforded to him in his London apartment.

Ten days later the court convened to discuss his bail application once again. The hearing had begun shortly after 12.30 p.m. District Judge Emma Arbuthnot, now presiding over this case, looked around the courtroom and said: 'This gives a sense of déjà vu?'

'Hope not too strong,' quickly added Clare Montgomery, Modi's counsel.

Arbuthnot and Montgomery had not long ago met each other in the same courtroom in the extradition case of liquor baron Vijay Mallya where Arbuthnot had ordered him to be extradited to India. The similarities in the two courtrooms were many, from the defence team to the Indian journalists in the press row. The sense of déjà vu was felt by almost all. However, unlike Mallya, who got bail on a bond of £650,000, Modi seemed to have the worst luck with his bail plea.

The diamantaire sitting in the dock in an open-collar white shirt and black trousers looked a man broken but perhaps not beaten. Modi sat with his head bowed through most of the hearing, only ever lifting his head to look straight with a blank expression.

The new barrister representing India was now the formidable Toby Cadman, who produced before the court a huge file with fresh evidence corroborating the allegations against Modi. Cadman has tremendous experience in human rights litigation and has represented CPS in many extradition cases. His knowledge of India and his willingness to engage with reporters has made him a

favourite among the Indian press. As was the norm, officials from
the CBI and ED were also present in court, and ED's Satyabrata
Kumar was deeply involved with the proceedings, supplying
Cadman with any additional information and pointing out any
material evidence that the court required. India's assertion that
Modi not be granted bail hinged on him not just being a flight risk
but also being an instrument of subverting the process of justice.

The court heard a story that could easily have been the script
of a Bollywood potboiler. The prosecution told the court a sordid
saga of coercion and intimidation, of threats and destruction. Modi
was painted as the villain who controlled his employees as puppets
and threatened them into submission. These allegations largely
convinced the court that it was safer for everyone concerned that
Modi remain behind bars.

'There could be no conditions that can be put forward to satisfy
the court to give him bail,' Cadman said in his opening remarks. He
told the court that Modi had threatened to kill a witness, Ashish
Lad, if he failed to accept a 'Rs 2 million (Rs 20 lakh) incentive to
provide a false statement'. Four other witnesses, including Subhash
Parab and Nilesh Mistry, 'who have knowledge of the fraud' were
sent to Egypt by Modi. It was alleged that they were also threatened
by Modi in an attempt to subvert justice. Modi had also allegedly
destroyed mobile phones and a server in Dubai to get rid of crucial
evidence.

What also worked against Modi was his attempt to secure
citizenship of a small island country in the South Pacific Ocean
called Vanuatu which has no income tax, capital gains tax,
inheritance tax or exchange control. Cadman told the court that
India suspects that Modi is a 'man of significant wealth' and has
the resources and willingness to settle in a jurisdiction that may not
be open to extraditing him to India.

It perhaps came as no surprise that Modi had now hired the
formidable Clare Montgomery to represent him and get him out
from behind bars. Montgomery argued that the 'notoriety' that the
case had accumulated in India should have no bearing on his bail

application and that he had a right to bail as someone arrested in a domestic fraud case. She insisted that his arrival in London was a planned move to establish 'UK as a central base' for his business and claimed that he had 'not travelled outside since his arrival to the UK'. This was later opposed by the CPS who declared that Modi had travelled to New York in February the previous year, which was subsequently found to be untrue.

Montgomery said that the bank issues that erupted were 'unexpected' but Modi was no fugitive as he was living in London in a 'highly visible way'—his property rental was in his name, he was employed under a contract by his company under his own name and was also opening a bank account in his own name. Modi's legal team was in contact with the police; the cops had also visited his office once.

Calling the fears of Modi escaping the UK 'just nonsense', she stressed that he 'is a wanted man and only qualifies to stay in the UK'. The Vanuatu application was made at the end of 2017 before the PNB scam emerged and is now history.

She offered the court a bail bond of £1 million (double of last time) and proposed Modi be put under 'effective house arrest' with electronic monitoring and also a 24×7 charged up and switched on mobile phone. He would also surrender his travel documents (some expired, some not) to Hong Kong, Singapore and the UAE.

District Judge Emma Arbuthnot, however, was not convinced. To her, the substantial fraud ensured large resources were at Modi's disposal. She also found a lack of community ties to the UK an important ground for his escape. His son, who had been studying in London, was now attending an American university, and as his family had moved to New York, Modi had no one in the UK.

Modi stood with tired eyes and a forced smile pasted on his lips as Arbuthnot informed him that he would now appear before her through video conferencing.

On 26 April, Modi joined the courtroom on a screen looking tired and ill. He coughed a few times. The hearing lasted less than ten minutes and the judge extended Modi's remand to 25 May.

On 30 April, Modi's team submitted new evidence to the court towards his bail plea.

On 8 May, at 2 p.m., Modi appeared in Westminster Magistrates' Court looking fresh and rested. He was clean-shaven, wearing a light blue shirt. No sooner had Modi sat in the dock, than he was taken away. There were whispers among those present that perhaps the court would not hear him yet. But within minutes, the judge entered and even before those who had stood for the judge's entrance could take their seats, Modi was once again brought into his glass cage. The court was hearing Modi's bail plea on the grounds of 'change in circumstances'.

The CPS was represented by a new barrister Nicholas Hearn, the third since the case against Nirav Modi began. 'What is clear on the basis of documentation is that these do not come from thin air. Documents show witnesses were threatened,' argued Hearn for India. Hearn looks deceptively young, but has over a decade of experience in extradition law and is an expert on the procedure for obtaining information from Interpol and on Red Notices. In 2018–19, he was involved in the high-profile prosecution of seven criminals who allegedly exploited over 250 victims of trafficking into modern slavery, the largest such investigation in Europe, and was featured on the investigative show BBC *Panorama* in September 2019.

'We have transcripts that show Nirav Modi's brother Nehal contacting witnesses,' Hearn argued, citing that the evidence provided to the court by Nirav Modi's team did not amount to any 'material change of circumstances' and the factors based on which Arbuthnot had refused Modi's bail earlier remained relevant. 'Modi had helped witnesses in setting up homes in Egypt and there is plausible account of witnesses being contacted by Modi where he gave them the illusion that they would be most certainly arrested in India,' he added.

Modi sat listening intently. Often, he was found scribbling away on his writing pad, intermittently looking up with an almost blank expression as the CPS barrister continued his monologue. 'There is nothing in the defence bundle at this stage to undermine those allegations,' concluded Hearn, urging the court to refuse Modi's bail.

Forty-five minutes later, Montgomery had her turn. She told the court that at 10.30 a.m., she was handed a very large file by India and insisted that while she did not have enough time to read the details, it did not establish that Modi has access to hidden assets.

'Any claims that he has assets that will enable him to flee are not true as there have been significant seizures in India of items that are precious, there is also a freezing order in place on funds in accounts with EFG bank and all other entities are now in receivership or liquidation,' she argued. 'The £2 million bail money was from his employer,' clarified Montgomery.

The CPS had made a strong assertion of witness intimidation. This had moved the focus of the case from a mere financial fraud to one that also involved mafia-like intimidation. No wonder the constant reference to Dubai and Egypt was making the court uneasy about Modi's intent towards his former employees whose testimony could be crucial to implicate him.

Montgomery, who has fought several extradition cases, was well aware of this dark cloud hanging over Modi. She adopted a nonchalant attitude in rebuking CPS' concerns. Referring to India's submissions that Subhash Parab was concerned that there was a risk to his life and threats to illegal confinement in Egypt from Modi, Montgomery questioned that if such threats existed, then how could Parab freely give statements to the Indian agencies?

Seeking to demolish the assertion that his employees were kept in Egypt under illegal confinement, Montgomery said that what had stopped these employees from returning to India was a possible threat of being arrested and charged by the CBI when they landed in India. However, when the employees were no longer afraid of an arrest, it was Modi who had arranged for their tickets to India. She also did not deny that Modi had offered Ashish Lad Rs 20 lakh. 'It was compensation for the witness to come to the UK to depose before the court,' she said in a matter-of-fact tone.

'There is no conceivable basis for obstruction of justice . . . he could have moved to plenty of countries who have no extradition with India, but he didn't. He would do nothing to risk his bail.' Besides, the court was told that Modi has no direct contact with the bank and neither did he deal directly with those who had landed in Egypt.

Then, quickly Montgomery's tone changed. It became softer and quieter, less aggressive, more humble. She now urged the court to consider Modi's bail plea. 'His experience in prison is vivid and damaging,' she claimed softly. Those in court sat a little forward to listen to what she had to say about Modi's life in prison, but she did not elaborate.

'Modi is in a state where he would do nothing to risk bail,' she said instead. She informed the court that Modi had agreed to a twenty-four-hour surveillance and promised to not contact his brother or any witnesses. He also offered £2 million as surety now, four times his initial offering.

'India wants to present Nirav Modi as a diabolical mechanic or a cold-blooded and hardened criminal, which he is not,' Montgomery said emphatically even as Modi, sitting in the dock in a light blue shirt and dark navy trousers, slowly smiled.

She also brought to the court's attention a tweet by the ED where it claimed that the seizures (from Modi) were Rs 7664 crore whereas the PNB scam was about Rs 6498 crore. 'It is a white collar case,' she said. 'It is incredibly rare that witnesses are intimidated and that escape is very rare particularly where a person has to provide high surety and meet other conditions.'

Modi had been in the UK since December 2017 to meet investors, even before the alarm was raised at PNB in January 2018 and an official fraud was declared in February. This was as much in response to the judge's query as to when Modi had arrived in the UK as it was to show how the Indian side was misleading the court by making unsubstantiated claims.

Modi was playing a catch-me-if-you-can game with the ED and CBI when the scam had broken out in January 2018. Just as he had availed of the LoUs from different parts of the world, he too, it seems, was following a circuitous route to escape the clutches of Indian law. But on that day, Montgomery was seeking to challenge the narrative of the GoI. She told the court that it was on 16 January that PNB raised the question of renewing facilities that Modi's company had availed of earlier. Few days after that, discussions took place between the bank and an employee of Modi on the need for security. It was only on 29 January that a complaint was made, but Modi, Montgomery pointed out, remained in England. Under advice from his solicitors, Modi informed Scotland Yard about his presence and remained under the 'protection of the British system'.

'He did not travel elsewhere,' said Montgomery. She threw a challenge: 'We have asked the government of India to make good the assertion that he (Modi) travelled to America.'

Hinting that India was fabricating stories of Modi trying to escape, she pointed out that in the previous hearing, India had claimed that Modi had travelled to New York in February 2019 even when Modi denied it. India had failed to provide any evidence of such travel. Then India claimed Modi had travelled in February 2018. But no evidence was supplied to support even that claim. 'It is now accepted that there was no such travel,' she said and looked straight at the CPS barrister.

When a ten-hour curfew for Modi was suggested by Montgomery to improve the prospect of bail, the judge interjected: What about a twenty-four-hour curfew?

Was Arbuthnot inclined to give bail if Modi was ready for a twenty-four-hour curfew? Modi and his team had to wait for Hearn's brief submissions before the judge gave an answer.

After a ten-minute break, the court reconvened. It was now Hearn's turn. 'This is not a documentary case where only papers are important or crucial. We need witness accounts and hence we have to rule out any possibility of witness inducements,' said Hearn. Describing Modi as a man with 'access to substantial resources', Hearn reinforced that 'there isn't sufficient evidence to disregard concerns'. This was a rather short submission by the CPS as it was Hearn who had opened the proceedings and did not have much to add. The suspense was fast building during the thirty-minute break the judge declared to reflect on the submissions.

The submissions provided an informative trailer to the extent of judicial wrangling that was sure to characterize the case as it moved ahead to fuller case management hearings and final trial. Bail had become a very precious commodity in the court of Emma Arbuthnot. A Pakistani tycoon, Arif Naqvi, founder CEO of Abraaj, a buyout firm with huge investments in the US and the Middle East, facing an extradition request on fraud charges from America, was granted bail by Arbuthnot at a whopping £15 million just the week before Modi's third attempt to get bail. It was Naqvi's second attempt to gain bail, which he was to defend in the high court as the US had filed an appeal.

Modi was in the dock flanked by two female guards, reminiscent of his trademark photo-ops, yet the circumstances couldn't have been more different. Was he going to be third time lucky? When the judge came back after the half-an-hour break, no one knew what to expect. What seemed certain was that the losing side would approach the high court. 'This is a large fraud and the doubling of security to £2 million is not enough to cover a combination of concerns that he would fail to surrender,' said Arbuthnot. 'Interference with witnesses will still affect this case. We are not done and dusted yet.'

She believed that Modi could tap into his large resources and his lack of ties to the UK created sufficient grounds for concern. The defence had put forth a compelling argument but it was not good enough to prevent Modi from going back to Wandsworth prison. 'I won't be granting bail,' Arbuthnot said to a forlorn Modi who stood quietly with his head bowed as she ordered him back to jail.

Shock. Anguish. Pain. Fear. A multitude of emotions passed through Modi's face in a matter of seconds. His defence team was clearly rattled. Bail was easily offered to economic offenders and Modi even had the means to pay a huge surety. Yet, the billionaire was left to languish in prison. The district judges were clearly not listening to Modi's bail pleas.

Everyone was baffled, including top legal minds. India had played its cards right. By bringing in the element of witness intimidation and destruction of evidence, they had converted a white-collar crime into one that promised unmitigated violence. Modi's lack of family links to the UK also did not endear him to the court as that meant he had no real reason to remain in a country where the extradition noose was tightening around his neck. There was nothing in the UK to stop the man from escaping to one of the many tiny island countries that could be safe havens for financial fraudsters.

Modi, though broken, was not beaten. Left with no choice, he took the battle to the Royal Courts of Justice.

The date was set. 11 June 2019. Modi's team was prepared. This was a battle Modi did not want to lose. Returning to his luxury pad in central London was all that he thought about, sitting put before a video conferencing screen in HM Prison Wandsworth as Montgomery stood before judge Dame Ingrid Ann Simler in the high court arguing for bail for her client.

'Nirav Modi is no Julian Assange. He is just a jeweller from India,' said Montgomery. And who else to know this better than Montgomery, who was representing Sweden against the WikiLeaks founder in his extradition case for sexual offences. Unlike the whistle-blower hiding away in the Ecuadorian embassy, Montgomery promised that Modi would not hide in any embassy to evade arrest but willingly cooperate with the authorities if he was granted bail.

The CPS argued that he had both the motive and the means to escape. Hearn also raised the issue of coercion and destruction of material evidence and termed it 'classic witness intimidation'.

Montgomery said that these allegations 'hold no water' and asserted that 'the reality is that at worst, his brother provided assistance to frighten employees into staying in Cairo to prevent their arrest in India'. Interrupting her, the judge said that this was 'not the worst' scenario but 'only one reading'. Montgomery, however, argued that the employees were in contact with the Indian authorities who were giving them advice on their actions, and as almost 80 per cent of them were graduates, they were consciously 'plotting their way through a difficult situation'.

Modi's team also produced in court a doctor's certificate highlighting the imprisoned jeweller's medical conditions. Softening her voice, Montgomery slowly said, 'The reality is that he is not a cold-blooded hardened criminal.'

Modi was suffering in the prison both physically and mentally and was willing to subject himself to strict restrictions, including sixteen-hour electronic tagging, if only he was given bail and sent home. Testimonies from Modi's geography teacher and his secretary Frances Hallworth-Noble, who runs the London Concierge Company, were produced and the £2 million was offered as a bail bond once again.

This made CPS' Hearn smirk. 'Nirav Modi pleaded poverty a number of times in these proceedings but the curious thing is that he has increased the offer of surety consistently in the proceedings.'

Montgomery said that Modi's bank accounts have been frozen in Switzerland and elsewhere. Significantly, she told the court that unsecured lending took place and traders took benefit of the cash flow in India and until 6 January 2018, there seemed to be no problem with this lending. Referring to Modi as 'careful, honest and coming from a family of jewellers,' she said that the UK is the country where he considers his interests will be best served.

The case was listed for 10. 30 a.m., but the bulk of the arguments were only heard post lunch, at 2 p.m. Considering the complexities of the case and the significance of this judgment, Justice Simler decided to give her verdict the following day.

At 10 a.m. on Wednesday, Justice Simler read out her judgment to a packed audience in courtroom 2 of the Royal Courts of Justice. 'There are still places in the world that one can escape to if they have means' and the offer of £2 million security provides strong evidence that Modi has means to abscond, she said.

Looking into the mental state of Modi in prison, Justice Simler observed that the fugitive billionaire could have been affected significantly by the possibility of returning to India, adding that the fear of a likely extradition provides a strong reason for him not to surrender, and hence, she decided to keep him behind bars.

Every twenty-eight days, Modi enters the courtroom through a video conference for a quick word with the magistrate on his prison conditions and bail extensions. On 27 June, his lawyer Jessica Jones asked for Modi to be provided with a laptop so that he has access to the 5000 pages of documents submitted by India. Judge Jonathan Radway, presiding over the remand extension, told Modi: 'I hope arrangements can be made for you to read the documents.'

On 6 November, the court was informed of a violent encounter that Modi faced in HM Prison Wandsworth. On 5 November, Modi was speaking to a work colleague over the phone from his cell when a fellow prisoner attacked him. He was punched in the face, pushed to the floor and kicked several times.

Modi's counsel Hugo Keith called it a targeted attack for extortion, and blamed the media for provoking hatred and violence against his client by calling him a 'billionaire diamantaire' and isolating him in prison. Modi is suffering from depression and anxiety, and even with medical reports given to the court, no counselling or prescriptions were provided to him, the court heard.

This over-crowded prison, built in 1851, is also one of the most notorious. An investigation conducted by the BBC in 2016 that involved filming in the prison for seven days, showed large scale drug abuse with corrupt jail authorities allowing the passage of cannabis and hard drugs to the inmates. Violence was rampant. Since then, measures have been taken to bring in prison reform including x-ray machines and physical checks, yet even in January 2021, allegations of drug abuse and contraband mobile phones were rampant with stabbing incidents reported routinely.

Keith requested the court to place Modi under house arrest to prevent such attacks in the future. Offering a bail bond of an unprecedented £4 million (by an Indian person), double the last figure offered, Keith suggested that private security guards monitor Modi at his residence with motion sensor cameras around the clock. 'We are ready for conditions suited to a terror accused,' said Keith.

However, District Judge Emma Arbuthnot was not convinced and still considered Modi a flight risk. The prosecution barrister James Lewis QC also said that Modi had previously threatened to kill himself if extradited to India and that in itself is the 'strongest motivation for someone to abscond' and interfere with witnesses and destroy evidence. Modi was denied bail once again. This meant the regime of appearing in court from Wandsworth prison every twenty-eight days was to continue.

* * *

From the sublime Edmond Dantès, Nirav Modi got transformed into a Jew in India as the case progressed. The nomenclature was given by Markandey Katju, retired Supreme Court justice, who was a witness presented by Modi's team in the UK court.

Nirav Modi's trial got divided into two parts. The extradition battle thus was broken down into two sets of separate but 'inextricably linked' cases. The first leg of the trial began on 11 May, a Monday, and was to last till Friday 15 May. It was to cover the two charges of fraud and money laundering. Both these charges were certified in 2019 by the UK home secretary. The two fresh charges of causing the disappearance of evidence and intimidating witnesses were made in 2020, and it was agreed, were to be the subject of a second leg of trial in September 2020.

In May 2020, Britain was under lockdown, and Nirav Modi appeared through video link and so did Helen Malcolm, the new CPS barrister. Malcolm is a natural in the legal robes, who brings a certain elan to her arguments, but doesn't carry the weight of her brief outside the courtroom and has a serene disposition. She was involved in the very first European Arrest Warrant case in the UK after it came into force in 2004. Along with Montgomery, she was in General Pinochet's defence team in the late 1990s.

Most recently she represented the Azerbaijan government seeking to extradite the wife of the chairman of a state bank in Azerbaijan who had spent £16 million at Harrods over a decade.

While Nirav Modi's legal team and the district judge were present in the court, nobody from the CBI or ED travelled to London, but were connected to the court through a video link.

Nirav Modi and his firms were accused of obtaining LoUs at highly advantageous rates without credit facilities, without providing the cash margins, without proper documentation and without paying proper commission. This was the gist of CBI's charge against Nirav Modi—defrauding PNB. Pursuing the charge of money laundering, the ED alleged that Nirav Modi had wrongly diverted the proceeds either for repayment of earlier LoUs or to companies controlled by him. Nirav Modi did not dispute the money flow, but took the line that all the transactions were authorized by the bank and that there was no dishonesty on his part.

The defence raised similar arguments that were made in the Vijay Mallya case, one such being the non-acceptance of the affidavits of investigating officers as admissible evidence. The CPS pointed out that as in the Mallya case, statements by investigating officers can be taken as informed explanations of or commentary on the documents, rather than as evidence of relevant events. The defence said that statements taken under section 161 of the Indian Code of Criminal Procedure cannot be relied upon to establish a prima facie case in extradition proceedings. The CPS countered that in several extradition cases, including Mallya's, courts in the UK have rejected this contention.

Another argument raised was that witnesses gave duplicated statements that raise a larger question about their reliability—the CPS pointed out that the court rejected this argument in the Mallya case, and that in making this assertion, the defence was being selective and ignoring the totality of the evidence.

Also, the defence argued that the prosecution failed to submit original statements which were later translated into English—the CPS countered that as the 2003 Act allows for a summary of the statement to be treated as a statement made by the person, then a complete translation of a statement could not be treated as inadmissible, when a summary is acceptable as well.

While Nirav Modi had fraudulently obtained LoUs since 2011, the case against him pertains to the 150 LoUs which were issued to him in 2017. These LoUs were issued to him between February 2017 and May 2017. Gokulnath Shetty, who had issued the 150 LoUs, retired on 31 May 2017, but the payments were due from 25 January 2018.

On 16 January 2018, Nirav Modi's firms requested the bank to issue fresh LoUs. With Shetty retired, the bank informed Nirav Modi that a cash collateral of at least 100 per cent was to be provided. The firms also failed to provide any sanctioned facility on the basis of which LoUs could be given; there was also no cash margin that was given. India's case is that as PNB refused to issue fresh LoUs, Modi defaulted on the repayment of the eight LoUs that were due immediately, following which the bank filed a complaint with the CBI on 29 January 2018. On 13 February 2018, the bank informed the CBI that their internal investigation showed that firms associated with Nirav Modi had fraudulently obtained 150 LoUs in 2017.

The case against Nirav Modi in the UK courts centres around these 150 LoUs. The defence took, what the CPS describes as, an alternative narrative, which presents the case as a pure 'commercial dispute'. But among several points, the CPS highlighted that if the 'commercial dispute' angle is to be taken, how could the bank extend credit of thousands of crores of rupees with no security and a commission of less than Rs 10 crore, instead of Rs 237.12 crore?

The CPS was clear that just because some LoUs (six LoUs issued between October and November 2017 were issued with 100 per cent cash margin) were repaid, it doesn't mean that no fraud had taken place. They claim that Modi's account of communications with the bank were a post facto attempt to legitimize his shady dealings. On 5 February 2018, Modi sent an email to PNB, in which he said that he owned less than 5 per cent since the last two years in the three companies—Diamonds R Us, Solar Exports, Stellar Diamonds—but was writing to them to come to some resolution as his moral responsibility.

Modi's firms got 1214 LoUs between 2011–17, but as it was the 150 LoUs that remained unpaid, they formed the subject of the CBI's case. The CBI, however, maintains that just because the earlier LoUs were repaid, it doesn't mean that they were not obtained fraudulently. Moreover, none of the 1214 LoUs were entered on the bank's system.

The CBI's case is that out of the 150 LoUs, 123 were used to repay the earlier ones taken in 2016 and 2017 instead of making payments for genuine imports. According to the CBI, 'In no circumstances can an LoU be used for repaying the liability of an earlier LoU.' Companies in Dubai and Hong Kong were shown as exporters to Nirav Modi's firm, whereas the foreign entities were actually shadow companies controlled by Nirav Modi.

The issues of dummy directors and shadow companies were to be taken up at a greater length in the second leg of the trial, but the CBI did not lose the opportunity to firmly connect Modi with the three firms. Between 2011 and October 2016, Rs 848 crore from the bank accounts of Diamonds R Us in Oriental Bank of Commerce, Punjab National Bank and HDFC Bank were transferred to Modi's personal accounts.

There was much less drama at the beginning of the Nirav Modi trial compared to Mallya when a fire alarm forced everyone to vacate the court building. It was only close to 11.30 a.m. that the video link to Modi could be reached. Lockdown restrictions meant that Modi could witness the trial only from Wandsworth prison. There were moments when the judge would tell Helen Malcolm that she was breaking up, which meant she had to repeat herself. Nehal Modi's role came up as well when the court heard that he played a significant part in the business and had a role in the destruction of evidence. There was some complexity on the

first day regarding the second set of (fresh) requests that India sent
and how that should be taken forward.

The court heard that several companies (which had dummy
directors placed by Nirav Modi) were uncovered in the UAE and
six in Hong Kong. Some of the transactions involved a company
owned by Nirav's sister Purvi, and that a property in Central Park,
New York, was bought with the LoUs issued by PNB. There's
not much complication in the case, Malcolm said, adding that the
charge against Modi has three simple aspects: the fraud, laundering
of the fraud and the rotation around the Modi empire. Modi and
his associates were accused of operating a 'circular Ponzi scheme of
borrowing'.

On 12 May 2020, the court sat for the second day of the trial
and the proceedings began with Montgomery making the defence
opening, and then considering the prima facie case. 'The assurances
by government of India are inadequate . . . there are huge strains on
the evidence . . . bank had multiple people, yet only a handful have
been picked and charged . . . it was the bank's incompetence, rather
than fraud and dishonesty on behalf of Nirav Modi that led to
the LoUs.' This was Montgomery at her best, and when the judge
asked, 'How come my bundle has no index?', India's recurring weak
spot came to the fore.

After lunch, Montgomery continued the charge and raised the
issue of identical statements given by witnesses, and the need to
produce the original statements that were made in a foreign (non-
English) language. Montgomery then raised the issues arising due
to India's second request. 'He (Nirav Modi) has spent a year in
custody only to find that GoI has made a second request,' said
Montgomery.

Malcolm's assertion was that if the court was to discharge Modi
on article 3, what would happen when the second request was to
be considered. 'We will end up in an endless loop,' she said. As far
as the second request was concerned, Malcolm said that Modi was
informed of additional charges, and that there was no plan to delay
the proceedings. There was thus an argument on whether the court

should consider the issues of fair trial and jail conditions during the current proceedings or deal with them when the second set of charges came up for trial.

The court was then shown a video in which six men were heard making allegations of being forced to leave Dubai for Cairo. They spoke in Hindi, Gujarati and English and the video played for over 20 minutes, following which the judge asked how it was adduced as evidence. At 3.58 p.m., the court was adjourned and the judge asked Modi to 'remain in the room as no doubt (your) legal team would like to speak before you go'.

On the third day, Montgomery told the court about an email she received from the CPS's barrister Malcolm in the night. The email had documents which provided further 'corroborative evidence' against Modi. As expected, Montgomery strongly objected to the new documents terming them 'highly contentious' and 'very troubling'. Malcolm told the court that additional materials— mostly bank statements and other documents—would add clarity to the case. Two witnesses—Justice (Retd) Abhay Thipsay, and Thierry Fritsch, a jewellery expert—were lined up to give evidence through video link.

The issue of whether the court should allow or decline the serving of additional materials was to be left for the end of the day as it was imperative to hear the witnesses. Due to technical issues, there were disruptions, but it turned out to be a busy and intense day in the first leg of the Nirav Modi trial. It is difficult to say whether Justice Thipsay had any indication of the storm his evidence would cause in India.

Fritsch, a Frenchman, took oath on the Bible, and was the first witness. Fritsch was on Nirav Modi's advisory board for three years starting 2015. 'In the course of that connection, did you personally see the quality in Modi's factory?' Montgomery began. Fritsch then went on to speak about Modi's passion, talent and perfect craftsmanship.

'He was very proud to be from India,' he told the court and added that all this was a 'huge surprise'. Montgomery then got him to speak about Nirav Modi's international splash, his knowledge of the industry and commitment to the business. This continued for close to an hour, after which Malcolm stood to cross-examine him.

She didn't take long and came straight to the point. The court was told that Fritsch was involved in just one aspect of Nirav Modi's brand. 'You have never visited his company in UAE?' she asked to counter his glowing description of his workshop in India, implying that he wouldn't know about the dummy directors running those companies. Among a few other questions, Malcolm got Fritsch to reinforce what he said in his evidence earlier about the business requiring liquidity. 'Yes, it is capital-intensive,' he told the court.

All through the proceedings, at least one person from the CBI and one from the ED were glued to the court's common viewing platform (CVP). The next witness was Justice (Retd) Abhay Thipsay, whose evidence became a major highlight of the Nirav Modi extradition trial and cast its shadow on subsequent proceedings. Justice Thipsay's affidavit was prepared in December 2019 and the CBI and ED must have been aware of his evidence.

For the public, though, it was only on 13 May 2020 that the full import of Justice Thipsay's evidence came out. His evidence revolved around the legal construction of deception, statements recorded by police, inadmissibility of certain statements, cheating and breach of trust. At one point the court heard from Thipsay, 'If a loan is taken for purchase of motor car and you use it for something else, it may not be cheating.'

Malcolm asked some pointed questions over the recording of statements by the police, and discussed ROAC—read over and confirmed—as a possible valve to ensure statements recorded by police have credence. 'You were asked about ROAC by Ms Malcolm; that is an assertion made by a police officer. What does that prove?' asked Montgomery when she stood up after Malcolm's cross-examination. 'Often the witnesses say they were never told what is in the statement,' quipped Justice Thipsay. The gist of Justice Thipsay's evidence was that the charges against Nirav Modi might not stand in the Indian courts.

When Justice Thipsay's evidence got over, it was time for lunch. But before the court took a break, Judge Samuel Goozee reminded Malcolm about her application to submit further evidence. 'I need very good argument for this late evidence.' The CPS had taken a decision to submit further documents even though this potentially meant that the trial would get delayed. 'What prejudice is caused to the government of India case in terms of not having the account is the area that troubles me, a lot of this is explanatory,' the judge noted. It emerged that the additional documents included bank statements.

On 14 May 2020 (Day 4 of the trial), while the defence continued to sit with a straight face in Westminster Magistrates' Court, the high court gave judgment in the Vijay Mallya case. It was a huge setback for Mallya as the court declined him permission to appeal in the Supreme Court. Modi still had a long way to reach that stage, and never mind the judicial setback, the real test for success or failure was whether the requested person would go back to the state that made the request. Nirav Modi must have come to know about the judicial defeat of Mallya, but was he assured by his legal team that Mallya was not going to India any time soon?

For now, the trial was painfully divided into two parts and the cell in Wandsworth prison beckoned him. Just before noon the court rose, but before that the judge told Modi that he hoped he would be physically present in court for the second leg and not through a video link. It was a month of setbacks for Indian money bags in UK courts. In the same month, May 2020, the high court directed Anil Ambani to pay $716 million to Chinese banks within twenty-one days. But unlike Modi, neither Mallya nor Ambani was in jail.

The lockdown made it difficult for Nirav Modi to meet his legal team in person and also put a stop to the consultation with the jail psychiatrist. None of his family members live in the UK, and his only window to the outside world were the brief trips he made to Westminster Magistrates' Court for his call-over hearing every twenty-eight days. Now, he appears in the court only through video conferencing. There were no more bail applications, but preparations for the September trial under lockdown conditions meant there would be a flurry of consultations with his legal team to prepare the case.

* * *

The hearings in September 2020 saw a request by the defence to conduct witness testimonies and cross-examinations in private. In none of the extradition cases was there ever any application to conduct the hearing in private. The application was done to prevent the evidence of Justice Abhay Thipsay being out in the public. This was necessary, the defence claimed, to prevent the kind of media backlash that happened in the wake of Union Minister Ravi Shankar Prasad's press conference on 14 May 2020, the very next day after Thipsay's evidence to Westminster Magistrates' Court.

Ravi Shankar's press conference is likely to appear in the ruling by the judge, not just because the defence mentioned it to make a case for a private hearing, but also because they argued that the court should stay the proceedings as the minister's conduct amounted to a potential abuse of process. The objectives of the press conference, the defence claimed, were to launch a personal attack on Justice Thipsay as 'retribution' for giving evidence on Nirav Modi's behalf; to further politicize the criminal proceedings against Modi; and to deter any professional from giving evidence which could have serious personal ramifications for any such individual.

This was not the first time that a press conference figured prominently in an extradition proceeding. The press conference held by former Mumbai Police commissioner R.H. Mendonca declaring Nadeem as responsible for the murder of Gulshan Kumar prejudiced the case against Nadeem. Ravi Shankar Prasad's outburst provided the defence a convenient stick to get back at the prosecution. Justice Thipsay's request to give evidence in private, instead of in the open court, was before the judge as one direct outcome of Prasad's press conference.

The prosecution told the court they maintained a neutral stand to the defence's application regarding Justice Thipsay's testimony, but there was a collective sense of dissatisfaction among the handful of journalists in the press gallery expressed only through raised eyebrows. Very soon, Naomi Canton, Sanjay Suri, Danish Khan, Aditi Khanna and Loveena Tandon stood up one by one to make the case for Justice Thipsay's evidence to be in public. Loveena's reason was the most ingenious. She told the court that even if Justice Thipsay's evidence was heard in private, there was still no guarantee that there won't be another press conference.

The CPS also shared with the judge a letter from Tushar Mehta, the solicitor general, which, among other points, pointed out that the press conference was held by Ravi Shankar Prasad in his political capacity as a member of the Bharatiya Janata Party, while Justice Thipsay belongs to a different party. The solicitor general's letter also dwelt upon the separation of powers between the judiciary, the executive and the legislature. Malcolm told the court that there was 'zero evidence' for the suggestion that the press conference engineered the media blitzkrieg and harassment that Justice Thipsay faced.

After a short break, the judge returned and gave the ruling that Justice Thipsay's evidence need not be in private. Ravi Shankar Prasad's press conference was given as a political commentary and Justice Thipsay would be aware of the high interest in the case. The threshold required for a private sitting, the judge concluded, was not met. It was a good start for the prosecution, because the judge, by not allowing a private hearing or other form of reporting restrictions for Justice Thipsay's evidence, by default had concluded that there was no need for the court to inquire into allegations of abuse of process as a result of that press conference. Montgomery, however, sought a written assurance from the CPS that there would be no commentary by the Indian government on the evidence by Justice Thipsay.

The stage was now set for the CPS to make out a prima facie case on the charges of criminal conspiracy for causing the disappearance of evidence and criminal intimidation to cause death, and for the defence to counter that. These charges were broadly spelt out with four instances—the transfer of documents relating to the LoU applications to Cyril Amarchand Mangaldas (CAM), a law firm; moving the Dubai-based dummy directors to Cairo against their will; threatening to kill Ashish Lad and destroying a server in Dubai which had data relating to Modi's companies.

Helen Malcolm then took the proceedings further by fleshing out the charges of destroying evidence. She began with the large-scale transfer of documents to Nirav Modi's solicitor in Mumbai to ensure that they were not available to investigators. 'The GoI case is that there is no legitimate reason to give such documents to lawyers other than to keep them away from investigators,' said Malcolm. CAM is a famous and respected law firm and the defence's stand was that Nirav Modi had engaged them, and hence, documents were given to them to be copied.

But it was not just documents that were transferred to CAM. Along with boxes of original documents, there were also rubber stamps, seals, blank letterheads and judicial stamp papers in the names of various Firestar Group entities. Besides, the prosecution argued that documents given to PNB in support of the LoU application were also sent to CAM which should not have been with Nirav Modi.

Before lunch, the court was shown a video of around twenty minutes featuring five employees of Nirav Modi. They could be heard saying that they were forced to sign documents and were kept in Cairo where they were totally under the control and at the mercy of Nirav Modi. Wearing t-shirts and speaking in both English and Hindi, a couple of them gave graphic accounts of how Nirav and his brother Nehal Modi kept them in Cairo after twice replacing their mobile phones. One of them, Ashish Lad, it was alleged, was directly threatened to be killed by Modi, and was also offered Rs 20 lakh to travel to Europe and make a statement before a lawyer.

Irrespective of whether these points would convince the court that prima facie, Nirav Modi had a case to answer or not, similar arguments successfully prevented Nirav Modi from getting bail on five occasions. Modi appeared in the court through video link and heard the proceedings surrounded by papers, and kept shuffling to keep pace with the materials referred from different files. He wore a black suit with a white shirt, and sported a beard and moustache.

The second video, shown after lunch, was of barrack 12 of the Arthur Road Jail, accompanied by a running commentary. The court was informed that currently there was no inmate in barrack 12—the last occupants were media baron Peter Mukerjea and Nationalist Congress Party (NCP) leader Chhagan Bhujbal. During the arguments in the Mallya case, the defence had claimed that the prison photos and video were designed to hide the real conditions. The video began with the claim that it had been made without artificial light sources and had a running commentary spelling out the dimensions of the cell and the facilities—twenty feet high, three windows, three ceiling fans, LED television and an attached toilet. The cell was described as having sufficient sources of natural light, and fresh air with cross ventilation. 'There is no one else in that barrack,' said Malcolm, while also giving an update on the COVID-19 situation inside Arthur Road Jail.

Describing the conduct of the 'dummy' companies belonging to Modi as an exercise of 'merry-go-round' of export and import, the court heard how planted directors conducted business between fictitious companies. The arguments were a poignant reminder of Summers making similar points in the Mallya case where he used 'washing-machine' activity to describe money laundering. But unlike Mallya, Modi's case had taken a criminal turn with allegations of destruction of evidence and threatening to kill witnesses.

After listening patiently to Malcolm, Montgomery told the court of the 'evidential black holes' in the case put up by India. It was wrong, she continued, to say that after the credit facilities were withdrawn, Nirav Modi did not try to set things right with Punjab National Bank. She spoke about the IPO plans and the correspondence between Nirav Modi and the bank as proof enough to restart the credit facilities. This was stated to counter the CPS which maintained that documents were transferred to the offices of the law firm when PNB declined to issue LoUs and the CBI had started investigations.

There was nothing to show that 'documents (transferred to the law firm) were to be destroyed to pervert the course of justice'. The documents were sent to the law firm for advice and not for destruction. The evidence given by India needed to be looked at with a 'certain degree of rigour', Montgomery said. On the charge of employees being taken to Cairo, Montgomery said they were party to circular trading and that no offence could be said to have been committed against them. She told the court: 'No offence is committed by one potential defendant giving advice, encouragement, and assistance to other defendant to ensure that they are able to stay away from detention by investigating agencies.' That was the defence's take on what the CPS described as kidnapping witnesses and destroying evidence.

On 8 September, the second day of the trial, Nirav Modi's mental illness, the state of jails in India, and the issue of fair trial in India were discussed. The legal teams and officers from the CBI, ED and members of the press had taken their seats. There were six passes allotted to journalists that were issued on a first-come-first-served basis after production of a valid press card. But as the proceedings could be heard over the telephone, some reporters had chosen to stay at home to listen in.

Right next to Anand Doobay, the defence solicitor, three cardboard boxes were stacked, turning them into a temporary three-tier stand for easy access to the bulky folders. At the end of the day, these boxes were wheeled out by juniors, to be taken back to the law firms. But as the five-day trial was set to be held in court 10, papers were left in the courtroom to be locked after the day was over.

At 10.10 a.m., the judge came and Montgomery began the proceedings. It was still not clear whether Justice Thipsay would be giving live evidence or not. The Arthur Road Jail was described as an old-fashioned sweatbox and the general state of prisons in India as shameful. She repeated the same argument made in the Mallya case when she said that while barrack 12 has sufficient space, the reality is that it is itself enclosed in a steel box, and does not get natural light. Nirav Modi will have 'limited opportunity to engage in any meaningful activity', she said.

High suicide rates and ineffective mechanisms to inspect and monitor the jails were cited to undermine the assurances given by New Delhi. Much time was spent discussing the level of preparedness for the pandemic at Arthur Road Jail. Alan Mitchell, the prison expert, was to give evidence to add further depth and heft to the defence's arguments, even though he remained handicapped due to his last visit to an Indian prison being several years ago.

The highlight on Day 2 though was the coming out in the open in full force of the extent of Modi's mental illness. The court heard that Nirav Modi, who took the global jewellery industry by storm, was accessing the counselling facility in Wandsworth prison. 'It's not his wish that he should become as ill as he has become,' said Montgomery. The defence was pursuing a legal battle to get private counselling for Modi, as the outbreak of COVID-19 had disrupted prison provisions. Modi's mental illness meant that the defence could link it with the provisions in Arthur Road Jail.

There was no assurance that Nirav Modi would be protected against further deterioration to his mental health. A high risk of suicide, she said, makes it imperative for the court to enquire whether there are proper facilities and appropriate arrangements in the requested state. An extended submission on the figures of overcrowding and ratio of doctors to inmates, shortfall of staff, area available per prisoner, etc., was made citing figures from various studies and reports. At one point, the judge asked whether these figures were overall figures (for the Arthur Road prison) and not specifically of barrack 12 which was shown in the video. 'Yes, there is space in that cell (barrack 12), but (inmates there) will be dependent on the central prison services,' Montgomery replied.

Terming the assurance given by the GoI as 'laconic', Montgomery said that Modi's psychiatric condition and the

COVID-19 pandemic rendered the assurance 'utterly inadequate'. A rather dense exchange on the technicalities and tools of managing the pandemic reflected the keenness to muster and master arguments from diverse fields, all to tilt the case in one's favour. 'We need to have a summary of what the doctor has to say,' said Malcolm, when Montgomery informed the court that Dr Richard Coker, professor emeritus of public health, London School of Hygiene and Tropical Medicine, would give evidence.

'She was copied on a mail sent on Friday,' Montgomery quickly added, to drive home the point that Malcolm was made aware of Dr Coker's evidence. Dr Coker was going to comment on the report prepared by the ministry of health and the various assertions made by the GoI relating to COVID-19. The judge then realized that the documents being referred to were missing from the set that was provided to him by the CPS. Nicholas Hearn, the solicitor, sprung up from his chair and offered a copy. 'I do not need additional documents,' the judge remarked, quipping that he preferred the missing papers to be in his set of folders. At this point, the court took a small break to facilitate the necessary papers being located in the judge's folders.

It also emerged that Justice Abhay Thipsay wouldn't give live evidence (but would provide a written statement), and as if to compensate for that, Justice Markandey Katju would be appearing before the court through a video link to give evidence on the erosion of the judiciary in India. Giving a flavour of Justice Katju's evidence, Montgomery said he would refer to the Supreme Court's ruling in the Ayodhya case and the conduct of the courts in the Delhi riots signifying 'significant deterioration in judicial independence'. Another defence witness was to be Dr Andrew Forrester, a forensic psychiatrist, who had examined Modi on four occasions between September 2019 and August 2020.

The second day thus largely served as the opening of the argument by the defence, after which Malcolm gave out details of how Modi masterminded the fraud upon PNB. 'He destroyed mobiles of dummy directors and threatened one of the witnesses with death,' Malcolm told the court. She took the court through the detailed witness statements by the dummy directors which included Ashish Lad.

For the two days of the trial, seeing the dexterity with which Modi shuffled the papers, one could have mistaken him to be in his office and not in Wandsworth prison. On the third day too, he appeared surrounded by files and papers. Montgomery began by taking the court through the evidence of Justice Thipsay. The written statement of Justice Thipsay claimed that the fresh charges brought against Nirav Modi—threatening witnesses and destruction of evidence—would not stand in Indian courts.

'It is necessary to prove that the threat is a real one and not mere words,' Montgomery said, quoting Justice Thipsay's statement which gave a reference to a judgment by the Calcutta High Court. Nirav Modi could be seen making notes even as the court continued to hear what Justice Thipsay had to say. The retired judge of the Bombay and Allahabad High Court opined that some of the offences for which Modi was charged were committed outside India (the alleged act of threatening Lad) and were extra territorial, falling outside the jurisdiction of Indian authorities.

Written witness statements were provided by two journalists whose full names were not disclosed in the court, but were subsequently learnt—they were Rajat Guha and Pushp Sharma. Their statements revolved around the working of the CBI and ED and the conduct of the 'biased media' in India. 'Due to immense public pressure, investigations and judicial process will be influenced if Nirav Modi goes back,' said Montgomery quoting from the statements. Just like in the Mallya case, where Rakesh Asthana came under special mention, the witness statements, which were read in the court spoke about certain favourite officers who get orders from the home minister and prime minister, and control the narrative that suits the government, the court heard.

Another statement that Montgomery read related to the concern that the media pressure created by comments or coverage could result in an impact on judges for which Guha quoted Justice Sikri, a retired judge of the Supreme Court, to the effect that there is constant pressure on what the outcome should be. The extradition of Nirav Modi was also linked to electoral victory. Guha, described as a former journalist, was based in India as an independent consultant, while Sharma, described as an investigative journalist, was now based in the UK.

The defence also referred to the extradition of Abu Salem from Portugal to India to raise the issue of breach of assurance. Abu Salem's case has been cited in UK courts in other extradition cases pursued by India, but has been found to not meet the required threshold. However, Montgomery was confident that based on the written evidence of Sudeep Pasbola, the Mumbai-based criminal lawyer who represented Abu Salem, the Indian authorities could be shown to have indulged in deliberate misleading and obfuscation to ensure breach of assurance. 'This is additional and new information even though the Abu Salem case has been used before,' said Montgomery.

The leak of a confidential report by Dr Andrew Forrester on Nirav Modi's mental health was also broached by Montgomery. It was brought earlier before the chief magistrate Emma Arbuthnot in November 2019, during a bail hearing. 'It will undermine the trustworthiness of the government of India if it were proved that they were responsible for the leak,' Arbuthnot had remarked. At the time, the defence had maintained that the leak could have only happened from the GoI, which was stoutly denied by the CPS. Nearly a year later, Montgomery had again raised the issue of the leak to the media to link it with the use of the media to build a positive narrative for the government.

Written evidence was given, among others, by Sajal Yadav, who was the advocate for Chhagan Bhujbal when he was arrested on money laundering charges and kept in barrack 12 of Arthur Road Jail; Vijay Aggarwal who also handled the 2G Spectrum case; and R.K. Rawal, who retired as deputy director, ED and investigated Godman Chandraswami. As these witnesses gave written and not live evidence, they were not subject to cross-examination, which meant the court would accordingly give weightage to their statements.

There was a noisy start to Day 4 as someone connected to the proceedings on the phone was listening to the news on the radio and had not muted their instrument. After a few minutes of interruption, and much to the relief of those present in the courtroom, the voice of the news from the radio was replaced by the court proceedings. The hearing was already delayed as there were problems connecting to Nirav Modi in Wandsworth prison. Dr Richard Coker was the first witness of the day, appearing through a video link from Bangkok. Quickly after being introduced as an expert in medicine and epidemiology, came some interesting percentages from him.

'My prediction is that there is a 5 per cent chance of Nirav Modi getting COVID and if he gets it then 15 per cent chance of dying,' said Dr Coker. Montgomery then asked him to elaborate on the management of COVID-19 at Arthur Road Jail, testing strategy, and the rate of infection in Mumbai with the percentage-wise COVID-19 prevalence in the slum population and the rest of the city. 'The immunology of COVID is very complicated . . . I can't say that there won't be any cases in Arthur Road Jail, prisons are extremely susceptible.' Dr Coker also raised questions on the data provided about the management of the pandemic at the prison and said that more information and clarity was required to assess the situation.

In live evidence, the counsel's task becomes doubly important. They remain on their feet and have to ask the right questions to get the right answers from the expert witnesses, emphasizing the most crucial bits to accentuate their arguments. The questions that they pose too, are supposed to highlight or expose the shortcomings in the case put up by the opposing party, and they do it rather directly. 'On 5 August (2020), 128 inmates were randomly administered the antigen test and none of them were found COVID positive,' Montgomery posed to Dr Coker quoting from submissions by the CPS, adding later whether it would mean there was 'no risk of the epidemic'.

'Why did they and how did they choose 128 and whether statistics power calculation has been used for the right sample size? Prisons are the perfect setting for an epidemic, the only way you can guarantee (no risk of epidemic) is by limiting the number of visitors and some form of incredibly robust quarantine . . . or herd immunity,' said Coker, with Malcolm listening to the conversation.

'I don't think it has been said by GoI that there will not be another spread,' said Malcolm as she began her cross-examination. She also disputed the date Montgomery had got for the lockdown in Arthur Road Jail. Dr Coker was the first witness to give live evidence in the second leg of the trial, and Malcolm didn't take much time in getting straight to the point. 'It is right that we are all immunologically naïve to COVID,' she said, building the base for a volley of forceful questions:

> Malcolm: *There are eighteen people here in court who have been to coffee shops, have kids at school, and at least three people (have) flown from India exempted from quarantine to attend this hearing. So we all are at risk?*
>
> Dr Coker: *Yes.*
>
> Malcolm: *Given that prisons are important in our society . . . so Mr Modi if returned to India is going to be in barrack 12 . . . do you accept that it will be less risk . . . considerable better risk ratio than at Her Majesty's Prison Wandsworth?*
>
> Dr Coker: *I haven't seen Wandsworth prison video.*
>
> Malcolm: *Is it not a reasonable evidence that Mr Modi staying among several inmates (at Wandsworth) will face less risk in the large airy cell separated by a 200-foot wall from the prison?*
>
> Dr Coker: *In any prison setting, inmate will be in touch with staff, jailers, cleaners and those who help with food . . .*
>
> Malcolm: *But if Mr Modi is kept in a separate cell and not with other inmates, isn't it better?*
>
> Dr Coker: *An enclosed barrack, inside an enclosed prison . . . risk of death for Mr Modi through COVID is 0.75 per cent.*
>
> Malcolm: *What would it (risk of death) be for malaria?*

Once Malcolm was done, Montgomery told the court about Varavara Rao, the eighty-year-old activist jailed since 2018 and who tested positive for COVID-19, and was yet denied bail. Summing up, Dr Coker told the court that from the information furnished by India, he couldn't form any final conclusions, and there was a need to be cautious as it was not clear how the tests were applied, the quality of the laboratory and other such issues. Dr Coker then spoke about how he did not agree with India's characterization that their data defeats his opinions and that he made sweeping generalizations.

'The route for transmission of COVID is aerosols that hang for fifteen to sixteen hours,' he said in an apparent reference to enclosed cells being comparatively safer than one with more inmates. The issue of enclosed cells, mental well-being and psychiatric support figured in the evidence of Dr Andrew Forrester who was next after Dr Coker's evidence ended at 12.15 p.m., forty-five minutes before lunch break.

'I first saw him in September 2019 and his condition has deteriorated and is severe. Deception is unlikely because he has a history of depression. He has developed more severe signs of depression,' remarked Dr Forrester in his opening statement. The court heard that Nirav Modi had been taking anti-depressants and the lockdown at Wandsworth prison had resulted in less time socializing, and greater time inside the cell had made the symptoms more severe.

'Depression can come and go; however, in Modi's case, numerous factors are around to perpetuate—like this hearing—and being in prison, he has not been receiving treatment that he needs,' said Dr Forrester. He further described Modi as someone who presents a 'high risk of suicide' and who could become 'unfit to plead in future'.

'You say he is on a deteriorating trajectory and has offered to pay for care, what if he was provided multi-professional health care in Mumbai . . . so if there was an assurance that he would get multi-professional care . . . and at least the stress of these proceedings would not be there, would it help?' asked Malcolm. 'We haven't been provided with any assurance or detail,' Montgomery was quick to respond. As if taking a cue from Montgomery, Dr Forrester added in a similar vein that he too would like to see the details, but warned that solitary confinement accentuates stress.

The third and last witness was Dr Alan Mitchell who like Dr Forrester was in court to give live evidence. Due to the COVID-19 restrictions, both the witnesses sat on chairs normally meant for defendants in the courtroom. Dr Mitchell had given two reports dated 8 January 2020 and 21 July 2020. He told the court that a video was no substitute for a visit. The video of barrack 12 was played again after Dr Mitchell said that he would only be able to answer after watching the video. Dr Mitchell's last visit to India was to Alipore Jail in West Bengal in 2015, after which he had been refused access to Indian jails.

There was a slight delay in getting the Arthur Road Jail video as Nicholas Hearn had stepped out briefly to attend to another case in the same building. There was a slight drama as the video was played out with Dr Mitchell asking for it to be paused at a certain point. 'That frame suggests that the cell is darker.' Malcolm quickly turned the laptop towards the judge exclaiming: 'Sir, it looks different on the small screen.' The suggestion was that the quality had suffered as the video was played on the larger screens in the courtroom. Dr Mitchell also referred to the evidence by Sajal Yadav, who visited Bhujbal in barrack 12, who referred to mosquitoes, rodents and insects in the jail in his statement.

> *Montgomery: There is no overcrowding problem in barrack 12?*
> *Dr Mitchell: Yes.*
> *Montgomery: Does that mean that overcrowding in Arthur Road Jail is irrelevant?*
> *Dr Mitchell: Overcrowding places enormous pressure on prison staff, they would be unable to do their job. Staff asked to look after Nirav Modi in barrack 12 may be asked to do tasks somewhere else.*

Dr Mitchell then dwelt on the adverse effect on Nirav Modi's mental health due to possible solitary confinement in barrack 12, even for a short period. He pointed out that there was no psychiatrist or psychologist in Arthur Road Jail. Malcolm's parting shot to Dr Mitchell was that 'nothing the government of India does will satisfy you'. 'What is important and appropriate is a psychiatrist cover,' said Dr Mitchell.

Unlike Dr Mitchell, Justice Markandey Katju, the star witness for the defence on the last day of the trial was more adept at listening rather than giving evidence. Ever since his retirement, Justice Katju has been active on social media where he has generated his own share of controversies. While he may not have any link to the Congress party like Justice Thipsay, the fact that he agreed to give live evidence was reflective of his rather outspoken personality.

The prosecution and the judge had a fair indication of what he was going to say as the defence had almost every day during the trial referred to what Justice Katju would speak on. On Friday morning, a few Indian journalists instead of racing inside to get their hands on the media pass and wait for doors to court 10 to open, were instead outside the court building. Sanjay Bhandari, subject of an extradition request by India, was expected to come to the court the same morning for his remand hearing.

Keenly aware of the media interest, Helen Malcolm looked a bit surprised seeing journalists wait outside the court building when Justice Katju's evidence was to begin in the next thirty minutes. Carrying a large and sturdy supermarket bag for her important papers, she told the journalists that she had no idea about Bhandari, but asked if any one of us was from the *Economic Times*. Justice Katju had spoken to the financial paper, an account of which was published on the same day.

The wait was short-lived as an official of the Indian High Commission informed that Bhandari's hearing was postponed. Still not wanting to take a chance, the journalists went in just before 10 a.m. driven by the logic that the last thing a person out on bail would do was to come late for his hearing. Besides, Justice Katju was going to be live soon.

'It is widely shared that the Supreme Court has shamelessly surrendered,' began Justice Katju. Montgomery interjected briefly to tell him that his evidence was being written down. He began with the Ayodhya verdict and referred to his three articles in the Wire which outlined how on one hand the Supreme Court admitted that the demolition of the mosque was a criminal act yet, paved the way for the construction of the temple. 'The CJI (Chief Justice of India Ranjan Gogoi) was made member of the Parliament.'

'The Ayodhya verdict was the most shameful verdict in fifty years which I would have dismissed in a minute as humbug. The BJP had just two seats and on the back of the Ram Janmabhoomi movement have now reached 303 seats,' said Katju.

'He was another shameless man,' thundered Justice Katju when Montgomery asked him to speak about Dipak Mishra, Gogoi's predecessor. 'He would send politically sensitive cases to relatively junior judges like Arun Mishra who was known to be pro-BJP . . . Justice Arun Mishra publicly praised PM Modi . . . called him a visionary . . . which was so brazen.' Expanding on his observation about Justice Arun Mishra, Katju asked, 'Now when a sitting Supreme Court judge publicly makes such a statement, what message goes to the public?'

He also referred to the government's refusal to elevate Gopal Subramanium to the Supreme Court, even though it was a recommendation of the collegium, as 'Subramanium had argued a case against Amit Shah' (a prominent leader in the BJP and India's home minister). Also Justice Akil Kureshi was, in Katju's opinion, unjustly made a chief justice of the smaller north-eastern state of Tripura instead of the collegium's recommendation to the larger central state of Madhya Pradesh. Katju also pointed out that Justice S. Muralidhar was 'overnight transferred' from the Delhi High Court to the Punjab and Haryana High Court after 'he made some critical remarks against the Delhi Police'. This, Katju argued, showed how the judiciary's independence in India had deteriorated.

There was not a single day during the trial when Ravi Shankar Prasad's press conference was not mentioned. It was unthinkable that Justice Katju would spare it. Terming the press conference as an indication that the GoI had made up its mind that Nirav Modi was a criminal, he told the court that as the law minister, Prasad should not 'pronounce a verdict against anybody', but instead could have stopped by saying that Nirav Modi 'faces serious charges'. The import of his evidence was that the court will do what the government says.

The media, ED and CBI were also spoken about by Justice Katju. He agreed with Montgomery's assertion that a media trial has an effect on a large number of judges, if not all. 'The media has also held a trial and pronounced him guilty . . . they benefit by their TRP ratings and various other ways.' Katju went on to say that India's leading investigating agencies—the CBI and the ED—are not independent, non-political bodies and will do what they are told to do by their political masters.

Taking a leaf out of history, Katju likened the BJP government in India to the Nazis in Germany. 'The Indian economy is collapsing, GDP is going down, businesses are closing . . . and the BJP government has no idea how to solve it so they must find some scapegoat. Just like Hitler found Jews, the present government has got Nirav Modi . . . he is the Jew of India . . . instead of trying to solve the economic problems, they want to divert attention and find a scapegoat for the down-slide of the economy.'

Justice Katju spoke relentlessly for an hour. At 11.21 a.m., Malcolm stood for the cross-examination. 'My Lord, as I understand, your evidence is broken into four parts—trial by media linked along with the dishonesty within CBI and ED; collapse of the rule of law; government influence on judges in India; corruption in judiciary.' Malcolm chose to address Justice Katju as 'My Lord' unlike Montgomery who used either Mr or Justice Katju.

Malcolm: This case arises because Nirav Modi admitted (that he) obtained more than a billion US dollars from PNB . . . are you aware that PNB officers have been charged as well?

Justice Katju: I can't comment because I have not seen the evidence, I can't comment on the merits of the case. I have said he (Nirav Modi) cannot get a fair trial in India.

Malcolm: Why did you choose to speak to the press?

Justice Katju: I got calls from the media, they contacted me.
Malcolm: You could have said no comments.

••••

Malcolm: Hindus believe that the birthplace of Lord Ram is in Ayodhya.
Justice Katju: How can you say that a person was born 5000 years ago
at a place where (a) mosque stands? Through propaganda, the whole
of Germany was made to believe that Jews need to be persecuted. If a
mosque has been made 500 years ago, can you go back and demolish
it? It is true that some Muslim invaders demolished temples. But this
is all politics.
Malcolm: Is it not right that whatever judgment was given, it would
have upset a large section of the population?
Justice Katju: By appeasement you don't succeed. Haven't you learnt
anything from the pact of 1938 (referring to the Munich agreement of
1938 signed by France, Italy, Britain and Germany which allowed
the latter to annex Sudetenland)?

••••

Malcolm: You were appointed Press Council (of India) chairman
after retirement.
Justice Katju: I was not appointed by the government of India.
Malcolm: The three-member appointment committee, composed of
the Speaker of the Lower House, chairman of the Upper House and
a Press Council member are completely apolitical and nothing to do
with the government?
Justice Katju: There are plenty of distinguished exceptions, retired judges
do get appointments. I was not appointed by government of India.

••••

Malcolm: Is it possible that you are a publicist seeking media attention?
Justice Katju: It is not for me to say.

The exchange between Malcolm and Katju turned fiery from then on. So far, her questions were designed to provide an alternative view to what Justice Katju had highlighted as flaws and shortcomings. It seemed as if Malcolm had planned her cross-examination to contain two parts: the first to fire a volley of questions to counter his evidence; and second to deploy his past utterances in an effort to undermine his evidence. The first part had ended and now the volley of uncomfortable questions began.

> *Malcolm: You are chairman of a body seeking annihilation of Pakistan and Bangladesh?*
> *Katju: We should peacefully come together, I didn't use the word annihilate.*
> *Malcolm: Did you say 90 per cent of Indians are fools?*
> *Katju: Yes, I did say that (in the context that people in India vote on the basis of caste).*
> *Malcolm: In 2014 you announced in your blog that gay relationships are unnatural . . . you announced that a woman has to get a man to look after her and women who remain single are prone to psychological problems . . . In 2015 you said Mahatma Gandhi was a British agent, and in 2017 you said that the Supreme Court erred in not giving death sentence in a particular case.*

Katju, of course replied to all of this, but his tone became shrill, and his voice high-pitched. By the end of it, it seemed quite a challenge for Justice Katju to manage his emotions. His response clearly reflected his growing irritation:

> *'Are you a Britisher?';*
> *'Have you read George Bernard Shaw';*
> *'At one point people saying the earth going around the sun was considered as outrageous, it was found to be correct in the end, I don't care if what I say is controversial.'*

Malcolm had finished her examination and Montgomery now took the floor. 'The main thesis put by GoI is that it is your personal vanity that got you to give evidence?' Montgomery asked Katju, who denied this saying that he held these views for a long time, writing three pieces in the Wire, which were published much earlier.

'There is a suggestion that you are alone in those views,' said Montgomery. Katju denied this, adding that people like Dushyant Dave, the president of the Supreme Court Bar Association of India, and a large number of people held these views. 'Freedom of speech exists on paper unless someone is there to enforce it. In recent years, judiciary has given up that role. Habeas corpus petitions are pending for more than a year. People like Safoora Zargar (student activist arrested for protests against the state) and Kafeel Khan (a doctor who accused the government of sectarian politics) have been held on trumped up charges, and the judiciary is turning a blind eye,' said Katju.

Just as the video link to Justice Katju was snapped at 12 p.m., a little over two hours after he started his evidence, there was an unusual buzz in the area where the Indian officials were seated. One of them had just walked in with a large stack of papers, whispering into the ears of Nicholas Hearn who sat right behind Malcolm. The next moment the papers were in the hands of Malcolm.

'There are two additional documents,' said Malcolm. The first was a written undertaking to the court that the Indian government would provide all the psychiatric help that Nirav Modi needed in Arthur Road Jail, and the second document gave clarity to the point raised by the defence about the difference between the 'original' and 'office' copies of the LoUs. Montgomery objected to the submission of these documents 'at the end of a long and exhaustive trial'.

'It is open for GoI to give assurance at any stage. I did put that to Dr Forrester whether assurances for medical facilities would be better,' replied Malcolm. The court then rose, marking the end of the second leg of Nirav Modi's trial.

In January 2021, the closing arguments of the trial saw Malcolm raise two extradition cases to argue against Modi being sent to India. The first case mentioned was of paedophile Raymond Varley—which this book explores in more detail in chapter seven. Varley was discharged when a witness statement on his mental health went unchallenged by India. In Modi's case too, India left it unchallenged until the last day and hence the court declined their request to have their expert examine Modi, agreeing with Montgomery that it should have been made earlier.

The other case cited was of bookie Sanjeev Chawla, which is explored in chapter three. The high court in the UK was convinced by assurances given by India that the prison conditions in Tihar Jail would meet with the ECHR guidelines and the CPS barrister requested that court that India should be given an opportunity to put forth any assurances that the court required to be satisfied with the jail conditions for Modi.

But what Modi would be pinning all his hopes on is the recent judgment by district judge Vaneesa Baraister in the extradition case of WikiLeaks's founder Julian Assange to the Unites States of America. Baraister began by upholding one after another the arguments put forward by the US for Assange's extradition, only to conclude that the extradition would be oppressive as there was a likelihood of Assange dying by suicide in a US prison. She mentioned that article 3 of the ECHR and section 91 of the (UK) Extradition Act 2003 provide the necessary safeguards to bar extradition due to poor mental and physical conditions rendering extradition unjust and oppressive. Modi's counsel Montgomery has cited both. Judge Goozee has declared February 25 as the day he would give out his judgment in Modi's extradition case. An appeal can then be made to the high court against his decision by either party.

But the repeated refusal of bail for Modi has added an interesting dimension to the extradition case. The many judges that have heard his bail plea have inferred that as a single man of relatively expansive means, Nirav Modi cannot be trusted to remain

in the United Kingdom. They also concur that his escape could put
the welfare of the many others who spoke against him at great risk.

As Modi languishes in Her Majesty's Prison Wandsworth,
the life of Edmond Dantès behind bars perhaps haunts him. 'Be
careful what you wish for', is advice Modi perhaps ignored as he
embraced Edmond Dantès as an alias when life was one of luxury.
The meteoric rise of a small-town jeweller into the global glitterati
circuit and his almost overnight fall from grace is symbolic of the
life events of his fictitious hero.

While Dantès was an innocent man wrongly imprisoned by
jealous peers who hated his kind, intelligent and ethical life, Nirav
Modi perhaps is anything but those things. It appears that life in
prison is affecting Modi's mental stability. If Modi plans to walk
in the shoes of Dantès, whose time in prison makes him lose the
capacity to feel any emotion other than hatred for those who have
harmed him, it might be better for his enemies to be well prepared.

3

BOWLED-OUT BOOKIE

'Hello, Hansie,' a faint voice mumbled.
'Hello, hi Sanjay,' replied a heavily accented voice.

An accent that was not Indian, not even British. Indian police were now sitting on the edge of their seats, clearly listening.

It was 13 March 2000. The officers in the crime branch of Delhi Police were tapping into telephone conversations of one Sanjeev Chawla, living in the UK, who they suspected was an extortionist and a part of the underworld gangs that operate in India. It was on a complaint filed by a man called Ramakant Gupta who believed he was being extorted by a man based in Dubai. The investigation trail led Inspector Ishwar Singh to various calls between specific numbers. One such number led to Chawla. Others led to a Delhi-based diamond merchant and property developer called Rajesh Kalra and one to the slain cassette king Gulshan Kumar's brother Krishan Kumar. Singh was curious to know the role UK-based businessman Chawla played in extortion.

What Singh had never imagined was to hear Chawla speak to, as was increasingly becoming clear, the South African cricket captain Hansie Cronje.

The South African team had landed in India a week ago to play one-day cricket matches. The conversation, they suspected would lead to an extortion threat, but what they discovered was much bigger and definitely more interesting. A volley of telephone

125

conversations was recorded between Chawla and Cronje, one even made from London by Chawla. SIM cards purchased by Kalra and given to Chawla were passed on to Cronje to keep the calls as untraceable as possible when conversations revolved around money transfers and rigged match outcomes.

On 7 April 2000, Dr Krishna Kant Paul, Delhi's joint commissioner of police, held a press conference. He announced to the curious press that a first information report (FIR) was registered at Chanakyapuri police station the previous day against Chawla, Kalra and Cronje. 'The information available with the police revealed that some businessmen were in contact with certain South African players for match-fixing in the Pepsi Cup,' said Paul. Amidst gasps and excited whispers among the journalists present, Paul continued, 'From the conversations between Sanjeev alias Sanjay Chawla and Hansie Cronje, it emerges that one-day international matches between India and South Africa in March 2000 were fixed for exchange or consideration of money.'

Hansie Cronje, thirty, and three of his teammates, Pieter Strydom, thirty-one, Nicky Boje, twenty-seven, and Herschelle Gibbs, twenty-six, were charged by the Indian police with match-fixing. A journalist in England called up Bronwyn Wilkinson, the communication manager of South Africa's United Cricket Board (UCB), for a reaction. Wilkinson quickly informed Dr Ali Bacher, managing director of UCB, whose only response was this is 'absolute rubbish'. He told Wilkinson to contact Paul in Delhi and demand an explanation for not getting in touch with the South African cricket board before making this public. Wilkinson dutifully did so. Paul was quite adamant in his refusal to entertain any interference in his investigations.

Dr Bacher announced that he was shocked and angry that anyone would doubt Cronje's integrity and stood behind his captain, rubbishing any news of match-fixing. Fans, too, rallied behind Cronje who had led the South African team for six years and was considered a man of good Christian values. UCB's president, Percy Sonn, called the allegations 'spurious' and threw doubts on the motives of the Indian police. He absolutely refused to entertain any suspicions about Cronje and his mates unless Indian police released the tape recordings. Several diplomatic efforts were also made to acquire a copy of the tapes with Harsh Bhasin, the high commissioner of India in Pretoria. The diplomat was queried on why Indian police would think it was okay to listen in on conversations of South African players on phones and in hotel rooms and asked to hand over the tapes to South African authorities. South Africa's high commissioner to India, Maite Nkoana-Mashabane, called the ministry of external affairs in New Delhi to request access to the tapes. The requests were denied by the Indian government. This, however, did not stop South Africa's deputy foreign minister Aziz Pahad from making a press statement that their high commissioner in India had listened to the tapes and could confirm that the accents were not South African.

It seemed no one in South Africa would take the Indian police seriously. Then the Delhi Police made public a part of the transcript of alleged conversations between Cronje and a bookmaker Sanjeev Chawla:

Chawla: Is Strydom playing?

Cronje: Yes, he is playing, yeah.

Chawla: Boje?

Cronje: Boje is playing.

Chawla: Yeah, Boje is playing . . . and who playing? Gibbs?

Cronje: Gibbs and myself.

Chawla: Ya, what about anybody else?

Cronje: No, I won't be able to get more.

Chawla: You won't be able to get more?

Cronje: No.

Chawla: OK, just tell me. But you have only four with you and not anybody else?

Cronje: No.

Chawla: Klusener and no one?

Cronje: No. No. Impossible. Impossible . . . No. No. They were saying that they were already doing Cochin. The other guys are already angry with me because I have not received their money, you know.

Chawla: No. But I told you, I have already given him altogether 60.
Cronje: OK.
Chawla: And tomorrow I can deposit the money in your account. It is not a problem because of the time difference. Tomorrow itself I can deposit the money.
Cronje: OK . . . OK, I have spoken. Yes, everything is fine. Spoken to Gibbs and to Strydom. Everything is fine.
Chawla: Already, OK? And how many runs for Gibbs?
Cronje: Less than 20.
Chawla: Less than 20?
Cronje: Yeah.
Chawla: OK. So everything is according to plan. They have to score at least 250?
Cronje: Yeah.
Chawla: And if you score 270, it is off?
Cronje: OK. And financially the guys want 25. They want 25 each.
Chawla: All right, OK.
Cronje: So that's 75 for those three and . . . what can you pay me? I do not know how much you pay me . . .
Chawla: You say.
Cronje: If you give me . . . 140 for everybody.
Chawla: 140 altogether?
Cronje: Yeah.
Chawla: OK, that's fine.
Cronje: OK.
Chawla: And we will sort something out for the previous one as well.
Cronje: OK, sure.
Chawla: Yeah?
Cronje: All right. So we definitely are on.

This released transcript provided some damning evidence against the South African captain.

What is clearly visible in the conversation are the strategies employed by bookmakers: the first is spread betting which involves wagering on the total runs on the board by a team. This can fluctuate as the match progresses but wagers are also taken on the number of runs a team will make in the first fifteen overs of a one-day international and on the individual runs a batsman will make. Another popular wager the bookmakers put forth is called line betting where bets are taken on the runs a particular batsman is expected to score or when he is likely to lose his wicket.

Though not all tapes were released, it was enough for Cronje to lose sleep. Two days later, Dr Ali Bacher was woken up by the team manager Goolam Rajah who told him that the captain had something to say to him. It was 3 a.m. No news at this time could be good news, Dr Bacher thought and held his breath.

'Doc, I haven't been honest with you,' said the faint voice of a broken man. Cronje confessed to Dr Bacher that he had taken money from Chawla to the tune of $10-15,000. Dr Bacher was heartbroken and ashamed.

He unreservedly apologized on behalf of the cricket board and himself to the Indian police and fans for supporting Cronje initially. He also asked the government to institute an independent inquiry into the charges.

Cronje's statement to the King's Commission of Inquiry that was held in Cape Town offered some dark insights. He admitted to being approached by a man named 'John' during the Mandela Cup in 1995 to throw the match, but he refused. Pakistani cricketer Saleem Malik had also asked Cronje if he had spoken to John, to which Cronje confessed, he nodded his head, out of shame. Cronje maintains he did not take any bribe from John, whose name had surfaced in 1998 in connection with the match-fixing allegations against Mark Waugh and Shane Warne during the Australian cricket team tour of Sri Lanka in 1994.

A year later, when South Africa was on a tour to India, Mohammad Azharuddin, the Indian skipper, had allegedly introduced Cronje to a bookie called Mukesh Kumar Gupta (M.K.) in a hotel on the third evening of the Test in Kanpur. M.K., who owns a jewellery showroom in Delhi, started the conversation talking about diamonds in South Africa and then swiftly slipped into his other avatar—that of a bookmaker—after Azhar left the two alone. M.K. asked Cronje to throw the last Test and paid Cronje $30,000 to talk to the other players to do so. South Africa were on the verge of losing the match anyway, so Cronje took the money and smuggled it out of India hiding it in his kit.

During the King's Commission, when Cronje confessed to the meeting with M.K., Brendon Manca, junior counsel for the UCB, asked him, 'At that time, when you left the room, didn't you think it strange that a person that Mohammad Azharuddin had introduced you to, had just handed you $30,000 and asked you to fix a match and I am asking you that in particular with regard to what you thought about Mr Azharuddin introducing you to this individual.'

Cronje explained that often players will get introduced to an autograph hunter or to somebody who wants a quick picture, and just leave you to it. 'Often in South Africa, I will introduce some of the Indian or Pakistani or Australian players to friends of mine and leave them to it.'

Cronje told the commission that M.K. had followed the Indian team to South Africa and paid Cronje $50,000 for information about team selection and daily forecast of the first Test and the score on which he would declare during the second Test. Cronje was emphatic in declaring that South Africa won both tests.

By now, M.K. had firmly decided that Cronje was on his side. He later contacted the South African with an offer of $200,000 to lose the last one-day international match. This offer was not rejected outright but formed the basis of a contentious team meeting. Cronje put it before his team where many members were vehemently against it. Some, however, were curious to see how high the offer could go, so Cronje asked for $300,000 and M.K. promised to take it up to $250,000.

Cronje told the King's Commission that since his team was largely opposed to it, he called M.K. and rejected the offer and no money was transferred then. 'I led him to believe I would. This seemed an easy way to make money but I had no intention of doing anything,' Cronje said. South Africa lost the Test nevertheless and Cronje received $30,000. He claims he did not feel guilty for taking the money as he had 'not actually done anything'.

When Cronje was repeatedly questioned about whether he believed Azharuddin was aware of the offers that were made to him by M.K., Cronje replied, 'No, he's not aware of it . . . I didn't for any reason think that he was doing business with Mr Gupta at all.' Cronje neither denied Azhar's connection to M.K. nor assumed that Azhar was unaware of M.K.'s business.

International Cricket Council (ICC) President Jagmohan Dalmiya promised a full-scale inquiry into the match-fixing scandal, pledging that 'those who seek to tarnish the image of cricket in this manner must be brought to justice'. While Cronje's culpability in match-fixing was met with much disbelief and angst, many were quick to assume that cricketers from India and Pakistan were hand-in-glove with the bookmakers. Not surprising if you look at the colonial history of cricket.

* * *

In the nineteenth century, Britain was the imperialist superpower with its spread across Asia and Africa and settler colonies in Australia and South Africa. British sport also made its entrance into these parts of the world and included cricket, football and equestrian events. Of course, as all things in the colonial world, the sports too were first played by the white settlers and the British Empire Games first held in 1930 in Hamilton in Canada were for white men only. Men of colour from colonial nations were excluded from this event until 1954.

While the origins of cricket in England were rural, in India it was the urban elite that took to cricket first. Prashant Kidambi in his 2019 bestseller book *Cricket Country* writes that in mid-nineteenth century Bombay, it was the Parsee bourgeoisie youth who first embraced this 'alien game, hitherto the pastime of British expatriates in the colonial enclaves scattered across the subcontinent' and in great detail shows how the inclusion of these so-called 'colonial mimic men' into cricket was fraught with much resistance and ridicule.

The Imperial Cricket Conference in 1909 had teams from England, South Africa and Australia. For men of colour to be accepted in the game was a journey layered with much struggle and discrimination. George Robert Canning Harris, who served as a governor of Bombay, believed in the imperial power of cricket and started a tournament between the Parsees and British residents in 1892. When he became president of the Marylebone Cricket Club (MCC) in 1896, he said that the game of cricket has actually done more 'to draw the Mother country and the colonies together than years of beneficial legislation could have done'.

Cricket was more than a unifying force, it came to exemplify 'whiteness'—purity, manliness, self-discipline, loyalty, courage, fair play, obedience to rules and even divinity. Cricket became a symbol of the empire and civilization. The Britannic nationalism became a centre-point for cricket tours, especially in the white settler colonies of South Africa and Australia where the imperial links remained strong through cultural ties through sport even when the political weakened.

The period between the two World Wars saw cricket emerge as a sign of normalcy and peace. Cricket was broadcasted on radio in the 1930s in England, Australia and South Africa, and this added to its popularity.

After World War II, a weak Britain lost its colonies to independence but maintained its sporting prowess through cricket. British journalist Mihir Bose in his book *Nine Waves* credits Jawaharlal Nehru with keeping India relevant in international cricket. Bose recalls that the *Times of India* newspaper would carry pictures of Nehru in his full cricket gear during the annual parliamentary match. And though the prime minister was not very good at cricket, he was good at ensuring the sport survived the political divorce with England. Nehru was adamant in his decision that an independent India would join the Commonwealth, even though there was much domestic opposition to this. When the Imperial Cricket Conference—founded in 1909 by England, Australia and South Africa—was convinced that India, even after becoming a Republic, was committed to being a part of the British Commonwealth, they made India a permanent member of the ICC, as it now fulfilled the basic criteria for its membership. India was a nobody in 1950s and this was the platform it desperately needed. Today it is a top team and Indians have held prominent positions in the International Cricket Council—the new avatar of the erstwhile Imperial Cricket Conference—which has now expanded to twelve full members.

Cricket was not very popular in India in the 1950s. Television in the 1960s and '70s won many more to the game and with the World Series Cricket in 1977, the game had truly become commercialized. The one-day match series played during day and night was introduced, and coloured uniforms replaced the whites. Today it is a cult.

Interestingly, when the rules of the game were first created in the eighteenth century, it was to facilitate dispute-free wagers on the match. Gambling was commonplace then and many in the British nobility enjoyed wagering on match outcomes. But by the nineteenth century, it became less and less common until finally, in 1817, wagers were banned from Lord's, considered cricket's home turf in England.

Despite the rapid commercialization of the game that followed, cricket was to its imagined community, a gentleman's game—pure and beyond reproach. When in 1998, news broke that Australian cricketers Shane Warne and Mark Waugh had passed on crucial information to an Indian bookmaker in exchange for money ($5000 and $4000, respectively) in the 1994 match in Sri Lanka, the Western media had put the blame on India and Pakistan for corrupting the game. The Australian cricket board had largely covered their actions, and let them off with just a fine. Now, with the Cronje affair, the Western media once again saw this largely as a problem of the Indian subcontinent, blaming Indian and Pakistani cricketers and the illegal bookmakers from the Indian subcontinent as being the nefarious elements out to destroy the sanctity of the sport of cricket.

An article in the *Mail & Guardian* on 10 April 2000 read: 'Allegations of match fixing are not uncommon, particularly on the subcontinent where illegal betting on the outcome of matches is rife, with bets running into Rs 22 billion ($4 billion) a year'. The Johannesburg *Star* conducted a poll where a staggering 94 per cent of South Africans believed Cronje was innocent of match-fixing.

This myth was shattered on 23 June 2000 when Cronje gave his testimony to the King's Commission that he was in touch with Sanjay and a deal was struck to fix the cricket match:

> *Cronje: Sanjay was staying in the same hotel as what we were staying in Cochin . . . I was trying to avoid any telephonic conversation with him the night before, but the morning of the match, I was reminded that he would like to speak to me. I went downstairs to breakfast, had breakfast, wanted to stay away from him, but on the way out, I picked up the telephone at reception, phoned his room and said 'yes, it is okay, we can go ahead'. I rammed off five or six names, I think it was five names and said that we will keep the score under about 250 and that we will try and lose the game. That is what I said to Sanjay.*
>
> *Commissioner: That is before the game. Was there any further discussion with him about Cochin, the game, either during the game or after the game?*
>
> *Cronje: The night that I got back to the hotel, Sanjay called me and was obviously not very happy with me because South Africa scored 301/3 instead of less than 250. The reason why we scored more is because I didn't in fact speak to any of the players and none of the players were aware that there is anything on the cards.*
>
> *Commissioner: You say Sanjay was not happy because you hadn't fulfilled your undertaking to him? Was there any discussion about any of the players being dissatisfied, was there any discussion of any monetary sums that would—allegedly owing, can you tell me?*
>
> *Cronje: The night after I got back to the hotel, I just said to Sanjay that he must keep his side of the bargain, then we will keep our side*

*of the bargain. But we didn't really specifically go into detail, he
was just very cross with me that we didn't score less than 250 as I
led him to believe that we would do. During the following game
at Jamshedpur, he phoned me again and not only wanting to get
information, but wanting to actually influence the result and the
excuse that I used in this instance was that I won't be able to get to
any of the players, because they are upset with me because they have
not been financially paid, using that as an excuse to keep him away
from me.*

*Commissioner: You say you told him that the players were cross
with you because they hadn't been financially paid; were numbers
mentioned, any amount, any figures?*

*Cronje: I am not 100 per cent sure what the figures were that were
discussed, I am actually not even sure whether numbers were discussed
before the Cochin game, as it was done in such a rush.*

*Commissioner: When you mentioned this to Sanjay, did he undertake
to make amends, to make any money available?*

*Cronje: Sanjay said to me 'not to worry, we've got an undertaking,
he has given me a deposit as well' and he is also going to transfer some
funds to my account in London, 'not to worry,' he said, 'not to worry,
we will sort out the others as well'.*

What emerged from the inquiry was that Cronje had got Chawla
to agree to pay three other South African players $25,000 each
but had told his mates that he would give them $15,000 each.
When repeatedly being questioned by Shamila Batohi, the leader
of evidence for the Commission, Cronje admitted that it was greed
that made him lie.

*Batohi: Your evidence is that on the previous night you had agreed
with Sanjay that the players would get $25,000 each, okay. The
following day, you offer Mr Gibbs and Mr Williams $15,000 each,
why did you do that?*

*Cronje: I offered them the equivalent of $15,000 and on my way out
of the room, I told them that I will try and get it up as high as I can.*

Batohi: But you had already agreed with Sanjay that they would get $25,000?
Cronje: Maybe I was trying to cut something for myself.

Cronje told the commission that he had taken at least $130,000 from bookies between 1996 and 2000 including a leather jacket from South African bookie Marlon Aronstam. During the Centurion Test in 2000, Aronstam had called Cronje's mobile on 17 January without an introduction but was soon invited into his hotel room where a deal was struck for Cronje to persuade Nasser Hussain and England to forfeit an innings to give England a run chase. Hussain agreed though he had no inkling of the meeting. Aronstam gave 500,000 rand to a charity of Cronje's choice and a leather jacket as a gift. There was no doubt any more, that it was the lure of easy money and greed that made Cronje indulge in match-fixing.

On 26 June 2000, Justice Edwin King declared Cronje guilty and gave him a life ban from playing and being formally involved in the game of cricket. He also handed out six-month bans and fines to Herschelle Gibbs and Henry Williams when they admitted to conspiring with Cronje to underperform in one-day internationals in India in March 2000. Nicky Boje was cleared by the commission and Pieter Strydom received no punishment. With this, the government quickly shut the inquiry before more skeletons popped out of the woodwork.

The Cronje affair was now at an end. Born Wessel Johannes Cronje on 25 September 1969 in Bloemfontein, Cronje's career started with his Test debut for South Africa against West Indies in March 1992 and ended with his final Test in India in 2000. He had 3714 runs including six centuries and an average of 36.41 runs. Cronje was a successful captain and a much-loved player of South African cricket. 'In the new democracy he was seen as a young Afrikaner who had a vision to transform cricket, to transform the country,' Bacher had once said. Cronje may have disgraced himself in the game of cricket, but to the South Africans, he was a hero.

While there were forty people who gave evidence at the King's Commission, only Cronje's evidence was widely televised. At the end of the hearing, Cronje broke down in tears and looked a man exhausted and tortured by guilt. He needed assistance to leave the room. 'In a moment of stupidity and weakness, I allowed Satan and the world to dictate terms to me. The moment I took my eyes off Jesus my whole world turned dark,' said the disgraced captain in his public confession.

Cronje's admission of guilt and his return to Jesus appealed to the Christian ethos of forgiveness, winning his disgruntled fans over. Cronje had requested a meeting with Nelson Mandela in 2000 before the King's Commission report was out. 'This is a young man who focused the attention of the world to South Africa, as far as cricket is concerned. The message I gave him is that a person can turn tragedy into triumph, and he has that capacity,' Mandela had told the press after the meeting.

Cronje moved his sporting interest from cricket to golf and tried to reinvent himself with a master's degree in business leadership and working as a financial manager with Bell Equipment, whose chairman, Howard Buttery, rubbished talks that Cronje's reputation would damage the image of his company. In fact, he said, Bell Equipment got several calls from the public congratulating them for giving Cronje a second chance.

To the South Africans, Cronje was a Christian, an Afrikaner, a great man who made a mistake. A mistake that could be eventually forgiven and forgotten. So in September 2001, Cronje appealed to have his life ban lifted, and a month later, he was allowed to attend and report on cricket matches.

On 31 May 2002, Cronje was delayed in Johannesburg when he visited the offices of Bell Equipment and had missed his flight to his home in the Fancourt estate, a luxury golf resort in George in the Western Cape where he lived with his wife Bertha. He called chartered airlines AirQuarius Aviation with whom he had a standing relationship to fly solo on their cargo planes. In turn, he let the pilots stay at his house in George overnight.

With a big smile, Cronje got into the small Hawker Siddeley 748 cargo aircraft that bitter cold evening, thinking of soon being in the warmth of his cosy home. Alas, that was never to be. On 1 June, news came in that Cronje was killed as the cargo plane crashed into Cradock Peak near his home in backwater George, 430 km from Cape Town. The wreckage was shattered on a frozen mountain and rescue teams found the remains of Cronje and the two pilots after hours of search.

Two thousand people attended Cronje's funeral at his alma mater, Grey College, in Bloemfontein. Tributes came pouring in and it was broadcasted live on television. 'Here was a young man courageously and with dignity rebuilding his life after the setback suffered a while ago. The manner in which he was doing that promised to make him once more a role model of how one deals with adversity,' said former president Nelson Mandela.

Many raised concerns that Cronje was murdered then, and once again when his former coach Bob Woolmer, 58, who became coach to the Pakistan cricket team was found murdered in his hotel room in Jamaica on 18 March 2007. Suspicions pointed to a match-fixing and betting syndicate. On 12 June, Jamaican police announced Woolmer died of natural causes.

Journalist and author Pradeep Magazine in his book *Not Quite Cricket* recalled a meeting he had fixed between Woolmer and Dr K.K. Paul, who was now the Delhi Police chief. Paul met Woolmer at his government residence in Lodhi Road in New Delhi on 18 April 2005. The meeting that lasted an hour saw Woolmer defend Cronje repeatedly, much to the annoyance of Paul who maintained that his investigation was 'fool-proof' and even asked Woolmer how he, being the South African coach then, was not aware of the contentious team meeting that discussed the bookmaker's offer. 'I was not asked to attend those meetings,' came the curt and defensive reply. Magazine remembers that Woolmer made some frivolous and unsubstantiated claims against a Pakistani cricketer to Paul and also mentioned that he was writing a book on corporate corruption in cricket.

The Cronje affair or Hansiegate spiralled into one that extended to several other cricketers across nations and matches. Azharuddin was later investigated for his links with M.K. and the CBI discovered that the Indian captain was deeply involved in match-fixing. M.K. alleged that he paid Rs 50 lakh to Azharuddin as an advance towards matches that Azharuddin would 'do' for M.K.

In his confession to the cops, Azharuddin accepted that he had fixed some matches—one against South Africa at Rajkot in 1996, one against Sri Lanka in 1997 and one against Pakistan in 1999. The last one was for another bookie called Ajay Gupta who allegedly paid him Rs 10 lakh. However, Azharuddin did not deny that Gupta and his accomplices paid for bills and shopping at Harrods in London during the World Cup in 1999.

Indian team physiotherapist Ali Irani alleged that underworld don Dawood Ibrahim's brother Anees Ibrahim had paid Azharuddin to throw matches. The CBI found Irani to be a conduit between Azharuddin and the bookie mafia. M.K. had met Irani as 'John' and had given him money to the tune of Rs 10-15 lakh to pass on to Azharuddin for 'doing' matches. Irani admitted to getting Rs 25,000–50,000 as a cut for his services. The CBI found an undeclared Dubai-based bank account of Azharuddin and several expensive personal items that were unaccounted for and estimated to be around $50 million.

Indian cricketers Ajay Jadeja and Nayan Mongia were named as Azharuddin's accomplices to fix matches. M.K. confessed that Jadeja visited him in his home and offered that he and Mongia could throw matches. He was paid Rs 50,000 for this meeting. Azharuddin and Jadeja were found to have made several phone calls to bookmakers. Ajay Sharma and Manoj Prabhakar were also named. Sharma's job was to handle Indian players while Prabhakar managed foreign players as per bookmakers' demands.

'It is clear Azharuddin contributed substantially to the expanding player/bookie nexus in Indian cricket. The inquiry has disclosed that he received large sums of money from the betting syndicates to fix matches, which resulted in this malaise making further inroads in Indian cricket,' stated the CBI report. By then Azharuddin's career in cricket was long over. But the fallen angel of cricket was also a much-loved figure and soon the Indian population was ready to forgive and forget any transgressions made by him. In the 2009 general elections, Azharuddin contested from Moradabad constituency in Uttar Pradesh on a Congress ticket and won with a huge majority.

On November 2012, Azharuddin got his final redemption, when the Andhra Pradesh High Court set aside the life ban given to him by the BCCI in 2000 as it could find no evidence against the former skipper. Bollywood made a biopic on him, with Azharuddin played by Emraan Hashmi.

Gupta, who rose from a mere bank clerk to a man of wealth with businesses in real estate and export in a decade, had named other international cricketers, many of whom were introduced to him by Azharuddin. But to get an introduction to Azharuddin, M.K. had paid Rs 5 lakh to cricketer Ajay Sharma in 1995 at the Taj Palace, New Delhi. A few years later, M.K. was replaced by Ajay Gupta (not related to M.K.) as the bookmaker Ajay Sharma worked with. For Gupta's introduction to Azharuddin, Sharma charged another Rs 5 lakh and arranged it in Taj Palace, New Delhi in 1998. Gupta also financed Sharma and his family's visit to the UK for the World Cup in 1999.

The CBI found that Manoj Prabhakar had links with various bookmakers, and had provided them with information on pitch and match conditions for money. He had also thrown matches away for monetary compensation. It was found that Prabhakar had demanded a Maruti Gypsy from M.K. for information given during the England tour in 1990. Prabhakar owned a Gypsy soon after the tour. Prabhakar also stated that Navjot Singh Sidhu was his accomplice in match-fixing but the CBI found only hearsay against Sidhu. M.K. also gave the CBI a long list of international players that Prabhakar facilitated an introduction to the bookies for money. M.K. disappeared soon after Cronje's testimony.

Later, Prabhakar turned a whistle-blower for news outlet *Tehelka* and made secret tapes of team meetings to implicate more players in match-fixing. He made a series of allegations against former Indian captain Kapil Dev. Dev told the CBI that the controversial South African businessman Banjo Qassim was known to him and he confessed to taking gifts including a BMW car and cash from bookmakers. A Bollywood film on Kapil Dev's grand World Cup victory is in the works where Ranveer Singh will play Dev.

After a six-month investigation, the CBI's report named England's Alec Stewart, West Indies' Brian Lara, New Zealand's Martin Crowe, Pakistan's Salim Malik and Asif Iqbal, Sri Lanka's Arjuna Ranatunga and Aravinda De Silva, South Africa's Hansie Cronje and Australia's Mark Waugh and Dean Jones. They faced inquiries in their respective countries to varying degrees.

The CBI consulted India's solicitor-general and found that it would not be able to bring a criminal prosecution against the cricketers, who were paid cash which could not be traced to the bookmakers and so a successful trial was almost impossible. It seemed the CBI was not going to pursue the case in courts in India then and it was soon forgotten.

On 1 February 2016, a request was made by India to the United Kingdom to extradite bookmaker Sanjay aka Sanjeev Chawla on charges of being a conduit between bookmakers who wanted to fix cricket matches and Hansie Cronje. The case, thought to be long closed, once again surfaced.

The case was not pursued earlier due to lack of evidence. The CBI had asked Chawla, who lives in the UK since 1996, to give his voice sample, but he had refused. Now the CBI had obtained assistance from South African authorities and had carried out a voice analysis on the telephonic conversation, and armed with the report that came in 2013, the CBI was confident that it had enough evidence to put Chawla in the dock. Meanwhile, a relentless Paul had also sought more information from Gibbs and Boje. A lengthy questionnaire and meetings ensured the two had disclosed crucial details.

Thirteen years later, a charge-sheet was filed in July 2013. Gibbs and Boje were no longer accused in the case, though the late Cronje is mentioned as an accused. No Indian cricketer is also considered an accused. Bookie Sanjeev Chawla is the main accused along with other bookmakers like Rajesh Kalra, Manmohan Khattar, Sunil Dara and Krishan Kumar, brother of murdered T-series founder Gulshan Kumar. They have been charged with fraud and criminal conspiracy. Kalra, Dara and Kumar are out on bail while Chawla and Khattar were considered absconding.

'While Sanjeev Chawla was in touch with Hansie Cronje, frequency of calls between him and his accomplices Krishan Kumar, Rajesh Kalra, Sunil Dara had increased manifold during the matches. This brings out the criminal intentions of the accused persons to fix matches in conspiracy with each other,' the charge sheet said. Clearly, the mastermind of the entire operation was the elusive Sanjeev Chawla who played the 'most vital role'.

Krishan Kumar was found to have bet Rs 40 lakh on matches that were clearly fixed between Cronje and Chawla as his name prominently figured in the conversations recorded. Kumar was also friendly with Kalra and clearly a part of the betting syndicate. However, as there was insufficient evidence to arrest him in April, he was simply interrogated and let off.

A nervous Kumar admitted himself into a hospital to evade arrest. When the first hospital discharged him, he moved to a corporate hospital and finally to the All India Institute of Medical Sciences (AIIMS) in New Delhi. By May, the ED had sufficient evidence to book him under the Foreign Exchange Regulation Act (FERA) and arrested him on money laundering charges. He was lodged in Tihar Jail and subsequently let out on bail.

The ED also arrested Kalra under FERA, and he led them to six other bookies. Five of them fled before the police could question them, one turned hostile. Kalra claimed he became familiar with the cricketers at the Siri Fort Sports Complex and the Hotel Park Royal gymnasium. He also allegedly told the police that Kumar and Chawla had paid Rs 60 lakh to Cronje to fix the matches. According to the police, Kalra confessed that he had accompanied Chawla and another accused Sunil Dara to the Taj Mahal hotel in New Delhi on 14 March 2000, and Cronje had invited Chawla to his room 346.

Raids were conducted on Kalra's properties and other locations suspected to be involved in match-fixing. The investigators claimed to have found some incriminating documents. One piece of evidence pointed to a South African man of Indian origin to whom calls were made by both Chawla and Cronje and who is suspected to have helped the laundering of match-fixing monies.

Armed with enough evidence against Chawla, the Delhi Police enlisted the help of the CBI and Interpol to bring the mastermind of the match-fixing scam to India from London.

* * *

Chawla had flown to London on 15 March 2000 and never returned. He lives in London with his wife Deepika Bali and two sons Ayman and Abir aged 15 and 12, respectively. Chawla had moved to the UK in 1996 on a business visa. He has been a resident of the UK since then though he made frequent trips to India until 2000 when his passport was revoked. In 2003, he secured an indefinite leave to remain in the UK and got a British passport in 2005. His family members are British citizens too. His son Ayman was operated on in 2008, to remove a benign tumour from his stomach. Deepika is a director in their catering business called ISK Caterers Ltd which runs a restaurant and leases another restaurant. Chawla is the accountant for this business. Deepika also has a few other businesses to her name in the hospitality sector, including Ruya London Ltd and Eastcote Restaurants Ltd. The Chawlas live in a £1 million home with six bedrooms, two bathrooms and two living rooms in north London.

When he was first contacted by the press at the height of the match-fixing scandal, a statement was made by his lawyer that said that Chawla 'denies that he was involved or had met or spoken to Hansie Cronje' and that he refuses to meet the press or make further comments on this matter.

Indian police suspect that he still continues his match-fixing operations from the United Kingdom. With an extradition warrant issued by the chief metropolitan magistrate in New Delhi on 27 February 2015 and an affidavit sworn by Bhisham Singh, deputy commissioner of police (DCP), Delhi Crime Branch, on 18 May, the Indian government approached the UK with the extradition request on 1 February 2016. Singh's affidavit provided the background to the investigations that led to the unearthing of the match-fixing, details of the telephone transcripts between Chawla and Cronje and with other bookies and the investigation and analysis of the call details and forensic evidence of voice records. It also contained the evidence provided by South African and UK authorities, investigation of the venues where the teams stayed and a detailed summary of the role played by Chawla and the others in match-fixing.

The secretary of state certified the request on 11 March 2016, and Chawla was arrested and produced in Westminster Magistrates' Court on 14 June. Chawla contested the extradition and the matter came before Judge Quentin Purdy in November 2016. Chawla hired top legal firm Bindmans LLP to represent him. A month later, a 'Statement of Issues' was produced on his behalf where his counsel argued that the prison conditions during his trial and after any conviction did not meet with article 3 of the ECHR.

The trial began in March 2017. Chawla's counsel produced a report by expert witness Dr Alan Mitchell on prison conditions. Dr Mitchell was a medical practitioner at Her Majesty's Prison (HMP) Shotts from 1998–2002 and a member of the Scottish Human Rights Commission since 2015. He has provided evidence in many cases of extradition to India, including Mallya's. In a report dated 26 February 2017, Dr Mitchell had stated that all the jails in the Tihar complex suffer from overcrowding and lack a national prison inspectorate. He also referenced many press reports highlighting the staff-prisoner violence that breaks out in the jail and stated, 'I believe there to be a very real risk that if extradited to India and if he were to be held in the Tihar prison complex, that Mr Chawla's rights in respect of article 3 would be at real risk'.

The government was quick to produce assurance in a letter dated two days after Dr Mitchell's testimony to inform the court that Chawla would be lodged in Tihar Jail in New Delhi and as per Delhi Prison Rules (1998), he would be put in a barrack as per the circumstances of his case. The letter assured the court that Chawla would be provided with necessary blankets and bedsheets, an adequate quantity of clean drinking water and three meals a day. The letter confirmed that there were also enough toilets and spaces in the yard to ensure no human rights of the prisoners were breached.

As a response to Dr Mitchell's report, the letter contained an annexe headed 'Best Practices in Delhi Prisons' which acknowledged that though the combined sanctioned capacity of the sixteen central jails in Delhi was 10,026 prisoners, there were 14,027 prisoners as on 30 November 2016, but also highlighted that the prisons provided education, vocational training, games and other recreational activities.

Three days of hearing took place in April 2017 but the case got delayed as District Judge Purdy was unwell. With a brief hearing scheduled for 19 May 2017, the final hearing was postponed to 25–27 September 2017. On 19 May, the court set the final deadline for producing evidence as 18 August and any evidence as reply to be served by 1 September. No party served any new evidence by 18 August and a letter from Bindman solicitors to the CPS enquiring about any new evidence from India went unanswered.

Yet when the trial began on Monday, 25 September in the court of District Judge Rebecca Jean Crane, the CPS told the court that the GoI would rely on the second assurance. This assurance was provided only on Friday, 22 September and forwarded to Chawla's team over the weekend. Chawla's counsel quickly put forth his objections on the basis that the second assurance came in too late and had violated the district judge's deadline of 18 August. Chawla's lawyer argued that 'the second assurance was given eighteen months after the initial request for extradition, fifteen months after the issue had been raised, and in breach of the order for directions on 19 May 2017'. The district judge agreed that the 'government had plenty of time to respond' and refused to admit the second assurance by India.

During the hearing, Dr Mitchell gave evidence on prison conditions and Prof. Martin Lau gave evidence on the Indian justice system. Both were cross-examined by the CPS. Chawla did not give evidence but relied on proof of evidence.

Chawla first evoked the 'passage of time' argument—from a 'rukka' (First Information Report or FIR) being filed by Bhisham Singh on 6 April 2000 to register the investigation under the Indian Procedural Law to a warrant being issued by the London court for Chawla's arrest on 17 May 2017—to bar his extradition. CPS barrister Aaron Watkins argued that Chawla was a fugitive and hence the 'passage of time' argument could not apply in his case.

Judge Crane observed that there was no suggestion on India's part that Chawla was informed or was kept abreast of the investigations or the charges against him, neither was he told about the warrant by an Indian court or the extradition request. He was only asked to provide a voice sample in 2004 which he refused. The judge declared that Chawla was under no obligation to provide a voice sample or to surrender to the Indian authorities and since he was under no bail conditions, did not seek to evade arrest and lived openly in the UK, India had failed to prove he was a fugitive.

Prof. Lau provided a report dated 12 January 2017 wherein he explained the criminal law procedure right from the FIR stage to that of the judgment in Indian courts. He raised the issue of delays in trial and since a co-accused Mr Khattar had not yet been arrested, Prof. Lau expected further delays in Chawla's trial unless he appealed to split the proceedings, as in India a trial can be split if doing so upheld the rights of the co-defendants to have their cases determined within a reasonable time frame. He also pointed out that the Indian police had not recorded the confessions of the co-defendants in front of a magistrate, and hence, they would not be admissible in the court.

Judge Crane said that she did not find anything that showed her that extraditing Chawla to India would be unjust and oppressive as the avenue to applying for a stay or to split the proceedings remained open to him in Indian courts.

With regard to prima facie evidence, Crane was satisfied with the evidence provided by DCP Bisham Singh. There was enough in four bundles provided by Singh to clearly show how Chawla shadowed Cronje by staying in the same hotels, including evidence by an employee of the Taj Mahal Palace, Mumbai, Arun Gonbare, who observed Cronje enter Chawla's room empty-handed and return with a bag. There were also detailed telephone records between Chawla and Cronje and also with other accused that threw light on the entire match-fixing scandal. 'There is sufficient evidence to show that Chawla acted with others to fix the outcomes of cricket matches by providing money to members of South African team,' the judge noted.

Just when everything seemed to be going well for India, Chawla's counsel Mark Weekes put forth his ace card. He argued that if Chawla was extradited, his prison conditions would be in violation of article 3 of the ECHR. This led to the longest deliberation in court.

On 16 October 2017, the district judge gave a judgment in the case after considering both reports of Dr Alan Mitchell, dated 13 November 2016 and 26 February 2017, which referenced several newspaper articles and reports, and took into account his experience of visiting Alipore central correctional home in February 2015 as he was denied permission to visit Tihar Jail for Chawla's case.

She also took into account a UK home office report titled 'India: Prison Conditions', dated November 2016, a Commonwealth Human Rights Initiative report and Amnesty International reports. The home office report had referred to a complaint about 'sub-human conditions' in Tihar, including the overcrowding and lack of medical facilities. One report had said that conditions are 'frequently life threatening' and also highlighted that prisoners are also 'physically mistreated'. Commonwealth Human Rights Initiative's 'Rights Behind Bars' (2009) report spoke about 'a huge gap between constitutional promises and the reality of the lives of prison inmates' and stated that inmates do not have access to adequate water and are likely to be tortured or exploited and 'the closed nature of the penal system makes it easier for any kind of abuse to go unnoticed or unattended'. While the 'Amnesty International Report 2015/16—India' detailed prolonged pre-trial detentions and that 'extrajudicial executions and torture and other ill-treatments persisted'.

This, along with Dr Mitchell's evidence on prison conditions, seemed to satisfy the judge. Judge Rebecca Crane found that India's own Supreme Court in 2016 accepted that overcrowding remains a problem and that prison reforms have led to little change in practice, and agreed that Dr Mitchell's report on Alipore prison reflects the picture painted by other reports of 'poor conditions within Indian prisons and a culture of officials acting with impunity'. The 'suspiciously high levels of deaths in custody' also raise concerns, so does the violence and the 'lack of robust investigation into the cause of death'.

The court characterized the assurance given by the GoI as being in 'general terms' and also ruled that there was not an 'effective system of protection against torture'. The second assurance was not considered as it was provided 'fifteen months after the issue had been raised'.

The district judge found 'that the level of overcrowding at Tihar prison was of itself sufficient to consider that there was a real risk of Mr Chawla's rights being breached if he was held there' and dismissed the extradition case against Chawla.

Chawla was spotted in a grey-blue suit with a blue tie on a white shirt as he left the district court, a happy man, though one still not comfortable in his skin. He used a newspaper to cover his face and evade the press photographers as he left the court, accompanied by his wife, dressed in black with a bright red scarf. The grey in his hair and the wrinkles around his eyes showed a man much changed from his rather carefree days of the pre-2000 era.

* * *

India appealed against the order of the district judge in the high court on 24 April 2018. The division bench of Lord Justice Leggatt and Justice Dingemans specifically looked at the assurances given by India to merit reopening of the case and more specifically the second assurance that was not considered by the district judge.

Chawla's counsel Helen Malcolm QC argued that the district judge was entitled to ignore the second assurance as it failed to meet the deadline set by the court and that there is a real risk of violence and degrading human conditions for prisoners in the Tihar prison. She argued that the second assurance does provide a guarantee of space but the photographs accompanying it are ambiguous and fail to establish whether the prison meets article 3 of the ECHR.

In a detailed judgment, Lord Justice Leggatt and Justice Dingemans concluded that 'there remains a real risk' of Chawla being subjected to inhuman or degrading treatment in Tihar Jail. The court noted that: 'We have looked at the terms of the second assurance to see if it will prevent a real risk of inhuman and degrading treatment and raised objections that the photographs do not identify whether what is shown is a cell (which seems likely) or a ward.' Focusing on the exact nature of the assurance that they wanted from New Delhi, the court spelt out three particular points: personal space that would be available to Chawla in Tihar; toilet facilities that would be made available to him; how would the jail authorities ensure that Chawla was kept safe from the risk of intra-prisoner violence in the high security wards.

The high court in London gave forty-two days to the CPS to provide further assurances regarding the facilities in Tihar Jail where alleged bookie Sanjeev Chawla was to be lodged.

The third assurance, dated 11 June 2018, was signed by a joint secretary to the GoI. The five-page document gave details of the accommodation to be provided to Chawla and also covered the concerns of the district judge when she ruled in Chawla's favour. It assured the courts that Chawla would be accommodated in a cell exclusive to him, thus ensuring proper safety and security. Four cells were identified—two in ward 9 in Central Jail 1 and two in ward 4 in Central Jail 3—to ensure operational flexibility. The document said that these cells were not in a high security ward and that Chawla would also be placed in a ward where inmates had not violated any prison rules and had satisfactory conduct, and not in the high security ward where there are outbreaks of violence.

The Indian government also assured the court that the cell would be approximately 6 square metres, excluding the toilet, and would comply with the standards UK courts adhere to regarding personal space and hygiene requirements, a partition separates the toilet from the living space and ensures privacy. More so, security cameras, monitored 24×7, would help meet any security concerns the courts might have. In terms of medical care, India said there were eighty-six medical officers available and a 200-bed hospital on the premises. India assured the court that Chawla would receive immediate medical attention if required.

On 13 November 2018, Chawla raised three issues in the divisional court (high court). They included inadequate medical provision, risk of intra-prisoner violence and whether there was any provision for alternative accommodation should the need arise.

Mark Summers of the CPS, representing India, argued that four cells had been identified to provide operational flexibility and none of them was in a high-security ward. He also reiterated that these were solemn diplomatic assurances provided to the court. He submitted that there was no evidence to support the district judge's finding of a risk of violation in this case.

After taking into consideration the third assurance (which was not provided to the district judge), the divisional bench quashed the earlier discharge of Chawla and concluded that the terms of the third assurance 'are sufficient to show that there will be no real risk that Chawla will be subjected to impermissible treatment in Tihar prisons'.

The court noted that there should be an assessment of Chawla's publicly funded legal costs. The case was remitted to District Judge Rebecca Crane, who was directed to proceed as if she had not ordered Chawla's discharge. In January 2019, Westminster Magistrates' Court considered the high court's judgment that India's assurances satisfied the requirement that the prison conditions would not breach Chawla's human rights and issued a fresh order in favour of Chawla's extradition. Judge Crane was, even in 2017, satisfied that there was enough to establish a prima facie case. 'The affidavit of Bhisham Singh, the deputy commissioner of police, dated 18.05.2015 (18 May 2015) also contains a very detailed summary of the evidence,' Judge Crane said again confirming that the prima facie case against Chawla still stands.

'There is nothing for me to decide. The case can now be sent to the home secretary. Sanjeev Chawla will continue to remain on bail, and if he breached bail conditions, he would be arrested and brought to court,' said Crane. UK Home Secretary Sajid Javid signed the extradition order on 27 February 2019. Chawla had fourteen days from the date of the order to file an application to seek leave to appeal against the order.

The embattled bookie quickly sought leave to appeal against the decision of the district judge. Chawla served a notice on 12 March 2019 seeking permission to adduce fresh evidence. He identified three grounds for the appeal, citing real risk of treatment contrary to article 3 of ECHR, a breach of article 6 (degrading treatment and use of evidence obtained by torture) and that there was a non-disclosure of material, rendering his extradition an abuse of process.

Sir Wyn Williams by an order made on papers on 9 July 2019 allowed an oral hearing where the application for permission to appeal, and if permission was granted, the appeal to be heard on the same hearing. The matter which was due to come up for a hearing in December 2019 was further delayed. A team of Delhi Police travelled to London, but since the prosecution lawyer had to go into hospital that day, the hearing was adjourned until 2020. 'We are waiting for a new date in the new year,' said Yasser Mehmood, CPS spokesperson.

Bookie Sanjeev Chawla has been largely successful in not just evading the law but also the press. The only image the press had of the man is the one the CBI gave Interpol of his younger days, prior to 2000. He now looks very different from his younger self. The fifty-two-year-old, Delhi-born bindaas bookie with sharp black eyes and a mop of shiny black hair, escaped law enforcement agencies at the height of the match-fixing scandal in 2000 and almost managed to wriggle out of the extradition proceedings that India brought against him in London. But no longer.

On 16 January 2020, courtroom 3 in the Royal Courts of Justice saw a lone man sitting in row three in a dark grey suit with a forlorn expression, nervousness visible in every twitch of his fingers as he curled and uncurled them throughout the two hours the proceedings for his appeal were heard. He was being represented by Russell-Cooke Solicitors, a top legal firm who hired Steven Powles QC to represent Chawla in the high court. A two-judge bench of Lord Justice David Bean and Justice Clive Lewis was to decide if they would give permission to Chawla to contest the district judge's decision, to send the case to the secretary of state or alternatively consider the reopening of the case.

CPS barrister Mark Summers was explicit in his argument that Chawla would use this permission to open the entire case, thus stretching it indefinitely. Lord Justice Bean was adamant that after all the delay, in this case, it was unwise to let it drag for long. 'Nobody wants this case to go off to another day,' he declared.

Powles argued that there was fresh evidence available now that raised concerns on the validity of the assurances given by India. He brought to the court's attention an article written in a popular broadsheet in India that spoke about a massive redevelopment in Tihar Jail that would affect jails 1, 2 and 3. India's assurance had specified that Chawla would be lodged in Central Jail 1 or 3. Powles pointed out that the development threw uncertainty on Chawla's lodgings in Tihar Jail and that makes 'nonsense of the assurance given to this court' by India. Summers argued that this evidence was just based on news reports and hence was highly speculative. The judges too were not convinced by this as the article did not mention any specific time or details of the proposed construction.

Next, Powles highlighted written evidence given by a retired Tihar Jail staffer Sunil Gupta who was a legal adviser to the Office of the Director General, Tihar Jail, till 2017. He had cited threats of possible violence to Chawla during his free time, and during training and travelling between the jail and the courts. Gupta had joined the jail in 1981 and retired in 2017. During the hearing, Justice Clive Lewis pointedly asked Powles to point towards a specific paragraph of his submission that directly contradicted or challenged the assurance given by India.

Chawla's counsel also told the court that co-accused Rajesh Kalra, whose testimony had implicated Chawla and himself, later alleged that he was forced to sign a blank document by the police. This, Powles argued, highlighted the possibility of torture Chawla would face in jail and by the police in India. This forced testimony dated back to 2000, and Powles was unable to tell the court what had happened since Kalra made these allegations. DCP Ram Gopal Naik and inspector Keshav Mathur were present in the courtroom, listening intently to the arguments. At this point, the judges wanted to know where the case had progressed in India to know whether these arguments were raised in Indian courts, and were surprised to find that the trial in the case had not yet begun even after twenty years of the crime being committed.

In a last-ditch attempt, Powles asked the judges to look at the photographs provided by India on the jail conditions. Summers interrupted the court and offered to pass on coloured photographs on A4 paper that would make better visuals. As the judges peered through the photographs, Powles raised the issue of curtains and rods that were depicted in the photographs. He said that

Sunil Gupta, who had worked in Tihar Jail for many years, had not once seen such curtains there, raising doubts over whether they were truly pictures of the jail. Powles also pointed out that a mere curtain separated the toilet area, thus raising issues of privacy and human rights.

It was 12.10 p.m. and the judges decided to take a short recess following which they would give their decision. Over the next fifteen minutes, Chawla convened with his lawyers in a corner of the courtroom, looking grim. The Indian team was nervous too but the CPS looked satisfied. When the judges returned, they did not mince words when they declared that their decision was to not give Chawla the permission to appeal, thus bringing the extradition saga to an end. They, however, conceded that they would explain their decision in a written order later but were satisfied that the assurances given by India were sufficient and there was no reason to appeal the decision of the district judge or to reopen the case.

A shocked Chawla stared into space, all colour draining from his face. As people began filing out of the courtroom, Chawla remained inside, huddled with his legal team, grasping at anything that would help save him.

Meanwhile, the Indian side was overjoyed, their smug grins lighting up their usually poker faces. Mark Summers was thrilled. 'He will have to go to India within twenty-eight days,' said Summers, convinced that no other avenues remained opened for Chawla to escape. 'He cannot apply at the Supreme Court and the judges have explicitly denied him permission to appeal,' he explained.

Chawla's young solicitor did not look hopeful either. 'We will convene a meeting to decide on the next course of action,' he said, requesting the press to understand how difficult this was for Chawla and respect his decision to not speak to the media. If Chawla was expecting that such talk from his solicitor would make the two reporters waiting in the corridors leave, he was grossly mistaken. As Chawla emerged from the courtroom, he was followed, and just as he stepped out of the majestic court building, was asked to comment and recorded on phone cameras. He swiftly covered his face with a scarf and disappeared into the sanctuary of the court where cameras are not allowed. He was escorted out of the court from another exit by his solicitor.

On 23 January, in courtroom 18, Justice Clive Lewis made a brief appearance to hand down the judgment. Right from the beginning, this seemed a case that Chawla was destined to lose. He had a new legal team and a new barrister standing for him. While both have excellent legal credentials, they still looked fairly unprepared for the legal arguments that Summers made confidently to the court.

During the proceedings, it was clear that Summers and Powles were taking divergent views, ones that also bordered on hitherto undiscussed finer points in the Extradition Act 2003. In the last paragraph of the judgment, the judges give an indication of the ambiguity that encompassed the hearing—whether the court had jurisdiction to entertain the appeal brought by Chawla or not. Hence, they noted that the permission to appeal the Westminster Magistrates' Court's January 2019 decision was refused as they had no jurisdiction to entertain such an appeal, and even if they do have the jurisdiction, that appeal is refused and so is the permission to reopen the decision made in the second Chawla judgment by the high court.

What tilted the case in India's favour was the five-page assurance that was given to the court. Given under the signature of a joint secretary-level officer, the assurance covered all possible concerns raised by Chawla to prevent extradition citing poor jail conditions. It was this unambiguity of the five-page assurance that put to rest any ambiguity that Chawla was raising in the 2003 Act to stay back in London.

Meanwhile, it emerged that Chawla had made another attempt to delay his extradition. However, Justice Lewis was adamant that Chawla had 'sufficient time to put his affairs in order' since the secretary of state had signed his extradition in February 2019. Chawla will be 'extradited within twenty-eight days from today, 23 January,' said the judge.

Chawla had a few days left to pack his bags, ensure his family's needs were taken care of, find someone to oversee his business interests and surrender to a police station. On 31 January 2020, a new company by the name of Holy Eats was incorporated by his wife Deepika, who in June had resigned from ISK Caterers Ltd. Sanjeev Chawla became a director of ISK Caterers but has no role in Holy Eats. In the company registers, his address is no longer his family home but that of his accountants.

Chawla did not easily come to terms with his inevitable extradition. Using standard textbook tricks to delay his extradition, Chawla approached the ECtHR in Strasbourg. In early February, the court refused his application for an interim measure to block his extradition to India. Chawla's extradition order was signed by the home office in February 2019, so as soon as the ECtHR order was made available to the UK authorities, measures were taken to extradite the bookie to India within twenty-eight days.

A week later, DCP Ram Gopal Naik at the crime branch in Delhi, came to London to escort the bookie to Tihar Jail in New Delhi. Sanjeev Chawla reached India on 13 February 2020 and remains in New Delhi as the court proceedings in the match-fixing case continue.

This extradition case was just like a nail-biting game of cricket where just when you think it is all over, one shot or one wicket changes the entire course of the match, making it almost impossible to predict until the final ball is bowled and the last man has crossed the line. Chawla has finally discovered that there are some matches that cannot be fixed.

4

GANGSTA GRANDPA

Iqbal Mohammed Memon alias Iqbal Mirchi was arrested in April 1995 and was discharged in September 1995 by the Bow Street Magistrates' Court. This was one of the shortest cases of extradition that India pursued and opened up the floodgates to a string of failures.

Mirchi's name conjures an image of the underworld characterized by cheeky nicknames, escapades between Dubai and Mumbai, and the metamorphosis of street punters into financial czars. Mirchi had survived the messy bloodbath of gang wars and the police crackdown of the 1980s and metamorphosed with the liberalization of the economy.

Another crucial reason for Mirchi's success was the relative lack of ostentatious lifestyle and the safe investment in real estate. Some observers say he kept himself out of the orthodox gangland activities and glamorous film financing, which ensured that while rival gangs targeted each other's cronies, Mirchi continued to flourish. Some accounts suggest he drove Bombay's famous kaali-peeli (black-and-yellow) taxi and also sold keema-naan along Mohammed Ali Road.

When the new architecture of Bombay's underworld was being made after the grip of old stalwarts like Haji Mastan, Varadarajan Mudaliar, Yusuf Patel and Karim Lala started loosening, several new figures emerged. One way of understanding the difference between the new and the old was that while both were in awe of Bollywood, the former would not terrorize the actors while the latter had no qualms about it. This also perhaps mirrored the shifting portrayal of baddies in Bollywood. Gone were the days of the suited-booted, sophisticated, cigar-chomping K.N. Singh and Ajit on the silver screen. Dawood Ibrahim, Bada Rajan, Sharad Shetty and Arun Gawli were no gentlemen dons.

While Dawood got enmeshed in the slimy web of personal and professional gang rivalry, Mirchi kept himself relatively clean. But much of this sanitization had to do with the rather cosy relationship he shared with the cops in Bombay. Mirchi always maintained that he knew Dawood's father Ibrahim Kaskar, a former constable in Bombay's crime branch, much better than the dreaded gangster. Mirchi's career, much like Dawood's, started from the tough and grimy by-lanes of south Bombay ghettoes.

This cosiness was also easier to maintain as Mirchi was involved in thefts from the docks and later the drugs trade which did not necessarily involve marshalling ruffians running amok on the streets. It was more of a behind-the-scenes role. Besides, there were other agencies like the Narcotics Control Bureau (NCB) established in 1987 and the Directorate of Revenue Intelligence (DRI) apart from the Bombay Police who were responsible for keeping a tab on the manufacture and transportation of drugs. Nothing could be more effective in creating a shield around you than having friends in a rival agency who find ways for you to escape from the other agency. This came to Mirchi's aid, and a similar model of Mumbai Police versus central agencies worked in favour of Dawood Ibrahim as well.

Mirchi's brush with the law began in his avatar as a dock hand in the late 1970s. In pre-liberalization India, a whole host of items like gold, silver, electronics, watches, textiles and chemicals were sought-after commodities. Before Mirchi, the docks had anchored the career of several dons like Haji Mastan and Varadarajan who had started out as petty dock thieves (*godichors*). Mirchi, too, began as a godichor, but unlike Mastan and Varadarajan, took to drugs in a big way, replacing the Pathans whose numbers and influence had dwindled in the 1980s.

On 8 January 1986, the DRI seized 602 kg of heroin, 4565 kg of hashish and 4 kg of Mandrax tablets from a farmhouse in Talasari which was then in Thane district on the outskirts of Mumbai. Valued at Rs 9 crore, this was billed as the biggest-ever seizure of narcotics in India. After an initial investigation, a reward of Rs 5000 was announced for information on Iqbal Mirchi and his associate Niaz Khan, who were named as suspects. The DRI issued a red alert to airports asking them to keep an eye out for Mirchi and Khan. At that time, Mirchi was clean-shaven.

The DRI was hot on the heels of Mirchi, but unlike the police, the DRI has restricted manpower. It had affected the biggest seizure and was itching to lay its hands on Mirchi, who had proved elusive. In 1984, Mirchi was issued a summons for detention under the Conservation of Foreign Exchange and Prevention of Smuggling Activities Act (COFEPOSA). For two years he had not bothered to pay any heed to the summons, but it was now perhaps the best time to visit jail. Passed in 1974 by the Indira Gandhi regime, COFEPOSA degenerated into a law just on paper, with those to be detained under it not bothering to pay heed to the summons issued.

On 21 January 1986, Mirchi handed himself over to the police who very efficiently lodged him at Arthur Road Jail to serve detention under COFEPOSA. This way he ensured that the DRI would still not get to interrogate him for the Talasari drug overhaul. After being at Arthur Road Jail for just over three months, he was summoned by the crime branch on 2 May in relation to a case registered four years ago in 1982.

The 1982 case pertained to smuggling of textiles and contraband goods wherein both Mirchi and Niaz Khan were arrested. It was perhaps one of the earliest cases involving Mirchi. After marking his presence at the crime branch, he was arrested by the DRI the same day and was released for Rs 2 lakh bail by the additional chief metropolitan magistrate. It's shocking that a person against whom a red alert was issued at airports was given bail without spending a single day in custody to answer questions relating to one of the biggest drug hauls of that year.

Was the crime branch shielding him? And did he use the three-month period of detention to work out a safe passage bail for himself without letting the DRI interrogate him? It is noteworthy that a former CBI chief used the example of Iqbal Mirchi to show how a small-time thief was able to transform into a high-profile underworld figure because of the huge patronage network that he ran. Mirchi's case found its way into the Vohra Committee Report which was set up to examine and suggest ways to delink the increasing hold of criminals in law enforcement agencies.

In July 1985, the police had detained Mirchi, described as a notorious dock thief under the National Security Act (NSA). With an increase in revenues and expansion of his operations, Mirchi started to allegedly maintain warehouses in Surat and Ahmedabad to facilitate the storage and distribution of drugs.

With cash overflowing, Mirchi had quickly diversified into real estate and one of his earliest investments was in Hotel Ashiana. Most of his investments centred in Worli, Crawford Market and Juhu in the city. But his most famous investment was the popular discotheque Fisherman's Wharf, which was also known as Hotel Gurukripa.

It was a hugely successful venture and had emerged as a famous pick-up point. Police lore has it that Fisherman's Wharf also ran one of the city's most popular striptease.

Mirchi told journalist Sheela Raval that he once hosted a birthday party for a textile baron with girls flown in from Dubai to perform a private striptease. On arrival, the businessman was presented with an ice-cream cake in the shape of a woman's breast. The man left the club extremely pleased and Mirchi secured himself a huge profit with an increased cut on the smuggled goods. The club was instrumental in helping Mirchi network with politicians, bureaucrats, businessmen and police officers.

Shaukat Patka, brother of Mirchi's wife Hajra, was looking after the day-to-day functioning of Fisherman's Wharf. In 1986, the CBI had prepared a report wherein Mirchi's rise from a petty thief to the owner of real estate worth crores of rupees was cited as an example of the links between the underworld and the Bombay Police. Mirchi was supposed to have made massive investments in Worli, Juhu, Crawford Market in Bombay, Mahabaleshwar and Panchgani.

In April 1987, Fisherman's Wharf was raided and thirty-one women were taken into custody. The police had sent four fake customers in an operation led by Assistant Commissioner of Police Minoo Faredoon Irani. The daily revenue from the hotel was rumoured to be Rs 1 lakh, a substantial sum in those days. But this was a minor hiccup and the Fisherman's Wharf was soon back in business. In March and September 1992, the hotel was raided by the vigilance department of the Bombay Police and around 200 prostitutes were held in both the raids. Despite the request by the police's vigilance department to cancel the hotel's entertainment licence, the state did not take any action.

By the end of 1987, Mirchi had moved to Dubai, where he invested in hotels and real estate. He continued to visit Bombay till the 1993 bomb blasts carried out by the D company, the underworld gang helmed by Dawood Ibrahim. What got Mirchi entangled in the blasts was the prime role played by Tiger Memon who shared the same surname. Mirchi was already present in police dossiers, where he was known to be an associate of Dawood Ibrahim, the man responsible for carrying out the synchronized bombings in Bombay that killed 300 people. The sheer enormity of the 1993 blasts meant that the Bombay Police was out with a magnifying glass to identify and hunt suspects. Iqbal Memon was initially described as a relative of Tiger Memon, and it did not take long for the belief that Mirchi was associated with the blasts to gain currency. Even though he was never an official accused, the tag remained with him forever.

But by then Mirchi's tentacles had grown far and wide. The lucrative drugs trade with operations in Africa, Europe and the

US meant he had made a base for himself in the UK. This was largely possible because his second wife Heena Kausar had already got a British passport—that facilitated his residency in Britain. In London, he owned a rice mill and ran restaurants including Dockmaster's House at Canary Wharf. He widened the portfolio by investing in the construction business and got his family and several relatives into gainful employment.

Mirchi had four brothers and four sisters and a large extended family of nieces and nephews who were also inducted into his business. He married twice. His first wife Hajra bore him two sons Asif and Junaid and a daughter Nadiya. His second wife Heena Kausar lived with him in London. They have no children. Asif was married to the daughter of the younger brother of Barrister Sibghatullah Qadri (QC), the first Pakistani queen's counsel in 1989 and a close confidante of slain prime minister Benazir Bhutto. Nadiya was married to Javed Malik, a businessman who also served as Pakistan's ambassador to Bahrain from 2015 to 2018. Malik's name featured in the Panama Papers, a leaked database of illegal activities of wealthy off-shore account holders of Mossack Fonseca.

* * *

Mirchi's story also highlights the ease with which many drug lords in the era could escape scrutiny by the law. In 1985, the Bombay High Court set aside the detention order served on Mirchi under the NSA. The court observed that the authorities had not applied their minds to the case. Between 1987 and 1988, not a single case came up for trial despite fifty-eight cases being registered by the anti-narcotics cell, as several of them failed the preliminary test that determined whether they were fit for trial, among other procedural reasons.

In the case of Mirchi, the same thing happened; the metropolitan magistrate could not commit the Talasari seizure case to the sessions court due to lack of evidence. The DRI approached the high court but nothing materialized. There was also a racial undercurrent to the police's offensive against drug peddlers. It was clear that the cops and courts were jailing Africans in a higher proportion than the locals. The African nationals were easier targets, as compared to their Indian counterparts, with the high-end drug lords even further away from the police's net.

Mirchi rose during the period when the field operations of the Bombay Police's anti-narcotics cell did not translate into judicial victories. In August 1993, Justice Arvind Sawant of the Bombay High Court passed strictures against Judge B.M. Gupta of the sessions court, prohibiting him from trying narcotics cases. Gupta was one of the eight judges mandated specifically with narcotics cases. It was found that Gupta had wrongly given bail in July 1993 to an offender in two cases filed by the NCB. The bail was cancelled and another judge was assigned to look into the cases. It's no surprise that Mirchi, who was detained under COFEPOSA, the NSA and was high on the police's wanted list as a drug lord, was not convicted in a single case while he was in India.

That Mirchi cast a much larger shadow over the judiciary was suspected when the erudite chief justice of Bombay High Court, Anandamoy Bhattacharjee, tendered his resignation over a book deal from a London-based publisher. Lawyers smelled a rat over the Rs 26 lakh ($80,000) that was offered to Bhattacharjee by Roebuck Publishing for his book *Muslim Law and the Constitution* which was first published in 1985. Courtrooms were abuzz with suspicions that the deal was a possible payback. The publisher, Sachdev Musafir, son of a former chief minister of Punjab, however, maintained that Bhattacharjee's book had a huge market in the Middle East and Africa and the company was sure to make a profit.

The crimes for which Mirchi was sought to be extradited from Britain were committed after he had not only shifted base outside India but had also stopped visiting the country. Mirchi tried to get himself discharged from some of the charges in Bombay courts before India had formally requested his extradition. After winning the legal battle in London, Mirchi's lawyer assiduously continued to work in order to procure a certificate of innocence from the courts in India.

The legal battle continues to be fought by his wife Hajra and sons as the ED tries to claw back prime properties in Mumbai which they maintain were purchased with ill-gotten wealth. A slew of court documents and submissions by the ED indicates that the ring-fencing of assets had begun when Mirchi was alive. The action by the ED thus was long in the making and it seems that the family is prepared for it.

* * *

What the family were not prepared for was the knock on their door by the Scotland Yard at 10.40 a.m. on Monday, 3 April 1995. Mirchi was arrested on the Red Notice issued by India and presented at the Bow Street Magistrates' Court the next day. The chief magistrate, Peter Badge, made it clear that a decision on Mirchi's bail application could be made only when the court could establish his immigration status. Mirchi had offered £300,000 as surety.

The prosecution told the court that two passports were recovered from Mirchi. Meanwhile, 'police sources' in Bombay were already pronouncing that getting Mirchi back to India would be a matter of a few days!

It seems that at the time of Mirchi's arrest, Scotland Yard had information of his involvement in two narcotics cases, for which he was sought by India, as per the Red Notice. The first was the recovery of over 2000 kg of Mandrax tablets and methaqualone powder valued at over Rs 2 crore. According to the prosecution, the anti-narcotics cell had received a tip-off that a jeep abandoned in a parking lot near the Jewel of India hotel in Worli was carrying Mandrax tablets. Officers reached the spot and seized 150 kg of Mandrax tablets on 2 September 1993. Based on further investigations, the narcotics cell arrested Angelo D'Souza,

Dhananjay Chalke and Milind Chalke and others over the next few days.

This led to more seizures of Mandrax tablets, taking the tally from 150 kg to 2000 kg by October 1993 valued at over Rs 2 crore. A total of fourteen accused were named, out of which six were shown to be absconding, including Iqbal Mirchi. A charge sheet was filed on 20 November 1993 and the case was listed in the sessions court. There were close to fifty witnesses in the case, and interestingly, none of them had named Mirchi.

Mirchi, through his lawyers, approached the Bombay High Court requesting that the charge sheet filed against him be quashed. A division bench of A.C. Agarwal and D.K. Trivedi dismissed Mirchi's application by an order dated 4 March 1994. Mirchi then filed an application on 15 September 1994 before the sessions judge seeking a discharge from the case, even as the sessions court was in the process of framing the charges.

While the sessions court was still seized of the application, Mirchi approached the Bombay High Court seeking a direction that the trial court dispose of his application (seeking a discharge) without insisting on his personal appearance. On 17 October 1994, a two-judge bench of G.R. Majithia and M.L. Dudhat directed the sessions judge to dispose of Mirchi's discharge application 'within fifteen days from the receipt of the copy of this order . . . without pressing for the personal attendance of the petitioner'.

This was a judicial coup by Mirchi's lawyers. The judgment had paved the way for an accused person, against whom was issued a non-bailable warrant, to fight a serious criminal case without the need to present himself to the court's jurisdiction. This order, in the immediate aftermath of setting up of the judicial process for a trial in the 1993 Bombay bomb blasts, incensed the state government, to say the least. It feared that absconding accused in the blasts cases, too, may file a similar application, and without being subject to interrogation, seek discharge from the court.

The state of Maharashtra went to the Supreme Court against the high court's order. Meanwhile, the sessions court in an order dated

7 November 1994, rejected Mirchi's application for discharge. The Supreme Court nevertheless deliberated on the special leave petition by Maharashtra. In March 1995, Justice P.B. Sawant and Justice S.N. Ray termed the Bombay High Court's order as 'unjustified' and 'uncalled' for. Thus, this became a case for which the Maharashtra government had to go right up to the Supreme Court to ensure that he did not get through the cracks. This was the background to the first case against Mirchi, which had now reached London.

The other narcotics case against Mirchi related to the seizure of around 5000 kg of Mandrax tablets between January and March 1994 in Bombay and Gujarat's Mehsana district. Considering that Mirchi was a prime accused, the remand application for him merely stated that 'Iqbal Mirchi was the main supplier of narcotics drugs'. Mirchi's name also did not figure in the first charge sheet filed in March 1994. It was only in the one-page supplementary charge sheet, filed hastily in August 1994, that Mirchi was named. The supplementary charge sheet too was rather tenuous. It recorded that Nitin Bhanushali, an accused, was told by another accused, Prem Shetty, that he was working for Mirchi.

When Mirchi appeared before the Bow Street Magistrates' Court in London at the second hearing on Thursday, 6 April 1995, the prosecution had added a charge of murder to these two narcotics charges. The defence objected to the fresh charge on the grounds that the Red Notice, based on which Mirchi was arrested, did not mention the murder charge. However, this was just the second hearing and the prosecution was within its rights to add a new charge.

Mirchi was alleged to be behind the murder of Amar Suvarna (the manager of his rice mill in London) who was gunned down in February 1994 at Kala Ghoda in Bombay. Suvarna was instrumental in introducing Mirchi to the drug syndicate in Europe and Canada, but for a large fee. This irked Mirchi's family members, especially his brothers, who were upset with Suvarna pocketing a huge cut of their profits. Mirchi then moved Suvarna to Dubai and later to Bombay. A disgruntled Suvarna started leaking details of Mirchi's operations to agencies both in India and the UK. Some accounts suggest that the 1993 Mandrax haul was due to Suvarna's tip-off. Suvarna was killed, allegedly at Mirchi's behest. It was a dying declaration by Suvarna, the magistrate was informed, which implicated Mirchi.

In what looked like a rebuke to the defence's assertion on the first court date that Mirchi was an international businessman, the prosecution said that Scotland Yard had received enquiries from anti-narcotics authorities in Australia, South Africa, US and Germany about Mirchi. An officer from Scotland Yard was cross-examined on the issue of enquiries from other countries. Mirchi was not given bail and remanded to appear on 13 April for the next hearing.

Stung by the suddenness of the murder charge, at the 13 April hearing the defence pointed out that the prosecution had to submit and share the necessary paperwork supporting the charges. The magistrate was requested to set a time limit for submission of evidence and a deadline of 9 June was set, with the rider that the court could review it. Mirchi was to be presented in court next on 12 May for a remand hearing. There was no bail application made by Mirchi.

In June 1995, a team of officers from Scotland Yard came to Mumbai (the new name of Bombay) in relation with Mirchi's extradition case. This was the first case after India–UK had signed an extradition treaty in 1993. The prosecution had to convince the court of a prima facie case against those who were sought to be extradited. In simple terms, the court was not to decide whether the requested person was guilty or not, it was to be satisfied that there was enough evidence for the requested person to stand trial.

There were some delays over filing of papers and arguments, and Mirchi remained in judicial custody. With shoddy paperwork and shifting charges against Mirchi, it was increasingly looking like the case would collapse during the case management hearings itself. On 19 September, after just five hearings and even before the trial began, magistrate Jeremy Connor quashed the case against Mirchi. The order was non-appealable, which meant that if India wanted to pursue extradition against Mirchi, they would have to bring more conclusive evidence and start afresh.

The magistrate observed that 'there is no evidence that the alleged crime has been committed by the defendant'. The affidavits by Cyrus Cooper, who was a witness to Suvarna's murder, and by Suvarna's lawyer implicated Mirchi. But the court observed that the affidavits were not authenticated properly to meet the standard of the extradition arrangement. This meant that the court could not give any consideration to these affidavits. Besides, Cooper's affidavit was dated more than a year after the murder of Suvarna, and the question arose that if Cooper was such an important witness in the case, why did it take so long for his affidavit to be filed?

The affidavits were authenticated by two notaries in line with the requirements of courts in India, which fell way short of what a British court would expect. According to section 27 of the British Act of Extradition 1989, the documents to be presented in the court were to be authenticated by a judicial authority or a minister in charge of the prosecuting department. The magistrate observed that neither of the two notaries who had certified the affidavits were 'officers of the state'. Besides, the English translations of the affidavits in Hindi were not certified.

As his wife Heena Kausar silently muttered prayers and his brother watched with anticipation from the public gallery in the courtroom, the judge declared Mirchi a free man.

Mirchi's release was a huge failure for India after a string of successes relating to extradition. He was represented by top solicitor James Lewis and barrister Clive Nicholls QC described as a flag-bearer in international criminal law. But unlike earlier cases wherein India fought a long and bitter legal battle, it was a different template in Mirchi's extradition case. India's loss was of its own doing, and there was not much of a sweat for Mirchi's defence team. For an extradition case to be dismissed before a proper trial shows an astonishing level of non-application of mind by the prosecuting agency.

Mumbai Police's crime branch, the CBI and the NCB were all involved in pursuing a drug lord on foreign shores with a poor set of documents, at least, that's what the magistrate's ruling indicated.

Another explanation for the lack of evidence against Mirchi was that Indian Police Service (IPS) Officer Rahul Rai Sur, posted in the anti-narcotics cell, had taken away the files relating to Mirchi and had failed to return them despite moving to a lucrative posting in the United Nations. Interestingly, this was the same officer who was accused by Mirchi of demanding a bribe.

After he was discharged by the Bow Street Magistrates' Court, frustrating India's attempt to get him back to Mumbai, Mirchi relentlessly pursued to clear his name in India. As discussed earlier, the state of Maharashtra had to go right up to the Supreme Court to halt Mirchi in his quest to file for discharge in the case pertaining to the seizure of 2000 kg of smuggled narcotics drugs in Mumbai. Mirchi, through his lawyers, went back to Bombay High Court filing a similar petition. Four months after his victory in the Bow Street Magistrates' Court, the Bombay High Court in a judgment dated 29 January 1996, dismissed Mirchi's case.

Advocate Rajendra Singh, representing Mirchi, pleaded in the high court that the Supreme Court's judgment meant that the discharge application of Mirchi could not be heard by the trial court in his absence. Singh implored that the petition before the high court sought to challenge the illegal order of the trial court and hence there was no need for Mirchi to be present in the country. He described the trial court's 7 November 1994 order rejecting Mirchi's discharge application as unsustainable in law.

But the discharge from Bow Street Magistrates' Court was different, and if Mirchi thought he could wriggle his way out in a favourable way from the courts in India, he was either mistaken or too optimistic. Justice Vishnu Sahai of the Bombay High Court made it clear that Mirchi would have to first submit to the jurisdiction of the court and surrender to the majesty of the law, and till then, any petition of the nature could not and should not be heard by the court.

Aslam Memon, Mirchi's brother, filed a petition in the high court seeking the quashing of the detention order issued by the state government against Mirchi. In May 1999, with Justice Arvind Savant and Justice T.K. Chandrasekhara Das ruling, the court upheld the objection of the Maharashtra government that since Mirchi was absconding, the petition should not be entertained. An absconding person cannot seek to quash the detention order issued against him, ruled the court. This effectively stopped any more attempts from Mirchi to clear his name through courts while being away from India.

Mirchi was simultaneously pursuing a return to Mumbai through the intervention of the court, but nothing materialized. Mirchi's lawyer Shyam Keswani moved the sessions court a few times, seeking judicial custody for Mirchi as a condition for his surrender till the trial in cases involving him got over. Shiv Sena Rajya Sabha member of Parliament and eminent lawyer Adhik Shirodkar maintained that it was the state government that was responsible for Mirchi's absence. 'My client is ready to come to Mumbai if he is given protection and taken into judicial custody,' Shirodkar told the sessions court. An offer which the state declined.

Mirchi had the financial muscle and clout to hire top rank lawyers to represent him in courts in India. And even though nothing much materialized in his favour in Indian courts, he had secured victory in the Bow Street Magistrates' Court which mattered the most to him. He was a free man who could effectively mount and fight legal battles. When Mirchi finally realized that his attempts to extricate himself from criminal cases in India were futile, he turned his attention to salvaging his assets.

In October 1998, the Bombay High Court rejected the application of the Maharashtra government that sought to attach six properties belonging to Iqbal Memon and his family members. The NCB had seized a total of eleven properties, including a locker in the Union Bank of India, Juhu branch. The process to freeze these properties began in March 1995, a month before Mirchi was held in London, and continued till February 1997, by when these eleven properties were frozen.

However, in October 1997, the competent authority under the Narcotic Drugs and Psychotropic Substances Act (NDPS) ordered the release of six out of the eleven properties. The bank locker was directed to be closed and a fresh notice was to be issued seeking its seizure. The remaining four properties were to be seized by the Central government. The six properties were shown to be acquired through legitimate means and hence could not be treated as illegally acquired properties. Furious that Mirchi had managed to secure the release of these six properties, the Maharashtra government approached the high court. The high court too turned down the state's application.

The assets were seized as per the NDPS Act to put pressure on Mirchi, but his lawyers managed to stave away six properties. In January 1999, the chief metropolitan magistrate ordered attachment of another set of Mirchi's properties. This reportedly included Hotel Minaz and two flats at Juhu, and three sea-facing buildings in Worli.

* * *

In 2019, the ED filed a charge sheet against Iqbal Mirchi's family members and friends in respect of properties in Worli, alleging that they were bought from ill-gotten money and escaped the ED's dragnet because of the involvement of a charitable trust.

Rabia Mansion, Mariam Lodge and Sea View at Worli are at the centre of the investigations launched by the ED and were confiscated under the Smugglers and Foreign Exchange Manipulators Act, 1976 (SAFEMA). NCP leader Praful Patel and Shilpa Shetty's businessman husband Raj Kundra were questioned by the ED in this case. According to the ED, Mirchi had purchased these properties from Sir Mohammad Yusuf Trust in September 1986 for Rs 6.5 lakh. However, when the authorities sought to freeze the three buildings, Haroun Yusuf, the chairperson of the trust, misled courts that the properties still belonged to the trust thus thwarting the attempt to take over the buildings.

These were tenanted properties, but according to the ED, over a period of time, the original tenants had moved out and were replaced by people who owed allegiance to Mirchi. With the help of friends and business associates, Mirchi started to negotiate the possible redevelopment of the buildings. The first one was Jayesh Soni of Joy Home Creation who allegedly met Mirchi in 2005 through the latter's friend Humayun Merchant.

A court in Mumbai unfroze the three properties later that year. The primary reason for the quashing of the confiscation was that these properties were owned by the trust and not by Mirchi. Thus, while Soni held meetings and discussions with Mirchi, the agreement about the properties were drawn between the trust and Joy Home Creation to continue with the mirage of the trust being the owner of the properties. As per the agreement, Joy Home Creation was to pay Rs 11 crore to Merchant and Rs 4.25 crore to the trust.

But the ED discovered that the trust ultimately got just Rs 25 lakh, which they allege, reinforces that the real ownership and control was with Mirchi since the early 1990s. Soni's inability to pay the promised Rs 11 crore incensed Mirchi. Besides, the real estate prices had escalated and Merchant started to look for another party. In 2010, a new deal was struck with M/s Sunblink Real Estate Pvt. Ltd with the help of broker Ranjeet Singh Bindra for Rs 225 crore.

The ED claims Mirchi received much of his share amounting to Rs 170 crore (the balance was shared between Joy Home and the trust) through hawala and the rest through cheques. It was this money that was used by Mirchi to buy a 5-star hotel in Dubai in 2010. A big twist came in the case when it was found out that Dewan Housing Finance Corporation Limited (DHFL) had given a Rs 2186 crore loan to Sunblink Real Estate. In the charge sheet filed by the ED in December 2019, Dheeraj Wadhwan is identified as the person behind Sunblink's deal with Mirchi.

DHFL, a non-banking finance company, was used to pay Mirchi through a Wadhwan-owned company in Dubai. Sunblink itself was linked to Wadhwan who had travelled to London in 2010 to crack the deal with Mirchi, according to the ED. Mirchi died in 2013, after which his sons continued to negotiate with Wadhwan, demanding more money for the properties. The previous agreements drawn were being challenged by Mirchi's sons and negotiations continued till 2015, which is when the ED got wind of the deal and served notices under the Foreign Exchange Management Act (1999).

In August 2019, the ED launched a money laundering case after which investigations gathered steam. Mirchi's family members have refused to join the probe, but claim that they have shared papers and answered queries raised by the ED. This was of course not the first time that the family had to face investigations and litigation relating to assets under the scanner of law enforcement agencies.

Mirchi's famous Fisherman's Wharf stood on the restaurant Gurukripa, which had become a centre-point of dispute. M.K. Mohammed was a tenant in the Sri Niketan building where he ran a restaurant called Gurukripa in the 1980s. The land on which Gurukripa stood was under litigation between the co-owners of the land and Mohammed. An interim order by the high court restricted Mohammed from carrying out renovations except for the work on the roof of the restaurant. A settlement between Mohammed and the court receiver saw the former pay Rs 7 lakh in a full and final settlement of the land and he became an absolute owner of the property in 1988. However, in 1986, Mohammed had given the rights in the property to Hajra Memon for Rs 9 lakh, thus making Mirchi the silent owner.

A suit by a co-owner Lalben Patel in 1999 challenged the validity of the consent decree which had given complete ownership to Mohammed. Effectively by filing this suit, the co-owners wanted to challenge Mirchi's ownership. However, Mirchi was able to get the co-owners to agree to consent terms wherein Hajra agreed to remove all the furniture and fixtures in lieu of a monthly tenancy of 14,000 square foot carpet area in Sri Niketan building on the third and fourth floors and six covered and one open parking spaces at a monthly rent of Rs 10,000. The co-owners also agreed that if the premises were to be converted into a co-operative society, the tenancy would turn into ownership. Hajra and her two sons were nominated as tenants. Sri Niketan building later went into redevelopment by Millennium Developers and Mirchi's family got ownership of two floors in Ceejay House in 2007. Millennium Developers is owned by Nationalist Congress Party leader Praful Patel and his wife Varsha.

Interestingly, a parcel of land in Murud-Janjira purchased in 1993 by Iqbal Mirchi is perhaps one of the earliest cases in litigation involving assets owned by the Mirchi family. A brief discussion about this case throws some light on the mechanics employed to save assets from being seized. The case related to this parcel of land went through various judicial forums including the Bombay High Court and it emerged that it was bought from the earnings of the Dubai hotel where Mirchi worked.

Mirchi was employed by the Imperial Hotel and another company Imperial Express General Trading since July 1992. Employment contracts drawn between Mirchi and the companies in Arabic accompanied by certified English translations were flaunted by Mirchi's lawyers before ED officers and in courts. The land was purchased in April 1993 for Rs 66 lakh. While the Bombay Police and the CBI neglected to have Mirchi's case papers certified properly for the extradition case, there was no such mistake from Mirchi. In March 1993, Mirchi transferred 2 lakh dirhams from his bank account to his family members to purchase the said land. He employed the services of a chartered accountant in Dubai who certified that the money transferred was indeed part of Mirchi's salary. This was also certified by the consulate general of India in Dubai.

This strategy was deployed to counter the argument that the land was purchased by ill-gotten money, and hence the seizure under SAFEMA was unlawful. Mirchi sought to sell a part of this land in 2003 to a Cuffe Parade resident Jai Hiremath for Rs 55 lakh.

This transaction was of course blocked by the competent SAFEMA authority with the assistance of the crime branch.

* * *

While his close associates and friends are now finding the investigating agencies closing in on them in India, it is interesting that after the failed extradition bid, it was a dispute with another close family member that landed Mirchi in deep trouble in the UK. Mirchi had taken his extended family members under his wing and had helped them in every possible way. At the insistence of his elder sister, Mirchi had fixed his son Junaid's marriage to his nephew Nadeem Kader's daughter.

Kader was also working with Mirchi in his marble business. However, in 2011, Kader broke the engagement and there was a huge row within the family. After the failed extradition bid, during which Mirchi was arrested, it was not even his inclusion in the US State Department's report in the list of narcotics kingpins that renewed Scotland Yard's interest in him. However, a rather tame case of a marriage being called off, and that too by a close relative, led to Mirchi being produced in a London court.

Kader lodged a complaint of 'threatening to kill' against Mirchi on 9 October 2011, following which the latter was promptly arrested on 13 October. After two days of questioning in custody, Mirchi was charged for threatening to kill Kader. He was taken to Redbridge Magistrates' Court where he was remanded to judicial custody till 20 October. Eventually, the charges were dropped due to lack of evidence. The CPS noted that 'if more significant evidence or information is discovered at a later date, the decision may be reconsidered'. It never happened.

Thus except for this brief brush with the law in London, there was nothing legally that contradicted Mirchi's claim of being a hardworking and successful businessman. A little less than a year after he passed away of a heart attack, a forgery slur emerged against his name as brought out in a high court judgment in London.

While Mirchi successfully warded off far more serious charges in his lifetime, it is an irony that after his death his name would get associated with the comparatively lesser offence of forgery of a will. Justice Gerald Edward Barling of the high court in a December 2013 judgment mentioned 'the surprising willingness of Mr Memon openly to encourage fabrication of a will . . .' The judgment was in a case relating to the validity of a will with intriguing subplots and turns involving close family members and friends spread across Mumbai and London.

The troublemaker for Mirchi was once again his nephew Nadeem Abdul Kader, whose evidence pointed to his role in the said forgery. Kader's evidence was in a case in which his friend and a former employee of Mirchi, Mehdi Hassan Syed, stood to gain substantial assets in London worth thousands of pounds. In a strange twist, it was again a matter of marriage that had strained Mehdi's relation with Mirchi in 2006 just as it later happened in 2011 between Kader and Mirchi.

Mehdi Hassan Syed had come to the UK in 2001 and was working in a restaurant owned by Mirchi. Mehdi was married to Mumtaz, daughter of Mirchi's life-long friend Ali Reza who is based in Mumbai. In October 2006, Mumtaz and Mehdi parted ways and even Mirchi's effort to work out a compromise did not work. This failed marriage eventually led Mirchi to fire Mehdi from his job.

According to Kader's evidence, when Mirchi found out that it was the estate of Ali Reza's sister-in-law Naseem that would go to Mehdi, he became angry and told Ali Reza that he (Reza) 'should do whatever possible to stop him from getting the estate, including preparing a will of Naseem if need be'.

Mehdi came to be the main beneficiary of Naseem's estate through the will of her husband Jaffar Ali Khan who died on 8 January 2011. Naseem had died in England on 17 July 2008 following which letters of administration for her estate were granted to her husband as she was supposed to have died intestate.

After Naseem's death, Mehdi had taken care of her husband, which included getting him admitted to a care home after he was discharged from a hospital. Mehdi's contention was that to show his gratitude, Jaffar Khan made him the sole executor and main beneficiary in his last will.

Opposing Mehdi's claim was Syed Ali Haider, son of Naseem's brother Akhtar Hussain. Haider sought revocation of the existing grant to Jaffar Khan of letters of administration in respect of Naseem's estate. This was because, claimed Haider, Naseem had not died intestate but had made a will. This purported will was made by Naseem in Mumbai on 25 December 2005 in the presence of three witnesses—her brother Syed Jaffer Hussain, brother-in-law Ali Reza and Reza's friend and neighbour Zaki Shah.

The case thus hinged on one issue—whether Naseem's signature on the will was a forgery. After hearing out all the parties and evidence including the three witnesses from India through video-conferencing, Justice Barling concluded that 'in the light of all the evidence Naseem did not sign the will and that her signature on that document is a forgery'.

According to Kader, it was 'two to three weeks' after the death of Naseem's husband, that Mirchi told Ali Reza on the phone that he would make sure Mehdi would not get a penny out of Naseem's estate. Mirchi spoke to Ali Reza from his office during which Kader was present. This was in January 2011, a few months before Kader called off his daughter's engagement with Mirchi's son.

As Mirchi spoke to Reza over the phone, Kader could not hear the other side of the conversation. According to Kader, Mirchi 'said that Ali Reza should do whatever possible to stop him (Mehdi) from getting the estate, including preparing a will of Naseem if need be'. Further, Mirchi also told Reza that he should bring a will to London and he would pay for his air ticket and for any legal expenses if the matter were to come to court.

In the cross-examination, Kader was asked whether Mirchi would have spoken to Ali Reza in his presence to which he replied that Mirchi was happy for him to hear the conversation and tell Mehdi 'because he would have hoped to scare the defendant

(Mehdi) having regard to Mr Memon's (Mirchi) wealth and connections'.

Justice Barling assessed Kader as 'a clear, straightforward and convincing witness generally' and concluded that 'Mr Kader is telling the truth'. 'I also accept his (Kader's) explanation for Mr Memon's surprising openness in his presence. This is not at all implausible given the evidence of Mr Memon's background and character.' The judgment had no material relevance for Mirchi as it came out after he had died. Had he been alive, he would have stoutly defended himself; perhaps whether the case would have gone to the court itself is a big question.

* * *

Journalists who have met Mirchi concur that the drug lord was a soft-spoken person with a calm demeanour. Mirchi hated tea but was fond of good food, and the restaurants that he ran served him well! A year before his death he had undergone heart surgery and his family kept a close watch on his diet. However, after a few months, it was difficult to resist his gastronomic cravings. In the large, expansive Hornchurch house, he was served rather simple and boring meals to protect his health. However, the family discovered that he had started eating his heart out along with friends and associates at the various Indian restaurants that dot London. In fact, it is said in Mumbai that Mirchi was a fairly good chef who loved his meat.

Mirchi stayed in the leafy Hornchurch suburb of London with his family since he moved to England in the early 1990s. In 2005, he moved into a bigger house just a few minutes away. A vast garden in the backyard with an old, shady tree and an elegant bench provided Mirchi with the perfect background for his walks, which he had come to enjoy a lot.

In fact, Mirchi died in London's famous Hyde Park where he had gone for a walk with his friend on 13 August 2013.

Mirchi's family, however, maintain that he was made a scapegoat and was caught on the wrong foot after refusing to toe the line of an IPS officer in Mumbai. The sprawling six-bedroom detached house in Hornchurch, once abuzz with people and activities, is now a skeleton of its original shelf. The wooden floors match the fawn fabric sofas and two pouffes in a black leather frame in the two reception rooms that open to a large dining area. Curtains in a similar beige, with a green trim, complement the odd plant thrown in the room. A cosy leather chair with a foot stool positioned before a huge television seem to be the most used. The crimson cushions and crystal chandeliers add a speck of character to a rather jaded decor. His second wife Heena Kausar, who lives there with a sole companion, recalls the time she first met her husband.

'I never knew that I would get married to him. He was introduced by a common friend who said he (Mirchi) was looking to produce a television serial and asked if I would be interested. So I met him and we spoke briefly,' remembers Heena.

Their marriage was arranged and a lavish reception was held at the Taj Mahal Palace hotel in Mumbai. Heena only discovered an hour after the nikah that 'Iqbal was married and had a wife'. Her mother Nigar Sultana, known for playing the jealous Bahar, a lady-in-waiting in the film *Mughal-e-Azam* that was directed by Heena's father K. Asif, advised her to be a dutiful wife. Heena made peace with her situation.

After marriage, she stayed wherever Mirchi took her—Bombay, Dubai and finally London. 'The Memons are very conservative and they do not like their women to work or leave the house. They expect them to take care of the house and stay away from the business,' said the starlet who quit Bollywood after her marriage. Heena Kausar is not from the Memon community and that also played a part in her being kept away from all his business dealings, she believes. Before marriage, Heena's motto was to work and earn and she greatly enjoyed her time as an artiste. A YouTube clip that wrongly identifies a woman in denim shorts as her still sends her fuming. 'I have never worn such shameful clothes,' she says angrily. She even admitted to leaving a comment below the clip to remove it. When that didn't work, she left another comment six months later that stated: 'Please remove the picture of the lady who is wearing shorts—that's not Heena Kausar!! Before uploading the picture, it's media's duty to make sure about the picture and the fake news.' The clip remains and so does her anguish.

At home, Mirchi wore a traditional white kurta-pyjama, or sometimes a lungi. He spoke Marathi, Gujarati and Kutchi, the last of which Heena admits she did not understand at all. Since his doctors warned him of a weak heart, Heena would serve him only light and healthy food. 'He was a lover of good food and despite my attempts, he would find a way of savouring kebabs, chicken and curries outside with his friends. That played a huge role in his heart condition.'

To her, her beloved Iqbal was a 'very simple man, who took care of his family members and always thought of doing good for everybody'. Heena lived in the Hornchurch house for more than twenty-five years, and now that's all she has left of her life with Mirchi. All his businesses and properties were allegedly taken over by Hajra and her children. She is disappointed that after his death, Hajra and her children did not stay in touch with her. 'It was a shock because we were on good terms when he was alive.'

Even living miles away from India, Mirchi was never free from speculations and accusations, recalls Heena. 'I remember once we were having breakfast and were watching Indian news when suddenly they spoke about Mirchi coming to India to plan to take part in some criminal activity and flying back to Dubai in a private jet. His jaw dropped, he left the food and stood up, walking away from the dining table,' recalls Heena, adding emphatically that all the talk of him being a Dawood man is complete hogwash. She describes him as 'a self-made man who achieved everything due to his hard work. But he was made a villain'. In a calm voice, she rubbishes all allegations against her husband, 'Iqbal *ne ek cheeteen bhi nahi maari hogi* [Iqbal would not have killed even an ant]!'

Heena will always remember the man whom India believes to be a dreaded drug czar as only Iqbal Memon, a loving husband, a caring father and a doting grandpa. And a man much wronged in his life. History, however, judges him differently.

5

MUSICIAN OF MAYHEM

The shrill tunes of the gaudy 1980s Bollywood had added to the despair of music-lovers who pined for the melody of the 1960s and 1970s. Banal lyrics accompanied by loud, tasteless music had become the norm. Then emerged a film which had its script woven around eleven compositions drawn from a music bank of thousands of songs. It broke the charts and reinforced the importance of music in Bollywood.

Aashiqui, released in 1990, became one of the biggest blockbusters on the strength of the music by Nadeem-Shravan. The duo was transformed, from being at the margins of the industry to becoming one of the most sought-after music directors. Around 20 million units of the film's soundtrack were sold. The gamble by Gulshan Kumar, who produced the film using fresh faces had paid off.

The unostentatiously simple lyrics set to immensely hummable tunes in *Aashiqui* brought back into fashion a genre of romantic music that characterized much of the early 1990s. Publicity posters of the film with the image of Rahul Roy and Anu Aggarwal kissing behind a large jacket covering their faces became a motif for all things romantic. Just a year before *Aashiqui*, Gulshan had produced his first film *Lal Dupatta Malmal Ka* in 1989, which sank without a trace. However, with *Aashiqui*, he was second-time lucky.

Gulshan's foray into the music industry (and films) was an extension of his father's industriousness. Chandra Bhan Dua came to Delhi as a refugee from West Punjab's Jhang district. To eke out a living, he started selling fruits on the pavement, and gradually opened a juice shop. But alongside, Dua also opened a shop dealing in pre-recorded music in Gulmohar Park. When Gulshan Kumar (he dropped Dua from his name) graduated from Deshbandhu College, his attendance marred by watching movies, it was no surprise that he took over the records shop and established Super Cassettes. Gulshan began by making pirated copies of HMV, India's largest record company. In the process, he provided a cheap alternative to the official, but expensive, records belonging to the HMV label.

The other model he deployed which stupendously added to his cash flow was re-recording old hits by unknown singers and selling them cheap. Taking advantage of the loopholes in the copyright laws, Gulshan's T-Series changed the dynamics of the music industry. He was thus, at the same time, busy capturing both the legitimate and illegitimate space in the music market. It was like a branded alcohol company also supplying hooch! The ever-ambitious Gulshan turned to music CDs and film production, taking the turnover of his enterprise to Rs 250 crore by the mid-1990s. His zeal for making money was matched by his religiosity. And he, a Shiva bhakt, had managed to merge the two as well.

The T in T-series represented the Trishul of Shiva. Along with romantic numbers, Gulshan is still remembered for the plethora of devotional songs he sold for the ever-growing cassettes market. And while he restricted his images to just the covers of film tracks, he didn't stop at that with the devotional cassettes. In the religious tracks, Gulshan would have a bhajan or two in his own voice. He had also started playing cameos, mostly leading bhajan-singing devotees, in the religious films he produced.

The visibility option, though limited, was used to the full extent in the case of commercial Hindi films. The only faces on *Aashiqui*'s audio cassettes were Gulshan Kumar's and Anuradha

Paudwal's. The film's marketing promo was such that it was only Anu Aggarwal's red flowing skirt and Rahul Roy's fawn baggy trousers that were visible on the cassettes. Gulshan didn't make any appearance in the films he produced but launched his brother Krishan Kumar in *Bewafa Sanam*. Gulshan's success and fame made a new crop of individuals popular. Sonu Nigam, Kumar Sanu, Alka Yagnik and Anuradha Paudwal were some of the most notable names, along with Nadeem-Shravan, who owed their big breaks to Kumar's entrepreneurship.

Shravan had received training under the tutelage of his father, a famous dhrupad singer. Nadeem and Shravan had met as co-judges in a school music competition in the late 1970s. Nadeem had no connection with music or films. Nadeem's father Yunus Saifi was a managing partner in Taj Office Book Depot, a landmark shop selling Islamic literature on Mohammed Ali Road in south Mumbai. However, in the days before Partition and several years after Independence, the shop published and sold all kinds of books and was frequented by the high priests of the Progressive Writers' Association. In 1945, Taj Office Book Depot published the correspondence between Muhammad Ali Jinnah and Congress leaders, edited by the secretary of the Muslim League leader Syed Pirzada. The copies sold like hotcakes.

The original owner of the shop was Nazir Ahmed, who hailed from Lahore and left Bombay in 1949. The Saifis became managing partners in the shop and continued to publish books. In the 1950s and 1960s, the shop also sold tickets to popular performances by the likes of Shakeela Bano Bhopali and other events like Indo–Pak mushairas held in Bombay. The shop decided to focus on Islamic literature; the Holy Quran with guaranteed sales, unlike the Urdu books and periodicals which saw a decline. While Taj Office Book Depot was moving away from novels, books and periodicals to religious texts, Nadeem was drawn towards music. ·

Given Nadeem's background, it is difficult to imagine that he would have a career in Bollywood. He grew up in Mahim from where the family moved to central Bombay when he was

still a boy. Studying at the prestigious Elphinstone College, the
family's prosperous business provided him with the cushion, if not
encouragement, to explore a career as a musician. Nadeem was
providing orchestras for musical and dancing nights in Bombay,
while the Quran published by his family business found its way
to mosques around the globe, including Islam's holiest lands. In
their own ways, both Gulshan and Nadeem's families were in the
dissemination of religious piety. The model and the scale—ornate
calligraphy and mass-produced audio cassettes—were of course
different.

Nadeem's creative instinct was informed by his Bombay
upbringing, growing around a world of Urdu literature that drew
a lot from all kinds of subtle imagery. Gulshan was a Delhi man
who made a base in Bombay to be closer to Bollywood in order
to satiate his appetite for success and moolah. It was more than
a decade after Nadeem-Shravan gave music for a Bhojpuri film
Dangal, that success and recognition came in the form of *Aashiqui.*
They composed music for Gujarati films and continued to look
for that big-ticket production. Mithun Chakraborty and Anuradha
Paudwal spread good words about Nadeem-Shravan in the industry.

When Nadeem-Shravan got in touch with Gulshan Kumar, he
was remixing old Hindi film songs. It was Kumar Sanu's success
with T-series' Kishore Kumar cover versions that gave the former a
chance in *Aashiqui.* Nadeem-Shravan started off composing music
for Gulshan Kumar's music bank, a system according to which
Super Cassettes would collect compositions from various music
directors and lyricists for use in films later. This was how *Aashiqui*
was made.

The popularity of *Aashiqui* propelled Nadeem-Shravan to
stardom. *Saajan, Phool Aur Kaante, Dil Ka Kya Kasoor, Dil Hai Ke
Manta Nahin* proved that *Aashiqui* was not a fluke. The industry
was abuzz that the asking price for Nadeem-Shravan had shot
up from Rs 50,000 to Rs 20-25 lakh. Harinder Baweja writing
in *India Today* called them the pied pipers of Bollywood. But
Gulshan Kumar was giving the credit for *Aashiqui*'s songs to

Anuradha Paudwal! 'I challenge her to come with one such score in a 100 years,' Nadeem told Baweja. Clearly, something was brewing between Nadeem and Gulshan, and it was not for the good. Things took a nasty turn when Nadeem accused Gulshan of not promoting his album *Hi! Ajnabi*.

Jackets were now carrying the images of Nadeem-Shravan on audio cassettes to shore up sales. They gained recognition like no other music director in the decade before. 'Just as there can be no other Lata Mangeshkar, there can be no other Nadeem-Shravan,' quipped Nadeem riding on the success of burgeoning sales of their music. Nadeem's confidence, bordering on the rude, reflected his upper-middle-class upbringing. He was a meritorious student at St Mary's in Mumbai, and had studied political science, unlike Shravan who did not finish his studies and Gulshan who barely completed his graduation. Nadeem was also in the National Cadet Corps and had won a medal for his marksmanship during his school years.

The rift between Nadeem and Gulshan was no secret. The cassette king and the reigning musical czars could not take their collaboration ahead. It was perhaps the success of *Aashiqui* that had made the professional road bumpy for them. But was it that bad, that instead of going their different ways, a Bollywood heavyweight gave out a *supari*?

On 12 August 1997, when Gulshan Kumar came out from a Shiv temple in Andheri, he was attacked by armed assailants. Gulshan was shot in his arm and waist. He managed to duck into a public urinal to seek refuge, but was followed by the killers. He then ran towards a nearby shanty and pleaded with an old woman to let him in and close the door. The shooters followed him and shot volleys of bullets, ending his life. According to author S. Hussain Zaidi, gangster Abu Salem had instructed his men to call him from their mobile at the time of the firing so that he could hear Gulshan wailing!

Just a week before, an attempt had been made on the life of *Gupt* producer Rajiv Rai. Gulshan Kumar's murder was the pinnacle of shock that the underworld inflicted on the psyche of Bollywood. This audacious murder had put into oblivion all the threatening calls and the visits to Dubai—voluntarily and involuntarily—by Bollywood stars. The Mumbai Police were in disarray. This was a direct challenge thrown at them, putting them under intense pressure to show results.

After the necessary formalities, Gulshan's body was taken to Delhi for cremation. The employees from his several companies constituted the majority of those present (one estimate pegged the number at 10,000) for the last journey from Gulshan's Greater Kailash residence to Nigambodh Ghat. The crowd following Gulshan Kumar's body was chanting *Jai Mata Di* and *Gulshan Kumar Amar Rahen* and also *Mumbai Police hai hai.* Gulshan Kumar's mortal remains were on a truck that was laden with flowers.

The police were already facing the music with the killings of trade union leader Datta Samant, mill owner Vallabhbhai Thakkar, and the attacks on Subhash Ghai and Rajiv Rai. Gulshan's murder was the proverbial last straw that triggered the inevitable change in guard of one of the most powerful posts in the financial capital of India. The affable 1966-batch officer Subhash Malhotra was made the Mumbai Police commissioner. Facing intense pressure, Malhotra said that Gulshan's murder was a case of extortion.

Malhotra's appointment as police commissioner was not to the liking of Shiv Sena chief Balasaheb Thackeray, who wanted R.D. Tyagi to continue. However, Gopinath Munde, the deputy chief minister, holding the home portfolio, had his say and Malhotra was installed as the twenty-sixth police commissioner in December 1996. In less than a year, a transfer was staring Malhotra in the face. On 19 August 1997, Natwarlal Desai, a prominent builder, was shot dead at Nariman Point as he was coming out of his car—the government had already decided to replace Malhotra.

On 21 August, Ronnie Mendonca became the new police commissioner. Mendonca was Thackeray's choice and was aware of the enormity of the Gulshan Kumar case. On Monday,

1 September 1997, Mendonca announced in a hurriedly convened, crowded press conference that Nadeem had given Dawood Ibrahim the contract to kill Gulshan Kumar as he felt that the cassette king was out to destroy his career. 'Nadeem feared that Kumar was intentionally trying to ruin his career,' Mendonca told the assembled reporters.

Nadeem was in London since July 1997 and was supposed to have returned to Mumbai two weeks earlier. His wife Sultana had a miscarriage and he had extended his stay. But with the cops, that too the police commissioner, naming him as the main accused in the murder of Gulshan Kumar, would he still come? One theory suggests that Nadeem was named as an accused to prevent his escape to the Middle East from London, from where, it was believed, it would be easier to nab him. If Nadeem moved base to Dubai, it would have been impossible to do anything.

The attempt on Rajiv Rai's life had got the police under tremendous pressure for failing to keep the underworld in check. The naming of Nadeem, however, as the main accused served to highlight the symbiotic relationship between Bollywood and the underworld. It created a narrative that Bollywood was hobnobbing with the underworld, and hence there were bound to be ramifications. This was one of the most potent defences that was offered by the Mumbai Police and the politicians who were rattled by the underworld's audacity.

The police claimed that the conspiracy to kill Gulshan Kumar was planned in Dubai in June 1997. On 12 June, the who's who of Bollywood had attended a musical night at the Royal Empire Hotel, to mark the opening of the hotel and a water park. The hotel belonged to Vicky Goswami at whose behest Nadeem played a big role in getting several stars for the Nadeem-Shravan musical night. Shah Rukh Khan, Salman Khan, Jackie Shroff, Deepti Bhatnagar, Atul Agnihotri, Mamata Kulkarni, Kumar Sanu, Alka Yagnik, Abhijeet and others had reportedly performed at the musical bash. The next day was the inauguration of the hotel, after which the film stars returned to India except for Nadeem.

According to the crime branch, Nadeem stayed back to discuss
and finalize the murder of Gulshan Kumar with Salem. Nadeem
had not charged for the bash, and this way had paid the supari in
kind for Gulshan's murder. Senior police officers were also briefing
journalists that some film stars, including Nadeem, met Dawood's
men during the same trip to Dubai. These meetings were done over
a hearty meal and were reflective of the cosy relationship between
these stars and members of the underworld.

The year 1997 was one of the worst for the Hindi film industry.
Dara Munawar Ali, the brother of the comedienne Guddi Maruti,
was shot dead by members of the Chhota Rajan gang in his flat
at Khar in March. Less than a week later, Dawood's shooters
killed producer Mukesh Duggal outside his office. Subhash Ghai
was being threatened by the D-gang demanding the overseas
distribution rights of *Pardes*.

The underworld was not just interested in the financial
aspect of Bollywood but had also started to dictate to producers
which stars should be cast in films. In 1995, producer Javed
Siddique was shot dead at the behest of Chhota Shakeel after
he refused to cast Pakistani actress Anita Ayyub in his film,
which was allegedly financed by the underworld. Well-known
producers refused to accept that the underworld was financing
movies, but it was a known fact that due to the increasing
budgets, a large section of producers and financiers had knocked
on the doors of the underworld for money. There were strong
rumours that Sudhakar Bokade, a former loader in Air India;
Mukesh Duggal, who owned a garment shop in Versova; Xavier
Marquis, an alleged drug dealer; Bobby Anand, on the fringes
of Bollywood were few of the several producers financed by the
underworld on the sly. Some other restaurateurs and small-time
businessmen became prominent producers signing mega stars,
making it obvious from where they drew their clout. It was as
if the killing of Gulshan gave the police a timely opportunity
to remind the film fraternity that some of its members were in
cahoots with the mobsters.

It was no less than the police commissioner who had named Nadeem. So, it would be preposterous to think that the cops would have not done their homework. What made matters worse for Nadeem was the narrative that he had become arrogant in the wake of his success. Nadeem was very accessible to film journalists and the absence of secretaries or public relations officers endeared him to a section of the media. He would ask journalists to do a *dhaansoo* (explosive) interview before the conversation would begin. But when the police named Nadeem as the main suspect, reporters started remembering with relish how he used to attack his competitors.

Nadeem's quotes in the media about fellow music directors and singers were effectively used to paint him in a bad light. Entertainment journalists had got the sense that success had indeed gone to his head. When the Bachchan-starrer *Hum* topped the music charts, he quipped '*Hum mein nahi hain dum* [Hum is weak]', as an insult to Laxmikant-Pyarelal's music. He labelled A.R. Rahman a 'good recordist' whose music was like a chorus of municipal workers. The Jain brothers who owned the Venus music company were described as 'music mafia'.

The biggest diatribe was reserved for Anu Malik whom he once called a monster. Seeking to explain Malik's popularity as a passing phase, he remarked that people flock to *karela* (bitter gourd) after an overdose of *mithai*, but people will ultimately come back to devour mithai and not karela. There were also talks that Kumar Sanu, Anuradha Paudwal and Alka Yagnik had fallen in Nadeem's bad books and hence he was promoting Udit Narayan and Kavita Krishnamurthy.

The more serious step that Gulshan took was buying the music rights from film producers, which apparently gave him an increased heft in the film industry. He started intervening on who the producers could hire and sign for their films and this meant keeping off Nadeem-Shravan. Gulshan had also said that the real credit for *Aashiqui*'s score should be given to Anuradha Paudwal and not Nadeem-Shravan.

But the police's theory continued to be questioned by a large section of Bollywood. Why would a conspiracy be hatched in the same period when the whole of Bollywood had descended on Dubai? Taking pot-shots at competitors and ridiculing peers was nothing new in Bollywood, but did it mean that the matter could go as far as getting someone killed?

* * *

Nadeem was arrested on Wednesday morning, 17 September 1997 from his cousin Nazish Chouglay's house in Kingsbury, north-west London. The arrest was largely symbolic as Nadeem had already agreed to cooperate with the cops. The Mumbai Police had alerted Interpol on 4 September, and when it seemed that Nadeem was not going to come to Mumbai anytime soon, nudged Scotland Yard to start the process against the musician.

Anticipating his arrest, Nadeem had already engaged the services of solicitor Henri Bradman. When he was taken to a police station, his solicitor was waiting for him. He was produced at the Bow Street Magistrates' Court where he was given conditional bail. Nadeem told the magistrate that his wife Sultana had suffered a miscarriage, which was why he couldn't travel to Mumbai after being named as an accused. He was directed to surrender his passport (which was already revoked by New Delhi) and appear on 24 September.

Supporters in the Nadeem camp maintained that Gulshan's power and influence in the industry was overblown and that brand Nadeem-Shravan were in a position to stand up to him. Nadeem too said that he and Shravan had chosen their producers and it was not the other way round. So if Gulshan couldn't do much to destroy Nadeem's career, there was no question of paying to get the cassette king killed. But Nadeem's arrest in London had changed the equation. Suddenly it looked plausible that Nadeem had a role to play in Gulshan's murder. Nadeem-Shravan had several big banners lined up which included the biggest names in the industry—Boney Kapoor, K.C. Bokadia, David Dhawan, Rajkumar Santoshi, Ramesh Taurani, Mehul Kumar and R.K. Films—all of which faced an uncertain future.

On 24 September, Nadeem appeared in court number 1 of the Bow Street Magistrates' Court in a blue suit. A £200,000 bail deposit and two sureties for £50,000 each had ensured that he would go back to his wife and kid after the proceedings were over instead of a British prison. He sat in the dock and quietly watched his barrister Clive Nicholls do most of the talking.

Nicholls fired the first salvo by asking why was it that the CPS, representing India, had asked for more time (sixty days) to submit evidence when Scotland Yard had pressed for Nadeem's arrest. 'In a case of conspiracy to murder, I imagine the Indian authorities would have the evidence before the provisional arrest,' said Nicholls. The CPS was within its rights to ask for a sixty-day period in order to submit evidence, but it gave an indication of the crime branch's unpreparedness in the case.

The magistrate granted a forty-day limit to the CPS to produce the evidence, setting a date of 3 November. Nicholls had vociferously argued that on a serious charge of murder, a foreign government cannot keep the accused in suspense for a long time. Nadeem had to report to a police station every Wednesday, a routine which he had to follow till the end of the judicial battle in London.

In Mumbai, the crime branch arrested Ramesh Taurani, the owner of Tips Video Cassette Private Limited, on Saturday, 4 October 1997, after he was called to the crime branch and interrogated by R.S. Sharma, the joint commissioner of police. Taurani was a self-made man like Gulshan and had in a short time gained soaring success. Owners of two other music companies, Dhirubhai Shah of Time Audio and Pradeep Vakil of Vatsa Music Limited, had also been interrogated by the cops.

Taurani's arrest was considered just a matter of time after the Shiv Sena chief Balasaheb Thackeray's googly that there was a larger conspiracy behind Gulshan Kumar's murder. Just after the police had identified Nadeem as the main accused, Thackeray had told journalists that there were three prominent businessmen who were behind the murder. Though he had not named anyone, it was widely believed that he was referring to Taurani, Shah and Vakil.

Taurani's arrest also provided a public display of inconsistencies in the police's version regarding the alleged hatching of the conspiracy to eliminate Gulshan Kumar. Till now the police were proclaiming that the plan to target Gulshan was made in June 1997, at the infamous party, whereas in Taurani's remand application, it was stated that the planning was done in January 1997. Never mind the discrepancy in the date of the alleged planning, the cops had made a connection between Taurani and Nadeem. Taurani's chauffeur, Joseph Selvaraj, had turned approver and told the police that his employer and Nadeem had handed the Rs 25 lakh supari in Juhu to people who ultimately passed the cash to Salem's men.

But in a remarkable turnaround, Ramrao Adik, celebrated lawyer and a former deputy chief minister of Maharashtra, managed to get bail for Taurani from the Bombay High Court on 23 October 1997. Adik told the court that Taurani's remand application, while highlighting that the conspiracy to kill Gulshan was hatched in January 1997, hardly mentioned his client's name. Justice A.B. Palkar concurred that it was difficult to believe, as the prosecution claimed, that Taurani would discuss with his chauffeur about carrying Rs 25 lakh cash for what would be a clandestine affair.

In less than twenty days after his arrest, Taurani was out on bail. The police machinery was furious at state prosecutor V.T. Tulpule, for not informing them about the bail application. Tulpule claimed that as was the practice, he had informed the crime branch constable about Taurani's bail application. Joint Commissioner R.S. Sharma held a press conference and lambasted Tulpule, claiming that instead of having a fill-in-the-blank approach, he should have personally alerted senior officers about Taurani's bail application.

If a high-profile accused, identified as a main player in the murder, could get bail right under the nose of the crime branch, what chance did they have of nailing Nadeem in a British court? Taurani's bail indicated a complete breakdown of communication between the cops and prosecutor. To add insult to injury, Tulpule told reporters that the case against Taurani was 'bogus and non-tenable'. A seething Mendonca ensured that Tulpule was taken off from all cases of the Mumbai Police!

The 3 November hearing was fast approaching and the crime branch had managed to get a 200-page document setting out the case against Nadeem. This included affidavits by the crime branch assistant commissioner of police, L.R. Rao, statements from witnesses including Bollywood stars and others who were arrested. It would be an understatement to say that public prosecutor Ujjwal Nikam sounded overconfident of their success. Joint Commissioner of Police R.S. Sharma, on the other hand, aware of the Mirchi case, was more circumspect of their success.

On Tuesday, 28 October 1997, Nikam and Rao flew to London for the 3 November hearing. They were confident of having strong prima facie evidence against Nadeem. Nikam and Rao were provided security by Scotland Yard in view of the high profile hearing, which turned out to be an anti-climax. The documents prepared by the crime branch were a source of immense satisfaction to Nadeem's counsel Clive Nicholls.

The 200-page document did not have evidence against Nadeem that was anywhere close to passing the court's muster. Nicholls termed it 'extraordinary' that the Indian government was not able to present evidence to the court despite the forty-day time that it was given. Alison Rowley, the CPS counsel, told the court that the forty-day time was not enough to prepare the case and sought a further extension of six weeks.

It emerged that several statements and confessions of key witnesses were recorded, not in front of a magistrate, but the police, rendering them inadmissible. 'If the Indian authorities had a good case against (Nadeem) for seeking extension or even extradition, they should have come up by now,' said Nicholls, who opposed the granting of any further extension. 'I pray that the Indian government has no firm grounds to support its case and Nadeem should be discharged.'

Ronald Bartle, the magistrate, gave three more weeks to the prosecution saying that if the CPS failed to comply with the new deadline of 24 November, Nadeem would be discharged. Bartle's 'final deadline' of 24 November exposed the Mumbai Police and sounded like music to Nadeem's ears who sat patiently all through the proceedings that lasted for around forty-five minutes. The defence clearly had an upper hand, but Rowley's assertion that the case was a 'serious murder conspiracy', which also included threats being issued to other stars, also gave an indication that the prosecution wouldn't let Nadeem off easily.

Displaying a rather clumsy approach, the papers submitted by the Mumbai Police used both Nadeem and Saifi to identify the musician. The CPS asked for necessary corrections to rule out any confusion on whether Nadeem and Saifi were two different individuals. Nikam and Rao returned to Mumbai with sullen faces, but the resolve to get Nadeem extradited did not waver. The Mumbai Police re-recorded the confessions of the fourteen accused under section 164 of India's Criminal Procedure Code (CPC), which meant that the confessions were recorded in front of a magistrate. Some other corrections were also carried out after K.L. Prasad, the deputy commissioner of police, crime branch, held extended talks with Anuradha Paudwal and Krishan Kumar at the police headquarters.

On Wednesday, 19 September, Nikam and Rao flew to London with the 250-page document. They would get two full days to confer with the CPS before the case would come up on Monday at the court. By the end of Thursday, a copy of the papers was posted to Nadeem's defence team, after the CPS had vetted it. On Monday, there was much jubilation in the Indian camp when the magistrate set 1 December 1997 as the date for regular hearing. Nicholls had asked for more time to study the papers, saying that they had received them only on Monday morning.

By now senior police officers, including crime branch chief R.S. Sharma, were more hopeful of getting Nadeem extradited. Two days after the hearing in Nadeem's case, the Supreme Court of India on 26 November 1997 cancelled the bail granted to Taurani and directed him to surrender to the magistrate. The crime branch had successfully closed in on two of the main accused. The tide was turning.

After stoutly opposing the extension given to the prosecution, it was now the turn of Nicholls to seek more time. When the court met briefly on 4 December 1997, Nicholls sought a new date, seeking to expound on the issue of Nadeem not getting a fair trial in India. He referred to Amnesty International's report, to bolster that Muslims were at a disadvantage in India and could not get a fair trial. At Nicholls's request, the magistrate set the next date in the new year—29 January 1998.

When the court met in January, Nicholls sought a further extension and the new date was set for 26 March. General elections were scheduled in three phases in February 1998 after the United Front government led by I.K. Gujral had collapsed. Thus by the next court date, a new government would be in place in New Delhi. Meanwhile, after surrendering to the police following the cancellation of his bail by the Supreme Court in December 1997, Taurani was again granted bail by the sessions court in February 1998. By then, it was absolutely clear that Nadeem would dwell at length upon him being made a scapegoat and not getting a fair trial in India, in addition to lampooning the evidence against him.

The Lok Sabha results were out and no single party managed to get a majority. But BJP's Atal Bihari Vajpayee-led alliance crossed the necessary 273 mark and he became the prime minister. Nadeem's case, however, continued to have an air of suspense over the final outcome. The prima facie test was turning out to be a semi-trial, and the crime branch was no longer talking about getting Nadeem in a matter of weeks!

Wisdom had dawned upon the Mumbai Police who made a huge push in the power corridors of Mantralaya to be allowed to hire private lawyers in extradition cases. This was partly due to the plans to get underworld figures like Dawood Ibrahim and Chhota Rajan extradited from the Middle East and South-East Asia, and partly from the bitter experience in the Nadeem case. Besides, the drubbing received in the Mirchi case was still raw.

The cops were particularly stung by the confidence shown by Ujjwal Nikam in getting a favourable order in November 1997, whereas all they got was scathing observations by the magistrate. Now, a year later, Nikam continued to do the rounds of Bow Street Magistrates' Court, and the prosecution faced the ignominy of being accused of delaying the case.

Nadeem had raised questions about getting a fair trial in India and that as a Muslim he was up against prejudice. The prosecution thus had to counter these serious charges, as they raised larger questions about the Indian state and the treatment meted out to the country's largest minority. The Mumbai Police had not anticipated that Nadeem would expand the ambit of the case and was caught off-guard.

The police became busy seeking opinions and pencilling in experts to challenge Nadeem's narrative. A force responsible to maintain law and order and detect and apprehend crime and criminals was thus forced to go beyond its domain. It was frustrating for the Mumbai Police that the London court was allowing Nadeem to move beyond the murder case by evoking religious discrimination and biased judiciary.

The case against Nadeem had four main witnesses—Mohammad Ali Shaikh, Arif Lakdawala, Keki Balsara and Taurani's driver Joseph Selvaraj. The prosecution's case was that Taurani and Nadeem carried Rs 25 lakh to an ice-cream parlour in Juhu where the cash was handed over to Arif Lakdawala and Keki Balsara according to Salem's instructions. Lakdawala and Balsara drove to Nagpada where they met and gave the money to shooters reporting to Salem.

According to Balsara's statement, he first came into contact with Salem in April 1996, due to a dispute with a person named

Mukhtar Ahmed over a plot near D'Monte Park, Bandra. Balsara had bought the plot in 1992, but Ahmed too claimed ownership for the same piece of prime land. In April 1996, Balsara received threats from the D Company and visited Dubai to sort out the dispute with Ahmed.

Balsara was assured by Salem that he would be paid Rs 75 lakh for handing over the land to Ahmed. On 27 June 1997, Salem called Balsara at his Bandra residence asking him to pick up Rs 25 lakh from Juhu. Balsara took his friend Lakdawala considering he had to take delivery of a large amount. Balsara was initially made to believe that the Rs 25 lakh that he was to pick up was supposed to be his first instalment.

Two boxes containing Rs 12 lakh and Rs 13 lakh, respectively, in cash were given to Balsara. Nadeem then called Salem from his mobile. 'Gulshan ka kaam kar do', Nadeem told Salem and gave the phone to Taurani who seconded what Nadeem told him earlier. After a few minutes, Balsara received a call from Salem who directed him to deliver the cash to his men at Sagar Hotel, Nagpada. Rather than an accomplice, the police saw it more prudent to make Balsara a key witness.

Balsara's testimony was damaging and clearly implicated both Nadeem and Taurani. But as Balsara's narrative had reference to calls made to Salem in Dubai, the only way to discredit his testimony was to get call details. Nadeem made an application to the sessions court in Mumbai seeking directions that Videsh Sanchar Nigam Limited (VSNL) and Maxtouch Cellular Phone Services be asked to provide records of phone calls made between January and August 1997. The calls records were for numbers belonging to him, Gulshan's brother Krishan Kumar, Ramesh Taurani, Arif Lakdawala and Keki Balsara. The sessions court rejected Nadeem's application.

While Henri Bradman and Clive Nicholls were holding the fort for Nadeem in Bow Street Magistrates' Court, Majeed Memon shuffled between Mumbai and London. Nadeem's aim was not just to block his extradition, but also clear his name in

India once the framing of charges was done. It was thus crucial that Bradman and Nicholls were kept up-to-date about the finer details of what transpired in the Mumbai courts.

On Monday, 14 December 1998, Memon was in the court in London. He had taken enough short trips since Nadeem first visited the Charing Cross police station in September 1997. The magistrate set the date for the trial in the week beginning 22 February 1999. The Maharashtra government had not taken kindly to the assertion that the Mumbai Police was biased against Muslims. Adding to their misery was the killing of Javed Fawda on 28 August 1997 by a team led by assistant police inspector Vasant Dhoble. The Samajwadi Party said that the person killed was not Fawda, who the police alleged had a role in Gulshan Kumar's murder, but an innocent peanut seller Abu Sayama. A.S. Aguiar, the principal sessions judge, conducted a probe and concluded in September 1998 that Sayama was not killed in the encounter as claimed by the police.

Before the February hearings, Nadeem's counsels had approached Home Secretary Jack Straw alleging that Nadeem would not get a fair trial in India and hence the extradition request be cancelled. Straw, however, declined to intervene and his office maintained that this was an issue for the courts to decide.

The hearings began in the last week of February 1999, and literally got lost in the melee of translations! 'It seemed it was magistrates in Bombay and not Nadeem going on trial,' wrote journalist Sanjay Suri for *Outlook* newsmagazine. The proceedings began with CPS barrister Paul Garlick, representing India, tracing the cracks in the relationship between Nadeem and Gulshan, which were said to have begun in 1997 after Nadeem's album *Hi! Ajnabi* flopped, and he blamed it on Gulshan.

The court was tied up in knots on the crucial issue of admissibility of the witness statements. Nicholls argued that the statements of six prosecution witnesses were inadmissible because the original statements were in Marathi and Hindi and what was presented before magistrate Christopher Pratt were in English. Nicholls's objection centred around the contention that the magistrate was not an expert and his translation must be dismissed as hearsay.

The statements were translated in English by a magistrate and Nicholls said there was no way to check the authenticity of the translated document. 'A magistrate's translation cannot be evidence as it is not on oath or affirmation and there is no statement as to his expertise,' said Nicholls. The defence demanded that the original copies in Hindi should be submitted.

Statements made by Gulshan's brother Krishan, his wife and Arif Lakdawala were given to the court. Gulshan's blood-stained clothes, pistol with live cartridges and bullets recovered from his body along with forensic evidence were also submitted. The most crucial of all was the statement of Mohammad Ali Shaikh, which Nicholls said should be dismissed as hearsay. It was Shaikh's witness statement that implicated Nadeem right from the alleged planning that happened in Dubai. The statement, attributed to Shaikh, and read out in court, recorded that he was in Dubai when Nadeem included him in the plan to eliminate Gulshan.

Nicholls regularly apprised the court that Shaikh had filed a writ petition in the Bombay High Court alleging that his statement was taken under duress. He also continued to highlight his underlying objection that as the witness statements were originally made in Hindi/Marathi, the prosecution by providing an English translation to the court, had not followed the norm. The original statements made in Hindi should have been produced, insisted Nicholls.

However, much as the defence wanted, the magistrate did not make any findings over the genuineness or unacceptability of the crucial evidence of Mohammad Ali Shaikh and others, except one. On 25 February 1999, the magistrate ruled that the evidence of Jyotidhar Desai, an employee of Gulshan Kumar who said that he received a call from Abu Salem who threatened Kumar and gave a telephone number for returning the call, was 'hearsay and inadmissible'. The magistrate observed: 'The caller could quite easily have been a disgruntled customer and to that extent, it seems to be irrelevant and progresses the matter not one instant.'

Nicholls then asked for permission to get the police witnesses flown down to London from India for cross-examination. Their strategy was simple and stemmed from the belief that the witnesses were either doctored or coerced into making statements that would implicate Nadeem. This was not a proposition which was to the prosecution's liking.

The non-admissibility of Desai's statement was a minor victory for Nadeem, especially as it came on the back of repeated pleadings by his lawyers that the prosecution was unnecessarily delaying the case. The Mumbai Police had a harrowing day assuring a section of the media that the London court had not rejected the witness statements presented by the prosecution, except Desai's. The magistrate, however, doubled the bail surety for Nadeem from £100,000 to £200,000—a substantial sum which was now inaccessible to him even as his legal bills kept mounting.

In the second week of March, the magistrate set a week-long window starting Monday, 10 May, for the case to progress. Keen to keep the case moving, the magistrate set a further date for Monday, 7 June. The adjournments and gaps were reflective of the requests made by the prosecution to get time for further preparation. The prosecution had contacted M.L. Pendse, former chief justice of Karnataka High Court and acting chief justice of Bombay High Court, and some reports suggest the veteran journalist Olga Tellis was also contacted to counter Nadeem's characterization of Mumbai Police as vindictive towards Muslims.

By the third week of April, the CPS filed the third set of documents of 755 pages. When the proceedings started in May, Garlick indicated to the court that a fourth set of documents would be submitted to the court. The defence was livid. They raised the objection that more than two years after Nadeem was arrested, the prosecution was still submitting documents.

And the fact that unlike the first two sets, the third set of documents was bulkier lent credence to the theory that the prosecution was deliberately delaying the case. The defence was annoyed that a fourth set of documents was on its way. Garlick

Courtesy of Danish and Ruhi Khan

4 December 2017: At 10 a.m., as everyone assembled in courtroom 1 at Westminster Magistrates' Court on the first day of the Vijay Mallya trial, the fire alarm rang, forcing everyone to evacuate the building. After a barrage of questions by the press, Mallya tried to make light of the situation with a joke, before he queued again to gain entry.

Courtesy of Danish and Ruhi Khan

5 December 2017: At the end of a long, gruelling day, Mallya could not resist a quick smoke before he left the court premises. Lunch was usually fast food—KFC burgers or pizzas—in a private room in the court and then he would emerge outside for a smoke. He told us that one positive outcome of attending the long court hearings was that he was forced to cut down on smoking.

The formidable Clare Montgomery QC (left) represented Vijay Mallya and now Nirav Modi. She also represented India in the trial of Hanif Patel. The petite barrister speaks with an authority that few possess as she forcefully confronts her opponents and politely challenges judges to think deeply on points of law.

Courtesy of Danish and Ruhi Khan

Courtesy of Danish and Ruhi Khan

Mallya has hired one of the sharpest legal minds in the UK on the extradition law—Anand Doobay of Boutique Law. Doobay also represents Nirav Modi. Doobay is reticent until you begin to discuss the finer points of law with him and then his passion for the profession, meticulousness and extensive knowledge on the subject shine through.

Crown Prosecution Service (CPS) barristers Mark Summers QC (left) and Aaron Watkins represented India in the Vijay Mallya trial. Summers was also the CPS barrister in Sanjeev Chawla's case. He has featured in important cases ranging from the 9/11 attacks, Madrid train bombings to spot fixing in cricket matches. Summers's calm demeanour changes to one of a firebrand barrister in the courtroom.

Courtesy of Danish and Ruhi Khan

Courtesy of Danish and Ruhi Khan

CBI's special director, Rakesh Asthana, made news outside and inside the courtroom. In our courtroom chats, Asthana would confidently tell us that whatever evidence the court demanded, he would ensure it was arranged and produced. One court hearing, however, proved fairly uncomfortable for Asthana, when Mallya's counsel raised questions on his professionalism, none of which were found convincing by the judge.

On 29 March 2019, Satyabrata Kumar, joint director, Enforcement Directorate, was in London for the Nirav Modi case (he has also attended all of Mallya's hearings) when it was announced that he was transferred. However, within a few hours, ED Director Sanjay Mishra revoked the transfer order. On several occasions, when the defence or judge raised questions and concerns, it was Kumar, always armed with a diary, who made quick notes and passed them on to the CPS team.

Courtesy of Danish and Ruhi Khan

Courtesy of Danish and Ruhi Khan

2 July 2019: The Mallyas had just emerged in the street opposite the Royal Courts of Justice after quickly grabbing lunch. What were the two so engrossed in on Sidharth's phone? Not the case in the high court, but the Cricket World Cup. India was playing Bangladesh at Edgbaston.

11 February 2020: Pinky Lalwani quietly slips out before Mallya makes an appearance and is thronged by the cameras. But she is constantly by Mallya's side on the court premises. Lalwani is often seen saying a quiet prayer or sharing a comforting look with her beau, and is Mallya's strongest ally in these troubling times.

Courtesy of Danish and Ruhi Khan

Courtesy of Danish and Ruhi Khan

13 February 2020: At the end of the three-day hearing, Mallya emerged with a cigarette between his fingers but did not light it. He said, out of consideration for the assembled journalists who were curious to know his gut feeling on the outcome of the appeal in the high court. 'After all the arguments in the Westminster Court, my gut said that I will win, but I didn't, so *gut se kya matlab hain.*'

Courtesy of Danish and Ruhi Khan

Overlooking Regent's Park in the heart of London lies Vijay Mallya's urban pad. With over thirty-five rooms, this property was big enough to generate interest for a private school, before it was snapped up by Mallya in 2007 and underwent four years of extensive refurbishment. Often, a couple of luxury cars from his extensive fleet can be spotted here. Many flaunt his signature nameplates.

Vijay Mallya's 30-acre estate is situated in the quaint village of Tewin on the outskirts of London. The property—Ladywalk and Bramble Lodge—includes a tennis court, swimming pool, gymnasium and several fairly large guest houses surrounded by open fields. Animal sculptures dot the grounds and the sound of cascading fountains with the chirping birds add to the melody of the quintessential English countryside where residents are often seen on horseback.

Courtesy of Danish and Ruhi Khan

Courtesy of Danish and Ruhi Khan

Vijay Mallya's canine housemates: golden retrievers Luna and Bella, Bichon lapdogs Elsa and Daisy, and a St Bernard, Spirit, are much loved and pampered. Promptly at 3 p.m., the dogs, each with their own dog walker, are off on their little stroll through the woods, though Bella is perhaps more interested in greeting us than accompanying her mates, even as Spirit lingers for her to catch up.

Courtesy of Danish and Ruhi Khan

Courtesy of Danish and Ruhi Khan

Nirav Modi pays a rent of £17,000 per month for his £8 million three-bedroom apartment at Centre Point in New Oxford Street. The thirty-three-storey tower has eighty-two luxury apartments that range from £1.8 million for a one-bed flat to £55 million for a two-storey five-bedroom penthouse. Modi's flat boasts of high-end luxury with gorgeous views of the central London skyline.

Nirav Modi got his flagship store on the supremely desirable Old Bond Street in February 2016 on a fifteen-year lease from a company registered in the British Virgin Islands, a tax haven. The property underwent massive renovations to house exquisite diamonds. A huge basement vault runs below the store. Modi was also suspected to be living on the top floor of the store before he moved to his luxury apartment nearby.

Courtesy of Danish and Ruhi Khan

Courtesy of Danish and Ruhi Khan

22 January 2019: Kaval Raijada faced extradition proceedings on serious charges of double murder, but that didn't make him mellow down. He had no qualms in showing his middle finger when he was photographed outside Westminster Magistrates' Court as his wife and co-accused Arti Dhir joined in for a smoke.

28 January 2020: Arti Dhir and Kaval Raijada leave the court premises for a quick lunch during the hearing in the high court. Raijada's behaviour was aggressive with the journalists, even with his legal team cautioning him against it. In her ruling, Chief Magistrate Emma Arbuthnot observed that the London Metropolitan Police could possibly investigate the couple as the planning for the alleged double murder was done in London.

Courtesy of Danish and Ruhi Khan

16 January 2020: The only image that the press had for many years of bookie Sanjeev Chawla was the one given to them by the cops from his pre-2000 days. Chawla seems to have mastered the art of hiding his face. He dodges the cameras with a rather dexterous deployment of a British broadsheet or with a muffler.

Courtesy of Danish and Ruhi Khan

16 October 2019: Iqbal Memon aka Mirchi had been living in the leafy Hornchurch suburb of London with his family since the 1990s. His sprawling six-bedroom detached home with a big garden now belongs to his second wife, Heena Kausar, daughter of Mughal-e-Azam director K. Asif. Over an egg-bhurji-paratha meal, Kausar shared her impressions of her husband on the condition that the camera would be kept away.

Courtesy of Danish and Ruhi Khan

September 2019: Ambassador Hotel in Mumbai hosted glitzy filmy parties and its revolving rooftop restaurant, The Pearl of the Orient, was the central attraction in the 1980s. The Narang brothers parted ways and the hotel is now a pale shadow of its former self, but remains a landmark. The two statues at the entrance, however, give an indication of the family's connection with art and antiques.

Courtesy of Danish and Ruhi Khan

Terry Adams was a much admired officer in the Bombay Police. When Mubarak Ali Ahmed was arrested by Scotland Yard in London, it was Adams who rushed to Britain to get him back. Adams retired as deputy commissioner of police in the 1950s. His son Terry 'Buddy' Adams (junior) got his Blue at the University of Oxford in boxing, a sport which Adams senior did much to popularize in Bombay. We thank Buddy for giving us this photo of his father.

The Bow Street Magistrates' Court in Covent Garden was synonymous with extradition cases in Britain until July 2006. Situated in a Graeco-Roman style building, a magistrate's office was established in 1740 and a decade later the first police station with the famous Bow Street Runners was established here. The extradition proceedings of Nadeem Saifi, Iqbal Memon, Manu Narang, Dharma Jayanti Teja and Mubarak Ali took place here.

Courtesy of Danish and Ruhi Khan

apprised the court of Justice Madhav Laxman Pendse's testimony, and was asked to ensure his presence when the case was next scheduled on 7 June.

Justice Pendse went to a school in Girgaum and studied at Wilson College. His evidence was supposed to give heft to the prosecution seeking to counter Nadeem's assertion of the police in Mumbai being anti-Muslim. On Monday, 7 June, he told the court that claims of obtaining confessions under duress were aberrations and 'few and far between'.

'You would be having similar aberrations in the London police,' said Justice Pendse in a riposte to Nicholls during a session of forensic cross-examination. Justice Pendse was the prosecution's rebuff to the witness statements of prominent lawyer Indira Jaising submitted by the defence. As regards the reports of organizations and bodies like Amnesty International and the US state department, Pendse said that they were too sweeping. Much of the cases cited in these reports were from the states of Jammu and Kashmir and Punjab where the situation was different than the rest of India, he told the court.

Pendse described as 'conjectures' when asked pointed questions by Nicholls on whether the Shiv Sena-BJP government in Maharashtra had an anti-Muslim bias. This assertion was a bit ironic as it was widely known that Nadeem shared a good relationship with the entire Thackeray clan. In fact, some political observers believed that Munde and Mendonca had shown undue haste in naming Nadeem as the prime suspect, as they feared that Bal Thackeray would shield him.

On 11 June 1997, a day before the infamous music show in Dubai, was the mahurat of Smita Thackeray's film. The entire clan led by Bal Thackeray was present. Nadeem was in Dubai but his video-recorded message was played at the mahurat. Subsequently, Anu Malik and Aadesh Shrivastava filled in for Smita Thackeray's film. Nadeem's video message might look a bit out of place, especially the circumstances under which Nadeem had his first brush with the Thackeray patriarch.

In 1993, a livid Mala Sinha—a popular Bollywood actress—had approached Bal Thackeray when all efforts to keep her daughter Pratibha away from Nadeem had failed. The Sinhas were not happy with their relationship, and the veteran actress knocked at Matoshree to rein in Nadeem. While what transpired when Nadeem was summoned is anybody's guess; both Thackeray and Nadeem accepted in later interviews that the Sena chief had intervened and the matter was resolved. That was in 1993, in the aftermath of the worst communal riots Mumbai had witnessed, and was the beginning of a close relationship between Nadeem and the Thackerays. Both Shravan and Shabnum, Nadeem's wife, were relieved that Nadeem was no longer involved with Pratibha who got the hugely popular *Pardesi Pardesi* number in *Raja Hindustani*, courtesy Nadeem.

But for now, Nadeem was singing a different tune to what he had composed for his popular 'I love my India' track for Subhash Ghai's *Pardes*. The entire force of the defence's argument was channelled to get the testimony of Shaikh declared ineligible by the magistrate. The intensity of the argument and the importance of Shaikh's statement throwing light on Nadeem's involvement meant that the magistrate had to rule whether the court would accept Shaikh's statement or not.

District Judge Christopher Pratt had to decide whether Shaikh's evidence passed muster under section 78 of the British Police and Criminal Evidence Act of 1984. This section says: 'In any proceedings the court may refuse to allow evidence on which the prosecution proposes to rely if it appears that having regard to all the circumstances, including the circumstances in which the evidence was obtained, the admission of such evidence would have such an adverse effect on the fairness of the proceedings that the court ought not to admit it.'

Shaikh had written a letter dated 25 September 1997 when he was in Thane Central jail. The letter expressed his willingness to make a confession before a magistrate. His letter was addressed to advocate R.B. Mokashi, asking him to facilitate the recording of confessions before a magistrate. Shaikh was promised a pardon in return for his testimony.

When the application for the grant of pardon came before the magistrate V.V. Palnitkar, he observed that in the absence of Shaikh's testimony, none of the co-accused in the Gulshan Kumar murder case could be convicted. The prosecution also had an affidavit by the Thane jail warden, Nana Wankhede, saying that Shaikh had written the letter in his own handwriting and in his presence.

Shaikh's confession pointed out that Nadeem was present in Dubai where the conspiracy to kill Gulshan Kumar was hatched. However, Shaikh retracted his confession and filed a petition in the Bombay High Court contending that the confessions were obtained by force. His petition was directed to the sessions court by the high court, but Shaikh knocked on the doors of the high court again after the sessions court turned down his plea.

On Monday, 30 June, the magistrate ruled that Shaikh's confession would be accepted by the court. 'I have come to the conclusion that the admission of a confession of Mohammed Ali Shaikh alias Chacha would not have such an adverse effect upon the fairness of these proceedings. I refuse to exclude it under section 78 of the British Police Evidence Act.' There was jubilation in the prosecution's camp. The magistrate had to now rule on whether the evidence produced by India, including Shaikh's confession, was good enough to warrant Nadeem's extradition.

Nicholls was now garnering headlines in the global media as he was defending the Chilean dictator, General Augusto Pinochet, from being extradited to Spain in the same Bow Street Magistrates' Court. Pinochet was facing a total of thirty-five charges ranging from sexual abuse to ordering killings between 1973 and 1990 during his reign. Pinochet's heinous crime fell into a category that meant he could be tried anywhere in the world—it didn't matter where they were committed. Nicholls was thus fighting to allow both Pinochet and Nadeem to remain in Britain, at the same time, and in the same court.

On Monday, 20 September 1999, Nicholls asked magistrate Pratt conducting Nadeem's trial that the case be dropped as there was 'insufficient evidence'. He described Shaikh's confession as 'worthless because of its inherent incredibility'. After the magistrate had ruled in July that Shaikh's confession would be accepted, it was assumed that it would be followed by a positive finding of a prima facie case against Nadeem.

On Tuesday, 21 September, the magistrate ruled: 'I am satisfied that there is sufficient evidence to justify a committal.'

Round one of the extradition battle was won by India, and coming as it did in the wake of serious allegations of impropriety, the prosecution led by Garlick and Nikam were doubly ecstatic. That an appeal would be made was a foregone conclusion, but Garlick was profoundly busy just after Pratt's ruling.

Not seeking to allow the defeat in Nadeem's case to affect him, less than a week later, Nicholls had to stand up for Pinochet. He told magistrate Ronald Bartle (who had thrown away Mirchi's case in 1995) that a former head of state could not be extradited in the absence of proper evidence. 'The responsibility, as opposed to a mere description of events, must be established by evidence. There is no such evidence and hence he is entitled to immunity,' Nicholls told the court. Pinochet's case was a landmark case for human rights across the globe. But it was Nadeem's case for which he had to eventually travel across the globe to India, to cross-examine the most important prosecution witness, Mohammad Ali Shaikh.

Nadeem made a request to the court that the bail surety amount of £200,000 be reduced, following which the magistrate reduced the bail surety to the original £100,000. The application was made to improve Nadeem's liquidity so that he could appeal in the high court. The magistrate's ruling had said: 'A properly directed tribunal could find Ali Shaikh's original evidence capable of belief.' Among other things, Nadeem's appeal was to convince the high court that this was wrong.

The appeal was filed at the high court in London, but the action had shifted to Mumbai. Pradeep Sawant, DCP, detection, had sought an appointment with B.P. Singh, the chief justice of the Bombay High Court, in the second week of July 2000 with an important missive. Based on an application by Nadeem, Justice Michael Burton of the Royal Courts of Justice in London had addressed a letter to Chief Justice Singh, which Sawant had to deliver.

'It is necessary for the purposes of justice and for due determination of the matters of dispute between the parties that you cause the witnesses who are within your jurisdiction to be examined,' read the letter from Justice Burton to Justice Singh. Nicholls and Garlick were coming to Mumbai to cross-examine Shaikh, his wife and their daughter.

Nadeem had requested the high court in London that Shaikh be examined on the limited issue of establishing the level of his literacy and whether he had indeed written the letter, in Hindi and signed in Urdu, to make a confession to his advocate B.R. Mokashi. Chief Justice Singh directed the sessions court to allow Shaikh's examination on Friday, 21 July 2000.

On Wednesday, Additional Sessions Judge Hemant Deshpande heard arguments from Nikam and Memon regarding the scope and outline of Shaikh's examination. Memon reiterated that Shaikh's examination was to be on the question of his literacy and neither the content of the letter nor the merit of the case would be discussed. Nikam was, however, opposed to any witnesses being examined. 'It was not permissible under the Indian law to examine any witness before the commencement of the main trial,' he argued.

Judge Deshpande ruled on Wednesday that as the charges were yet to be framed in the Gulshan Kumar murder case, it would not be possible to allow the examination of a crucial witness before the charges were framed. He, however, allowed that Shaikh's wife and daughter be examined. Garlick and Nicholls had arrived on Tuesday and got a taste of both the Indian judiciary and Mumbai's monsoons in ample measure.

The British counsels took over from where Nikam and Memon had left. At the centre of the examination was the question of the letter written by Shaikh in Hindi and signed in Urdu to his advocate B.R. Mokashi. The original letter was not produced in court as the prosecution said the letter was not with them. Shaikh was in Arthur Road Jail. On Wednesday, Judge Deshpande said that the Bombay High Court in consequence to the request from the London court had directed whether an examination of Shaikh could be done or not.

Shabnam agreed with Garlick that she had letters written to her by her father from prison. However, Nicholls countered saying that there was only one such letter and that too was written by a fellow prisoner. This was a direct counter by Nicholls to Garlick's assertion. For Nicholls not only disputed the number of letters Shaikh wrote to his daughter but also that the sole such letter from him was written by another inmate. Shabnam said the letter was at home. The judge asked if the letter could be produced but Garlick at the prodding of Nikam termed it not necessary as it would delay the proceedings.

Nicholls was not going to let it go so easily. He asked a pointed question to Shabnam over whether she herself had seen her father write in English or Hindi, apart from putting his signatures. Shabnam replied in the negative. This question was critical as Garlick had produced Shaikh's passport and embarkation and disembarkation cards which had Shaikh's signatures in English and were identified by Shabnam, who was subject to a two-hour session of questioning.

Shabnam's fluency in English facilitated her examination by Garlick and Nicholls. Both decided against putting Shaikh's frail and ailing wife in the dock and left it at Shabnam's examination. The transcript of Shabnam's evidence was to be forwarded to the high court in London. His daughter had identified Shaikh's signature but had also said that she had not seen him write anything except signing on documents.

So was Shaikh literate? Acutely aware that this remained an open-ended question, Nadeem, through Memon, filed an application in the Bombay High Court seeking to challenge

Sessions Judge Deshpande's order disallowing the examination of Shaikh. This last-ditch attempt to gather evidence directly from Shaikh, to add to the reams of documents before the high court hearing Nadeem's appeal, failed.

On Monday, 4 September, Justice Vishnu Sahai of the Bombay High Court rejected Nadeem's petition. The sessions court was correct in not allowing Shaikh's examination before the main trial. But strange are the ways of fate, and the judiciary. Just as the Bow Street Magistrates' Court was hearing Nadeem's extradition, all attempts by Shaikh to get redressal on his plea of being tortured to make a confession had failed.

Now on the back of Justice Sahai's refusal to allow Shaikh's examination, the high court had decided to turn his letter into a criminal petition. Shaikh had written to the high court's registrar on 29 September 1999 that he was forced to turn approver by the police. The letter went on to say that he was picked up on 25 August 1997 (thirteen days after Gulshan Kumar's murder) along with a few others and had been in jail ever since.

The police had promised him a taxi and a house and had also given money to his family on three occasions since his arrest. He thus gave statements as asked by the police under pressure and threats to his and his family's well-being. This letter was written in Marathi and was signed in Urdu along with the signature of S.M. Sonawane, the jailer of Byculla prison. This development quickly found its way to Nadeem's pleadings being prepared in London by the team led by Nicholls.

After a long-drawn-out legal battle that reached the House of Lords, Nicholl's most famous client Augusto Pinochet was to be extradited to Spain. But in March 2000, the British home secretary, Jack Straw, the final authority, ordered Pinochet's release and return to Chile despite vigorous objections by organizations like Amnesty International and others. Straw had chosen to ignore the House of Lords' decision to extradite Pinochet.

In September 2000, when Straw visited India at the invitation of Home Minister L.K. Advani, it was expected that he would raise the question of British national and arms dealer Peter Bleach who was languishing in a jail in Calcutta. Bleach was arrested in the sensational 1995 Purulia arms drop case along with others.

In February 2000, Bleach and five Latvians were given life imprisonment by a court in Calcutta after being convicted of dropping an arms cache from an aircraft in Purulia. In July 2000, all the other accused were granted a pardon by President K.R. Narayanan after his Russian counterpart Vladimir Putin had threatened to cancel a later visit to India.

Now the pressure was on Straw to get the Yorkshire-born Bleach released as well. This was compounded after Bleach's aged mother told the media in England that she had more faith in the Indian President, whom she had directly written to, than the British government. If the Latvians could be freed, then why not a Briton?

Also on Straw's schedule was a visit to Mumbai's principal mosque, the Jama Masjid. It was built and maintained by Konkanis, a community to which Nadeem belonged. Now one of their most famous sons was involved in a case for extradition. All Straw was prepared to say when asked about the delay in Nadeem's case was that there was the need to improve our over-complicated procedures.

On Monday, 22 November 2000, Nicholls and Garlick made their way to the court of Lord Justice Rose and Justice Newman at the Royal Courts of Justice. It was the first of the scheduled four-day hearing. Nicholls had challenged the lower court's decision on five grounds. It was agreed during the trial at the Bow Street Magistrates' Court, by both Garlick and Nicholls, that Shaikh's confession was crucial evidence that established Nadeem's involvement in Gulshan Kumar's murder.

The first two grounds were both related to Shaikh's confession. Nicholls told the court that Shaikh's evidence was inadmissible in extradition proceedings as it was the English translation and not the original given in Hindi which was provided to the magistrate. Shaikh's evidence thus should have been excluded under section 78 of the Police and Criminal Evidence Act, 1984, was the second ground.

The third ground was that the evidence provided was insufficient and the magistrate's analysis of it was inadequate as well. The fourth ground was that the charges against Nadeem were made in bad faith and hence it would be oppressive to extradite him. The fifth and last ground was that if extradited, Nadeem would face a prejudiced trial because of his religion.

Nicholls stressed on the importance of having Shaikh's evidence in Hindi rather than just its English translation. To buttress his point he highlighted a major discrepancy in the transcript of a telephone conversation between Gulshan and a newspaper editor on 9 August 1997, just a few days before the murder. This discussion referred to threats made to Gulshan, but unlike the original Hindi transcript, the English translation given to the court contained a reference to Nadeem!

Nicholls told the court that there was a fine line between an authenticated document and its admissibility. Shaikh's evidence, said Nicholls, was indeed properly authenticated but it was (the English translation of the evidence in Hindi) a 'product of non-independent, unchallengeable translation from Hindi by the Indian magistrate or his clerk'.

The magistrate had also failed to make findings of several disputed matters which were germane to the case, said Nicholls. He then went on to detail at great length the chronology of Shaikh's arrest and incarceration to point out that if the magistrate had gone into the details—the foisting of advocate Mokashi who was compliant with the Mumbai Police on Shaikh, the allegations of torture and claim of innocence that Shaikh made on several occasions when produced before magistrates after his arrest—the decision would have been different.

Nicholls referred to the 'introduction of Javed Fawda as a co-conspirator' at a much later stage by Shaikh in his confession, which reflected the urge by the Mumbai Police to use him as a convenient ploy to implicate individuals in the murder of Gulshan. Fawda was later killed in an encounter with the police. The findings of Judge Aguiar, that Fawda was not involved in the murder of Gulshan, were also discussed.

Judge Aguiar's conclusions were overturned by the Bombay High Court, but the defence did not fail to point out the lacunae in the latter's findings. While Judge Aguiar had concluded that Fawda was shot from close range, the Bombay High Court accepted eyewitness accounts from cops that Fawda was shot at from a distance. In doing so, Nadeem's defence apprised the high court in London that expert forensic evidence had found the fatal shot was fired within a distance of one or two feet, but this was ignored.

Garlick's measured counter-arguments signified a pragmatic response to Nicholls. He was aware of the intensity of the feelings in his camp, especially the references to torture and intimidation, and the intense discussions on how Nadeem would not get a fair trial as he was a Muslim. What had particularly irked the prosecution were the three reports by Prof. Martin Lau averring that the Mumbai Police was biased against Muslims.

But this was neither the forum nor the occasion for Garlick to win a battle of narratives. His brief was to deliver Nadeem from the safe confines of London to the Mumbai Police. Without seeking to 'diminish the significance of the human rights complaints', he addressed the court that these complaints must be looked at in reference to Nadeem's case. Besides, he told the court that there had been a change of government in both India and the state of Maharashtra.

Garlick contested that under the extradition proceedings there was any requirement to present evidence in the language of the witness. He compared the situation to a magistrate in Wales, saying that just as a Welsh-speaking magistrate would translate evidence taken in Welsh into English without any assistance, a magistrate in India too could take evidence in the local language and translate it into English.

On the reliability of Shaikh's confession, Garlick submitted that two credible witnesses, a prison officer and advocate Mokashi, had given evidence on its authenticity. In any case, should Nadeem be extradited, all the contested aspects relating to Shaikh's confession would go through judicial scrutiny. Nadeem was a well-known and prominent music director, besides in the wake of large-scale publicity to the case, the police and the judiciary would be all the more careful to proceed properly.

In seeking to counter the grounds raised by Nicholls, Garlick was not averse to draw his arguments from where Nicholls had left off, even at the risk of appearing to be conceding grounds. An impartial, competent, vigilant judiciary in India, Garlick pointed out, would provide the proper balance to allegations that the accusation against Nadeem was made in bad faith. Besides, Garlick also reminded the court that there was a possibility that it could be Judge Aguiar who could try Nadeem if he returned to Mumbai.

After four days of intense arguments, analogies and references to cases which were as imaginative and wide-ranging as the likely conduct of a Welsh magistrate to Mumbai's Srikrishna Commission and to whether some officers of the Kingdom of Saudi Arabia were entitled to sovereign immunity or not, the court declared that it would give the judgment before Christmas.

At the high court in London, a divisional bench of Deputy Chief Justice Rose and Justice Newman delivered on 21 December 2000 a judgment that was as much about the exoneration of Nadeem as an indictment of the unprofessional approach of the Mumbai Police. Terming Shaikh's confession worthless, the high court noted that the magistrate had not 'considered all the circumstances of the original confession and the ambit and character of the retraction'. Had the judgment limited itself to technicalities or generic issues like poor conditions in prison or lack of medical facilities, it would have provided some scope for the Mumbai Police to salvage its image.

Justice Rose castigated Ronnie Mendonca, Mumbai Police commissioner, for naming Nadeem in a press conference in September 1997 as being involved in the Gulshan Kumar murder even though there was no 'legally admissible material available'. 'The assertion of the Mumbai Deputy Chief Minister (sic)

gives rise to like concern,' the judgment noted, weighing why
the request for extradition was not made in good faith or in the
interest of justice.

Nadeem had secured a huge victory riding on the reputation of
the Mumbai Police. The depth of humiliation the Mumbai Police
suffered in the British court lies buried in the case files in the archives
that will not be open to public scrutiny for some more decades.

'The appearance of misbehaviour by the police in pursuing their
inquiries and the significant risk that the activities surrounding that
misbehaviour have so tainted the evidence as to render a fair trial
impossible,' the high court declared. The only consolation was that
the divisional bench did not agree that Nadeem was at risk of being
prejudiced because he was a Muslim. The bad faith which guided
the accusation was not, ruled the court, because of a religious basis
or motive.

Nadeem would remain on residential bail while Indian
government appealed to the House of Lords against this high
court judgment. But while his passport would not be returned, the
court exempted him from reporting to the police and waived the
£200,000 surety.

'For me this has been a great victory, but a terrible experience
which nobody should have to endure,' Nadeem told the press soon
after the verdict. 'Only my music, my family, the support of my
friends and lawyers as well as my love for the people of India to
whom, I pray, I will safely return one day, have sustained me.'

Nadeem's exoneration led to a media blitzkrieg by Majeed
Memon and Ujjwal Nikam in Mumbai. Both Memon and Nikam
flew to London on more than twenty occasions and were effectively
the main sources for the happenings in the London court for
journalists who were in India.

The case had become too big for India to not take it to the
House of Lords. Despite the rather scathing observations by the
high court, an appeal was lodged. Experts had already opined that
there was not much of a chance for India, but further humiliation
was on the way.

Three months after the high court decision, the House of Lords rejected India's appeal and that was the end of the road for the Mumbai Police, their hopes to bring back Nadeem to face trial in India had truly crashed and burnt.

As Nadeem had not secured legal aid and had borne the cost of his legal team including Majeed Memon's twenty-two visits to the UK, the UK government paid Rs 6.7 crore to Nadeem as part of his litigation charges. Erroneous press reports in the Indian press that attributed this amount to be paid by the Indian taxpayer, created much hue and cry. However as per the extradition arrangements, the cost of litigation is borne by the home country—in this case the UK.

The most shocking declaration in this case came much later—on 22 October 2014—in an unrelated event. The House of Lords select committee on extradition law had gathered at 10:30 a.m. in the chambers to listen to three expert witnesses, Daniel Steinberg, Ben Keith and Paul Garlick QC, all notable legal minds with decades of experience in extradition law on their views regarding human rights concerns.

Lord Inglewood, who was the chair of the committee—comprising Lord Brown of Eaton-Under-Heywood, Lord Empey, Baroness Hamwee, Lord Hussain, Baroness Jay of Paddington, Lord Jones, Lord Mackay of Drumadoon, Lord Rowlands and Baroness Wilcox—had asked the barristers how a swift and efficient extradition process allowed for the examination of human rights concerns. In his evidence, Garlick recalled his experience working as the CPS barrister representing India on Nadeem's extradition case.

'During the course of a lengthy extradition hearing, where we had to take evidence in India, it did become abundantly clear that the application—which on paper looked faultless—was being made in bad faith by the Mumbai Police,' Garlick told the committee.

The comment was of course made in his effort to help lawmakers understand how compatible the process of extradition was with human rights concerns. Nadeem is perhaps not even aware that Garlick finished his sentence by saying: 'Fortunately, although I was for the prosecution, the High Court refused extradition.'

Could there have been a more scathing remark against the Mumbai Police's investigations in Nadeem's extradition case?

* * *

India remains out of bounds for Nadeem as the Mumbai Police did not drop the case against him. As late as 2007, the Mumbai Police opposed the petition of Nadeem's father in the Bombay High Court seeking a passage to India for his son. Nadeem's goodwill and the support of his partner Shravan ensured a steady stream of work while he remained in the UK. Producers would fly over to London for meetings with Nadeem, a practice that continued since the musician was stuck in London. Nadeem-Shravan gave some hits like *Dhadkan*, *Kasoor*, *Ek Rishta: The Bond of Love* and *Raaz* after the extradition battle was over, but they were past their prime. Offers dried up and in 2005, the pair split.

Shravan is now concentrating on establishing his sons in Bollywood. Nadeem has moved to Dubai and runs his perfume business—Arabian Attars and Just Sheesha and makes music videos featured on YouTube. In 2015, on a business visit to the UK, he met journalist Nabanita Sircar at a café in London and lamented on the cases against him in India. 'I am not an absconder. I have faced justice and been exonerated,' he told Sircar, boldly adding that he was 'not afraid to go back to India' but was being respectful to his mother who at one point 'put a *kasam* on him' (made him swear) to not return because 'he wouldn't get justice in India'.

The case in India continued. After the huge media presence when the stars were called to the crime branch, it was inevitable that they would do the court run as well. In November 2001, eight months after the House of Lords' verdict, Shah Rukh Khan, Salman Khan and Chunky Pandey were summoned as prosecution witnesses at the Mumbai sessions court. Shah Rukh Khan did not turn up due to a pressing professional engagement and had accordingly informed Nikam. Judge Tahilyani did not take the superstar's absence kindly and stated that he could issue a bailable warrant against him. At this point, Nikam asked that Shah Rukh Khan be discharged as his evidence was not going to be of much use for the prosecution.

Pandey bore much of Nikam's brunt and was in the dock for close to two hours. He declined giving a statement to the police that he knew Abu Salem or had attended a party in Dubai where the conspiracy to kill Gulshan was hatched. At one point, Nikam sternly told Pandey that the actor was in an actual courtroom and not on a stage. Nikam declared him hostile and asked whether he had any animosity towards the Mumbai Police.

Salman Khan, though called into the witness box, was spared the examination as Nikam told the court that he did not want to add to the list of hostile witnesses. The Gulshan Kumar trial in Mumbai had all the filmy trappings. After the drubbing in the UK courts, superstars being declared hostile did not bode well for the police's case in Mumbai as well.

The same month, Judge Tahilyani visited the spot where Gulshan was shot dead. He travelled in a bulletproof car for a thirty-minute inspection. The judge visited the Shiv temple; Shiva Hair cutting saloon where the alleged Salem shooters were waiting for Gulshan; the hut where Gulshan pleaded for his life and the coconut tree from where one of the witnesses had seen the murder. Around forty witnesses had appeared in the case and the judge wanted to verify their depositions by taking a look himself. It was Majeed Memon who had made an application for an inspection of the murder spot which was agreed to by the prosecution.

At the end of the trial, the court acquitted eighteen out of the nineteen accused in the case. In April 2002, Judge Tahilyani dismissed the conspiracy theory and rejected six key charges of conspiracy for want of evidence. Abu Salem, Nadeem Saifi and Salem's aide Abdul Qayyum were declared absconding and only Abdul Rauf Dawood Merchant was pronounced guilty. Rauf was given a life sentence on two counts; one for killing Gulshan Kumar and the second for attempting to kill Gulshan's driver Roop Lal. The nature of the conspiracy and the identity of the conspirators has not been established.

Earlier, on the morning of 26 June 2001, Balsara was found dead in a toilet at the Mumbai Police headquarters. It later transpired that he was summoned by the crime branch to brief him about the Gulshan Kumar murder trial. Doctors at the nearby GT Hospital, where Balsara was taken, said he had died of a heart attack, but his family members were sceptical.

But the bigger mystery was the disappearance of Taurani's driver Joseph Selvaraj. Selvaraj was believed to have overheard an incriminating conversation between Taurani and Nadeem. Mohammad Ali Shaikh turned hostile in 1998. After Shaikh, it was the testimony of Arif Lakdawala that was crucial for the prosecution. Lakdawala claimed that he had dialled Salem's number for Taurani to speak. Majeed Memon turned it upside down saying that Gulshan's brother Krishan Kumar too had dialled the same number, and Lakdawala who had a connection with Dawood Ibrahim could not be relied upon. Lakdawala's testimony was discarded by the court since his role was more of an accomplice. Adik Shirodkar had argued that Lakdawala was an accomplice of Salem and his evidence could not be the basis for a conviction.

But controversy has not left Nadeem. In the last few years, media has flashed news discussing Nadeem's links with members of the underworld. Gulshan Kumar's brother Krishan alleged that Salem threatened him to offer work to Nadeem. At regular intervals, Nadeem has made emotional appeals of hoping to visit India, but in the absence of the case against him being taken back, he can't unless he is ready to face incarceration.

6

TERROR TIGER

A sixteenth-century mosque that had stood erect for more than four centuries became the topic of many heated debates and discussions in the early 1990s, when members of the right-wing Rashtriya Swayamsevak Sangh (RSS) and Vishva Hindu Parishad (VHP) alleged that Mughal emperor Babur erected the mosque on the exact location of Hindu deity Lord Ram's birthplace after destroying a temple that once stood there.

RSS is the ideological power centre for the Hindutva groups including the political Bharatiya Janata Party (BJP). On 6 December 1992, over 1.5 lakh RSS and VHP *'karsevak'* cadres and supporters, following the war cry of BJP leader Lal Krishna Advani, joined the *rath yatra* (march) to Ayodhya, to 'reclaim' the land of one of the most popular 'Indian' deities.

The entire nation was glued to their television sets; many gathered together on the roadside listening to the radio broadcast with trepidation. This was unprecedented and everyone waited with bated breath to know how this would unfold.

As the yatra neared its destinations, the sloganeering grew louder and fears stronger. Policemen and volunteers stood guarding the mosque. Journalists and photographers stood on the fourth floor of a building overlooking the mosque, recording history in the making. Around noon, the mob turned threatening, broke through the police cordon and started attacking the volunteers and even the press.

As the mob picked up their iron rods, shovels, axes and rocks and began breaking through the 400-year-old structure, riots broke out.

The centuries-old Babri Masjid was demolished to reclaim that land for the Hindus and construct a grand Ram *mandir* (temple). This sparked off several clashes across the country between the Hindus and the Muslims. Headlines in Indian newspapers shouted of 'a betrayed nation', calling the event a 'national shame' as the government failed to defend the shrine even with the country's apex court opposing any destruction to the mosque and BJP leaders promising to abide by the Supreme Court's diktat.

To Hindus, the destruction of the mosque was to correct the perceived wrong done to the Indians by the foreign Mughal rulers; for the Muslims, it was a direct attack on their religion and identity as a minority in India.

The country was consumed in communal riots, the worst of which were in Mumbai where 900 people were killed, most of them from the Muslim community. While the focus was largely on the metropolitan commercial capital of India, the small trading town of Surat in Gujarat too witnessed brutal violence. Irfan Engineer writes in the *Economic and Political Weekly* (EPW) in 1994 that 'hundreds of people belonging to the minority Muslim community were done to death in an extremely cruel manner, women were subjected to repeated rapes and were humiliated by hoodlums of organized communal outfits like BJP, VHP, Shiv Sena and Bajrang Dal'. He goes on to write that 'Muslims provided the necessary spark by giving a bandh call to protest' against the Babri Masjid demolition and by 'indulging in violence either due to anger or frustration'. According to him, each side was using the riots to garner support for the upcoming elections in the state.

Calling it a 'nightmarish day' (7 December 1992), Kalpana Shah, Smita Shah and Neha Shah, who interviewed fifty-nine Muslim and Hindu victims of the Surat riots for *Manushi*, a women's bi-monthly journal, show how the city 'swiftly degenerated into a free-for-all as lumpen and communal elements stepped in to let loose an orgy of bloodletting and brutality'. They argue that between 7 and 12 December, anarchy and lawlessness prevailed as the police force was inadequate and highly communalized and even the government machinery failed to provide rescue and relief during the peak of the mayhem.

Even when the army took over the policing of the city and the riots subsided, the city continued to simmer as the death toll, injuries and brutality became the news. Migrant workers returned to their villages as factories were destroyed and production came to a halt. Businesses suffered, houses were damaged and many suffered from extreme trauma of the events that unfolded during the riots, the scars of which ran deep.

The chasm between the Hindus and Muslims only got wider resulting in two events that once again shook the fabric of Surat:

28 January 1993. It was a breezy morning as workers and traders hurried with their business at the Mini Hira Bazaar (mini diamond market) along Varachha Road in Surat. This was also a high impact site during the riots and was only just beginning to see normalcy return. But not for long. Twin grenades were thrown near Sadhna school near the market. As hell broke loose, one eight-year-old schoolgirl Alpa Patel was killed, and eleven more were injured including another young student Jigna Pansuria.

22 April 1993. A loud bang thundered at the busy Surat railway station. Russian grenades were thrown at the Gujarat Express stationed on platform 1. While no lives were lost, thirty-eight people sustained injuries.

The grenades were alleged to be part of a cache of arms diverted to Surat by an Ahmedabad gangster Abdul Latif. Police arrested twenty-seven people in the two cases. All of them were let off by the special Terrorist and Disruptive Activities (Prevention) Act (TADA) court two years later for lack of evidence.

But just when it seemed the blast cases met with a dead-end, another arrest was made almost a decade later, which then spiralled into further arrests shedding new light on the modus operandi and perpetrators of the blasts.

* * *

On 12 March 1995, the Umra police arrested fifty-two-year-old Kharva Chawl resident Mushtaq Patel who apparently confessed to his involvement in the two blasts during one drunken stupor. Patel claimed that the cops picked him up for possessing a revolver without a licence while he was on a family holiday on Surat's Dumas beach. Days later, he was declared an accused in the railway blast case.

On 14 March 1995, Keshubhai Patel of the BJP took oath as Gujarat's chief minister. On 19 March, the eleven-member special investigative team led by police commissioner Sudhir Sinha, and his deputy Pravin Sinha, formed to probe this case after Patel's claims, arrested a prominent Congress leader and former Gujarat minister Mohammad Surti who they claimed procured hand grenades from the underworld and planned the two attacks.

Nine more arrests followed, including members of the local Congress party, along with the recovery of arms and ammunition. Six foreign grenades, two AK-47 rifles and 199 live cartridges were found on them. Those arrested included Hussein Ghadially, Iqbal Wadivala, Salim Chawal, Ahsan Ismail Patel, Aziz Ibrahim Patel, Mehboob alias Baba Ibrahim Mastar, Fazal Dawood Nagori and Saeed Nadi alias Abdul Saeed Abdul Majid Navdiwala. In 2000, one Yusuf Dadu was also arrested. They all languished in jail until 2001 when they were granted bail.

They were all charged for the blasts at both Varachha Road and Surat railway station. The stringent TADA provisions were applied to them. The police also extracted confessional statements from the accused which the defence claimed were given under duress.

On 4 October 2008, after a rigorous trial where over 150 witnesses had deposed followed by two months of study of the material evidence, the TADA court judge R.P. Dholadia sentenced

Mohammad Surti, Hussein Ghadially, Iqbal Wadivala, Mushtaq Patel and Yusuf Dadu to twenty years' imprisonment. Surti, Ghadially and Wadivala were slapped with a fine of Rs 2 lakh each while Patel was asked to pay Rs 1 lakh and Dadu, Rs 50,000. Salim Chawal and Ahsan Ismail Patel were awarded ten years' imprisonment while Asif Bashir Sheikh, Aziz Ibrahim Patel, Baba Mastar, Fazal Nagori and Saeed Nadi were released due to lack of evidence.

The family of Alpa Patel who lost her life in the Varachha road blast was given a compensation of Rs 2.1 lakh while one Pravin Gandalal who lost his eye was given Rs 25,000. Those injured were given compensation of Rs 11,000 each.

Other men the police identified as involved in the blasts were found to be absconding. Surti's son Farooq was one of them. He is believed to be in Pakistan. Others the police were searching for included Salim Lala alias Salim Abdul Hamidlal and Gazanavi alias Gajno Mohammad Betwala, Ahmedabad Rasul Pati alias Yakubkhan Pathan, Abdul Latif and Hanif Patel alias Tiger.

* * *

Tiger Hanif was a small-time textile trader operating out of Ved Road, which like Varachha Road had seen some brutal atrocities during the riots. As several houses were set on fire, lives were lost and possessions destroyed, many in the vicinity were made homeless and destitute. A relief camp in the Ranitalao area was set up by Tiger along with Surti, Ghadially and Wadivala. They also created a makeshift office next to the camp to hold their meetings.

The genesis of this camp lies in the heightened communal feelings created post the Babri Masjid demolition. According to investigators, Tiger and his mates nurtured feelings of betrayal by the government and the police during the riots which disproportionately affected Muslim lives. In a bid to protect the Muslim community and to hit back at the majority Hindu community, Tiger and his allies decided to use the camp to arm themselves and others seeking shelter there. It began by collecting weapons like iron rods, swords, firearms and country-made bombs but soon they decided to import better weapons from a notorious Ahmedabad gangster, Abdul Latif, who was operating from Dubai. Eventually, Latif was arrested by the police and even produced in court but was killed in an encounter by the cops.

Tiger had also set up a fund to collect monetary donations. These donations, the cops believe, were used to procure weapons to carry out the blasts seen as revenge for the riots. According to the police, Hussein Ghadially and his wife, and Iqbal Wadivala went to Ahmedabad in a Maruti van (GJ 5A 5178) with their driver Bhupat Makwana. A concealed compartment was created in the vehicle into which a cache of arms and ammunition including grenades, AK-47 rifles and cartridges were loaded and brought into Surat and were then quickly distributed to various locations to be used in carrying out attacks.

The police claim that Tiger is no stranger to crime. He is believed to be a close aide of underworld don Dawood Ibrahim, prime accused in the 1993 bombings in Bombay, which followed the Babri Masjid demolition and the riots that ensued. Hundreds of innocent lives were lost in carefully synchronized attacks on Mumbai's iconic and busy locations.

Tiger's association with the D-gang goes back to the days when Dawood was a smuggler living in Bombay. Tiger handled the don's smuggling operations in Gujarat, whose rugged coastline was used to land contraband including drugs and arms. The police believed that as Dawood moved away from smuggling to terrorism, Tiger followed suit and is privy to crucial information about terror organizations like Lashkar-e-Taiba and their association with the Indian underworld.

As the police began making arrests in the Surat bombings and closing in on Tiger, he quickly escaped the country. He was believed to have fled to Pakistan. An Interpol Red Notice was issued. Yet for seventeen years, no one knew where Tiger was hiding.

On 16 February 2010, a team of Scotland Yard officials in armour and guns swooped in on an address in Astley Street, in an otherwise quiet neighbourhood of Halliwell, Bolton. They walked out with a forty-nine-year-old seemingly docile and timid man. Neighbours could not fathom what the man who lived a quiet life and worked as a greengrocer at Barkat Enterprises in Derby Street, Daubhill, could have done to bring the heavy arm of the law down on him.

No wonder when news broke that Hanif Patel was the most-wanted fugitive 'Tiger', suspected of masterminding the bomb blast in Surat in India in 1993, killing an eight-year-old schoolgirl and injuring many more, it was received with both shock and disbelief. That he had successfully evaded the law for seventeen years was something none could fathom.

When India intimated Interpol on Tiger, his photograph and description under the name Tiger Hanif were circulated to nations across the world, but this Patel from Bolton had dropped the honorific Tiger from his name when he entered the UK. He was now simply Mohammed Hanif Umerji Patel.

* * *

Headlines across India shouted that '1993 Surat blast accused held in UK'. UK newspapers, both local and national, ran stories on his arrest with varying degrees of shock and angst. 'Grocer held on terror charges' shouted the local *Bolton News*. 'Terror suspect Hanif Patel faces extradition to India' read the BBC headlines.

On 11 May 2010, Hanif (Tiger) Patel was granted bail on a personal surety of £50,000 and others providing sureties of £2,00,000. He had to give up his passport, reside in his house and not leave Lincolnshire except to meet his lawyers and with consent.

Two days later, India swiftly appealed to the high court against the district judge's decision to grant Patel bail. The CPS argued that the charges against Patel were severe and that his alleged terrorist offences had cost many lives. Also, since Patel had escaped from India, they argued that he was a flight risk. Lord Justice Patrick Elias and Justice Brian Keith heard the case in the high court.

Justice Elias observed that Patel had been living in the UK since 1996 and 'has lived an apparently unblemished life in that time in a house in Bolton'. The judge was convinced that Patel had been known to the authorities throughout because until 2004, he had to report to the police once a month, till he received leave to remain in the UK. 'We have been shown his application for asylum, which was made in July 1996, where he told the British authorities that he was being accused of these serious offences but which he denied,' he said.

What worked in Patel's favour was that the British authorities had been well aware of his presence in the UK and he had not sought to conceal from them the fact that he had been accused of these offences. Also, his strong roots in Bolton, where his family and friends reside, served as a deterrent for his escape. The court refused India's appeal and agreed that bail would simply continue on the basis of the conditions which were imposed by the district judge.

The extradition hearing continued in Westminster Magistrates' Court, albeit with Patel out on bail, much to India's consternation. And Patel had a fair share of support. People from his locality in Greater Manchester travelled to London to give him moral support.

The CPS, on behalf of India, argued that Patel had set up the relief camp post the Surat riots to secure donations to buy grenades to carry out the revenge blasts in Surat. A witness statement was produced in court, allegedly written by Hussein Ghadially, in which he had confessed to a meeting with Patel and two others. 'It was agreed by this defendant and three other witnesses that the fund would be employed to buy weapons . . . for revenge,' CPS barrister Clare Montgomery told Westminster Magistrates' Court in October 2010.

Patel's team argued that the confessions of those arrested in India in the case had been gained through third-degree torture during the interrogations. Montgomery further explained how the plan was to throw a live grenade into a busy market on 27 January but it had to be aborted due to police presence. It was carried out the next day and an eight-year-old schoolgirl was killed. She also told the court that the grenade attack at the railway station was to disrupt a planned rally of Hindu *sadhus* (religious men) but 'mercifully no one was killed'.

Patel was also alleged to have given cash, weapons and a fake passport to help one of the conspirators escape. Patel, who arrived in Britain in 1996 and gained citizenship in 2005, speaks only Gujarati, Urdu and Hindi, and could only tell the court his name and date of birth, a mandatory requisite before every hearing, after the request was translated by his interpreter.

He was represented by power-house legal firm Birnberg Peirce and Partners who have successfully represented several high-profile terror-related cases, including the Guildford Four and the Birmingham Six, wherein Irishmen who were convicted for bombings in England in 1975 were eventually let off after long legal campaigns; the family of Jean Charles de Menezes who was shot dead at a tube station in London in a terrorism raid gone awry; and Guantanamo Bay detainee Moazzam Begg and Shaker Aamer. Patel is one of the many terror suspects whose cause the determined human rights lawyer Gareth Peirce has taken up, as Patel fears torture and threat to life if extradited to India.

Patel's counsel Ben Cooper told the court: 'There is a real issue concerning torture. In his case, there is an abuse of process submission. The offences alleged date back to 1993 and arise out of a factually complex political background in India.'

Patel's legal team had opposed his extradition on the grounds that he would be tortured in India, but the district judge dismissed them calling him a 'classic fugitive'. Judge Evans said that even before leaving India, Patel was aware of police interest in him, and it is accepted he fled India in breach of his bail condition and to avoid arrest on these terrorism charges. He also did not believe that Patel was tortured and considered it to be a likely false claim. 'Most probably the claim is only advanced in an attempt to defeat this extradition request. His credibility is therefore seriously compromised.'

The trial court was also given a witness statement by Maninder Pawar, deputy commissioner of police, Surat crime branch, which stated that the other co-accused had made allegations of torture and violence. These facts were brought by them before the court in Gujarat and police officers were cross-examined. The court, however, rejected the allegations of torture and ill-treatment. In the case of Patel, Pawar stated that he would be in judicial custody on arrival in India and the police would have to take the court's permission to interrogate him.

Even a plea to evoke the passage of time did not alter the judge's decision. 'He travelled to England arriving on 16 February 1996. On 8 May 1996 he claimed asylum . . . On the face of it that brief historical account renders any submission under section 82 of the Act quite hopeless.'

On 2 May 2012, District Judge Evans ordered Hanif Patel to be extradited to India. The secretary of state signed the order on 26 June. On 9 July, he approached the high court to appeal against his extradition.

* * *

A two-day hearing took place in the high court on 28 February and 1 March 2013 before Lord Justice Alan Moses and Justice Kenneth Parker. In the high court, CPS's barrister Julian Knowles told the court that the attacks 'formed part of the ongoing violence between Muslims in India' and the Bolton grocer was involved in the 'revenge attacks'.

The 1993 bomb blasts masterminded by underworld don Dawood Ibrahim, now a fugitive in Pakistan, were widely believed to be 'revenge' for the destruction of Babri Masjid by right-wing Hindutva factions and the riots that followed. Knowles told the court that 'it is alleged the bomb blasts were revenge attacks for previous attacks, undertaken by Mr Patel and others' including Hussein Ghadially, Yusuf Dadu, Iqbal Wadivala, Mushtaq Patel and Farooq Surti who were arrested in India.

Patel had identified six grounds for the appeal. The extradition appeal was termed as an abuse of the process of the court as India had made an extradition request to undertake 'an unviable prosecution'. The second ground was that the extradition would be a violation of article 5 of the ECHR. The third was that the trial court had wrongly held that there was a prima facie case to answer. The fourth was that it was a very old case for which his extradition was sought and hence it was barred by lapse of time. The fifth and sixth grounds were that the extradition would violate articles 6 (denial of justice) and 3 (risk of torture) of the ECHR, respectively, with new evidence on the latter which was not available to the district judge.

This was a tall order for Patel's counsels Edward Fitzgerald and Ben Cooper in the light of the emphatic judgment by the district judge that a prima facie case was made out against Patel. For the abuse of process ground to succeed, the starting point was to be that the extradition request was not made in good faith by India.

The CPS had maintained that there was no evidence against Patel, except the statements of the co-defendants. A statement was produced by the co-accused Iqbal Wadivala which confirmed that Patel was 'one of the main leaders of the camp' and when a Muslim woman was brutally attacked, the desire for revenge increased manifold. Wadivala, it seems, confessed to attending the meeting when the Varachha Road blast was planned.

Prof. Martin Lau had appeared before the district judge and was cross-examined by Montgomery for the CPS. In the high court, Prof. Lau provided a third opinion. The thrust of Prof. Lau's opinion was that it was only under section 15 of TADA, that statements made by one defendant are admissible against a co-defendant.

But a further safeguard provided that in such a scenario (where an accused gave a statement implicating another) all of them should be charged and tried in the same case. However, as there was no formal framing of charges against Patel in India, and the other co-accused (including Wadivala who had named Patel) had undergone trial, there was no way that Patel would be tried together with them in the same case. The court thus had to decide whether section 15 of TADA would be applicable for Patel or not.

Also produced before the court was an affidavit by Nayan Sukhadwala, who was the public prosecutor in Surat, which said that the statements by the co-accused could be admissible in the Indian court. This was contrary to a Mr Chaliawala, who as an assistant government pleader in Surat, made a statement dated 29 February 2012 that was at odds with that given by Sukhadwala and India. These conflicting versions were dissected by Fitzgerald to derail the prosecution's case by showing that two members of the same prosecuting agency had divergent views.

The high court was not willing to get drawn into the technicalities of the trial in India. While accepting that there were indeed differing views offered by the prosecutor's office, the judge said he did not have to resolve these issues but simply take a position. At this point, he chose to go with the CPS, while also making it clear that the trial court in India may take cognizance of Patel's arguments which may work in his favour.

But in rejecting Patel's first ground of appeal, the high court gave importance to the 'ultimate position of the requesting state' that the statements of the co-defendants would be admissible at Patel's trial. Notwithstanding the technicalities over the acceptance of section 15, the guiding principle was that there was strong presumption that a requesting state would make a request for extradition in good faith.

The second ground of unlawful detention (article 5 ECHR) would not hold if the court was convinced that the request was made in good faith and as per the due process of law. Thus this too was overruled by the court.

It was the third ground—lack of a prima facie case—that most engaged the court. This question, too, revolved around the statement of co-defendants. Unlike Mirchi and Nadeem, the witness statements against Patel were authenticated following the due process as stated in the Extradition Act 2003.

On this aspect, too, Fitzgerald sought to make light of the statements made by co-defendants. He cast aspersions on the witness statements from another angle. Now he said that the statements were not taken for the express purpose of extradition proceedings. Thus, because those who had made the statements implicating Patel had not reaffirmed the truth of the content of the statements to be used in an extradition case, it should not be accepted, maintained Fitzgerald.

'There is simply no scope in this context for the judicial gloss of the kind suggested by Mr Fitzgerald,' the court noted in the judgment. In extradition proceedings, lawmakers anticipate that live evidence might not be possible, but instead authenticated witness evidence allows statements taken in different countries to be submitted. 'In this case, the correct characterization of the co-defendants' statements is not as out-of-court hearsay evidence but as statements of evidence which the witnesses would give on oath if they were called to do so,' noted Justice Parker.

The court thus held that there was a prima facie case against Patel, by holding that the authenticated witness evidence passed muster despite the statements not being made specifically for extradition proceedings.

Invoking article 6 of the ECHR—the right to a fair trial—can also bar extradition, and Patel raised it by submitting that as the co-defendants were not competent witnesses, facing a trial just based on their evidence would be tantamount to an unjust trial. The court did find this arguable but held that if Patel was to be extradited he could point out during his trial in India that it would be unsafe and unfair to convict him just on the basis of co-conspirators. In short, he would have the opportunity to address the lacunae in his case, but in India.

To buttress its point, the high court referred to a Supreme Court of India judgment in 2005, which said that there should be corroborating evidence in cases where the conviction is sought solely on the basis of statements by co-conspirators under section 15 of TADA. The Supreme Court of India was thus invoked to drive home the point that the court in India 'is likely to be fully alive to the needs of a fair trial in the present context'. The high court held that it would not be correct to prejudge the issue and to conclude that a fair trial would not be possible.

The passage of time ground was dismissed by the district judge and the high court, too, agreed with that. At the time of his escape from India, Patel was out on bail facing serious charges. Describing Patel as a 'classic fugitive', the court found that the 'evidence falls well short of establishing that delay, in this case, would cause oppression or injustice.'

The sixth argument about the possibility of torture used the case of Abu Salem Abdul Qayoom Ansari, who was extradited to India from Portugal. Salem had claimed that despite assurances, he was tortured by police officers. 'The allegations made by Ansari must be treated with extreme caution. He has powerful incentives to make such allegations,' the court noted.

In dismissing the risk of torture, the court took into account the statement provided by the Surat police commissioner. This was in addition to the statement given by Pawar to the district judge. The high court took the Surat police commissioner's statement as a 'detailed response' to the concerns raised by Patel. The commissioner in his statement maintained that Patel would not face specialized units of Gujarat police, who were alleged to have ill-treated other terror suspects.

In a last attempt to secure freedom for his client, Fitzgerald raised the issue of specialty. Article 13 of the Extradition Treaty obliges both states to comply with the rule of specialty which means that a person extradited for a particular offence cannot be tried for a completely different offence irrespective of whether it was committed before or after the said offence, and he will not be re-extradited to a third state. The issue of specialty was raised to appeal the decision of the secretary of state to extradite Patel following the district judge's ruling.

Patel used the example of Abu Salem to show that India would violate specialty, which was not accepted by the high court. Since then, in quite a few cases of extradition involving India, requested persons have cited the example of Salem to bar their extradition, but UK courts have declined to accept that because of the determination in Patel and Shankaran's cases (chapter nine) that Salem's case cannot be invoked to cite violation of specialty.

Abu Salem Ansari was extradited from Portugal to India in 2005. In India, Salem was charged with offences other than the ones for which his extradition was sought. Salem then initiated proceedings in both Portugal and India stating that the terms on which he was extradited were not followed. The high court and then the Supreme Court in Portugal accepted that India had violated specialty. The Supreme Court in India, however, held that there was no violation of specialty.

There was thus a conflict between India and Portugal, which the UK high court held partly due to the lack of an extradition treaty between both the countries leaving enough scope for disagreements. The high court also took into consideration that the GoI subsequently accepted that certain charges against Salem should be dropped as they potentially violated the principle of specialty.

This was further reinforced by the email from Pritam Lal, first secretary (co-ordination) at the High Commission of India, dated 14 March 2013, giving more detailed information on the charges that were added and withdrawn against Salem, which was instrumental in convincing the court that 'the Government of India is diligently seeking to comply with its obligations regarding specialty as laid down by the Supreme Court of India'.

Besides, on 22 February 2013, the secretary of state received a letter of assurance from the GoI that sealed Tiger's fate in British court. There was no doubt in the minds of the high court bench that Hanif Patel aka Tiger Hanif had to return to India to face trial.

* * *

Meanwhile, the accused in India approached the Supreme Court to appeal against the district court verdict. In July 2014, a Supreme Court bench of Justice T.S. Thakur and Justice C. Nagappan heard the appeal by the accused. The state also assailed in the appeal and sought enhancement of the sentence to those convicted by the lower courts that ranged between ten to twenty years imprisonment. The genesis of the blasts lay in the demolition of Babri Masjid in 1992 that led to nationwide communal riots, senior advocate Yashank Adhyaru, appearing for the Gujarat government, told the court.

In Surat, the riots caused massive damage to life and property of the Muslim community and built resentment against the state. The accused used the cover of a relief camp in Ranitalao to collect firearms, country-made grenades, gelatin bombs and weapons—swords, spears, iron rods, to protect the members of the Muslim community who were failed by the state police. Bombs were also procured from a notorious gangster, Abdul Latif, killed later in a police encounter.

The brief for Adhyaru was clear: stick the TADA charges to the accused. TADA was the Terrorist and Disruptive Activities (Prevention) Act, an anti-terrorism law enforced between 1985 and 1995. The defence lawyer contended that the proper course was not followed for the TADA provisions, and hence, it could not be applied. Under the rules, it was the deputy superintendent of police who was the sole authority for the application of TADA.

In some of the cases, TADA was applied a few months after the offence was committed. However, on 24 April, it was decided that TADA would be dropped as per the TADA advisory committee's recommendation. Accordingly, the accused were no longer under the draconian net of TADA, but were instead to be tried under the

Explosive Substances Act, 1908 and other provisions of the Indian Penal Code (IPC). When P.C. Pande became the Surat police commissioner, TADA was again applied. In some other cases, the assent of the Gujarat home secretary and that of the additional commissioner of police was taken to apply TADA.

The point raised by the defence was that this practice of bypassing the office of the deputy superintendent of police, even though in favour of a higher and senior official to apply TADA, was bad in law and made it unsustainable. The court accepted the objections and unanimously held that only an officer of the rank of deputy superintendent of police could authorize the application of TADA because as the officer in charge, the statute had identified the holder of that post as competent enough to give the necessary assent.

The court then inquired whether there was evidence against the accused, which could be shared in the court that would cancel their acquittal. Adhyaru candidly admitted that there was not enough evidence for the same after which the court ordered the discharge.

With the case in India collapsing and the co-accused set free, questions arose whether their statements, the only evidence that India relied on to convince UK courts to extradite Patel, held merit any more. Patel was ordered to be extradited in 2013, yet there was no news about his extradition until 2020. In July 2015, we wrote to Birnberg Pierce Solicitors, who represented Patel, seeking an update, but despite our request they did not offer any comments.

Meanwhile, Britons were getting restless with Patel sitting put in the UK and the £2,00,000 bill taxpayers have footed to fight his extradition. In 2016, a glaring headline in the *Sun* dated 8 August read: 'Terror Suspect Protected: Theresa May allowed Muslim bomber "wanted for terrorism" and death of a schoolgirl to remain in Britain' and rebuked the prime minister for not signing Patel's extradition order while she was the home secretary. A similar news item in the *Daily Mail* on the same day pulled up Amber Rudd, the then home secretary for the delay and quoted a Home Office spokesperson saying that 'further representations have been made to the home secretary in this case and they are currently being carefully considered'. The hope that Tiger Patel will ever return to India was, at best, bleak. But in January 2020, Edward Fitzgerald confirmed to us that the home secretary, after considering this new evidence, has decided not to sign on Patel's extradition order.

As per the 2003 Extradition Act, for category 2 countries, after Westminster Magistrates' Court gives a ruling, the case is sent to the home secretary for final consideration. Representations can be made to the home secretary to bar the extradition on new developments on the issues of specialty, death penalty and human rights. In Patel's case, after the district judge found a prima facie case in May 2012, the then home secretary Theresa May ordered his extradition in June 2012. Patel lost the appeal in April 2013, but approached the home secretary, raising concerns over human rights based on new evidence. The final decision came in August 2019 wherein Sajid Javid, the then home secretary, refused Patel's extradition, and he was discharged. This was perhaps the last such decision made by the home secretary, as following the recommendation of the Baker committee, the Extradition Act was amended in 2013 to remove the ability of the home secretary to consider human rights issues, for which requested persons would have to go to the appeal court.

This extradition case is perhaps symptomatic of the eerie turn a jubilant victory for India can suddenly take; the echoing silence covers the cacophony of painful failure.

7

PILGRIM PAEDOPHILE

The idyllic trance music was replaced by blaring police sirens and screeching cars as armed police rushed out to surround a small orphanage near Colva beach in Goa. Gurukul, the orphanage, operated under the supervision of an Anglo-German priest called Freddy Peats.

Another police team laid siege to a small flat behind a petrol pump in the Fatorda suburb of Margao. The flat belonged to Freddy Peats. To the horror of the cops, both places were found to be the den of nefarious crimes, a hotbed for paedophile activities where innocent boys and girls were 'leased' to foreigners for sexual acts in a state proudly called the tourist paradise of India.

No longer all about the sun and sandy shores, this little Portuguese-influenced state of Goa, with its pristine beaches and shimmering golden sand, was now a thriving commercial market for child sex abuse.

For seventeen years, white-bearded Peats carried out this trade under the guise of being a 'priest' associated with the Catholic Church. Gurukul housed 150 boys and girls, some orphans, others left at the doorstep due to the poor financial conditions of the parents who could no longer afford to feed them. The children had nowhere to go and no one to hear them out, making them the perfect victims.

Until one victim spoke and was finally heard.

In March 1991, Peats approached a young boy playing out on the streets like many young boys do, made small talk like most neighbours do, and casually mentioned that he had several foreign stamps and currencies, knowing fully well that it would pique the boy's interest, just like such things often do. He sweetened the offer by telling the boy he could take some of them home. The stamps and currency he offered were worth a princely Rs 4! He saw the joy in the little boy's eyes, the eagerness in his stride as he walked beside the man of God into his den of iniquity.

But the rest is not history. In fact, it is just the beginning of the end of Freddy Peats and his band of unholy criminals.

This boy, unlike the hundreds under Peats's watch, was not an orphan. He lived with his parents. Over dinner that night, the boy struggled to sit well, wincing every few minutes, closing his eyes shut tight as the pain shot through him. His father, an assistant mining engineer, stopped eating and quietly watched his son for a few minutes. The boy struggled to eat, the pain turning him pale and making him lose his appetite. When he caught his father watching him, the tears began to flow and silent sobs took over. His mother hugged him and enquired as to what had happened. 'Terrible pain . . . I can't bear it. It's hurting,' he murmured to her between his sobs pointing to his genitals.

The parents quickly inspected them and found several scratch marks on the boy's testicles. 'What is this?' thundered his father and the boy burst into loud wails, punctured by slow narration of the events of that afternoon to his shocked parents.

The boy confided in his father that Peats had injected his testes and also fondled him repeatedly. Though in a state of shock and rage, his father began pacing up and down the small room shouting expletives and wanting to commit murder. His distraught wife held his hand and with a tear-streaked face looked up at her raging husband and muttered, 'Be quiet. If people heard this, our reputation would be ruined.'

With his wife's words ringing in his ears, the distraught father was hesitant to lodge a complaint. On one of his morning walks, he met the deputy superintendent of police, Santoba Desai, and confided in him. Desai asked him to meet him at the police station later.

The next day, the troubled parent walked all the way to the police station. He sat before Desai and poured his angst out as he reiterated what his son had told him about Peats. The man in the uniform sat up straighter. This is what he wanted, a complaint to raid the orphanage and investigate the man he had suspicions about for some time but no legal resource to verify.

But with the victim's father reluctant to lodge a First Information Report (FIR) that would secure the cops the warrant to raid Peats's properties, nothing could be done. So he spent the next precious few minutes convincing the poor father to go on record with his complaint, alternating between appealing to his humanity and threatening him with dire consequences, until the man relented and lodged an FIR against Peats. Thus began the unveiling of a great international paedophile ring.

Police raided Peats's flat and walked out with a bounty of child pornographic material: two cameras, 2305 obscene images of minor boys and girls often engaged in sexual acts with older white men, 135 negative film strips that promised more images of the same kind, a cache of narcotics and syringes. It appeared that Peats injected anti-spasmodic drugs into the testicles of minors to inflate them for sexual activities. As most of the children used for these sexual acts were pre-puberty, these drugs were used to stimulate erections. The children told the court that Peats would take them to his room, ask them to remove their clothes and indulge in oral sex to help him masturbate. He would also do the same to the children to enhance his pleasure.

Peats also supplied several foreigners with children to take to their hotel rooms, hostels or guest houses for a day or several days to carry out similar and more such sexually depraved activities. He was paid by these foreigners. The photographs captured some of them in various sexual acts. Images obtained showed a six-year-old boy with blindfolds on and hands tied to a wall with drugs being injected into his testicles. Another image showed a two-year-old, her arms clutched tightly by a pair of hands, and her privates being violated by one stiff penis. The photographs narrated the untold saga of unbearable pain, sheer brutality and unthinkable violence committed on minor boys and girls in the heart of India's tourist haven.

* * *

'Who is this?' the superintendent of police asked his junior as he went through the cache of photographs. One man stood out among the photographs—tall and pale with a pointed nose and a protruding jawline. The gleaming eyes and cunning smirk failed to belie the cruelty of his intentions. 'Looks European, perhaps English, and a tourist,' said the junior, who promptly began making enquiries at local hotels, motels, guest houses and hostels. Police investigations confirmed him to be a British citizen and unearthed his identity as a forty-year-old man called Raymond Varley, a schoolteacher from Halifax, a town in West Yorkshire in England. Varley was a regular visitor to Goa and Peats's Gurukul during the 1980s and early 1990s.

Armed with the photographs, another officer approached the terrified children and slowly asked them if they knew who the man in them was.

'Raymond from Thailand,' one boy said.

'Yes, he said to call him Raymond. He is from Thailand,' said another.

The third nodded and mumbled, 'Raymond . . . Thailand.'

To the children whom he abused in India, he was simply 'Raymond from Thailand', a moniker that stuck. The cops had a long list of children he had abused, but four boys and one girl (all minors) were on record. The police were quick to register thirty cases against him, including criminal conspiracy, for the commission of various sexual offences on children between 1989 and 1991, identified by reference to dates that he stayed at a particular hostel in Goa and testimonies given by the children.

A domestic warrant for his arrest was issued in India on 15 October 1996, but before Indian authorities could cast their net on him, he escaped from India. Varley thought he could live a life sans worry shuttling between Britain, Mexico, Slovenia and Thailand and by creating a new identity for himself. He was now Martin Ashley, a name he adopted through a deed poll in 2000.

But his deeds caught up with him when the Indian authorities tracked him down in Bangkok in 2012 through a Red Notice, where his passport was seized. Before India could provide Thai authorities with any details, Varley was deported to the UK in less than a day. India made an extradition request to the UK on 25 April 2012, and the case was certified by the home secretary on 15 May 2012. Varley was arrested at his home in Halifax on 29 May 2012 and was soon out on bail. But what began now was one of the most interesting extradition cases between India and the UK.

* * *

Raymond Varley's story does not begin in Goa, but a small town in the Yorkshire moors. Born on 7 September 1947, Varley lived at Rugby Terrace, Ovenden, Halifax, West Yorkshire, a minster town known for the popular mouth-watering Quality Street chocolates and fear-inducing gibbet, a rudimentary guillotine used in the mid-seventeenth century to execute criminals by decapitation.

Varley's life story in Halifax is one of crimes, though perhaps in the twentieth century he did not have to fear the gibbet. Varley was in his twenties when he got involved with a vicar, a teacher and a doctor in what was one of the biggest paedophile rings of that time in Britain.

Vicar Reverend John Fairburn Poole, fifty-three, of Holy Trinity Church, was the ringleader who abused young boys on the premises of the church, took their pictures and circulated them among the members of the ring. But the lure of a quick buck got him to soon begin selling them to pornographic magazines in Copenhagen and Amsterdam. Varley met Poole in 1972 at a gathering that called for equality for homosexuals in Huddersfield and soon found shared interests. Varley admitted to Poole that he had been, for many years, sexually abusing young boys and taking their indecent sexually graphic images.

Impressed by this, Poole introduced Varley to Dr John Roussel Byles, a doctor in the posh Kensington neighbourhood of London. For many years, Varley developed films for Byles. Poole was the go-between—he received the films from Dr Byles and gave them to Varley, and later took the photographs from Varley and supplied them to Dr Byles of Earls Terrace in Kensington through post. This went on for almost eighteen months until Dr Byles left for Australia. Poole then introduced Varley to Clive Wilcox, thirty-six, a schoolteacher in Huddersfield, as a 'commercial artist' who was then tasked with doing photography for Wilcox, perhaps the most depraved of the lot.

Thus began a series of photographic sessions of young boys in the nude, physically abused, sexually assaulted, beaten and broken, all to pique the interest of the dark society of paedophiles under the watchful eyes of the man of the cloth. Vicar Poole even let them use the church and crypt to carry out their crimes. Varley admitted to taking photographs of a boy in the nude on the balcony of the church without Poole's permission, but later sought the vicar's nod before he photographed a boy in the church's crypt. Poole, in fact, bought many of these photographs from Varley at the rate of £1 for four. Thus began the production of hundreds of such photographs of young boys sexually abused in not just Yorkshire but also London, Durham and Lancashire. Varley had found his calling. He was now not just sexually abusing boys for his pleasure, but found a path to reap monetary profits from the sordid enterprise.

But in 1975, it all came to a crashing end when a young girl spotted two young boys in Varley's car and her suspicions were raised. Jacqueline Oldfield, 14, of Portland House, Elland spotted the car the next day and called 999 with the registration number and shared her concerns. Thus began a massive police crackdown on what is known as the Huddersfield Paedophile ring, with Varley as a prime suspect leading them to the vicar, the doctor and the teacher, all men who swore to protect the vulnerable and better society, but had turned rogue. On 5 February, Poole and Wilcox were taken into custody. Poole tended his resignation after seventeen years of service at Holy Trinity Church.

At Leeds Crown Court, Varley pleaded guilty to seven charges of conspiracy, indecently assaulting boys between nine and fourteen under the Sexual Offences Act, the Obscene Publications Act and the Post Office Act. He was jailed for four years. On 21 March, Poole pleaded guilty to three charges of conspiring with Varley to commit sexual abuse with boys under seventeen and to publish obscene pornographic material and admitted to sending indecent photographs through the post to Dr Byles and Varley. Wilcox, of Hollinwood Avenue, Moston, Manchester, denied his six charges but Varley told the court that he took colour photographs of a boy in the nude for Wilcox in the presence of another man by the name of Jack Nichols and the evidence stacked up against him.

Dr Byles had a history of such allegations. In 1963, he was alleged to have assaulted a sixteen-year-old boy with the intention of committing grave offence. He was declared not guilty and discharged by the Central Criminal Court of London. Dr Byles, who later moved to Sydney, Australia, had been arrested on 17 December and charged with indecent assault on a boy there. He was granted bail against a surety of Australian $2000 but soon absconded. Later he committed suicide in Proserpine hotel in Queensland on 20 January, as his crimes began to close in on him.

On his release from prison, Raymond Varley left the UK shores to embark on a new career as an English tutor in Serbia, Albania and Thailand. During this time, he frequently took holidays to India and in particular to a small orphanage in the touristy state of Goa. Far away from the laws of England, Varley found himself free to indulge in the passions of his depraved mind and found a like-minded soul in another man of the cloth, 'Father' Freddy Peats, and his band of miscreants.

* * *

From the late 1960s all through the 1990s, Goa was a hippie paradise and attracted foreign tourists from across the world in droves. Wonderful tropic climate with the sun smiling down in the heart of December, an exchange rate that favoured the West and a lax political and police will to secure the area from drugs, sex and substance abuse, sent thousands of hippies from across the globe to the shores of Goa to lose themselves in psychedelic and trance music.

A Portuguese colony from 1510 until 1961, Goa is an eclectic mix of modernity and tradition, of openness and secrecy, of freedom and confinement. While almost every global hotel chain has one or more beautiful luxury resorts here, there are also several seedy inns, motels and guest houses dotting the shoreline and in the many villages where few questions are asked about the identity of the guest and fewer still about his activities.

Decades ago, even fewer eyebrows were raised if some older white men brought in companions to their rooms, even if the unwilling companion was a little girl drugged and unconscious or a little boy frightened out of his wits. Goa was a dream destination for people like Varley, who once bitten, refused to be twice shy.

Being in the dock a few times for his nefarious crimes seemed to be no deterrent for Varley as he allegedly took full advantage of the conducive environment of 'Hippie Goa' and the opportunities afforded by Peats's orphanage—according to the investigators, he embarked on a series of visits from 1989 to 1992, planned implicitly to sexually abuse children in India. But just like in Huddersfield, his crimes caught up with him when Peats was arrested and the net cast out for him. Two decades later, on India's request, Varley was finally arrested from his home in the UK for his crimes in India. What should have been an easy prosecution of a serial sexual predator, became a tedious judicial process that eventually failed to bring the notorious sexual offender to book.

* * *

The formal request from India to extradite Varley was dated 5 April 2012 which was certified by the home secretary on 15 May. Accordingly, Varley was arrested on 29 May and produced at Westminster Magistrates' Court on 30 May. He was granted conditional bail and remained free during the trial. Varley's case can easily qualify as one of the most prolonged ones.

This was due to questions raised about prison conditions and the fact that not one, but two experts visited the prisons in Goa to ascertain whether Varley's stay there could breach his human rights. Matthew Butt, representing Varley, raised three challenges to his client's extradition. The first was the passage of time; second, human rights—prison conditions under article 3 of the ECHR; third, health conditions by raising concerns of a tentative diagnosis of dementia and threat to commit suicide.

A short mention of the timetable within which the case was heard at the Westminster court gives an indication of the protracted legal battle. The hearing commenced on 3 October 2012, when the court heard details of the prima facie evidence against Varley. On 19 November, the court adjourned as India presented new chunks of prima facie evidence which Varley's counsel needed to study. As was expected, the defence had also raised the question of the conditions of Indian prisons. No information was forthcoming from the CPS representing India on this, perhaps due to lack of effective communication and bureaucratic delays. So the judge welcomed a discussion on whether an independent inspection of the prison should take place.

When the matter came up for hearing on 20 December, David Ramsbotham, Baron Ramsbotham of Kensington, was identified as the expert who would visit the likely prisons where Varley was to be lodged upon the extradition. Lord Ramsbotham served as the Chief Inspector for Prisons for England and Wales from 1995 to 2001.

However, it was still not clear if Lord Ramsbotham would get access to the prisons. On the next hearing on 18 January 2013, CPS counsel Peter Caldwell informed the court that India would allow Lord Ramsbotham to inspect the prisons under the escort of Indian officials. This was a substantial development and reflected the confidence and the eagerness of the Goa state to get Varley back.

But it seems that there were some delays on India's part. On 14 February, Butt brought to the notice of the court that he was still waiting for some crucial evidence to be shared by the CPS that was needed to prepare his defence. On the prison inspection front, it was agreed that Lord Ramsbotham would inspect the prisons on 19, 20 and 21 February and would submit a report. He visited three prisons in Goa, but even though he was an expert brought forth by Varley's team, he submitted his report to India, which was to be then shared with Butt.

When the hearing resumed on 9 April, Butt complained to the court and demanded that another expert, Prof. Rod Morgan, be allowed to inspect the prisons as the protocol was not followed. Even though there was no suggestion that sharing the report first with India would have made any material difference, Lord Ramsbotham's error was considered grave enough to warrant another inspection of the prison conditions.

It was also on this date that the court was informed that Varley had spoken about committing suicide if he was sent to India. Lord Ramsbotham's report, as was disclosed later, was clear that Varley's human rights would not be violated if he was extradited to India and kept in the prisons which he inspected. This had perhaps unnerved Varley, who must have known the contents of the report when it was shared with his counsel. The court could not take a suicide threat lightly and was adjourned for 'any psychiatric report and any further prison report'.

After nearly a month, when the case came up on 7 May, it was still not clear if Prof. Morgan would get permission to visit the prisons. But while the decision on whether access to inspect the prison would be granted to Prof. Morgan hung in the balance, on 7 June, the CPS counsel informed the court that India would be submitting further evidence. This meant that the defence needed more time to study the new evidence and in the absence of any clarity about the prison access, it was clear that the case would spill over to the following year.

At the next hearing on 4 July, Indian officials were in attendance and Caldwell informed the court that a decision on allowing Prof. Morgan access to the prisons could only be expected by mid to end August 2013.

Nothing of significance took place in the next hearing on 6 September, but when the case came up on 7 November, both the counsels had already seen the two prison reports prepared by Lord Ramsbotham and Prof. Morgan. Both the experts had concluded that the prisons met the requirements of article 3 of the ECHR.

Just when it seemed Varley was losing ground in the courts, a new twist was added to his sordid tale. The court was informed that Varley was showing signs of dementia. This was a step up from the earlier claim of committing suicide and should have alerted the CPS and India to take the necessary counter steps. It was known that a diagnostic assessment for dementia on the National Health Service (NHS) would easily take a few more months, giving that much time for the CPS to plan for it. The next two hearings on 22 January and 25 April 2014 revolved around the issue of diagnosing dementia and the submission of further evidence by India.

The court had set aside all the usual conditions that are put by the defence to thwart an extradition. The case was tilting in India's favour. It was also unusual that India accepted and allowed not one but two experts to make an assessment of the prison conditions. Both reports found the prison conditions satisfactory.

The Westminster court threw away two challenges to Varley's extradition raised by his counsel—passage of time and prison conditions—but found merit that on health grounds, it would be 'unjust' and 'oppressive' if he was sent to India. It was thus the claim of dementia that saved Varley.

Little did India realize that it would be a report from a chartered psychologist, who was neither a registered medical practitioner nor a consultant psychiatrist, that would be their undoing. The report dated 2 February 2014 by Linda Atterton, a psychologist who examined Varley on his personal request, provided enough ammunition to Butt to give the court further written submissions. Atterton, in her report, claimed that Varley's 'concentration, attention and working memory are all severely impaired' and while he was not clinically depressed, he 'is vulnerable to depression'. She concluded that Varley had 'moderate to severe dementia already'. One of the most clinching observations in Atterton's report was that Varley 'must have immediate daily support, both practical and emotional to keep him safe'.

Cases of sexual grooming of children and child pornography in England always find their way to the British press and often create much uproar in public and political spheres. Varley's case was closely monitored by some activists who were concerned that he would get away, both in the UK and India. They were alerted early on during the trial after Varley's suicide threat, and suspected that the dementia claims were only made to secure his release after all other attempts had failed. Surprisingly at that stage of the hearing (March 2014), there were no written submissions from India in response to the report by Atterton. No experts were brought in to contest the defence claims or request made to examine Varley by a prosecution recommended psychiatrist. A major slip-up on the part of India and CPS that gave the case away.

To be fair to Caldwell, he requested and got the opportunity to cross-examine Atterton on 25 April. In her oral hearing, Atterton declared, 'I do not believe he is well enough in any respect to be currently facing proceedings. It would be impossible for his functioning to improve to a level where this would not be the case. Deterioration is almost inevitable and there is no medication that will significantly improve his functioning or any other means of doing so.'

She took a volley of piercing questions from Caldwell which he delivered in a sardonic style—Did her report lack rigour? Was she competent to examine and prepare a report on Varley's mental health which she submitted? Could Varley be faking his condition? There seemed to be a two-fold strategy deployed by Caldwell. The first was to frustrate the claim of poor health (threat of suicide and dementia) made by Varley. Additional submissions by Caldwell pointed out to the court that the threat of suicide was not supported by expert witnesses but was only a bald statement of intent. The second was to assure that if at all Varley required medical assistance for mental health, he could be taken to the Institute of Psychiatry & Human Behaviour in Goa.

Caldwell relied on the affidavit by Mihir Vardhan, head of the prisons department in Goa, assuring that if the need arose, Varley could be referred to the Institute of Psychiatry & Human Behaviour which was 25 km from the prison. But Vardhan's affidavit was characterized as 'very belatedly served' which Butt said he wouldn't entertain. The defence counsel countered that even if the treatment regime offered by India was accepted, it could not negate the injustice of putting a dementia patient through 'preparing for and facing a trial of the instant kind involving events over 20 years ago'.

In his closing submissions, Caldwell suggested that Varley might have been exaggerating his symptoms, to which the district judge asked, 'Why not have your own report then?'

As Varley, if extradited, would be kept in prison right from the pre-trial stage till his discharge or completing the sentencing if found guilty, the court placed emphasis on Atterton's report that, as a dementia patient, Varley could not be expected to defend himself right from the pre-trial stage while being kept in an Indian jail. The judgment noted that Varley 'is to face trial' and not simply serve a sentence.

Explaining why extraditing Varley would be unjust and oppressive, District Judge Quentin Purdy said: 'By that I mean regard has to be had to the basic and fundamental requirements of instructing one's lawyer, following proceedings and potentially giving evidence oneself. This is in contrast to a convicted serving prisoner who faces no such demands. Given the recent report and oral evidence, which I find compelling, from Mrs Linda Atterton, I am driven to conclude Martin Ashley is now—May

2014—a vulnerable individual due to dementia which is viewed as necessitating immediate daily support to keep him safe.'

The biggest mistake during the trial was that Caldwell, representing India, did not make any request for the commission of its own expert to challenge the evidence presented by Atterton. But Caldwell could only make the request if India had instructed him. The CBI, on their part, were upset that the CPS did not insist on examining Varley by an independent expert. It is understood that the CPS decides on using independent experts on a case-by-case basis and funding could have been a factor.

It will remain a mystery whether it was the CPS's incompetence or India's legendary bottlenecks that stopped Caldwell from requesting the court for another medical test. As it turned out, merely challenging Atterton's expertise was not going to prove much in court. What was required was the evidence of another expert which the magistrate indicated had the CPS requested, would have been approved. In his judgment, the magistrate mentions that 'India has chosen not to commission its own expert, merely to challenge the competence of Mrs Atterton'.

A CPS spokesperson said: 'In examining the (medical) report, the CPS and experienced extradition counsel concluded that the medical expert obtained by the defence was unqualified to make a diagnosis of dementia. It was also concluded that the medical report did not establish that the defendant did in fact have dementia, and that the report did not satisfy the required test that extradition would be "unjust or oppressive". These arguments were presented by the prosecution through cross-examination of the expert and submissions to the district judge.' It later emerged that Varley had found Atterton's details on the internet and had driven to her clinic several miles from his house for the consultation. It is believed that Atterton was not informed of the extradition trial when she examined him for the first time.

There was an outcry in sections of the British press and the magistrate, too, came under some criticism. But in the end, it was the refusal to not commission another medic that cost India the case and gave Varley his freedom. Whether it was due to cost consideration, miscommunication or bureaucratic delay, it was certain that only a miracle would now allow India to succeed in its appeal.

On 7 July 2014, the case came before Master Gidden in the administrative courts of the Court of Appeal where a timeline was agreed to take the appeal forward. By 21 July, the CPS had to present evidence on why Varley should be examined by an independent expert and the defence counsel would submit their replies by 11 August. The CPS then had time to file counter arguments till 16 September and the final response by Varley was to be filed by 23 September.

On the eve of 21 July deadline, in an unprecedented move, the CBI chief Ranjit Sinha requested India's foreign secretary to take up with the British government the issue of the CPS being non-responsive in the Varley case. It is believed that Michael Omo, specialist extradition prosecutor, CPS, initially agreed to video-conferencing, but when the CBI gave him various dates, he did not follow-up. The CBI was clearly frustrated that their communication with the CPS had fallen through, which they figured would have a negative impact on their appeal in the high court. When we explicitly asked the CPS to comment on this, a spokesperson said: 'The CPS is acting professionally on behalf of the GoI and is co-operating with all relevant authorities to achieve the extradition of Raymond Varley.'

As part of the appeal process, the CPS requested for a mental health check-up, but Varley's counsel refused. He told the high court that any further examination was bound to take a toll on his client's health. During one of the hearings in the high court, the judge told the CPS counsel that 'you are asking us to do something very significant'.

The court maintained that the CPS had been given more than a fair opportunity to examine Varley during the extradition trial but had 'expressly declined to do so'.

On 10 October 2014, Lord Justice Patrick Elias and Justice Gary Hickinbottom dismissed India's appeal, and Varley remains free.

8

PARASITE PARENTS

'**F**uck the fuck!' shouted Kaval Raijada raising his middle finger at a journalist who had clicked him with the sour-faced Arti Dhir puffing a cigarette outside Westminster Magistrates' Court on a rare pleasant January day in 2019. At thirty, Raijada looked like a grumpy teenager whose attempts to fit in with the English blokes only made him stand further apart, as his fifty-four-year-old wife looked on with a dull resigned look of a passing stranger witnessing the tantrums of a spoilt brat.

There was nothing in the behaviour of the two that showed them as a loving couple keen to establish a happy family or the mature compatibility required to raise a boy of eleven. Dhir and Raijada were at Westminster Magistrates' Court in London to fight their extradition to India on charges of murdering their adopted son to claim money from his life insurance.

This is how their version of the story begins: the love story of a British woman Arti and an Indian boy Kaval, and their adopted son Gopal. Kaval, who came from an affluent family from a village in Gujarat, moved to London as a student. He was joined by his friend Nitin Mund, also a student from India. Arti, born in Kenya with family in Gurdaspur, Punjab, was a British citizen. The two Indian students lived as tenants in Arti's house in Hanwell, London. Kaval and Arti fell in love, got married and since Arti was childless and had crossed menopause, they decided to adopt a child from India. Kaval's father helped secure the adoption. Mund helped the child secure a visa to move with his new parents in London. Somewhere during this, a freak attempt at kidnapping took the child's life and that of the child's brother-in-law who was facilitating this adoption and visa.

But the emerging reality is different. For this, we perhaps first need to acknowledge that some students come to the UK with the sole intention to settle here by any means possible. The UK has cracked down on several Mickey Mouse colleges that were created to lure foreign students with promises of a 'good' life in the UK. Attendance at these colleges can be bought to be produced for visa extension purposes while the student indulges in full-time employment (often cash jobs) or simply merriment. The degree on offer (if the student completes the not-rigorous course) is one which may have less relevance to the UK labour market, though those in India are often content with simply having a foreign qualification to boast. But this study path can only stretch your stay in the UK for so long. More ingenious ways are required to make this temporary stay permanent.

One such method is to marry a British citizen. Kaval and Mund wanted to live in London. Arti wanted money. Of the two Indian boys, Kaval was more influential and an undisputed leader, though perhaps more bark than bite. In the drawing room of the house in Hanwell, a scheme was drawn up, in which Arti, who worked on a meagre pay as an air freight representative for Worldwide Flight Services at Heathrow, could get rich quick and Kaval and Mund could live in the Queen's country.

Arti and Kaval got into a 'contract' marriage with a hasty lunchtime ceremony at the Ealing Town Hall in 2013 where their neighbours, David Coombs and his wife, served as witnesses. Mund, who was also a witness at the court ceremony, ratted out that the marriage was solely to extend Kaval's visa and to foster adoption for Arti. Arti and Kaval then worked together in the warehouse of Worldwide Flight Services at Heathrow but were dismissed from service due to a breach of contract in 2016. While

Arti is remembered as a party-goer and was often a regular at drinks after work and trips with colleagues, Kaval was a regular absentee, staying away from the shadow of his overpowering wife. The cracks in their marriage were visible for all to see.

Here we must confront another reality, of foreigners and non-resident Indians (NRIs) flocking to Indian shores to adopt babies. Most are willing to pay between Rs 30–45 lakh for a child, but the beneficiaries are often not the child's parents or guardians but the middlemen fostering the adoption. A report in the *Daily Mail* dated 9 February 2019 highlighted how 600–800 Indian children are easily adopted by foreign nationals, mostly from Europe and the US, sometimes by 'fraudulent means aided by unscrupulous agencies', fostered by a lack of guidelines and after-adoption checks on international adoptions. A public interest litigation (PIL) in 2012 was filed in the Supreme Court by lawyers from Advait Foundation and Sakhee who were seeking a moratorium on foreigners adopting Indian children.

India's premier investigating agency, the CBI, in an affidavit to the court, said it has no resources to conduct a probe of such a huge magnitude into adoption scandals as it is limited by lack of knowledge on the number and names of agencies involved and parties to each of the thousands of adoptions that take place every year. An important ruling in the case came in July 2019, when the Supreme Court made it mandatory for any foreigner looking to adopt a child to get a 'no objection certificate' from their country.

Earlier in October 2016, the Indian government had sent out an order to fertility clinics to stop all surrogate embryo transfers for foreign nationals. Since surrogacy was legalized in India in 2002, Anand in Gujarat had become a popular destination for those wanting to rent-a-womb. With over 3000 surrogacy clinics across the country, the business was flourishing, making £65 million annually. However, lack of regulation on the international level and exploitation of women by these clinics and the biological parents had raised red flags, forcing the government to bring in legislation against surrogacy.

With adoption and surrogacy being so common in Gujarat, no one batted an eyelid when, in 2015, Kaval's father Mahendrasinh, who worked as manager of the Junagadh Jilla Sahakari Bank in the small village of Malia in Junagadh, Rajkot district of Gujarat, began advertising for a child the newlyweds could adopt. One would have thought that Mahendrasinh would go the conventional way and approach an orphanage. But orphanages would ask questions, demand paperwork and would require a hefty payment. Besides, this was no conventional adoption. The motive was never really to adopt a child, but to find a suitable cast to play a tiny but vital part in a pre-written script.

With less than 20,000 people in the village, it wasn't difficult for Mahendrasinh to zero in on Gopal Sejani, a fatherless child, abandoned by his mother when he was two and living with his sister Alpa and brother-in-law Harshukh Kardani. Gopal had five siblings. The family's sole income came from farming a small holding of five acres. They were neither educated nor worldly-wise. Raijada Sr easily convinced the Kardanis that if Gopal was adopted, he would be living in London and his life would be improved.

Gopal's pictures were sent to Arti who immediately approved of Gopal and instructed Mahendrasinh to prepare the adoption papers. She visited India in July 2015 to 'look the boy over' but there were no lingering looks that spoke of a mother's joy at having a new son. Neither Arti nor Kaval contacted Gopal after that day. Gopal, though, ecstatically announced to all his impending trip to London. He even started learning English words and his family, with their meagre savings, bought him a Gujarati-English pocket dictionary.

The adoption deed was registered on 23 July 2015 and Gopal was now christened Gopal Arti Dhir. A momentous occasion like this would have called for some celebration, some outpouring of love from the desperate mother on finding her new son, some joy of a father and grandfather in seeing their family grow.

Yet what the mother and grandfather did next was shocking. They began bank-shopping to get life insurance for Gopal. While there is nothing wrong with trying to get a 'wealth builder plan' for your child, the thing that sent alarm bells ringing was that getting life insurance was the *only* thing that Arti was interested in doing for her adopted child.

On 22 July, a day before the adoption papers were signed, Arti visited banks and opened a savings account in the ICICI Bank in Keshod. She provided the bank with her documents and Mahendrasinh also produced his identity card. 'The two wanted to take out an insurance policy. Since we don't do that here, I sent them to another branch,' said a bank official.

They promptly contacted that branch. 'I had a telephone meeting with Arti (in India) and Kaval (in London) to jointly take out a wealth builder plan which, in the event of the death of the insured person (Gopal), would pay ten times the value of the annual premium,' an official from ICICI Prudential Life Insurance company explained. But since the amount of the annual premium of Rs 13 lakh was not in the bank account in July, they did not proceed with the application then.

A month later, Mahendrasinh informed the insurance agent that the money was in the account to pay the premium and they could start on the insurance plan. So on 26 August, an insurance policy was taken out in Gopal's name, the first premium of which was paid through the newly opened account in ICICI Bank. This was the only transaction ever made from that account.

Later in 2015, Gopal acquired his first-ever passport, yet his new parents seemed in no hurry to have him in London. Gopal continued to stay in the tiny shack with his sister and her husband, not in the palatial home of his grandparents. His new parents had all but forgotten him. There were never any conversations between the parents and the child. All communication came through grandpa Mahendrasinh to the Kardanis and they were limited to only instructions on the journeys Gopal and his brother-in-law had to make to Rajkot for 'visa purposes'.

* * *

Here enters Kaval's old buddy from London, Mund. Mund had transferred Rs 4 lakh from his Lloyds Bank account in Southall to Kaval's Lloyds Bank account in Hanwell as part of the first premium paid in August 2015, making him a partner in the insurance payout.

The initial plan for the couple to go to India and kill Gopal themselves changed to Mund doing the task when he failed to get his visa extended and could no longer afford to pay his share of the insurance premium. Since the couple had put money in helping him secure a visa and now had to foot the entire amount of the premium, they began putting pressure on him to murder Gopal. They sweetened the deal with promises to get his visa extended and find him a willing partner for a contract marriage in the UK. In the event of Mund getting arrested for the murder, the two promised to pull all strings and spare no expense to secure his release. Finally, Mund was convinced. The lure to return to London and have the right to live there like his buddy Kaval proved too tempting to let fear or conscience overrule it.

Kaval called Mund on 15 or 16 August 2016 and instructed him to meet Gopal through his father. He also told him that under the guise of getting Gopal a visa, Mund was to lead him to Maliya Hatina railway station where Gopal could be killed.

Mund hired a contract killed called Bavaji who demanded Rs 5 lakh for the murder. Kaval agreed to pay Rs 1 lakh upfront but the remaining Rs 4 lakh after fifteen days when they would get their insurance payout. Bavaji agreed.

An eager Gopal, accompanied by his unsuspecting brother-in-law, landed at Maliya railway station earlier than expected and this turned out to wreck the plans of the murdering duo (Mund and Bavaji) who were following them on a motorcycle. The targets were soon lost in the crowd at the Maliya railway station. Mund and Bavaji returned without accomplishing their task. A furious Kaval yelled at Mund to get on with 'the work'.

As the murder was being plotted on phonelines across continents, Mund requested Kaval for money to buy an unregistered

SIM card so that the calls could not be traced back to the various conspirators. Kaval sent Rs 25,015 through Thomas Cook Money Gram money transfer on 10 January 2017. Mund paid Rs 20,000 of this money to Bavaji to expedite the murder.

On the pretext of submitting more documents for the visa, Gopal and his brother-in-law were once again drawn to the Maliya railway station. Bavaji had another chance to kill the boy. Yet, fortune favoured Gopal once again. A policeman intercepted Bavaji and his mate to check their vehicle documents and identity card. This ticked precious minutes off the clock. When the duo was finally asked to leave, they rushed into the station but could no longer spot Gopal. They had lost their target. They returned with yet another failed attempt to report to their already restless boss.

This sent Kaval through the roof and he now threatened Mund and his family. A terrified Mund coaxed Bavaji to complete this task over the next three to four days. The two then reconnoitred the place where the attack would take place and meticulously planned every detail. It was no longer the Maliya railway station where the boy would be hit. Repeated failed attempts there was enough reason to now look for a place very unlike the crowded transport hub. A quiet strip of the highway was chosen now to take an innocent life.

* * *

Every time the pretend visa processing was involved, Gopal and his brother-in-law Kardani were led to an internet shop in Rajkot. They were informed that the visa was submitted online and so several documents were scanned and emails were sent to convince the naïve villagers that crucial steps to secure Gopal's visa were being conducted.

Later, several emails were found where the Adoption Deed was sent back and forth. This, according to Mund, was to justify the many trips to Rajkot to show that the (non-existent) visa application was progressing. Around four such trips were made at the behest of Raijada Sr and accompanied by the unflappable Mund.

On each trip, the same travel arrangements were made. Kardani and Gopal travelled by train. They were collected by Mund and after some 'business' was conducted at the internet café, they were returned to the village in a car driven by Mund's driver.

The same itinerary was followed every single time.

On that fateful day of 8 February, Alpa dressed her brother in his best clothes, brushed his hair back and kissed his forehead before thrusting a packed lunch in her husband's hand and bidding the two adieu. Gopal holding his *mota bhai*'s (big brother) hand once again headed to the Maliya railway station to board the afternoon train to Rajkot. Kardani was told this would most likely be the last time the visit was required as a few crucial documents needed signatures.

Excitedly planning Gopal's future in the UK, the two munched on lunch and practised English greetings that Gopal would soon be using in his new English home. The dictionary had indeed proved useful! Gopal confessed that he was excited to see the world he had only glimpsed in Bollywood films. He also admitted that he would miss his family and think of them fondly as an emotional Alpa kissed him goodbye.

Mund met the pair in Rajkot and ushered them into the 'online office' to sign some papers. One delay after another kept them within its walls until it was dark outside. At 9.30 p.m., Gopal and Kardani got into the car with Mund and his driver for the return journey to their village. They stopped at a dhaba (roadside eatery) to have dinner.

No sooner did they get into the car, the driver stopped at a quiet stretch of the road near Manekwada village, some distance from Keshod, to answer a call of nature. In the wee hours of 9 February, all hell broke loose.

A motorbike approached the car stationed at the side of the road. One of the men on the bike shouted, 'Let us kidnap the boy and we may find something of value.' To this, the other responded by opening the car door and lifting Gopal out.

Squashing the wailing boy between the two, they were about to speed off when Kardani grabbed Gopal's hand and tried to pull them out. 'Help! Help!' shouted Kardani to the other two men in his group who seemed reluctant to come to his aid, even as Kardani was fighting what seemed a losing battle quite bravely.

The pillion rider pulled out a sharp knife and stabbed him in the stomach. Gopal's hand slipped out of his brother-in-law's grasp and the motorbike sped off into the night. A blood-soaked Kardani fell on the side of the road. The driver came to Kardani's aid but Mund did not rush to help. They took Kardani to the hospital rather than chase the motorbike that took Gopal away. Kardani was unable to identify the men on the bike and succumbed to his injuries in the hospital, a week later on 17 February.

Not long after Gopal was snatched from the car and not far from the scene of the kidnapping, the young boy was thrown on the roadside after being repeatedly knifed. An auto-rickshaw driver found him with multiple stab wounds and injuries and rushed him to a hospital in Keshod. He was shifted to a bigger hospital in Rajkot and died during treatment on 11 February. There was no consoling Gopal's distraught sister as her wails echoed through the hospital first on losing her young brother and then her husband to what she refused to believe was a random kidnapping-gone-awry murder.

Why a seemingly poor and inconsequential boy was kidnapped and then stabbed a few minutes later, left the police in no doubt that foul play was involved. Digging into the background, the police discovered that the young orphan loved to pretend play as Bollywood's legendary cop Bajirao Singham. But the sordid saga of the adoption and the crumbling dreams of the wide-eyed boy, left no doubt in the minds of the sleuths that there was more to it than met the eye.

Kardani's statement was recorded and Mund and the driver Trivedi were quickly arrested. This was followed by the arrest of two contract killers Rajpari Goswami and Lakshman Gadhvi who confessed to being hired for Rs 5 lakh to murder the boy.

It wasn't long before the investigators linked the murder of the child to his adoptive parents and ascribed the motive as to cash in on the insurance cover that paid them Rs 1.3 crore on their son's death.

* * *

The Indian government requested Britain to extradite Arti and Kaval to stand trial in India on six counts: conspiracy to commit murder, murder, attempt to commit murder, kidnapping, abduction for the purpose of committing murder and abetting a crime. On 29 June 2017, a provisional warrant was issued and the two were arrested that same day and produced in Westminster Magistrates' Court. Initially, they were remanded into custody. When substantial securities were paid, they were remanded on conditional bail. On 29 August, a certificate was issued to pursue the case under section 70 of the Extradition Act 2003 where India, being a category 2 territory, had to show a prima facie case before extradition could take place.

After the case management hearings, a two-day trial was fixed for 21 and 22 January 2019 in Westminster Magistrates' Court, being presided over by Chief Magistrate Emma Arbuthnot who a month before had ruled to extradite liquor baron Vijay Mallya to India. With what seemed like an open-and-shut case, many were confident that this case too would meet with the same conclusion. Alas, it was never meant to be so!

Dr James McManus, who represents the UK on the European Committee for the Prevention of Torture and Inhuman or Degrading Treatment or Punishment and had also served as chairman of the Parole Board for Scotland, was the prison expert who visited Junagadh prison for three days in April–May 2018. He concluded that the prison conditions met with the guidelines of the ECHR.

During his visit, the prison population was 247 males and thirteen females as opposed to the official capacity of 250 males and fifteen females, and the number of toilets, bathrooms, window sizes and other provisions were satisfactory. He, however, admitted that there were no beds and prisoners slept on 'essentially a bare floor but a mat and blanket (were provided)'.

However, Kaval's counsel Peter Caldwell brought in photographs of the prison notice board which showed headcounts taken daily. He picked random dates throughout the year to show how the prison population was higher on other days than those visited by McManus. For example, on a day in October 2018, there were 311 inmates against the official capacity of 265. In December, this number rose to 350. And on 12 January 2019, it was 367. It was the highest in August 2017, when 413 inmates resided in the prison.

McManus agreed that the occupancy 'consistently remained above capacity' and 'perhaps they (the prison authorities) prepared for my arrival as it is not unusual for population to change during inspection'. However, the judge remarked that while the male prison population seemed to be higher than capacity during most months, the female population in the two large cells provided for them had remained consistent.

Issues of Arti's health conditions were also raised by her counsel Edward Fitzgerald, who said she had spent many years taking care of her old parents, and was suffering from depression and back problems. Her counsel said she required psychiatric help and physiotherapy. McManus said there 'was appropriate medical care in prison and 99 per cent medication is free' and a psychiatrist visits the prison every week for two hours. There is also a hospital nearby that has a secure ward.

On the second day of the trial Dr V. Suresh, a human rights lawyer and the national general secretary of the People's Union for Civil Liberties, gave evidence from India through video conferencing on the procedures and time frame of such trials.

The defence raised the issue of delayed trials and a long period of stay in jail as undertrials, mentioning that while the average time is two to two-and-a-half years in Junagadh prison, some stay in jail for as long as eleven years without bail. 'In my opinion, they will be unlikely to get bail as they will be considered absconders,' Dr Suresh told the court.

Fitzgerald was also worried that Arti Dhir and Kaval Raijada would be tried for double murder, but the CPS maintained that since their intention was to kill the child for insurance, they would be tried for his murder and the other would be a culpable homicide.

The trial was slated to continue to a third day with Dr Alan Mitchell, a prison expert who provided testimony in both Mallya's and Chawla's cases on the conditions of Indian jails, taking the witness stand. In Mallya's case, Arbuthnot was convinced that barrack 12 of Arthur Road Jail in Mumbai met article 3 of the ECHR, and she looked seemingly satisfied in this case too with the evidence already provided by McManus; she was not convinced about how Mitchell could further contribute to the case.

For Arbuthnot, the essential evidence lay in the emails that the Gujarat Police had claimed to obtain from Mund. CPS counsel Toby Cadman admitted that while Indian authorities have obtained the emails and claim that some were sent on the day of the murder, neither the forensic report of the hard drive nor the contents of the emails have been supplied to the CPS. 'There are two critical questions,' said Arbuthnot. 'The contents of the emails and the confession evidence.'

Also, Arti 'lied on arrest' about the adoption and murder of their ward and the subsequent failed insurance claim worked against them. But the contents of the email sent hours before the murder could provide the clinching evidence required to establish a prima facie case to extradite them to India. The court gave India two months to submit the emails as evidence.

* * *

On 2 July, as Indian journalists flocked the high court to hear the decision of the divisional bench in the sensational Vijay Mallya appeal to overturn the order of Emma Arbuthnot to extradite Mallya to India, the chief magistrate was preparing to deliver her verdict in yet another extradition case where India wanted the killer parents brought to Gujarat to face justice for their crimes.

Alas! India suffered a massive defeat that day. First with Mallya winning his right to appeal and then with Arbuthnot refusing to send Dhir and Raijada to India. Interestingly, Arbuthnot found prima facie evidence of a conspiracy to murder but was not convinced that certain laws of the state of Gujarat met with article 3 of the ECHR.

After intense arguments by Toby Cadman of the CPS and Edward Fitzgerald and Tim Maloney representing Dhir and Raijada, respectively, Arbuthnot decided 'to rule on only two points: issues of prima facie case and article 3, the irreducibility of the sentence'. Arbuthnot said that India's evidence against the defendants was 'circumstantial'. There was money sent to Mund from London and also a crucial email sent from Arti to Mund four hours before the murder.

Arbuthnot concluded that the 'wealth-builder policy which was in essence a life insurance policy set up for Gopal' would benefit Dhir if Gopal died and she would be paid ten times the premium and she found it strange that a 'penniless farm boy, unaccountably was targeted by the murderers'.

'There is only one person who would financially gain from this little boy's murder and that is Ms Dhir. The insurance policy gives Ms Dhir and through her, her husband Mr Raijada, a motive for killing him,' said Arbuthnot.

* * *

If convicted, Dhir and Raijada would receive a sentence of life imprisonment with no possibility of a review either by the state of Gujarat or by the President of India. The hearings in Westminster Magistrates' Court in London saw defence lawyers raise the issue of human rights in Indian jails and the long waiting period for cases to reach their conclusion in the courts to convince against the extradition of the two to India.

However, what clinched the case in their favour was the evidence provided by Dr V. Suresh, the human rights lawyer, who spoke from India through video conferencing in January 2019, on the procedures and time frame of such trials.

He followed this by his report dated 24 March 2019, where he made it clear that if the defendants were found guilty of culpable homicide, they could still be excluded from considerations of remissions under the 2014 remission policy of the state of Gujarat. He also said that the defendants, if convicted, did not have the right to remission or pardon under article 72 of the Constitution of India as the crime they were accused of did not fall under either the state list or the Union list of offences that would allow a Presidential pardon.

India neither challenged Dr Suresh's testimony nor produced any evidence to contradict it. He was also not cross-examined by the CPS, which meant that his evidence was accepted and the judge said she was left with 'uncontradicted evidence that there is no system of review of these life sentences'.

In England and Wales, an important principle is to provide the offender 'hope' and a 'possibility' of release in exceptional circumstances 'which render just punishment originally imposed no longer justifiable'. The UK courts have long accepted that there cannot be one rule in this jurisdiction and a separate rule for extradition in another.

'I find there are substantial grounds for believing that they are at real risk of being subjected to treatment, a lack of review of a life sentence which would be inhuman and degrading and a breach of article 3,' said Arbuthnot, discharging the case against the duo.

Minutes before Arbuthnot was to announce her judgment, she received an email from the CPS attaching an assurance sent by the GoI that 'notwithstanding the remission policy of the State of Gujarat' the couple would be 'eligible to apply for remission', but the letter by a joint secretary to the GoI reached just forty-five minutes before the court was due to give judgment. Since its consideration would mean further delays and 'in the light of the lateness of this assurance', Arbuthnot decided to proceed with pronouncing her judgment.

The judgment, however, left ample room for appeal. Arbuthnot said that if the state of Gujarat changed the rule of irreducibility of sentences, it might be in accordance with article 3 principles. If that happened, the case could come back to the court where the judge would then look at prison conditions and other issues raised by the defendants. India had fourteen days to appeal against this decision in the high court.

She also said that since it was alleged that the agreement to murder was made in the UK when Mund was here and there was 'strong evidence that money was sent from the defendant's UK bank accounts to the man who organized the killing', and there were relevant email exchanges between London and India, it was 'not impossible for a prosecution to be initiated here'.

On 2 July, Arti and Kaval walked out of Westminster Magistrates' Court, free. The Indian government appealed the decision in the high court in London.

On 28 January 2020, India's appeal was to be heard in court number 3 of the Royal Courts of Justice. The same court in which Mallya's appeal was heard. It was a chilly day but the sun shone very bright. At 10.30 a.m., Toby Cadman of the CPS stood to address Lord Justice Dingemans and Justice Spencer. The court sought to confirm with Cadman whether he agreed with the chronology of the case as submitted by the defence. 'One can't have extradition proceedings derailed by giving materials last minute,' observed Lord Justice Dingemans.

A simple assurance from the Gujarat government offering the duo such a chance for remission would have sealed their return to India. However, India produced an assurance by the government in New Delhi, which was neither satisfactory nor on time, which prompted the district judge to refuse the extradition.

The high court heard from Cadman how delays were inevitable as it required communication between both state and the Central government but failed to convince the court to rethink the district judge's decision. 'At least from January 2019, the chief judicial magistrate had made it clear that unless you get assurance you might lose,' said Justice Spencer. Cadman seemed to be in a tight spot. It was in January 2019 that Emma Arbuthnot had heard the case when the substantive arguments were made. Yet it was only on the day—2 July 2019—when she was to give her ruling that the assurance from India reached her.

Something similar happened in the high court as well, which clearly did not go well with the two judges. Taking the lead, Lord Justice Dingemans termed it 'disappointing' and a waste of time that India provided the same assurance to them which was given to Westminster Magistrates' Court. The court was clearly peeved that a few hours before the hearing on Tuesday morning, they were provided materials, but there was nothing new or updated. For once the usually eloquent and confident Cadman looked at a loss for words. 'Our point is that the case must be remitted to the district judge for consideration as she had not agreed to adjourn the judgment,' said Cadman.

There is a 'strong obligation to honour the (extradition) treaty', said Cadman, adding 'she could have allowed time for parties to make submissions'. Cadman's principal point seem to be that the allegations against the couple were very serious and the lower court should have taken into consideration the assurance provided by India.

Besides, he pointed out that the judgment mentioned that if the state policy (on granting of parole to those accused of double murder) was changed, then the outcome would have been different. All through Cadman's arguments, the judges were reiterating the importance of meeting the agreed deadlines to serve new evidence at the trial stage. Justice Spencer then remarked that it seemed Indian courts were too indulgent in accepting evidence at the last moment. 'It (the assurance) took a number of months, regrettably,

I can say. The assurance was provided (to Westminster Magistrates' Court) the moment CPS received it,' said Cadman.

At 11.30 a.m., the judges rose and came back after two minutes. It was now Edward Fitzgerald's turn. Over the years, Fitzgerald has emerged as a champion defence lawyer, with the British press calling him 'a Rolls-Royce in the cab rank of barristers'. 'The assurance was not provided on time. It was in November 2018 that the issue was raised, and in January 2019 we set out the case in full,' said Fitzgerald. Arti and Kaval were all ears as Fitzgerald elaborated on how, despite having several months in between, the assurance was not being sent. He also highlighted the shifting stance of the CPS regarding the cross-examination of key defence witness Dr Suresh. According to Fitzgerald, on 25 March 2019, the CPS said 'we will examine and then in May, CPS said we won't cross-examine Dr Suresh.'

Fitzgerald termed the assurance from India as 'hearsay'. 'We have got a hearsay statement from the federal government,' he said to highlight that the assurance should have come from the Gujarat government.

Lord Justice Dingemans then asked Fitzgerald to speak on the points of financial consequences and the gravity of the crime. 'If the gravity of the crime is so much, India could have been prompt in giving assurances. Financial consequences are on both sides.' And as if to highlight a casual approach from India, Fitzgerald added that the assurance had still not come from the right authority.

Cadman also reasoned with the court that if their appeal was refused, India would start fresh extradition proceedings in the case and this would incur additional expenses. The judge said that since the delays were caused by India, it seemed only appropriate if they incurred more costs to pursue this. 'Those financial consequences were brought about by the government's failure to obtain directions regarding assurances or to provide an assurance at an earlier date.'

While the judges agreed that the chief magistrate did not give any directions requiring an assurance to be provided at any time, the bench also noted that the GoI also did not suggest that they 'were able to provide any relevant assurance which would meet the irreducible life sentence point' and that two extradition hearings were adjourned because of delays by the government in complying with directions and the third and final hearing was adjourned part heard to enable the government to deal with the irreducible life sentences point.

A piece of paper bearing the solemn promise by the Gujarat government to consider a reduced sentence for good behaviour, should Dhir and Raijada be convicted for the double murder, was all that was required to extradite them to India. Yet, the government failed to produce it.

Kaval had donned his best three-piece suit for the hearing but still carried the demeanour of a spoilt privileged teenager. Arti was wearing her usual dark suit that contrasted her blood-red nails and surprisingly a smile. In the lunch break, as the couple emerged from the grand building of the Royal Courts of Justice, wearing identical sunglasses, and walked with confidence to a sandwich bar across the street, they were confronted by a journalist and photographer from the *Daily Mail*, a reporter from the BBC and us, the authors. An agitated Kaval swished his hand with enough force to cause a journalist's phone camera to drop. This was recorded on the camera of another journalist. Notwithstanding that this act could have got him into trouble, he walked into the restaurant with a swagger, even as the paralegals accompanying him whispered words of caution.

On 6 February 2020, the high court in London discharged the appeal by India against Westminster Magistrates' Court's refusal to extradite the duo to India in July 2019 because of the delays caused by the GoI in providing the crucial assurances that could have clinched the case in its favour.

India can bring about extradition proceedings should the law change in Gujarat. They could also apply for a new extradition proceeding and simply give an assurance that the Gujarat state policy of irreducible life sentences would not apply to the duo. Something which they could have easily done in this case. Now, the government has not just lost this extradition battle, but also set two alleged child murderers free.

Meanwhile Dhir and Raijada live in London, free today from the shackles of the law, free from standing trial for the murder of a young boy in cold blood. Who would have thought a stringent law in the state of Gujarat would actually rescue them from the proverbial long arm of the law?

9

WAR ROOM LEAK LIEUTENANT

Take one air defence directorate officer, mix with an extramarital affair, add to it a large dose of Big Brother Air Force Intelligence department and slowly stir electronic surveillance. What do you get? But of course, 7000 pages of highly sensitive information leaking from the supposedly airtight navy war room cauldron.

For many days, the Air Force Intelligence had put Wing Commander Sambhaji Surve under the scanner for his relationship with one Raj Rani Jaiswal, a honey trap to obtain classified information from the commander. Finally, in April 2005, they had enough evidence to raid his house. They found a 128 MB Kingston pen drive and seized it. It contained secret documents with sensitive information on India's maritime preparedness and plans for the next two decades. The Indian Navy was informed.

Naval intelligence traced the leak to the high-security war room in the Directorate of Naval Operations (DNO) in New Delhi, a highly secure building with electronic swipe access and sentries. The 'prohibited' Indian Navy war room falls under section 2(8) of the Official Secrets Act, 1923 (OSA) which makes it a criminal offence to distribute any of its classified documents.

By December, Naval intelligence had followed the trail of the leak to one Commander Vijendra Rana of the Marine

Commando Force, who was posted to the DNO, and navigation and operations specialists Commander Vinod Kumar Jha and Captain Kashyap Kumar. During the course of the inquiry, Rana surrendered to Commander Anupam Kaushal a 256 MB Transcend pen drive, which was forensically examined and then handed over to the CBI Superintendent Ramnish Geer, heading this investigation.

The trail then led to middlemen and arms dealers. Prominent among them stood a young retired naval lieutenant with a charming persona and a strong preference for blonde babes.

As a young man, Ravi Shankaran simply followed his famous uncle's footsteps when he joined the Indian Navy in 1986. Shankaran's aunt was married to the Naval Chief, Admiral Arun Prakash. As a young lieutenant, Prakash had risen to fame with a bravery award in the 1965 Indo–Pak war and a Vir Chakra in the 1971 Indo–Pak conflict. One of the most decorated war heroes, Admiral Prakash's career trajectory had seen him command the Eastern Naval Fleet, become the chief of personnel at naval headquarters, then commander-in-chief of the Western Naval Command and finally the twentieth chief of the Indian Navy in July 2004. He retired in October 2006.

But Shankaran was too impatient to aspire for a long naval career. He quickly learnt that the navy had to offer him more than just deep-sea diving and a few medals to decorate his uniform. So in just eight years, citing medical reasons, he retired from the navy as a lieutenant.

While in 1994, this may have looked like the end to the naval career of Lieutenant Ravi Shankaran, it was actually the birth of the ambitious, enterprising and social charmer Shanx—as he would often introduce himself. Shanx knew this moment would only define his meteoric rise to fame and fortune.

It is little wonder that soon Shanx Oceaneering was born. Shankaran, along with another retired naval lieutenant, Kulbhushan Parashar, who quit the Navy in 1995, incorporated Shanx Oceaneering Private Limited on 11 September 1996 with an authorized share capital of Rs 100 lakh with a 64.03 per cent paid-up capital. The company was declared to be 'involved in architectural, engineering and other technical activities' and was registered at 8 Clark House, Woodhouse Road in Mumbai. A posh office opened in south Goa later that year. Situated at S-58, Varna Industrial Estate, Phase II-B, Salcette, the 1100 sq. m. plot housed staff quarters and a residence.

But neither Shankaran nor Parashar believed that only Shanx Oceaneering could fulfil their ambitions. A year later, they started the Indian arm of a Swedish firm Interspiro, a company that specializes in breathing apparatus for firefighters, divers and other emergency services. Thus Interspiro India Pvt. Ltd was born. Under the umbrella of these two firms, Shankaran and Parashar also provided 'consultancy' to foreign companies seeking to sell defence equipment to India and served as representatives and liaison between the foreign companies and the Indian armed forces. CBI investigations later found a host of shell companies they suspected were floated by the duo, including Expert Systems Pvt. Ltd, Basic Pvt. Ltd, Kelvin Engineering Pvt. Ltd and Unitech Enterprises.

* * *

One of Shankaran's partners in crime—whether on the dance floor of a social event or within the confines of the power corridors of the politico-business class—was arms dealer Abhishek Verma.

Verma's parents, journalist Shrikant Verma and Veena Verma, both served as members of Parliament and held prestigious positions within the Congress party. Handpicked by the then prime minister, Indira Gandhi, Shrikant also served as a general secretary and Veena as a vice President of the Indian National Congress and also the chief of the Mahila Congress, the party's women's wing.

While studying at Georgetown University in Washington DC, Abhishek Verma was the editor-publisher of *India Worldwide*, a magazine for non-resident Indians in the US. On his return to India, he declined to contest elections on a Congress ticket in 1996 and set up his business in the arms sector earning him the moniker 'Lord of War'.

A November 1997 cover of *India Today* hailed the 1968-born as the youngest billionaire in India. His empire only grew. He soon started a communications venture called Atlas Interactive India Pvt. Ltd that tied up with the government to run the state-owned Bharat Sanchar Nigam Limited (BSNL).

Verma made several headlines: His marriage to Miss Universe Romania Anca Neacsu in 2006 was the talk of every tabloid; in 2011, he became the chief evangelist of Olialia World, a multinational FMCG brand splashed on every business daily; and in 2017, business papers reported on the young man winning the contract to construct (and own for the next fifty years) Maldives International Airport which he planned to christen Olialia International Airport.

But this journey was not easy. It was fraught with allegations of corruption and money laundering. Several cases were registered, Verma and his wife faced arrests and spent years fighting battles in courts. One such was a result of his close friendship with Shankaran that found him embroiled in the navy war room leak.

Shankaran and Verma were kindred spirits. Both loved to party, travel to exotic locations and grow their network and net worth. While Verma was politically well-connected, Shankaran boasted of friends in high places in the armed forces. It seems the duo spent the 2006 New Year in Mauritius and then extended the party to Dubai later that week, even while the investigations in the navy war room leak were unfolding.

* * *

The CBI filed the first charge sheet on 3 July 2006 against Shankaran, Parashar and others for allegedly conspiring to commit offences under the OSA. The leaked files included a war game marked 'Top Secret' that contained intelligence inputs given to the navy; details of 'vulnerable areas' and 'vulnerable points' in India's air defence network; details of navy preparedness and requirements for the next twenty years; operating procedures for a missile project; armed forces preparedness during talks with Pakistan; the joint response in case of aggression by Pakistan, among many other important and sensitive details.

The CBI noted that some files pertained to 'a strategically very sensitive study which is being taken up by the Air Force, Navy and the Army to identify their vulnerable areas and vulnerable points, update threat perceptions to the nation', while others, in particular one obtained from Parashar's pen drive containing 3264 pages of 'secret network-centric operations', contained the Navy's acquisition plans for the next two decades.

The charge sheet clearly states: This information for big multinationals engaged in defence supplies implies planning their business and networking strategies for the next twenty years, because this gives them a clear insight as to what the requirements of Indian Navy would be in this area, hence affording a market edge. The worth of this information, when translated into currency could run into billions of dollars.

'Some Sly Truths', shouted the 17 July 2006 issue of *Outlook* magazine, always persistent in its reporting on the case. Mocking the defence minister for calling the leaked files 'commercial information', the journalist Saikat Datta wrote, 'How many contradictions does it take to bury the truth? Union defence minister Pranab Mukherjee's repeated efforts to gloss over the culpability of Kulbhushan Parashar and Ravi Shankaran—named as the prime accused in the naval war room leak case—have come to naught.'

The charge sheet did not mince words when it named Shankaran and Parashar as the main accused working for 'unknown persons' of a communications company called Atlas. The plan was to 'unauthorisedly trade off classified documents/ information relating to the ministry of defence'. Parashar, the CBI said, started working as a vice president (marketing) of Atlas Defence Systems after being introduced by Verma to one Phillip who was the managing director of Atlas Telecom, a UK- and

Canada-based company. Verma looked after the Atlas group's interests in India.

Parashar and Verma hosted several parties where high-ranking defence personnel mixed with arms suppliers and agents including several foreigners. This shows that the telecom company served as a front to push the agenda of its defence sister company. The CBI also found several incriminating documents about Atlas Defence Systems from Parashar's residence.

The CBI raided Verma's residence on 23 June 2006, seizing documents that were crucial in filing a second charge sheet that now included Verma for allegedly conspiring to obtain the secret naval documents. It was alleged that Verma received remittances of about Rs 6.5 crore to pay bribes to defence personnel to obtain necessary information that would prove conducive to strike a deal between the military and Atlas group for procurement of equipment that the military hoped to acquire. Verma's links with Atlas group were irrefutable and it was found that the company had submitted several bids to supply communication equipment to the armed forces.

* * *

The CBI registered the case only on 20 March 2006. But before the CBI took over the case, an in-house investigation by the navy conducted in December 2005 held Commander Vijendra Rana, Commander Vinod Kumar Jha and Captain Kashyap Kumar guilty of the leak. They were all sacked without trial under a provision of article 311 of the Constitution which states no trial is required if 'the President or the Governor, as the case may be, is satisfied that in the interest of the security of state, it is not expedient to hold such inquiry'.

While the judgment of the Board of Inquiry (BoI) mentions that an affidavit was filed by Naval Chief Admiral Arun Prakash who denied any kind of involvement or to show any leniency to protect his relation, investigations by *Outlook* magazine revealed that the BoI ignored the telephone records that could have been crucial to the inquiry. These included a call from Admiral Arun Prakash's residence to Parashar's mobile in November 2004; a call from Shankaran's residence in Mumbai to the Admiral's wife, his aunt, Kumkum Prakash's mobile but not routed through the exchange as is the norm; and many other calls by Shankaran to senior naval officers including those directly involved with the board like Captain Jason Thomas, who got a call the night before the inquiry began. Shankaran's relationship with Admiral Prakash also led to speculation about why the navy did not investigate civilians involved in the case or even lodge an FIR against them.

In his autobiography, former president of India, Pranab Mukherjee wrote that when Shankaran's name was linked to the navy war room leak case, Admiral Prakash called him up and offered his resignation, which Mukherjee turned down. 'I was influenced in my decision by the dictum that every individual is responsible for his or her own action, and the relatives of an accused do not have to bear the burden of any criminal or improper act unless there is some evidence to the contrary,' wrote Mukherjee who was then the defence minister. Calling Admiral Prakash a man known for 'high integrity and professionalism', Mukherjee left vindicated when no evidence was found that linked the Admiral to the leaks.

Jha, Rana and Surve were arrested by the CBI and chargesheeted. They were later granted bail. Raj Rani Jaiswal, the woman with whom Surve was allegedly associated, was also arrested but she was not declared an accused in the charge sheet. Abhishek Verma was also arrested and granted bail. However, Captain Kashyap Kumar, named in the FIR, was neither arrested nor chargesheeted.

The BoI had sacked Surve, Rana and Jha for misconduct under section 19 of the Air Force Act. Rana and Jha challenged the BoI decision in the Armed Forces Tribunal (AFT). They alleged that the 'brain and mastermind' behind the naval war room leaks was Shankaran, and the BoI inquiry was 'aimed at shielding' him, 'a relative of the chief of naval staff'. Their plea was dismissed on 30 June 2010.

They then approached the Supreme Court. On 7 July 2018, a Supreme Court bench comprising A.M. Khanwilkar and M.M. Shantanagoudar and headed by Justice Dipak Misra refused to interfere with the AFT's decision.

Captain Kashyap Kumar approached the Delhi High Court to quash the FIR against him. In 2018, the high court informed Kumar that the case against him by the CBI has been closed 'on the strength of the relevant documents'. The CBI's report to the high court stated: 'The investigation in respect of petitioner Kashyap Kumar has concluded and the CBI has decided to close the case against him'. Since his dismissal from the Armed Forces, Kashyap found it difficult to find employment and had to take on low-paying jobs to make ends meet. A clean chit by the CBI has now helped Kashyap challenge his dismissal from the Navy at the AFT.

A trial held in the special CBI court in Delhi in 2006 pronounced Verma guilty and sentenced him to imprisonment under sections 3 and 5 of the OSA. Verma approached the high court, and in May 2008, he was granted bail on a personal bond of Rs 10 lakh.

Meanwhile, two former naval officers were also named in a second charge sheet filed by the CBI in February 2007 which included Captain (retired) Salam Singh Rathore and Commander (retired) Jarnail Singh Kalra, a deputy general manager (customer services) in the Bangalore-based Hindustan Aeronautics Ltd (HAL). Kalra allegedly passed on confidential documents to Captain Rathore who was in naval procurements in 2005 and he allegedly passed those documents on to Parashar.

Both Rathore and Kalra were accused of leaking military secrets under the OSA and the IPC in charges framed by the CBI in 2014. On 7 July 2018, the court convicted Rathore under section 3(1) C of the OSA, 1923, but acquitted Kalra of wrongdoing in the case.

The CBI had told the court that it seized seventeen official documents from Rathore's possession—nine secret, four restricted and one confidential. Special CBI Judge S.K. Aggarwal awarded seven years of rigorous imprisonment to Rathore stating that the documents found in his possession belonged to the navy and were 'directly or indirectly useful to the enemy in one way or the other' and the offence was 'against the very national security'.

Judge Aggarwal gave permission to Parashar who was also out on bail to travel to several countries including France, Spain, Greece, Czech Republic and Russia from 4 June to 1 July 2018, for meetings regarding his business of food imports. The dramatic arrest of Parashar had taken place at the airport when he returned from London on 5 April 2006. While granting Parashar permission, Judge Aggarwal warned him not to extend his visit abroad (even due to medical reasons) and not enter the UK to meet his co-accused Shankaran.

Shankaran had left India on 10 November 2005 never to return. He could travel within the European Union as he had availed himself of a Schengen visa before leaving India and the CBI tracked him across Europe until he reached the UK where Shankaran applied for asylum citing political persecution in the war room leak case.

On 2 April 2006, Shankaran in a press statement said: 'I am a respectable non-resident Indian, I can never dream of getting involved in anything that could undermine national security. I have absolutely no connection with the transaction of the purchase of Scorpene submarines nor with the War Room Leak case of the navy.'

Investigations revealed that Parashar had met Shankaran in London and the CBI had tracked Shankaran's relatives in the UK. They cancelled his passport and issued a Red Notice through Interpol in May 2006. But the CBI's request to the ministry of external affairs (MEA) to ask Scotland Yard to arrest Shankaran was shockingly turned down. The MEA response read: 'The Ministry of External Affairs vide its letter dated May 31, 2006 had intimated that since the case was still under investigation stage, it would be premature to process the case for extradition or making a request for provisional arrest for the purpose of extradition.' The CBI had then issued a proclamation notice in *The Times* (London) on 11 August 2006 asking Shankaran to appear before the CBI for questioning.

The CBI, while pursuing the many accused in the case, also kept making requests to the MEA for Shankaran's extradition from Britain. The MEA revoked his travel documents on 1 April 2006. After Shankaran failed to appear before the investigating officers, the CBI on 12 September 2006 attached Shankaran's property— the office of Shanks Oceanographic Pvt. Ltd in Goa—and accounts with HSBC Bank of his firm called Besix India.

Finally, a formal request was made to the UK for his extradition, following which an arrest warrant was issued on 10 April 2007. Shankaran evaded the law for years until he was arrested by Scotland Yard in April 2010.

The case in India is currently at the stage of hearing of evidence. Meanwhile, all the CBI's attempts to get Shankaran to India from London have met with failure.

* * *

In the course of the investigation by the Board of Inquiry, on 7 August 2005, Commander Rana surrendered a 256MB 'Transcend' pen drive with a unique serial number (72989-0314-OC-6C), which was sent to the Andhra Pradesh Forensic Laboratory on 19 May 2006. The lab report contained 112 active (but non-unique) files and 343 deleted files capable of being retrieved. It listed the 432 files (active and deleted) common to both the 'Transcend' pen drive surrendered by Commander Rana and the 'Kingston' pen drive seized from the home of Wing Commander Surve. Within these 432 files were eight Microsoft Office Word files (numbers 416– 22 inclusive, and number 425) totalling about eighteen pages that were sent by an email address cdr_rana@yahoo.co.in to one Vic Branson on vicbranson@aol.com.

The copies of the files that contained information about the Indian Navy's operations along the Sir Creek area on the border with Pakistan were marked 'Secret'—a classification between 'Confidential' and 'Top Secret'—and were created on 16 May

2005. An email was sent to Branson on that same day at 6.30 p.m. with the subject line '*Hi there!!!*' and the body text as:

> Dear Vic, Please find attached some useful information on the creek area. Read it as I got to make the user rqmts for BSF tonight, which I shall send for any amendments if reqd.

In less than fifteen minutes, a reply was received from 'Vic Branson' simply saying '*ROGER*'. This email was followed by another email with the same subject but one with an attachment named 'User Reqmt BSF Boats.doc'. On 17 and 21 May 2005, 'Vic Branson' sent more emails to Commander Rana with the subject '*Hi there Again!!!*'.

* * *

In Spring 2010, extradition proceedings began against Shankaran. Requests were sent to the UK, France, Sweden and Spain for the arrest of Shankaran. Shankaran was wanted by India for crimes under various sections of the OSA and section 120-B (criminal conspiracy) of the IPC. The CBI had registered a case on 20 March 2006 and a charge sheet was filed against Shankaran along with former IAF Wing Commander Sambhaji Lal Surve, ex-naval Commanders Vinod Kumar Jha and Vijendra Rana, Kulbushan Parashar and arms dealer Abhishek Verma.

The CBI investigation revealed that all these accused could be grouped in three categories: Group 1—accused who were serving in the Indian Navy and Indian Air Force; accused Vijendra Rana, V.K. Jha and S.L. Surve fall in this group; Group 2—accused who have retired from the Indian Navy; Kulbhushan Parashar and Ravi Shankaran; and finally Group 3—accused like Abhishek Verma who were private persons and have never served in the Indian Navy or Air Force.

On 21 April, Shankaran was arrested by the London Metropolitan Police. Shankaran was produced in Westminster

Magistrates' Court on 22 April and was given a court bail. He was confined to his residence and his movements were monitored by a police guard.

Key evidence that the CPS on behalf of India produced in Westminster Magistrates' Court were statements by a witness, P.H. Khushwaha, who was an employee of Shanx/Interspiro based in Goa, for over a decade. Three statements were produced before the district judge. In his first statement to the CBI on 3 June 2006, Khushwaha said that he was 'not aware' of any other email ID being used by Shankaran. Then on 5 June 2006, Khushwaha told the CBI that Shankaran always used his laptop and never any office computer for sending emails. His email ID was interspo@vsnl.com and shanx@vsnl.com.

But the evidence the CBI wanted the court to focus on came in Khushwaha's third statement dated 6 June 2006 where, after the CBI showed him certain papers, he confirmed that 'these papers relate to a purchase order from V. Branson of Inmaty Ltd, Vogolheid, 9052, Gent Belgium regarding purchase of diving equipment. All these purchase orders were sent by Ravi Shankaran by courier'. He went on to say that 'Victor Branson and Vic Branson were none other than Ravi Shankaran. And the email ID for this identity was vicbranson@aol.com. He also stated that being an employee, he was simply following orders and was unaware of Shankaran's motives for the transactions.

Shankaran told the court that the CBI had gone out of the way to 'cover up false and fabricated evidence' and it should be considered inadmissible as it had 'no merit whatsoever'. The District Judge Nicholas Evans determined that the third statement was admissible evidence and held that there was no need to call Khushwaha to give oral evidence to explain any discrepancy with his earlier statements. There would be no unfairness to the appellant as he would have the opportunity to controvert the statement during the trial in India.

Judge Evans also said that extradition between India and UK was bound by 'good faith' and he was confident that if the prosecution in India later found that there was no 'credible and admissible' evidence against Shankaran, then India was duty bound to end the proceedings and withdraw the extradition request.

On 27 March 2013, the district judge at Westminster Magistrates' Court in London said in his ruling that he had been presented with no evidence to prove that there wasn't a 'case to answer' and ruled that based on sufficient prima facie evidence there existed a conspiracy between Commander Rana and Vic Branson to disseminate classified information for commercial purposes. He agreed that Shankaran should be extradited to face trial in India. The case file was then sent to the UK Home Secretary Theresa May for a final decision. May signed the extradition order on 22 May 2013.

Shankaran appealed against this decision in the High Court. The case came up for hearing before the president of the Queen's Bench division Sir Brian Leveson and Justice Nicholas Blake. Justice Leveson is known for leading the public inquiry, ordered by the then prime minister David Cameron, into the role of the press and police in the wake of the phone-hacking scandal. Some British tabloids were found to have hacked into phones of not just celebrities but also some unsuspecting victims of crime. The Leveson inquiry report was published in November 2012 and garnered much headline in the British press.

Before the high court bench, Shankaran had raised two substantive grounds against the decision of the district judge. First, could it be conclusively proved that Shankaran was in fact Vic Branson? Second, was the disclosure of information in this case particularly damaging under India's OSA (1923)?

The court acknowledged that India's 1923 Act almost mirrors the UK's OSA (1911). However, the UK act was amended in 1989 and the bench believed that the amendment made it important to look more closely at whether the information was actually damaging rather than just being classified as confidential.

Sir Leveson believed that the latter could have easily been resolved by the CBI if one of its officers had provided evidence to show that one or more of the attachments of that email constituted a damaging disclosure. But since that was not done, James Lewis, QC, Shankaran's counsel, urged the court to consider that there was really no basis on which the material could have been considered damaging. However, CPS barrister John Hardy, QC, told the court to take into account the 'sensitivity of the border' and the likely damage such disclosures would cause to the security along the Indo–Pak border, to establish a prima facie case. District Judge Evans had seen the documents and was satisfied that they were damaging even without any expert evidence accompanying it.

The high court too inspected the documents in the presence of an Indian police officer and allowed Hardy and Lewis to make closed (private) submissions on them. Neither the documents nor the submissions made on them are in the public domain. Sir Leveson said that while he was no expert on the matter in the files and going solely based on evidence, he found six of the eight files of 'little substance' but the remaining two appeared to be of 'obvious significance to issues of Indian national security' and capable of establishing their disclosure as damaging. He agreed to accept the CPS contention and 'assume the worst'. Even though the case against Shankaran was for commercial sale of the documents, the judge agreed that some of those documents in the wrong hands could pose a high-security risk for India.

'The likelihood of the disclosure being damaging is actually exacerbated by the uncertainty of the identity of Vic Branson,' the judge said. He reprimanded the Indian government for its 'informal approach' in the district court and not providing expert evidence which led to the high court too facing a 'lack of clarity'.

The critical question before the high court was whether Shankaran was indeed Vic Branson. Sir Leveson was also disappointed with India for not pursuing the many 'potential lines of evidence' but choosing to base its case on 'one piece of direct evidence', the third statement by Khushwaha.

The judge noticed that all the three statements of Khushwaha were typewritten and signed by the police officer. None of them was an affidavit or in any format that is recognized by UK courts.

'There is no statement or endorsement of truth, nor, indeed any warranty that the witness has read and understood the statement,' the judge said.

In the district court, Shankaran had also filed evidence that included a report by an expert on Indian law, Prof. Martin Lau, an affidavit by his co-director at Interspiro, Jennefer Mirza, and a fourth statement from Khushwaha. This fourth statement by Khushwaha, dated 14 December 2011, was a sworn affidavit that confirmed that during his employment with Shankaran's firms, Khushwaha had never received any email from vicbranson@aol.com. He claimed to be 'unaware of this email ID until the CBI during the recording of my statement told me that they had evidence to show that this email ID was used by Shankaran. I am not aware why the CBI said that or what evidence they had as the same was not shown to me'.

Mirza's affidavit asserted that the email address vicbranson@aol.com had never contacted Khushwaha's company email address. This raised questions on how Khushwaha would have any knowledge on who owned the email address vicbranson@aol.com.

Prof. Lau gave expert opinion as to evidential procedures in Indian criminal cases, drawing attention to the distinction in the IPC between section 164—statements taken by a magistrate—and section 161—statements taken by police officers. Lau told the court that the former are generally admissible as primary evidence at trial, but the latter are not. This makes the first three Khushwaha statements (under section 161) evidence that can only be relied upon in cross-examination for previous inconsistent statements.

Sir Brian Leveson held that the district judge was wrong to dismiss the expert evidence of Prof. Lau on the limitations of section 161 statements that was now before him, as simply 'an interesting debate, but one I need not consider'. Sir Brian Leveson was clear that 'his failure to do so constitutes an error of law' as all those factors were 'relevant to the reliability of the critical Khushwaha statement' to admit it as evidence where a prima facie case had to be made out for the extradition.

'I am satisfied that it would be wrong, as a matter of English law, to admit into evidence the single key hearsay sentence in Khushwaha's third statement upon which the link between "Vic Branson" and the appellant depends,' declared Sir Brian Leveson. He also called it 'far too slender a basis for founding this case', especially as, he said, the Indian government had several avenues open to them to establish the link between the name Vic Branson and Shankaran, none of which they explored in the three years the trial was considered in Westminster Magistrates' Court. 'I have little doubt that it should not have been admitted as the only evidence linking the Vic Branson email to the appellant. Without that link, the prima facie case that must be established collapses,' concluded Sir Leveson. Shankaran was also awarded £1,25,000 in legal costs.

Many questions arose after this judgment. How did India's premier investigating agency fail to meet even the simple expectations of the courts in the UK? Why was this case that threatened the security of the country allowed to crumble in such a shoddy fashion? Why were there no attempts made to produce more evidence and impress upon the judiciary in the UK the severity of the charges against Shankaran? This was India's biggest failure and yet no heads rolled in New Delhi.

This extradition case disappeared into oblivion when on 1 April 2013, the disgraced former naval lieutenant marched out of the high court, now a free man having the last laugh.

10

FILMY MOORTI CHORS

In September 2020, three fifteenth-century idols of Ram, Lakshman and Sita, stolen four decades ago from India, were repatriated from the UK. This wasn't an easy feat. One of the idols was spotted four years ago on the website of the British Antique Dealers' Association by a member of the India Pride Project, a group that works to locate stolen Indian artefacts. The bronze of the idol was identified as that from the Vijayanagara Empire—founded in 1336 in south India. But after many rigorous checks and false alarms, they were still clueless as to the identity of the idol.

Then another similar looking idol—with a slightly different crown and posture—was spotted on the website over a year ago, which is when the search changed from looking for solitary idols to an entire stolen set. Months later, in the rusty archives of the French Institute of Puducherry in India, they hit the jackpot!

A photograph taken on 15 June 1958, blurred at the edges and wearing its age on its sleeve, solved the great mystery by showing not just the full set of the idols but also the location of their real home—Sri Rajagopala Swamy Temple in Anandamangalam village in Tamil Nadu. The Idol Wing of the state police was roped in, and after days of digging through abandoned piles of written records, they unearthed a police complaint filed on 24 November 1978 of the theft that had taken place the night before. Three men were arrested and sent to prison in 1998, but that is where the trail died as there was no clue to the buyer of those idols. How they made it to the UK is anyone's guess!

The High Commission of India in the UK was now roped in to search for stolen idols. The Indian diplomats approached the Art and Antiques unit of the London Metropolitan police and traced the collector based in the UK, who had bought these idols from a vendor. Interestingly, the vendor had also supplied the Art Loss Register Certificates, which are certificates authenticating that the artefact was not on the global database of stolen items and disputed art and antiques. Since the vendor was now deceased, no further investigation could be opened in the UK.

However, when the Indian mission told the collector that these idols were stolen from a 'living' temple and requested the return of the idols, the collector, once satisfied it was a genuine match, agreed to return them. And so the three idols were sent back to India with much pomp and fervour. A rare success in what is definitely not a rare occurrence!

The lure of stealing priceless idols and artefacts from the numerous ancient temples that dot the length and breadth of India has a long history.

Several Bollywood films in the 1970s and 1980s had baddies who were *moorti chors* or idol smugglers. They epitomized the villainous conduct of robbing India's national treasures by selling them abroad at a hefty price. The thrill of the chase made this crime one of the most exciting to be immortalized on the silver screen, though the representation is now dwindling. What happens when it moves beyond the Bollywood scripts to real life? You may be able to take the moorti chors out of Bollywood, but can you take Bollywood out of the moorti chors?

Manohar Lal Narang was a permanent fixture at film premieres and also directed and acted in few films, one of them was titled *Manu—The Great* (1989), chronicling the life of an industrialist who marries piety with charity. He shortened his screen name to Manu. It is ironic that Narang was also one of the popular surnames of smugglers and dons in Bollywood. Much like the underworld dons, who had a fetish for Bollywood, Narang had a strong obsession with films.

The Narang brothers—Manu, Rama and Om—came to India as Partition refugees barely in their teens and began life as petty hawkers selling wares on the streets of Delhi, having already lost their father Sewa Ram. Early days were spent in refugee camps, and if a romanticized account is to be believed, the eldest brother Manu had got the youngest Om admitted to the prestigious Delhi Public School. Manu would ferry his brother to the school on a cycle, pretending to be his servant to shield his brother from uncharitable remarks.

The brothers had their business interests in antiques, real estate, films, hotels and in-flight catering. South Bombay's Ambassador Hotel belonged to the Narangs, to which they had added the iconic revolving restaurant. It still remains in the family.

It was the acquisition of the Ambassador Hotel in the mid-1960s that had got the Narang brothers into the limelight. By virtue of the Ambassador Hotel, they got access to the airline catering business, which became lucrative with every passing year. The Ambassador Hotel building belonged to Messrs Sultan Brothers, which was owned and controlled by the Bohra head priest's family. For the longest time, it was leased to an Australian, Jack Voyantizis, before the Narang brothers snapped it up.

In 1969, the brothers got a flight kitchen unit with modern equipment set up near the Santa Cruz airport to supply food to 900 passengers daily. The hotel counted eight international airlines as its clients and the move closer to the airport saved time from transporting the food from the hotel's premises in Churchgate. This was a strategic decision, which some observers allege was instrumental to the expansion of their business. The brothers owned around a dozen limousines that catered to their large family. In the sweltering heat of Bombay, they would move around in suits.

It is still a mystery as to how they got into arts and antiques, but it was perhaps facilitated by the policy of the government that items less than 100 years old could not be termed antique, and hence, could be shipped abroad. This generally meant that a piece of paper from an 'expert' or the owner certifying the provenance and date of the item to be less than 100 years was enough to goad a section of inefficient and corrupt officials of the Archaeological Survey of India (ASI) to allow its export.

There was another factor that led to the proliferation of antiquities smuggling. The abolition of the privy purse (which ensured fixed payments to the ruling princely families by the government in return for the merging of their states with independent India) in 1970, meant that the descendants of the princely families were further hard pressed for cash. This aided in the enlargement of the supply side logistics. Besides, they could always claim that the article in question was less than 100 years old. Still wary of dealing directly with the lower end operatives, the swish set socially close to erstwhile royal families doubled up as important cogs in the giant wheel of international smuggling, giving much scope to operatives like the Narang brothers. In some cases, members of the minor branch of royal families themselves got their hands dirty to cut out the intermediaries. Rumour has it that the wife of a senior Indian diplomat was known to organize auctions for a select and hand-picked audience in New York in the late 1970s. She herself came from a royal family.

The ambitious and resourceful Narang brothers were in the game for high stakes, allegedly lording over a well-oiled empire that could procure antiques, hoodwink the bureaucrats, and deliver it to the highest bidder—mostly to foreign shores.

The Bombay crime branch meanwhile started keeping a watch on the exploits of the brothers since at least 1964. The brothers primarily operated from Delhi and Bombay, but the acquisition of Ambassador Hotel had made them stay more often in the filmy *nagri*. Manu had started gravitating towards the film industry, but it was not till the early 1970s when he transformed into an insider from an outsider to Bollywood.

The first major case against the Narangs surfaced in October 1965, when the customs authorities in Bombay detained four consignments containing sixteen cases of brass trays that were being exported by M/s India Products, the Delhi-based export firm belonging to the family. F.J. DeMello, an appraiser with Bombay Customs, was on overtime duty at the Alexandra Docks on 28 October 1965 with his assistant Patankar in tow. Around 7 pm, DeMello received a tip-off that India Products was attempting to export banned goods aboard the S.S. Yoshinosan Maru bound for New York.

DeMello immediately instructed the tally clerk to stop the loading of the consignment. There were four shipping bills in the name of M/s India Products which covered sixteen cases. The experienced DeMello quickly realized that the packages appeared heavier than the weight mentioned on the shipping bill. The signatures of the customs officers on the shipping bill of M/s India Products were found to be fake. When one of the cases was opened, it was found that instead of brass trays, as declared, it included stone antiques.

The matter was cascaded and it was decided to summon an expert in order to assess the market value of the antiques. The total declared value of the consignment was Rs 27,460, but upon examination in the presence of Dr Motichandra, the director of Prince of Wales Museum (now Chhatrapati Shivaji Maharaj Vastu Sangrahalaya), the brass trays were confirmed to be an exorbitant Rs 4 lakh. What were shown to be brass trays in shipping bills were actually exquisite stone sculptures.

It also emerged that in May 1965, twelve cases were exported to New York by Narang Overseas Ltd, which included a very rare tenth-century stone sculpture of Shiva Parvati mounted on Nandi. Perhaps there was no DeMello and certainly no tip-offs that could prevent the May 1965 shipment!

The CBI registered a case and the trial began in the judicial magistrate court in Delhi. The three brothers, Manu's wife Saroj and two of their employees were the accused in the case. As the court proceedings continued, Manu Narang occasionally travelled outside India with the court's permission. Between August 1968 and July 1974, he travelled to foreign shores on six occasions and continued to attend court as and when required. But when he left India for the seventh time in July 1974, his career and life too took on a different flight.

Om Narang was already in London since 1970, and with Manu gone, Rama was left alone in India to face the wrath of the administration. On 5 October 1974, Rama was arrested under the Maintenance of Internal Security Act popularly known as MISA on the orders of the Bombay Police commissioner. He was nabbed as he was leaving his Pali Hill bungalow by the CID on the grounds that he was involved in smuggling since 1964. MISA was passed by the Parliament in 1971 and gave immense and wide-ranging powers to law agencies to detain individuals and search properties without a warrant. It was of course used much more punitively when Prime Minister Indira Gandhi announced Emergency in June 1975 which lasted till March 1977. Thousands of activists, scholars, academics and opposition politicians were detained without trial for months.

The Narangs, several smugglers and other criminals got a taste of the state's excess, months before the Emergency officially began. Local police, the ED, the CBI and other agencies had started detaining the cream of the rogues' gallery in a massive crackdown on hawala transactions, smuggling and breaches of foreign exchange control regulations.

On the day Rama Narang was picked up from his bungalow in Bandra, the police had also arrested Santan D'Souza from Bombay's Ballard Estate and Ali Koya from Dongri. Was this a coincidence or an affirmation of the wearing-on-the-sleeve secularism that MISA was applied equally to every Amar, Akbar and Anthony?

These arrests happened under the direct supervision and the watchful eyes of K.J. Nanavatty, the last Parsi police commissioner of Bombay city. Under the provisions of MISA, D'Souza and Koya were sent to Thane jail, while Rama was lodged in Yerwada jail. D'Souza alias Charlie began life as a cigarette vendor, while Koya began as a helper in a timber shop. But now they were playing in millions, being at the helm of busy foreign exchange rackets.

In the days of telegrams and trunk calls, Manu and Om Narang must have got to know their brother's travails after a considerable delay, which would be unthinkable today. But except feeling helpless and guilty, there was not much that they could do. Fifty officials of the investigation wing of the income tax department swooped down on properties belonging to the Narang brothers. Twenty lockers in the Ambassador Hotel, which were not used by any hotel guests, were sealed. Narang Overseas Private Limited, the antiques shop at Bhulabhai Desai Road, was searched and sealed. The police had always suspected that the shop was a front to camouflage the smuggling of precious antiques outside India. Now, an armed constable was posted outside the sealed shop.

But the biggest surprise awaited the raiding team which went to the Pali Hill bungalow of the Narang brothers. The sprawling house had become a landmark of sorts, a reflection of the wealth amassed and social heights that the brothers had scaled. The team recovered tape recorders, television sets, transistors, binoculars, blue films and various other items. The checklist of items seized was indeed quite lengthy.

The awe-inspiring feature of the bungalow was a swimming pool with a glass flooring, and a suite under it, from where those in the pool could be looked at. The discovery of this swimming pool created a huge splash in the public psyche. People read with relish as newspapers conjured images of the hosts treating their guests to watch beauties take a dip in the pool.

The swimming pool found a mention in Parliament as well. In December 1974, during a discussion in the Lok Sabha, Atal Bihari Vajpayee, in his speech taking on the assortment of dons, smugglers and black marketeers, referred to the meteoric rise of the Narang brothers. A member nudged Vajpayee to not forget the 'swimming pool' as a marker of the opulent lifestyle of smugglers.

'And look at their flooring of glass, under which there is a room,' said Vajpayee, alluding to what became the nation's most notorious swimming pool.

'Is it not the job of the income tax people to inquire where all this wealth came from? Rama Narang purchased the Ambassador Hotel for Rs 76 lakhs. Was he asked where the money came from?' asked Vajpayee in Parliament, and then went on to answer it himself. 'He did it very cleverly. Without paying estate duty, he bought a controlling interest in Sultan Brothers. Narang could successfully evade stamp duty of seven lakh rupees. No income tax was paid, nor estate duty, nor wealth tax. But could the income tax people not have asked where the wealth came from?'

In 1973–74, Rama had paid Rs 1.4 lakh as income tax. But clearly, many believed that the figure was not the correct reflection of the family's income. While Rama remained in jail, pressure was mounting on Manu as well. As part of the crackdown against smugglers and foreign exchange regulation offenders, Manu too was served with a detention order under MISA in October 1974. Manu knew that there was no escaping jail if he came back to India. His elder son Ashok and nephew Ramesh (Rama's son) initially bought time in the metropolitan magistrate court saying that Manu was not well. They kept submitting Manu's telegrams saying that he wanted to come to India, but was not able to due to medical reasons. During one such hearing, they submitted a certificate by Dr Ralph Evans of Harley Street certifying that Manu was under his treatment for a peptic ulcer.

For around a year, the second generation of the Narangs, using the services of lawyers like Ram Jethmalani, managed to delay the inevitable order to attach Manu's properties due to his non-appearance in court. They pleaded before the metropolitan magistrate in Bombay that Manu had left India even before he was put under the MISA detention order, and hence he should be given some leeway.

On 19 September 1975, the magistrate ordered the attachment of Manu Narang's property while giving fifteen days to appeal. Ramesh Narang approached the city sessions court to challenge the magistrate's order declaring Manu as an absconder and to attach his property. A month later, the city sessions court confirmed the magistrate's order proclaiming Manu Narang as an absconder.

* * *

The other notorious smuggler who too was detained under MISA in September 1974 was Bali Ram Sharma. Sharma, who resigned from his job as a peon with the ASI, was detained by the Delhi crime branch. All such characters were put under MISA, and later COFEPOSA, another stringent law. Sharma was the uncrowned king of antiques smuggling with the obvious advantage of having worked in the ASI. The Narang brothers, however, were more suave and more widely travelled than Sharma. And there was one particular prize catch, which went a long way in establishing their hold in the lucrative antiques market.

This was the antique bronze Sivapuram Nataraja idol which had a dancing Shiva, believed to have been smuggled to the US in 1968. When the premises of Narang Overseas Private Ltd was raided, documents recovered showed the involvement of the brothers in the smuggling of the Sivapuram Nataraja. The story of how this ancient idol travelled from a small village in Tamil Nadu to Bombay and then to the US from where it moved to the UK is reflective of the tentacles of the hydra-headed monster that antiques smuggling had become.

After being discovered in 1952 from the precincts of a temple, it was passed on to a craftsman for repairs, which was when it was sold to Lance Dane, an Anglo-Indian art collector in Bombay. Dane was well known in the arts circle and had co-edited a book on Kama Sutra with the famous writer Mulk Raj Anand. The idol remained with Dane for more than ten years, after which it was bought by Boman Behram, another avid art collector. Dane maintained he exchanged the four-foot Nataraja idol for ninety pieces of sculpture from Behram, as the Nataraja was considered to be a bad omen.

Manu Narang had paid Rs 5 lakh to Behram for the Nataraja idol. The payment was done through a cheque dated 7 December 1968, drawn on National Grindlays Bank, Cumballa Hill branch through the joint account number 10418 belonging to the three brothers. Manu maintained that he had bought the idol from Behram for Harnam Singh, a Delhi-based metal trader. The Tamil Nadu CID had begun investigations into the disappearance of the Sivapuram Nataraja after an official of the British Museum confirmed that the idol in the temple was fake. Manu showed receipts given by Harnam Singh to support his contention that he was just acting as an agent between Behram and Singh, as the two did not know each other, and he was just the common link to effect the sale. But there was a catch.

The receipt by Harnam Singh with Manu was signed in Urdu, but the Tamil Nadu CID established that Singh used to sign in English and not Urdu. Meanwhile, Interpol and officials of the Indian embassy in Washington confirmed the presence of the Nataraja idol in the possession of millionaire industrialist and art collector Norton Simon. Simon had bought the idol from Ben Heller, a known arts connoisseur, in 1973 for around $1 million. Just a few months after the purchase, Simon sent the idol to the British Museum in London for restoration. Meanwhile, it did not take long to establish that Lance Dane, Heller and the Narang brothers were known to each other. In the late 1960s, Heller and Dane had attended the marriage of Rama Narang in Delhi.

In 1973, India filed cases in the US and the UK to gain custody of the magnificent Nataraja. A London court ordered that the 1000-year-old idol be kept in a bank vault, after Scotland Yard seized it. India and the Norton Simon Foundation entered into negotiations for a settlement. As per the agreement, India was to allow the Norton Foundation to display the idol for ten years, after which it was to be returned to India. The foundation was given an assurance that India would not question the antecedents of other articles with the foundation that were with them before 1973.

However, India made it clear that it would pursue those involved in the criminal act of smuggling the Nataraja. The Nataraja's return to the US from London was thus the first step in India ultimately getting it back in 1986 as per the settlement with the Norton Simon Foundation. The audacity and the deftness with which precious objects were smuggled comes out starkly when a little drama that entailed the transfer of the Nataraja idol to the US from London played out. The security agency with the responsibility to transport the idol from the bank to Heathrow airport declined to carry out the job unless Scotland Yard was ready to provide an extra layer of security. The airline supposed to fly out the idol refused unless it was provided with complete immunity. At the last moment, another airline agreed to step in but only with enhanced insurance cover.

Sitting in London, Manu and Om must have exchanged a grin learning about the brouhaha over the Nataraja's transport. They were reputed to have smuggled hundreds of antiquities outside India in novel ways. From forging signatures of customs officials to hiding objects in jute and cotton consignments, the Narang brothers, Indian agencies believed, had mastered the art of delivering exquisite items effortlessly to cities around the world by cunningly using people and the logistics of their existing businesses to carry out the smuggling.

According to Dane, the Sivapuram Nataraja reached New York through Paris. It was shipped to a destitute Parsi student, who was stuck in Paris having fallen on bad times, in bales of cotton. The student then shipped it to New York, where the arrival of the idol from France, unlike India or other South-east Asian countries, did not attract much suspicion. In fact, when the controversy regarding the Sivapuram Nataraja arose, Heller went on record to say that the US customs had assured him that there was nothing illegal in the arrival of the idol in America. However, the Sivapuram Nataraja was not the only object in London in which the Narang brothers had a hand in removal from India. This was also not their only modus operandi.

The other model they used for smuggling was to substitute the real sculpture with replicas, and whisk away the originals to the right buyer. The seizure of two ancient pillars in a warehouse had led Scotland Yard to the London pad of the Narang brothers. On 6 May 1974, Manu Narang was arrested on the charge of receiving sculptures stolen from an Indian temple by the Antiques branch of the Yard and was taken to Marylebone Magistrates' Court where he was given conditional bail.

On 28 May 1976, when Manu Narang was leaving Marylebone Magistrates' Court, he was accosted by detective sergeant Alan Wright.

> *Wright: Are you Manu Lal Narang, born on 20th July 1933 in Pakistan?*
> *Manu: Yes.*
> *Wright: I have a warrant for your arrest for extradition to India.*
> *Manu: Yes.*
> *Wright: I am arresting you for offences shown in the warrant and you will be taken to Bow Street police station to be charged.*

The CBI already had a dossier on the activities of the brothers, but the discovery of the pillars in London made their job somewhat easier in the UK courts. It was only after the discovery of the pillars that India started the extradition proceedings against Manu and Om. Within days of Manu's first arrest in London, the CBI on 13 May 1976 registered a case against the Narang brothers in relation to the theft and smuggling of what came to be known as the Amin temple pillars. Based on the registration of the case and India's request, the extradition process was set in motion.

* * *

Manu told the Bow Street Magistrates' Court that he was on a brief stopover in London to meet his wife and child before joining the Liberian embassy in Paris. However, at the very first appearance, the court rejected his plea for diplomatic immunity. Besides, there seem to be very feeble or no efforts at all from Liberia to press the case of Manu with the British establishment.

The court declined bail to Manu in the wake of stout opposition from Bhagwan Hiranandani, the solicitor for the GoI. At the second hearing on 7 June, Manu was represented by Sir Dingle Foot, who described the charges against him as 'very stale'. 'What is charged here is that my client was guilty of some offence between January 1963 and October 1965,' said Sir Dingle Foot.

The court was also told that Manu Narang had become a citizen of Liberia in 1975. Louis Blom-Cooper, representing India, told the court that Manu Narang had last attended the criminal proceedings in India against him in September 1973 and came to Britain on an Indian passport. 'The proceedings in India have become abortive since he has not been back.'

The legal battle at Bow Street Magistrates' Court was reminiscent of the extradition case of Dharma Jayanti Teja (chapter 11) in 1970–71, but unlike him, Manu Narang was granted bail by the chief metropolitan magistrate Kenneth Barraclough. Barraclough, described as a judge who sentenced with a Christian spirit, had famously ruled in 1968 that there was no law that dictated a cab driver to take the most direct route to the passenger's destination. He granted Manu Narang bail on the condition that he would surrender his Liberian diplomatic passport, reside at his brother's residence in London, and report to the police once a day.

An overconfident Manu, perhaps due to an important task that he may have had then, approached the divisional court seeking a variation to his bail terms. He sought permission to not report to the police every day and also that he should be allowed to stay wherever he wanted.

Manu's freedom was short-lived, as in the wake of opposition from India, the higher court not only declined to relax, but cancelled his bail and remanded him to custody till 5 July. He acted snobbishly during the proceedings by saying that he was in London on a secret diplomatic mission which he could not discuss as officials from the Indian high commission were present in the court.

Meanwhile, acting on India's requests and further information, Om Narang was also arrested and brought to the Bow Street Magistrates' Court on 8 July 1974.

Manu faced two sets of charges: the forging of signatures of customs officials on shipping bills to facilitate the export of twelve cases of antiques and the illegal import of sixteen items of sculptures were clubbed together constituting the first set; the second set related to the fraudulent possession of two antique stone pillars dating back to 200 BCE, which were originally kept in the Suraj Kund temple in village Amin situated in Karnal, Haryana. The pillars were valued at a minimum of £1,50,000 by Scotland Yard, though a general consensus considered it much higher. Court papers revealed that the pillars were in the London warehouse of Spink & Co. Om was charged only with the second case, relating to the Amin pillars. However, unlike Manu, Om's case for bail was on a stronger wicket, as the court released him on a £20,000 bond at the very first hearing.

Operators like the Narang brothers and Bali Ram Sharma were responsible for India becoming one of the biggest exporters of arts and antiques. The whole process of smuggling also perhaps added to India's exotic image for the Western clientele. But this insatiable appetite for India's heritage was in sharp contrast to the comparatively poor response and patronage to the works by contemporary Indian artists. The unsavoury part was that the hunt for old treasures had taken a widely imaginative criminal hue. All sorts of characters were involved in procuring treasures from the hinterland and smaller towns to feed entities like Narang Overseas Ltd to the metropolitan cities of Madras, Delhi, Calcutta and Bombay.

The smuggling of the Amin pillars had all the elements of an intriguing plot, which had become the hallmark of big ticket smuggling. It also separated the boys from the men. It is believed that the Amin pillars were an unfinished project, which the Narang brothers took over from Bali Ram Sharma. The pillars had disappeared from the temple on the intervening night of 31 March/1 April 1967. Sharma was apprehended and during his trial, the pillars were in the custody of the court, where they remained since the time they were recovered on 2 May 1967 from Faridabad. Sharma was ultimately acquitted in this case.

In February 1968, the Narang brothers got a whiff of the pillars and planned a devious move. Using their contacts in the judiciary, they goaded H.L. Mehra, the chief judicial magistrate in Karnal, to misuse his position and allow one Narinder Nath Malik, described as 'an eminent archaeologist', access to the pillars to carry out a detailed private study. From 1 March to 27 May 1968, the pillars remained with Malik.

Three months were more than enough to accomplish what the Narang brothers had in mind. Malik's workplace was actually a posh house in Delhi's Defence Colony belonging to the Narangs and the study was as fictional as the house being a genuine site for archaeological preservation. Expert craftsmen Balkishan Rawal and his brother Nathubhai Rawal, who was recognized with a National Award, were roped in to make replicas of the Amin pillars.

The Rawals had asked for Rs 1900 for each pillar, but the benevolent Narang brothers—keeping in mind the huge profits they would achieve—paid the craftsmen a lump sum of Rs 5000. Just a few days after the work commenced, an English lady living next door objected to the constant 'khut khut'. It was no longer safe to continue. On the direction of Om Narang, the original pillars and the work-in-progress replicas were taken in a horse cart to their godown in Kotla Mubarakpur to finish the work. In April 1968, the pillars were finally completed and the brothers could not contain their joy.

A month later, Balkishan was again contacted by Rama Narang to produce two more replicas. This time it was more challenging as the task was to be accomplished without the originals and only by looking at the tracings and photographs. The original pillars were too precious to be kept in a godown, whose location was known to outsiders. But there was a casualty to that decision. The additional two replicas were not of great quality and the Rawals were paid at the original asking rate of Rs 1900 per piece. Post-completion, the tracings and the photographs were all taken away by Rama Narang.

Malik returned the pillars to the court on 27 May 1968, and they were eventually installed in the temple. All seemed well until the Bombay customs officers in December 1968 seized one set of the replicas as evidence of—what they thought was—the smuggling of valuable antiques. The CBI registered a case and two separate examinations confirmed that the pillars in the temple were fake and so were the ones seized by Bombay customs. Having found two sets of replicas, the CBI found itself facing the prospect of locating more such fakes. But the daunting task was to locate the real pillars. A natural course of action was to alert the international community about the pillars, especially in the lucrative art markets of London, Paris and New York.

The CBI arrested Malik and Mehra in 1970. Investigations continued and a charge sheet was filed against the duo in 1972. There was no trace of the original pillars though. But the situation changed dramatically when Scotland Yard seized the pillars in May 1976 from a London warehouse and arrested Manu Narang who was trying to sell them. An expert from the British Museum confirmed that the pillars indeed belonged to the second century BCE. The CBI was intimated about the seizure in London and it was then that a case was lodged against the three brothers. Not only were the original pillars recovered, but the alleged main culprits were identified and apprehended as well.

Now all these facts were put before the Bow Street Magistrates' Court. Malik was paid Rs 70,000 cash, given a Fiat car, and plied with fully-paid pleasure trips to Bombay which he took with his wife. And a rather interesting gift in the form of a revolving metal bed! All this for his crucial role to pose as an archaeologist, get access to the pillars and ultimately help the brothers get three replicas made, one of which was returned to the temple. It was not surprising that the Amin pillars figured prominently in the extradition proceedings.

Malik had turned approver, which helped the CBI gather evidence against the Narang brothers, but the move also came under some scrutiny in the extradition proceedings by the counsel representing Manu and Om Narang. The granting of pardon to Malik by a court in India was criticized by raising the banner of impropriety, hinting at a quid pro quo.

The frequent attempts at bail and the high amounts offered as sureties give an indication of the Narang brothers' deep pockets. The Narang brothers paid for their own legal expenses.

Ram Jethmalani, who had appeared for Manu Narang in the sessions court in Bombay, gave evidence on behalf of the brothers before the Bow Street Magistrates' Court. Jethmalani, a fierce critic of the Emergency and Indira Gandhi, had left India in April 1976 and moved to the US where he was given political asylum. He came to London from Michigan, where he taught law at Wayne State University, to appear before the magistrate in September 1976. Jethmalani gave oral evidence and was subject to cross-examination on his claim that the Delhi magistrate had no jurisdiction to grant pardon to Malik. This was because, he pointed out, the Amin pillars case was before the Ambala magistrate court, and only the latter was authorized to do so.

For the prosecution, the star witness was a hurriedly arranged member of the English bar—Ellis Raymond Meyer—who had started his career as an advocate of the Calcutta High Court in 1938, and became Senior Advocate of the Supreme Court of India in 1952. Meyer belonged to that crop of legal eagles who came to Britain after the end of the Raj led to the inevitable Indianization of the administration and the judiciary. Some stayed back in India for good and some like Meyer gradually came over to England. Meyer commenced practice in London in 1968, and thus came across as a formidable witness, drawing from his rich experience in India. Jethmalani too had commenced his legal journey as an advocate during the British rule in India, having enrolled as an advocate of the High Court in Sindh in 1942.

'Assuming a pardon was not in accordance with law, the pardon is still in existence until it is overruled by any judicial act,' said Meyer. The final submissions, including evidence and cross-examination of Jethmalani and Meyer, took place in the last two weeks of September 1976.

On 21 September, the brothers were described as involved in a 'James Bond' style plot by Leonard Caplan, QC, who was representing India. The reference to the James Bond plot was made to describe the replacement of the Amin pillars by replicas and the attempt to sell them in London. 'When Manohar Lal Narang felt the net begin to tighten, he became the adopted son of the President of Liberia and claimed diplomatic immunity with credentials issued by the Liberian Embassy in Paris,' Caplan told the court.

On 5 October 1976, W.E. Robin, the magistrate, held that there was a prima facie case that was made out against the Narang brothers by the GoI. It was imminent that the brothers would appeal in the high court. The case in the divisional court came up for hearing before Lord Widgery, the chief justice, Justice Talbot and Justice Slynn from 22–26 November 1976. The defence's contention was that the alleged crimes were committed several years ago and that, due to passage of time, it would be unjust to extradite the brothers. The court was told that either Manu or his counsel had attended seventy-six hearings in the customs paper forgery case in India and that there had been no conclusion.

The thrust of the defence's argument was that the GoI had made a thin case and the emergency legislation in operation in India (suspending or removing fundamental rights guaranteed by the constitution) as also MISA and COFEPOSA would effectively mean that the brothers would be detained, and witnesses who would have otherwise helped them, would not be able to come forward. Besides, as proceedings under MISA and COFEPOSA were subject to courts, the Indian government would not be able to intervene, thus contravening the extradition arrangement—section 4 (3) of the Fugitive Offenders Act 1967—that Manu Narang would not be dealt with in respect of an offence committed before his return, unless he had the opportunity to return to the UK or be restored.

The court, however, did not agree with this point by virtue of the home secretary's assurance that necessary arrangements had been made as the Indian government had given an undertaking that Manu Narang would not be dealt with otherwise than for the offences specified. This may have not worked in Manu Narang's favour in the extradition proceedings, but it actually helped him get his properties back, which were subject to confiscation proceedings. However, the court accepted that extraditing the brothers for forging customs documents to smuggle antique items outside India would be unjust and oppressive. As stated earlier, the conspiracy with regard to the forging of customs documents was done between 1963 and 1965 in relation to May and October 1965 consignments. In 1968, the police had filed a charge sheet, and charges were framed by the court in July 1970. All these points, reiterated by John Wilmers, QC, the defence counsel, had a bearing on the judgment.

'It is plain that a very long time has elapsed since these events occurred. To investigate these events which occurred eleven years ago is inherently difficult, whether they happened in India or, as they are said to have happened in one case in New York. What in fact happened was that proceedings were allowed to drag on for a very long period. By June 1974, when Manu had left India, already nine years had elapsed since the shipments and six years since the prosecution charges were first commenced. In my judgment, even by 1974, it would probably have been unjust to send him back because of delay. Since then two more years have passed,' observed Justice Slynn in the order dated 26 November 1976.

In an indictment of sorts for the slow response of the Indian government, Justice Slynn noted in the judgment that while the 'passage of time' principle does not include any delay on the part of the prosecution, 'on the material to which we have been referred, I am not satisfied that they did make real efforts, or that it can be said that the lapse of two years can be ignored because Manu was putting himself out of the reach of the government'. The first group of charges—relating to forging customs documents to smuggle antiques from India—was put only against Manu, while both Manu and Om were charged with the crime related to the Amin pillars.

The defence stressed upon the fact that Malik's evidence— establishing the involvement of the Narang brothers—was obtained in July 1976. 'In the first week of May 1976, we are told that the government of India for the first time discovered the whereabouts of the pillars and learnt of the possible involvement of Manu and Om. On 26 June of this year (1976), Malik applied to the court for a pardon and on 3 July a conditional pardon was granted. Once again one has the story only revealed fully for the first time on the evidence of an accomplice who was granted a conditional pardon.'

Caplan, representing the GoI, maintained that the prosecution itself came to know rather late about the involvement of the Narang brothers in the smuggling of the Amin pillars. The court, however, considered that while Malik and Mehra were charged at an early stage, 'from 1972 little appears to have been done to get on with the case'. In essence what the court was pointing out was that if Malik gave a statement incriminating the Narang brothers in 1976, was there a possibility that the investigators could have done the same earlier? 'If there had been a reasonable expedition in the proceedings it may be—one does not know—that Malik might have given his statement earlier and the two applicants would have been in a stronger position to prepare their defence.'

Nevertheless, the divisional court was not impressed with the tardy pace at which both the groups of cases had progressed. 'It is plain that investigating these events which took place in 1967 and

1968 would be difficult at this distance of time. At the end of the day, I consider that because of the passage of time and the difficult issues raised it would again in this case be unjust to send the two men back for trial at this time.' Justice Talbot too concurred with Justice Slynn who gave the leading judgment.

The issue of poor paperwork which has dogged India in the recent cases of Nirav Modi and Vijay Mallya seems to be an old story. Incorrect or confusing paperwork has come in for criticism, never mind India's success in the Vijay Mallya case. In the Narang case, it was no less than Lord Chief Justice of England and Wales John Widgery, who criticized India's shoddy paperwork. Justice Widgery gave an indication of the vast amount of material served by India when he mentioned: 'We have here a bundle of papers perhaps 18 inches high. A great deal of this is concerned with the law of India, and it follows that if a magistrate is treating himself as having to apply the law of India he must sit with an expert Indian lawyer at his elbow at the time. It is quite impracticable.'

Justice Widgery was driving home the point that a magistrates' court, in deciding upon cases of extradition, is concerned whether 'in England by English standards and English law the evidence is strong enough to justify a committal, then that is sufficient to justify the return' of the requested person. The reversal of the magistrates' order meant the Narang brothers could soak up the Christmas and New Year celebrations in London.

* * *

On 20 December 1976, the appeals committee of the House of Lords allowed India's application for leave to appeal. Both the parties had a change of barristers. This time two Queen's Counsels, John Hobhouse and Richard Du Cann, were instructed by V.C. Kothari, who was the solicitor for India in the high court as well. The Narang brothers were represented by Robert Alexander, QC, and Kenneth Machin, instructed by Jonathan Hirst, who rose to become chairman of the Bar Council in 2000. Over four days in the last week of February 1977, Viscount Dilhorne, Lord Morris, Lord Edmund-Davies, Lord Fraser and Lord Keith heard the counsels for the Narang brothers and the GoI.

In this appeal application, India sought to only challenge the divisional court's conclusion—unjust and oppressive due to the passage of time—with regard to the Amin pillars and not the customs forgery case in which only Manu was the accused. This was perhaps done to counter the 'passage of time' reason as the Narang brothers were formally charged in the Amin pillars case only in 1976. Unlike the customs forgery case, which was a long-drawn-out legal quagmire, the offence against the Narang brothers in the Amin pillars case was only registered in May 1976, just days after the pillars were located in London. This was also a smart move as the GoI argued that the brothers had not said much about their involvement in the pillars case except denying their guilt. The divisional court had discharged the Narang brothers under section 8 (3) of the Extradition Act of 1967 by reason of the passage of time, which Hobhouse claimed was actually 'fully explained and accounted for'.

Hobhouse put forward six reasons to establish that the divisional court was wrong in discharging the Narang brothers. The first was that the divisional court did not take into account that the burden of proof or persuasion is on the requested persons. The second was that the case was not shown by reason of the passage of time to be exceptional. The third was that it was not shown that due to the passage of time, the Narang brothers would be subject to injustice or oppression, and that much of the blame for the passage of time was due to the clandestine nature of the crime. The fourth was that in ordering the discharge, the divisional court wrongly considered the complicated issues raised by the case. The fifth was that the court had misconstrued the Fugitives Offenders Act 1967 and its exercise of discretion was wrong. Finally, the sixth was that the decision was inconsistent with previous authorities and was based on a wrong view of the facts.

On 23 March 1977, the House of Lords overturned the decision of the divisional court and committed the Narang brothers for extradition, pending—as per the convention—the assent of the home secretary. In a detailed judgment, the House of Lords emphasized that the divisional court was not correct to conclude 'as to what issues of fact will arise at the trial or as to their complexity' because the Narang brothers had not put forward any arguments relating to the case except a plea of not guilty.

'Since the discovery of their involvement in May 1976, it must be remembered that, despite the lapse of time, the Indian authorities have since then been able to secure sufficient evidence to warrant their committal for trial had the offences charged been committed in this country. Where, with respect, I think the Divisional Court erred was in concluding that complex issues of fact would arise at the trial without any materials before them to justify that conclusion,' said Viscount Dilhorne who delivered the leading judgment.

* * *

The successful appeal of the GoI to the House of Lords was in some ways a landmark proposition. This case proceeded under the Fugitive Offenders Act 1967, which replaced the Fugitive Offenders Act 1881, and was the first case under the updated Act in which the divisional court discharged the requested person/s and the requested state appealed to the House of Lords.

A key difference was that section 10 of the Act of 1881 provided scope for some discretion to courts, but the relevant section 8 of the Act of 1967 narrowed down the jurisdiction. This was because, under the Act of 1881, a court could discharge a fugitive if the offence was trivial or the application was not made in 'good faith in the interests of justice or otherwise'. The presence of 'or otherwise' could be constructed to mean that the court may exercise its discretion to order the discharge of a requested person as if not doing so would be unjust. This was tantamount to a wide construction amplifying the scope of discretion.

In a number of cases, judges gave a wide construction. However, there was also a possibility of a limited interpretation which would essentially mean that the court might release a requested person only on the grounds of triviality of offence or of bad faith on the part of the requesting state. In some cases, as per this limited interpretation, even if there were any other reasons for the extradition to be unjust (apart from triviality or bad faith), courts held they had no power to act.

The Act of 1967 did away with the 'or otherwise' phrase, thus having a limiting effect as the court had to take into account only the specific conditions mentioned. However, section 8 (3) (b) of the 1967 Act made the passage of time a specific reason to decline the return of a fugitive. Under the Act of 1881, the magistrate was to be satisfied that the evidence pointed to a strong or probable presumption of guilt to order the return of the fugitive. As per the Act of 1967, the magistrate has to be satisfied that the evidence submitted is enough to warrant a committal.

But the Narang brothers were not going to give it up so easily. They had launched multiple court proceedings in India to frustrate the extradition process. Besides, after the House of Lords decision, the case went back to the home secretary, which got them some more time.

On 22 June 1977, the Delhi High Court stayed all proceedings against the Narang brothers, after an application challenging the extradition warrants issued against them was admitted. So, while in England the case had moved from the magistrates' court to the high court and had reached the House of Lords, the Narang brothers were trying to nullify the whole process. For if the Delhi High Court was to rule that the extradition warrants issued—based on which they were arrested in London—by the Delhi magistrate court was unwarranted, their release from Pentonville prison, where they were kept, would be imminent.

The famous Her Majesty's Pentonville prison, located on Caledonian road in central London, was a men's only separate prison built in the mid-nineteenth century where an innovative design of wings radiating from the central hall allowed for prisoners to be kept in individual cells. Following the closure of the dreaded Newgate Prison in 1902, Pentonville was used as a site for executions and a training ground for executioners. It was in 'The Ville' that revolutionary Udham Singh, who shot General Michael O'Dwyer responsible for the Jallianwala Bagh massacre, was held and later hanged in 1940. Now it was home to India's modern thugs.

Regular follow-ups from the Indian High Commission and close interaction with the foreign office and the home office brought the date of extradition closer. The home secretary signed the extradition orders on 22 June, following which the brothers were scheduled to fly from Heathrow on 26 July.

Just a day before their departure, they approached the high court in London. It was a last-minute attempt by the Narang brothers to avoid extradition. John Wilmers, QC, representing the brothers, told the court that since the home secretary signed their extradition order, the situation had changed as the only witness against them—Malik—had died. Wilmers also informed the court that the Delhi High Court had stayed the criminal proceedings against the brothers pending the hearing of an application to have them quashed. Harry Wolf, appearing for the home secretary, told the court that all legal options had been exhausted by the brothers, and hence, the extradition to India was inevitable. The three-judge bench led by Lord Widgery, Lord Chief Justice Eveleigh and Justice Forbes told Wilmers that they could not do anything.

It seems what worked in favour of the GoI was that there was no specific order by the Delhi High Court to stay the extradition proceeding. It was only on 26 July that the Delhi High Court directed that the authorities in Britain be informed that the extradition proceedings against the Narang brothers had been stayed by it. But by then, it was too late.

Call it the tyranny of distance, amplified by the lack of instant communication, the brothers had taken off from Heathrow at

9.30 a.m. The Indian government's line was that before the Delhi High Court's directive could be communicated through official channels to the British government or the CBI team, the flight had taken off. If the Delhi High Court had come with the directive just a day earlier, the Narang brothers could have stayed back in London.

But now, they found themselves in Delhi on the morning of 27 July, under the strict vigil of a CBI team led by Deputy Superintendent of Police Abnash Chander. The brothers were produced before the Chief Metropolitan Magistrate Mohammad Shamim and were remanded to judicial custody till 11 August.

On 16 August, the Delhi High Court granted bail to Om Narang with the condition that he should report to the CBI on the first of every month and should not leave India without the permission of the court. Manu Narang was denied bail as he was considered a flight risk. Manu made a few more attempts to get bail but was unsuccessful. The only tangible relief he got was the permission to visit Bombay for a week to see his ailing eighty-year-old mother Lajwanti Kaur, who was also a co-accused in some cases along with her sons.

* * *

Further legal setbacks awaited the Narang family. In January 1978, the Delhi High Court dismissed the petition by the brothers that sought to quash the proceedings against them in the Amin pillars case. The brothers submitted an appeal which was dismissed a year later in January 1979 by a division bench of the Supreme Court comprising Justice Untwala and Justice O. Chinnappa Reddy. The Supreme Court ruled that the extradition warrant issued by a lower court against Manu and Om could not be quashed and that there was no illegality in the investigations being done by the CBI. This meant that the three brothers had to appear before the trial court in Delhi in connection with the Amin pillars case. It was only in March 1978 that Narang was able to get bail from the Delhi court under strict conditions, which included reporting to the police every Monday.

The entire family was also under the dragnet of COFEPOSA and the SAFEMA (Forfeiture of Property) Act. Rama and mother Lajwanti Kaur had approached the Delhi High Court in July 1978 challenging the constitutional validity of COFEPOSA and SAFEMA to get their attached properties back. Manu Narang, who was declared an absconder too, had his assets attached since September 1975.

Armed with the undertaking that the Indian government gave to the British home secretary, he approached the chief metropolitan magistrate in Bombay in October 1978 and sought to dismiss the suit filed by the Maharashtra government to attach his assets. Among his known properties were a building named Garden House at Apollo Bunder, two flats on tony Malabar Hill, half of the shares in Narang House in Fort, and Glenrose Building in Colaba. Manu owned 500 shares in Narang Overseas Limited, 10,750 shares in Messrs Narang Hotels, besides shares in some other companies.

Manu Narang got permission from the Delhi High Court to visit Bombay to attend to his business and the various cases, including proceedings by the income tax authorities, at regular intervals. Subsequently, he got relief from the Bombay High Court, which quashed his detention order under COFEPOSA. Four years after his assets were attached, the metropolitan magistrate court in Bombay ruled that his properties must be released.

On 28 November 1979, B.P. Saptarshi, the magistrate, ruled that India had given an undertaking to the UK that Manu Narang would not be tried for any other offence committed before, other than the one for which he was being extradited, and hence, he could not be tried under COFEPOSA. It was thus ironic that the extradition which Manu Narang had fought with all his strength aided the restoration of his attached properties! Unlike the extradition case, Manu's brush with the courts in India were producing positive strokes.

Manu, meanwhile, had less time to strut the racecourse in his silky short kurtas like he did in the late 1960s and early 1970s.

In 1983, he re-released the multi-starrer film *Paanch Dushman*, which was produced by him in 1973, as *Daulat Ke Dushman*. It had some memorable songs with a star cast that included Vinod Khanna, Shatrughan Sinha, Prem Chopra, Pran and Manu Narang. Slowly but surely, the Narangs dug out to gain judicial reprieve. In December 1986, nine years after Manu and Om were extradited from London, the sessions court in Delhi acquitted them, but found Rama Narang to be guilty, in the case related to the forgery and smuggling of the Amin pillars. All three brothers were acquitted on charges of dishonestly receiving stolen property (section 411) and breach of trust (section 406), but unlike his brothers, Rama Narang was found guilty of being present where an offence was committed (section 114), cheating (section 420) and criminal conspiracy (section 120B).

Rama Narang was sentenced to rigorous imprisonment for two and a half years and fined Rs 5000. But that's not all. V.S. Aggarwal, the sessions judge, came to some startling conclusions. The most striking was that the CBI had failed to prove that the (returned) pillars that were installed in the temple were *fake*.

Rama Narang was later discharged by the Delhi High Court in the Amin pillar case in 1995. This meant that the case was finally decided twenty-seven years after the offence was registered. Justice Vijender Jain of the Delhi High Court set aside Rama Narang's conviction by V.S. Aggarwal, the additional sessions judge in December 1986. Justice Jain ruled that it was wrong to convict Rama Narang on the uncorroborated evidence of Mehra, a judicial officer who acted in a most injudicious manner. Besides, in the wake of the release of the two brothers, there was little merit in keeping Rama on the hook.

But the startling disclosure was that the prosecution had failed to establish that the pillars returned to the village in Karnal were fake! And hence, there was no case against Rama Narang as the making of replicas and whether the pillars were stolen or not became irrelevant.

Understandably, the court is at the mercy of the evidence put on record—oral and documentary—but it still seems preposterous that the status of the pillars seized in London and returned to the Indian High Commission by Scotland Yard was not made a reference point. The inference from the session's court's judgment could be that the pillars recovered in London *were not original.* Is it possible that these pillars were also replicas? Seems highly unlikely as the pillars were returned to Delhi and kept at the National Museum, and were examined by experts in London as well as Delhi on their return.

The extradition case had brought to the fore the dangers of dealing in sculptures having unclear provenance. Auction houses were as usual eager for new products to adorn their catalogues, but the buyers too had become circumspect. In 1982, Sunita Pitamber, Bombay's well-known socialite, whose party list was the envy of the town, was unable to sell the golden throne of the Maharaja of Jamnagar. The throne to be sold by Sotheby's did not find a buyer as it did not inspire confidence among the collectors that it was legit. Pitamber insisted that she had all the paperwork and the required permissions, having bought the throne from the royal family in the late 1970s for close to Rs 4 lakh, but a negative report in a British newspaper had reduced the golden throne to dust. Even Pitamber's assertion that—the throne was made in 1907 (backed by a declaration made by the ex-owners) and hence, it did not come under the ambit of being 'antique'—was not good enough to cajole potential buyers.

Life for Manu, though, had taken on a turn for the better. Freed on the sole charge on which he could be tried, and getting access to all his assets, Manu Narang embarked on a second innings in Bollywood and this was when he produced and starred in *Manu— The Great* in 1989.

Essaying the role of a philanthropist businessman, he mouthed dialogues like '*Paapi ko paap ka dand bughatna padta hain, chahe woh bhakti kare ya Ganga snaan kare ya kurukshetra jaaye*' (A sinner has to pay for his sins even if he turns into a devotee, goes for a dip in the holy Ganga or visits holy places). Shots in the film showed him as the owner of factories and mills established in 1855, to reflect the trappings of an old commercial family, a role which was far from reality. The signature lyrics of the film were '*Kyun karta hera pheri, daulat teri hai na meri*' (Why do you indulge in cheating, the worldly wealth belongs to no one).

Manu—The Great might have been unsuccessful at the box office, but it gave the next generation of the Narangs a celebrity quotient without the taint of smuggling. Manu's son, Sanjay, is a very successful hotelier, who once dated actress Sushmita Sen. Rama Narang's sons continue to run the Ambassador Hotel and one of his sons—Timmy—is married to Isha Koppikar. One wonders if the swimming pool in the Pali Hill bungalow still exists!

11

POLITICAL PIPER

Dr Dharma Jayanti Teja exemplified the flexibility a wannabe industrialist could get under Nehruvian socialism. Dr Teja appeared from nowhere in the late 1950s and became India's biggest shipping magnate, traversing the globe. He had everything that would appeal to New Delhi's swish set—fairly well-known parents in the pantheon of freedom fighters, degrees from Indian and Western universities, being on the staff of the prestigious European Organization for Nuclear Research (CERN) in Geneva, enviable work experience in New York, and an American–Russian wife. But all this came to naught when the bubble burst and Indian agencies came after him with all the might at their command.

Teja's extradition case represented the modern face of India's post-colonial industrialization gone wrong. If only Teja had managed to sustain his enterprise ethically, it would have set a template to first-generation entrepreneurs. In the courts of London, he was charged with criminal breach of trust, fraud, forgery and misappropriation of company funds to the tune of millions of dollars. This was a massive fall for someone who claimed he only came back to the motherland to prove that there was plenty of scope in Delhi for an enterprise to be nurtured in pursuance of a New India. And as his fall was not as quick as his rise, Teja's case became emblematic of the dangers posed by giving the reins of crucial sectors to private players—quick but unsustainable capacity building.

By all accounts, Teja was a financial wizard who mesmerized the power echelons with his confidence and contacts. But right from the beginning, there was an orthodox set, in business and bureaucratic circles, that was apprehensive and uncomfortable of his smart manoeuvres. But his meteoric rise overshadowed whatever reservations a section of the political class and bureaucracy had. Teja started from nothing and in just about three years, had twenty-two vessels; the company clocked Rs 7 crore profit in 1964–65. Little did anyone know that in just about five years after the launch of Jayanti Shipping in 1961, Teja would be hounded by Indian authorities from Europe to America. Finally, it was England from where India managed to get him extradited in 1971. This makes Teja's extradition case one of the most interesting in modern India.

* * *

Teja's parents Venkat Narayana Teja and Suramma Teja (née Konduru) were known to the senior leaders of the Congress party due to their involvement in the freedom struggle. Venkat Narayana resigned from his government job, became a committed Arya Samajist and spent considerable time with Gandhi. One of Teja's favourite anecdotes (and he had many that were often dismissed as tall claims) was that Mahatma Gandhi was present in his house during the time of his birth which prompted his parents to name him Dharma! With some sense of achievement, he would let people know that he spent a year working at Gandhi's ashram in Wardha after finishing his graduation. He had studied mathematics and physical chemistry at Andhra University and Mysore University and did further research at Madras University, before leaving India in 1948. He lived in England for a brief period and went to the US to pursue higher studies. He moved between biochemistry and physics, alternating fellowships at the universities of Purdue and Chicago.

Teja then came under the wing of Enrico Fermi, the creator of the world's first nuclear reactor, and turned seriously to nuclear physics. At the recommendation of Fermi, Teja joined Mystic Tape, a company that made magnetic tapes, at a senior management position. But he turned to his true calling, successfully completing a doctorate at CERN, Geneva. He made a good impression on the research community and seemed to have effectively capitalized on his research findings. According to C.D. Deshmukh, the first Indian governor of the RBI, Teja's research had led him to a 'new process in steel-making' for which he got a patent. Deshmukh's wife, the feisty freedom fighter Durgabai, was a close family friend. Teja married a Russian–American girl Betsy and they had two children—a daughter and a son. In one of their trips to the US in the 1950s, the Deshmukhs had met Teja and his family.

But success abroad did not bring much recognition to Teja in his home country. Besides, till now there is not much clarity on whether he actually achieved all that he claimed, so there was not much traction for him in India based on feats accomplished on foreign shores. He had although managed to convince and impress those who mattered in the power echelons that he was a man of considerable means.

That he turned his gaze to India was not surprising. But given his background and panache, he clearly did not have the patience and demeanour to excel in the role of a technocrat, confined, as he would have been, within the strict and inflexible set of rules and regulations. Yet, Teja knew that he had to be a part of the establishment, without being a part of it.

During a trip to India in 1960, he met Jawaharlal Nehru at his official residence. The prime minister took an instant liking to Teja and was impressed with his plans. Some accounts suggest that two sectors—steel and shipping—were discussed in the meeting. Teja claims Nehru had known him since he was a child of seven. And now he was expecting much more than a loving, fatherly pat. But before he spread his network in India, tragedy struck. On their return journey, Betsy passed away in Rome and his detractors made the most of this tragedy. What added to the rumour mills was Teja's rather quick marriage to the beautiful Ranjit Kaur who had studied in America and had also worked for him. Within a year, he came back to India, holding parleys in Nehru's drawing room. The same year he came back to India holding talks in Nehru's drawing room, accompanied by a new wife, attorneys from the US and an Irish shipping magnate.

It was in November 1960 that Teja suggested to the GoI a plan to acquire 3 lakh DWT of bulk carriers and tramp ships in the third five-year plan. Teja had drawn up an elaborate plan to make use of only about Rs 7 crore of the Rs 55 crore that was earmarked for the development of shipping in India. Accordingly, a loan agreement was signed between Jayanti Shipping Ltd and the Shipping Development Fund, the government agency formed to finance shipping companies, in February 1961. As per the agreement, Jayanti Shipping was given a loan of Rs 20.25 crore which was to be paid directly to the shipyards. Ten per cent was payable at the time of delivery and the remaining 90 per cent in seven instalments. Teja owned a 73 per cent share, and the Greek shipping tycoon Michael Kulkundis owned 25 per cent in Jayanti Shipping. The managing director of Jayanti was Teja's nephew Narayana.

In January 1963, Japan's Mitsubishi Shipbuilding & Engineering Company delivered India's first bulk carrier, *Bharat Jayanti*. It created a splash in the shipping world as an Indian vessel started plying between Europe and America, putting Indian shipping in the spotlight. Bharat Jayanti was followed by Gautama Jayanti, Akbar Jayanti, Chandragupta Jayanti—the list got bigger. Between October and November 1962, the company purchased thirty-two ships. Jayanti Shipping and Teja were on a roll. His company was now handling 40 per cent of the country's shipping tonnage.

In February 1962, the *Economic Weekly* (now known as the *Economic and Political Weekly*) questioned whether the 'government is wise to grant such unduly generous facilities to shipowners'. But as Teja discovered, parliamentarians and journalists were not bound by the civility of the *Weekly*, especially as details of the massive wrongdoings emerged later. The scale of his financial misdemeanour, Nehru's death in May 1964, the coming together of the opposition, and fault-lines within the Congress made Teja an easy and potent target. To tide over the cash crunch, Teja proposed to sell four vessels abroad raising further questions of mismanagement.

Another decision which attracted attention was the appointment of Lieutenant General Brij Mohan Kaul, as senior adviser to Teja in Jayanti Shipping's Tokyo office. Kaul's appointment, after the debacle in the Indo–China war, at a salary nearly double of what he got in the army raised eyebrows. Kaul was already looked upon as Nehru's favourite and rumours abound that he had got this plum posting because of his mentor's benevolence. He resigned from the army, just a few days short of his retirement, and took up the position as adviser to Teja. In his book *The Untold Story*, Kaul remembers his first meeting with Teja at a party in April 1963 after which Teja sent a letter stating his intention to have Kaul take charge of his office in Tokyo at a salary of Rs 8000 per month. After acquiring a sanction from the government, which was aided by Teja himself approaching defence minister Y.B. Chavan, Kaul sent Teja his written acceptance. For Kaul, this provided an opportunity to escape 'depressing surrounding' and get away from the 'scene of my recent disenchantments'. Kaul denied that Nehru had any role to play in his association with Teja.

There is, however, little dispute that Teja knew how to humour politicians. In June 1965, Teja took a group of members of Parliament including Dahyabhai Patel, H.V. Kamath and several journalists to Mormugao harbour aboard the *MV Kanishka Jayanti*, the biggest bulk carrier in his fleet. He was already looking at new initiatives to raise his public profile. In 1963, after his shipping empire had taken off, he prepared a blueprint to set up a 20,00,000 kW thermal power station at Ramagundam in Andhra Pradesh.

It was incredible that this entailed putting up the necessary capital himself and then selling the plant to the state government. He was ready to accept the repayment in instalments spread over fifteen years after the plant was commissioned.

Despite such public relations exercises, Teja was already under the scanner of investigative agencies on allegations of financial mismanagement. According to Teja, his relations with the new prime minister, Lal Bahadur Shastri, were not as cordial as they were with Nehru. When Shastri mysteriously died in Tashkent in Uzbekistan in January 1966, some suspected Teja, who was also believed to be in that country at that time, was behind his murder. Teja never denied his strained relationship with Shastri. 'Within months of Shastri becoming the prime minister, continuous statements were made that my company would be taken over,' lamented Teja who made no secret that the private secretary to Shastri, Chandrika Prasad Srivastava, was someone who was opposed to Jayanti Shipping even during the time of Nehru.

Srivastava's antagonism perhaps sprang from his early association with the Shipping Corporation of India (SCI), India's first public sector company in shipping, formed around the same time as its competitor Jayanti Shipping. Srivastava was at SCI's helm between 1961 and 1964, and during his second tenure (1966–1973), Jayanti Shipping was amalgamated into SCI in January 1973. Srivastava went on to be the secretary general of the International Maritime Organization in London for a record fifteen years (1974–1989). In 1990, Srivastava was knighted by the British monarch Queen Elizabeth II.

Unlike his nemesis, Teja was not destined to play a key role in the global shipping industry. Teja's bravado, prolonged absence from India, and the quest to diversify quickened the bursting of the bubble. When in Delhi, he would splurge on a suite at the grand Ashoka Hotel, even when vessels belonging to Jayanti Shipping were getting arrested in different parts of the world due to non-payment of dues to port authorities and staff members. The Akbar Jayanti was arrested in Naples in 1964.

There was a clamour in India to investigate Teja, which continued even when Indira Gandhi became the prime minister in January 1966. In March 1966, the Sukhtankar committee was appointed to investigate the affairs of Jayanti Shipping Corporation. As the heat turned up, the Tejas sneaked out of India in May 1966 creating a political storm, much like Vijay Mallya. Questions were raised as to why he was not arrested earlier.

Whether it was bureaucratic inefficiency or calculated indifference by top politicians, Teja was now beyond the ambit of the Indian judiciary. In June 1966, the government took over the management of the company for a period of five years. It was only in October 1966, that an arrest warrant was issued followed by an Interpol notice. 'Teja bashing' became the national obsession with the press and Parliament taking the lead.

Leaders like Raj Narain, Madhu Limaye and Dahyabhai Patel led the charge against the Indira Gandhi government in the Parliament. Madhu Limaye charged senior cabinet ministers of turning down the ED's request to arrest Teja which paved the way for his escape in May 1966. N.R. Sanjiva Reddy, the transport minister, in September 1966 told the Rajya Sabha that Teja had swindled about Rs 2.9 crore. The government was attacked for not disclosing full details about the fraud, to which Reddy accused Dahyabhai Patel of using Teja's chartered plane. It was clear that Morarji Desai and S.K. Patil were the two biggest supporters of Teja.

Narain had alleged that Teja had presented an air-conditioned Lincoln car for the use of Sanjay and Rajiv Gandhi. In a letter to Zakir Hussain, the chairman of the Rajya Sabha, Narain claimed that Teja had presented Indira Gandhi a necklace, besides an expensive mink coat and financed the family's foreign holidays. The allegations of Teja's close links with Indira Gandhi and her family did not go away.

In February 1978, appearing before the one-man Justice A.C. Gupta commission, inquiring into the Maruti affairs (the Japanese car maker whose entry into India was helmed by Sanjay Gandhi),

Dharam Yash Dev testified that Teja had financed the stay of Sanjay and Rajiv Gandhi in England. Dev was employed by Teja in Delhi who was also India's first high commissioner to Mauritius in 1948. Dev told the commission that Teja had spent between £7000–8000 on the brothers.

Sanjay Gandhi was in London for a three-year apprenticeship with Rolls-Royce. Dev said he was privy to this information as he was an employee of Teja in Delhi till 1964. Teja's plan was to make Sanjay Gandhi an automobile tycoon. Giving graphic details, Dev told the Gupta commission that once when he was having breakfast with the Tejas in their London flat he heard Teja say: '*Sanjay beta, paisa chahiye?*' He then asked Sanjay to collect money from his office.

Meanwhile, political gossip was abuzz with the infinite possibilities of where the Tejas could have gone to escape the political heat in Delhi's sweltering summer. They had offices in New York, London and other places in Europe. It turned out that it was the salubrious climate of Cannes that had beckoned the trendy couple. Teja owned Villa Cashmere which was tastefully decorated, situated as it was in one of the most exclusive neighbourhoods. It had a swimming pool, a huge garden and offered a picturesque view of Cannes. Except for the princely families, it is difficult to imagine any other prominent industrialist of the time from India who could match Teja's flair. While he liked to be seen as a follower of Gandhi, he had never embraced frugality.

The French Riviera was the magnet for the rich and the famous who partied hard and soaked up the amber sun along the pristine beaches. So while the political establishment in India was rankled by the Teja affair, the Tejas were rubbing shoulders with Hollywood stars and global financers. Indian agencies did discover Villa Cashmere in August 1966, but by then the couple had left their house. They had embarked on something more exciting—a road tour of the Continent. The arrest warrant for the couple was issued in October 1966, and the same month, the Bombay High Court directed the attachment of Teja's 2,12,472 shares in Jayanti

Shipping Corporation. But funds posed no problem, as Teja's Varuna Corporation, incorporated in the tax haven of Liechtenstein near Switzerland, offered enough liquidity.

Teja and his wife always had more than sufficient friends and avenues outside India to provide them shelter. But his personality and ambitions were too pronounced and prominent to afford him a life of calculated subterfuge. In April 1967, the couple's presence in New York was confirmed, and extradition proceedings commenced in May 1967. Teja claimed that he was a guest scientist at the Brookhaven National Laboratory of the atomic energy commission.

In his book, *A Ringside Seat to History*, IFS officer Pascal Alan Nazareth, who had taken charge as Consul (Passport/Visas) in New York in January 1967, recalls his first assignment in the form of a 'Top Secret' telegram from the Consul General of India (CGI) Shanti Swarup Gupta to locate and help extradite Teja and his wife, for committing a fraud on India's Shipping Development Fund. Nazareth's first stop was The Sherry-Netherland Hotel, which was Teja's last known address just few blocks away from the CGI office.

But the couple had checked out and the hotel had no knowledge about their location. Nazareth made the rounds of several consulates in New York with a detailed note on Teja's activities to prevent him from getting a visa. Nazareth also approached the New York Justice Department and Immigration office with the necessary information on Teja and his wife. On 27 May 1967, recollects Nazareth, he got a call from the Immigration office that the couple was arrested for overstaying their visas and would be produced before the US district court of New York the next morning.

On their very first appearance in court, the couple was granted bail much to the annoyance and dismay of Nazareth. It seems that it was an impassioned plea by Ranjit Teja that moved the District Judge John McGohey. 'The good-looking and elegant Mrs Teja stood up and told Judge McGohey that she and her husband were victims of political vendetta in India because they had been close friends of Prime Minister Nehru and had been assisted by him.

She asked whether the allegation of criminality against them was credible to him. The judge, visibly moved, granted them bail on a surety of US$10,000 each,' records Nazareth.

Teja opened two fronts to thwart his extradition—the obvious one in the US and another in India. He approached the Delhi High Court in September 1967 requesting that the government be restrained from seeking extradition. The argument was made that as there was no valid treaty between India and the US, they couldn't be extradited! It was turned down by the Delhi High Court which also refused an application for leave to appeal to the Supreme Court.

And it was in September 1967 that the district judge was informed by the couple's lawyer that they had left the country having lost hope of securing justice in the US. The judge forfeited their bail bonds and ordered their extradition to India. The focus now shifted on finding out which country the couple had escaped to from the US. The Tejas had mastered the art of giving the slip.

This time it was the Latin American nation of Costa Rica. Indian efforts suffered considerably as there was no diplomatic presence in Costa Rica and the consulate general in New York had to stretch itself. The annual report for the year 1968 of the Indian consulate general of New York reports the 'important' and 'out of the ordinary consular case' of Dr and Mrs Dharma Teja.

While India assumed that the case was bolstered by the fact that the couple had jumped bail while the extradition process was on in New York, it did not cut much ice with Costa Rica. The back story to the Tejas' escape to Costa Rica is very interesting and speaks much of their ability to cut a deal. According to Nazareth, Teja allegedly paid José María Hipólito Figueres Ferrer, Costa Rica's former president, US$30,000 and all possible help with his presidential campaign in return for entry visas to be issued on the instruction of the country's Ministry of Foreign Affairs. This ensured that despite India's alert not to issue visas to the couple, the consul general of Costa Rica in New York had plied the Tejas with visas facilitating their escape.

Nazareth was alerted about this by none other than a diplomat with the consul general of Costa Rica. This diplomat was related to the then Costa Rican President Jose Trejos Fernandez and had his own interest in exposing Ferrer's link in the escape of the Tejas to San Jose, the capital of Costa Rica. Nazareth and the helpful Costa Rican diplomat got an audience before President Fernandez who, according to Nazareth, set the police behind the couple.

It seems Teja and his wife had made deep inroads within the establishment in Costa Rica. For a long time, the Tejas remained untraceable after the Costa Rican government cancelled their visas. Despite Nazareth's assertions, it seems clear that Costa Rica was not eager to either deport the Tejas or arrest them. At the right moment, the Tejas emerged from hiding with a sob story of political vendetta to make a splash in the local newspapers, garnering public support. The couple sought political asylum, which was rejected in January 1968.

A formal request for extradition was made to the Costa Rican government, which kickstarted a complex process. India soon discovered the reality of Teja's case being metamorphosed from the smoothly moving ambit of the US court to obstinate obstacles being hurled by Costa Rica.

Teja and his wife were arrested based on a warrant issued by a magistrate, but his counsel in Costa Rica objected to the warrant saying it had no judicial validity as the magistrate had issued it as an executive magistrate. The President of Costa Rica raised it with the President of India and after going through the judicial channels, Costa Rica was informed that the magistrate had acted as a judicial officer, and not as an executive magistrate. India had to fortify another key defence. The papers relating to the Tejas' extradition were to be translated into Spanish from English. This task was undertaken for around 1000 pages of documents at a considerable cost, as time was of the essence. Meanwhile, Teja got enough time to ingratiate himself further with the top echelons in Costa Rica.

It took almost two years before the matter reached the Supreme Court of Costa Rica. In June 1969, out of the fifteen judges, eight voted against the extradition, five voted for the extradition and two voted for the extradition of Teja alone. There were whispered allegations that Indian officials had made a half-hearted attempt to get Teja. His entry to Costa Rica was largely because of his link with Ferrer, but that was no guarantee for Fernandez, Ferrer's political rival, to simply hand over the couple to India. The Lok Sabha was informed that till 31 January 1970, India had spent a whopping Rs 4.9 lakh on the extradition process, all of which had come to naught.

But when Ferrer replaced Fernandez to become the President of Costa Rica for the third time in May 1970, Teja got an official position in the establishment. He got a Costa Rican diplomatic passport and continued to do what he did best—striking deals for the President and scouting business and investment avenues for Costa Rica. His name in the passport was tweaked, making it doubly difficult for immigration and customs officials to question an individual travelling on a diplomatic passport. In the meanwhile, Ranjit had given birth to a boy. The Tejas were away from India, but had clearly moved away from the fugitive tag. Teja, confident in his ability to thwart arrest, continued his jet-setting ways, which turned out to be his undoing.

* * *

On 24 July 1970, Teja visited London for the third time since he moved to Costa Rica. Contrary to the popular saying 'third time lucky', this visit shattered his self-assured hubris. He was approached by detective sergeant Robin Constable of Scotland Yard, holding a circular which clearly showed his picture. Constable looked him up and down, checked his passport and then, looking him straight in the eye, asked, 'Are you the wanted man in this?'

'Yes,' replied Teja nonchalantly, confident that his Costa Rican diplomatic passport would come to his rescue. Teja had visited

London twice earlier and had no trouble. This time however, he had met his match in detective Constable.

'Why are you travelling under a false name on a Costa Rican diplomatic passport?' the detective asked pointedly.

Teja boasted that he had personally got the passport from the President of Costa Rica. But the Costa Rican passport had 'Konduru' and not 'Teja' as his surname. Teja had taken some calculated precautions, yet his reckless acceptance that the wanted man on the circular was him was enough for the detective to arrest him.

It was 9.53 p.m. when Teja was officially arrested at Bow Street police station, where a clearly agitated Teja told Constable that he would do everything in his power to avoid going back to India. Unknowingly, Teja had spoken too much and too clearly to Constable.

Constable recounted in Bow Street Magistrates' Court that Teja told him that notwithstanding the diplomatic passport, he was not an accredited diplomat and that he worked only for the President of Costa Rica. This statement was used against him, although it was later claimed by the defence in the court that he was going to be appointed the economic advisor to the Costa Rican embassy in Switzerland.

With his arrest, Teja had now entered the British records as a fugitive. He took forward his freedom-fighter parents' legacy of being jailed by Britishers, but the circumstances were entirely different, to put it mildly. The first entry in the register of Bow Street Magistrates' Court in respect of Teja is dated 25 July 1970. It records: Jayanti Dharma Teja, forty-seven years old was arrested on the basis of a warrant dated 22 July 1970. The charges: In collusion with his wife Teja Ranjit, he produced a forged resolution of the board of directors authorizing him to be the sole beneficiary of a letter of credit for $1.2 million which was initially granted to the company. This sum he paid to the SBI, London (Great Britain)—'against the law of India'.

The second entry is dated 31 July 1970 where he once again appeared at Bow Street Magistrates' Court and had the following charge added: By using forged documents and making false statements he withdrew from the account of the same bank the sum of $11,36,800 belonging to his company and of that sum, transferred $19,600 to his wife's personal account. He misappropriated $87,600 of the money paid by a Norwegian company for the charter of a ship, declaring to his own company that a lesser amount had been charged for the charter. He fraudulently took for himself a 2 per cent commission on the amount paid by his company to Mitsubishi International Corporation for the building of eleven boats. All contrary to the law of India and Extradition Act 1967.

In short, he was charged with criminal breaches of trust, cheating, forgery and falsification of accounts—misappropriating company funds totalling $7,50,000. On his second appearance, Teja made the first of his three bail applications, which was rejected. He was remanded to custody for seven days and was sent back to HM Prison Brixton in South London.

The next entry is dated 7 August 1970, and instead of a handwritten note, the charges were on a typewritten paper stuck in the bulky register, which had entries of fugitives sought by various countries. But Teja was a fugitive with a difference. Unsuspectingly, he got stuck in the British dragnet as he had come to meet his two children from his first wife—a boy and a girl—who were studying in schools in London.

Meanwhile, Ranjit Teja started writing letters to ministers in the UK. The first such letter, traced in British archives, dated 1 August 1970, is addressed to Sir Alec Douglas-Home, minister for foreign and commonwealth affairs. She stated that Teja was arrested while he was on a special mission which was of interest to 'all central American countries'. She blamed the Indian High Commission in London for instigating the detention of Teja. 'On account of the public interest and political ambitions of my husband, the government of India has been persecuting us since 1966 by confiscating our Jayanti Shipping company in India worth about $68 million in India without compensation,' and went on to describe the charges as 'false and malicious'.

Further sympathy and consideration were sought by giving a brief description of the 'untold hardships and anxiety' their minor children had faced over the last four years. The eldest daughter who was studying in London's St Paul's Girls' School went to Israel 'for want of a home'. The second child, a son aged fifteen, studying at Tonbridge School, was described as 'so shocked that his educational career is seriously being impaired'. The third child, a British citizen who was seven years old, had to leave England. The fourth child was a boy aged twenty months with her in Costa Rica. 'Please give due consideration to the fact that it is an entire government bent upon annihilating our small family,' she urged in her letters.

Shorn of any emotion were the letters that the President of Costa Rica, José María Hipólito Figueres Ferrer, wrote to the British prime minister. Crisply worded and direct, on the face of it the President was within his right to demand the release of a person travelling on a Costa Rican diplomatic passport. The British offered standard and safe replies, an approach informed by the combination of persistent follow-ups by the Indian High Commission and the spectacle of British taxpayers taking the legal tab of a foreign diplomat whose release was sought by none other than the country's President, but without paying for his defence.

It also seems that officially the Costa Rican embassy in London was keen to come to the aid of Teja, but in informal diplomatic meetings, opinions about Teja were not very glowing. The Costa Rican ambassador described Teja as a 'strange bird' to C.D. Wiggin of the American department in the Foreign and Commonwealth Office (FCO) and disclosed that Teja's lawyer had approached the Costa Rican embassy to check if they could be paid by the embassy.

No doubt, the President was the greatest supporter of Teja and accordingly, the embassy had sounded to their British counterpart the possibility of having Teja accepted as a counsellor in the Costa Rican embassy in London. This was gently shot down by British officials who told them in no uncertain terms that a formal request would be declined. It was also disclosed that as Teja had visited

Britain twice, 'Indians seem to have been slow in catching up with him'. Thus there was plenty of action both inside and outside the courtroom.

On 28 August 1970, a second bail application was made, which was rejected by the magistrate. The court was told that Teja had cerebral hypertension and that the defence had to examine several documents. Teja was in prison for more than a month and he was desperate to secure bail. It was during this hearing that the Costa Rican government intervened with Britain saying that Teja was visiting London on its behalf. Britain's judiciary was aware of the vast possibility of misuse of the 'diplomatic immunity' status, and while it was admitted that Teja was not yet accredited, the continued confabulations between Costa Rica and Britain did cast a shadow on the proceedings at Bow Street Magistrates' Court.

Teja applied to the court to try as a preliminary issue before the committal proceedings took place, the question of his 'immunity from process under the Diplomatic Privileges Act, 1964'. This was a smart move on Teja's part to ensure he got an exit before the court could decide whether prima facie he had a case to answer. And with Costa Rica's ambassador in London, Manuel Escalante, having forcefully taken up Teja's brief, he perhaps thought there was no need to give India the opportunity to present her case against him in an open court, which would entail lurid details of financial bungling.

On 27 October 1970, Sir Frank Milton, the magistrate, rejected claims that Teja had diplomatic immunity. This paved the way for a full-fledged trial, but not before some anxious moments in the court for India just a day earlier. As proceedings began in Bow Street Magistrates' Court on the morning of 26 October, it emerged that Escalante was at the foreign office to extract diplomatic immunity for Teja. If the foreign office was to tell the court that Teja had diplomatic immunity, that would have meant he had no case to answer and the proceedings would have collapsed. Defence counsel Jeffrey Thomas, also a Labour member of Parliament from Wales, requested for an adjournment in anticipation of favourable news to emerge from Escalante's meeting in the foreign office.

But with no glad tidings from the meeting for Teja, the court proceedings commenced. Thomas was reprimanded by the magistrate when India's counsel Louis Blom-Cooper pointed out that the defence's assertion that Teja left for Costa Rica with the knowledge of the court in New York was wrong. Blom-Cooper was an able general in India's battle to get Teja extradited. In fact, he remained a legal adviser for India, helping in negotiations on extradition arrangements with Britain in the mid-1980s.

The opposition had done much to link Teja with Indira Gandhi and her family. That he came in the limelight due to Nehru's initial push was no secret, so his extradition would not have been in the interest of the Congress party. It was thus surprising that during court proceedings in London, Teja made some sensational claims exposing the Congress government if not the Nehru-Gandhi family directly.

He claimed that he was asked to make a donation of Rs 10 lakh to *National Herald*, a newspaper run by Uma Shankar Dikshit. Dikshit, who was the managing director of the paper, later became treasurer of the Congress party. The requests were made between March 1964 and May 1966, he alleged. He was made to understand that the donation to *National Herald* would help ease out the criticisms against him.

Making no bones of his affiliation with Nehru, Teja told the court that after the death of Nehru, 'young people' in India were being targeted. Giving the example of Biju Patnaik and Bakshi Ghulam Mohammad, he pointed out that young people close to Nehru were being selected for special treatment. Opposition leaders in India made the most of Teja's sensational utterings in Bow Street Magistrates' Court. The defence produced pictures of Teja with Jawaharlal Nehru and Indira Gandhi. Was he peeved that the Indian government had come after him in full force despite the alleged favours he had done for India's first political family?

Perhaps his counsel was trying to prove that Teja, being a Nehru man, had become a target after his death.

Teja had plenty of support from India too. The defence produced a letter from Morarji Desai, dated 24 July 1969 by when he had resigned as the deputy prime minister, written in reply to a letter sent to him by Teja. Desai's letter confirmed the claim made by the defence that the Indian government had put pressure on Mitsubishi Company to give evidence against Teja. Thomas had attempted to prove that D.N. Rao, chief accounts officer of Jayanti Shipping, and officials from SCI and Mitsubishi Company of Japan had lied to prove the fraud and misappropriation of funds.

It seems Teja was on a mission to embarrass the Indian establishment. He told the magistrate that he had jumped bail in New York after consulting his friends and officials including the Indian ambassador in Washington!

He also gave the example of Naga leader General Nowu Angami who was detained without trial for having links with China. Teja tried to convince the court that he too faced a fate similar to General Angami, as he was privy to the secret Henderson-Brooks report on the failings of India in the war against China. 'Since I am aware of the contents of the Henderson-Brooks report which is classified as top-secret, if I am sent back to India, the government will arrest me under the same sort of thing as General Angami.'

Teja told the court that the transport minister in Indira Gandhi's cabinet was his 'deadly enemy'. The prosecution took umbrage at the assertion that Teja would not get a fair trial in India, terming it 'extravagant'.

Teja shot back: 'The calumny against me is also extravagant.' To further his point, Teja pointed out a letter he had received from a barrister saying that it was almost impossible to defend him in Indian courts. Teja dropped a thunderbolt when he told the court that the barrister was none other than C.D. Deshmukh, a former finance minister of India. Teja also declared in court that he had renounced Indian citizenship and was a national of Costa Rica.

Seeking to insulate his wife, the defence pointed out that under English law, husband and wife cannot be guilty of conspiring as they are taken as one unit. The law states that if the husband–wife duo conspired with a third person X, then the husband could be charged with conspiring with X to commit a crime and the wife could also be charged with conspiring with X to commit the same crime. However without the presence of a third party X, the husband and wife would not be charged of conspiring to commit any crime. Blom-Cooper attacked it as an old-fashioned view and argued that even if it was to be accepted, Teja and his wife were co-directors and not just spouses.

During the trial in the magistrates' court, P.C. Govil, an official of the Indian High Commission, appeared as a witness. Govil produced Teja's application for an Indian passport on 27 June 1966. And two of the five passports he had used from 1961 to 1966. Teja's date of birth was registered as 22 September 1922. But perhaps the most important confirmation that came from Govil was that the name of Teja's mother was Konduru Suramma—it was his mother's name that he had added on his Costa Rican passport. Govil told the court that New Delhi had not received any application from Teja renouncing his Indian citizenship.

On 29 October 1970, just before the court was to be adjourned, the defence moved a third bail application. Offering four sureties of £5000 each and the residence address of a friend, Teja made an unsuccessful attempt for bail. Sir Frank Milton rejected the bail application saying it was made too late and that Teja had jumped bail in America making him a flight risk in Britain too. Teja appeared before Bow Street Magistrates' Court twenty-six times—including his first appearance on 25 June 1970 till the magistrate's decision on 11 December 1970 following the completion of trial.

The entry on 11 December in the court register simply notes 'committed in custody to await decision of SOS'. But hidden within these words was the emphatic victory India secured in the court.

Sir Frank Milton was convinced that a prima facie case was made against Teja and that it would be incorrect to term the charges against him as politically motivated. A visibly upset Teja stood up in the court when the magistrate read the charges against him.

Interestingly, it was the same sergeant, Robin Constable, who had arrested him, who ferried Teja the last time from Bow Street Magistrates' Court to jail. Teja's daughter from his first wife was present in court and before being taken away, he briefly spoke to her and kissed her goodbye.

* * *

Teja ushered in the new year—1971—from behind the bars of Brixton prison. With its over two-centuries-long history, the prison, tucked away on Brixton Hill, has housed many—from children as young as six who came from the notorious band of pickpockets called The Forty Thieves to philosopher Bertrand Russell and even singer-songwriter Mick Jagger of the Rolling Stones. Interestingly, this was the first prison to introduce a treadmill for the prisoners—not as a mode of recreation as prisons do today, but as a mode of sadistic punishment.

In the nineteenth century, the treadmill—conceptualized by engineer William Cubitt—represented large wide wheels fitted with steps. At a time, twenty-four prisoners, with partitions between them, spent ten hours a day climbing the steps that rotated the wheels connected to a millstone that ground corn for bread and pumped water for the use of inmates. They were allowed a twelve-minute break every hour. This gruelling labour was the perfect Victorian punishment. Many inmates suffered greatly. Writer Oscar Wilde, who was also subjected to this punishment during his time in Pentonville prison in 1895, suffered serious health issues and died two years later, at the young age of forty-six. Fortunately for Teja, the use of penal treadmills was stopped in the early twentieth century.

In January 1971, the action shifted to the high court where Teja filed an appeal against the decision of Bow Street Magistrates' Court. Sir Dingle Foot, Solicitor General in the first government of

Harold Wilson in the 1960s, a member of the UK Parliament and brother of the legendary Labour leader Michael Foot, represented Teja, while Sir Elwyn Jones, a former attorney general of England and Wales, argued for the GoI.

A three-judge bench of the high court led by Lord Chief Justice Parker, Lord Justice Cairns and Justice Melford Stevenson dismissed all the five grounds forwarded by Teja.

The first was that Teja was a diplomatic agent in transit—the court held that at the most he could be termed as a commercial agent with no diplomatic status; the second was that the Costa Rican Supreme Court had dealt with the issue of the extradition and had decided in Teja's favour—the court said that the Costa Rican Supreme Court's order was only advisory; the third was that he wouldn't get a fair trial in India—the court held that there was no evidence to prove that; the fourth was the passage of time—the court held that this was not due to India but because of the conduct of Teja; and the fifth was that the charges under section 409 of the IPC had been wrongly made out—the court held that Teja would get the opportunity to remedy this in the Indian court.

There was one more hurdle to cross before Teja could land in India. Teja petitioned the House of Lords appeal committee. On 24 February 1971, Teja's counsel Sir Dingle Foot appeared before Lord Dilhorne, Lord Reed and Lord Morris raising the same issues of diplomatic immunity, passage of time and political targeting. All the issues were dismissed by the lordships, and though technically it was the home secretary who had to sign the extradition order, there was hardly a chance he wouldn't do so in the wake of decisions reached by the high court and the House of Lords committee.

All through the Teja affair, the British were concerned about the bad press they would get in India. A.V. Hayday, the British high commissioner in Chanakyapuri in Delhi, was sending regular dispatches to London about the media coverage in India on the Teja affair. Diplomats exchanged notes which made it clear that the Indian High Commission and Indian journalists in London had noted that he was being defended by British taxpayers. The

British were eager to see that Teja's legal bills issue was not discussed in the press. Meanwhile, N.L. Vaidyanathan, the legal adviser at the Indian High Commission in London, was holding extended discussions with V.K. Ahuja who was in the embassy of India to Costa Rica.

The Indians were also worried about the delays from the home secretary's side that might have allowed Teja to escape. Vaidyanathan wrote to the South Asian department in the FCO in March 1971 asking whether the delay from the home secretary to carry out the extradition within two months of the rejection of Teja's appeal to the House of Lords on 24 February would invalidate the extradition order under section 10 of the Fugitive Offenders Act.

There was another delicate balancing that the UK had to do. I.M. Hurrell, the British ambassador in San Jose, suggested in April 1971 that the British prime minister should write a further personal message to Costa Rica's President, as the latter was about to take a decision on the purchase of civil aircraft. 'We have good hopes that Costa Rica will buy BOC III's (she's done so before), but an emotional reaction by Sr Figueres might cause things to go sour.'

Giving a window to the backchannel diplomacy that happens in extradition cases, Prakash Kaul, the deputy high commissioner, wrote a series of letters to the FCO, concerned that the Easter break might delay the signing of the extradition order by the home secretary. Besides, Kaul was also giving all kinds of assurances and undertakings to the British that were required to bring Teja's extradition to fruition. Mr Dewan of Messrs Stocken and Co. Solicitors representing the Indian government was also in touch with the British officials.

But there was a proverbial twist in the tale. Unknown to the staff at the Indian High Commission, a comment by a visiting senior member of the Indian Police Service (IPS) nearly derailed the extradition of Teja. Legendary super cop Ashwini Kumar, an officer of the erstwhile Indian Police (IP) service, told a senior British security official—they had worked together in the IP—that cabinet minister Swaran Singh did not want Teja's extradition to take place. Kumar was visiting England as an official of the Indian Hockey Federation, and must have made that remark to someone very senior in the security hierarchy for the British foreign office to react so swiftly.

The UK immediately set down to tackle this latest curveball. The FCO sent a missive to the British high commissioner in Delhi on 2 April that they 'have received an unofficial representation from Ashwini Kumar who claimed to speak on behalf of Swaran Singh to the effect that the Indian government do not wish Teja to be extradited because as a former protégé of Nehru his trial would reveal activities embarrassing to the present government'. Kumar claimed to be a personal friend of Singh hailing from the same town of Jalandhar.

Nevertheless, the British were deeply concerned with Kumar's assertion to the senior security agent, whose identity remains protected. They immediately got down to ascertaining Kumar's position and reliability and whether Singh had confided in him to pass on the message regarding Teja. British diplomats seemed clear that the only way the extradition could be stopped was if New Delhi made a formal request to halt it. Moreover, in the almost euphoric follow-ups being made by officials of the Indian High Commission in London, they couldn't do anything to the contrary.

John Gordon Hibberdine, the first secretary in the British High Commission in Delhi, discussed Kumar's intervention with someone senior in the cabinet secretariat on 5 April 1971. His contact confirmed that Kumar was a senior police official and that he had visited England, but also that he was a 'well-known name-dropper who likes to meddle in politics'. Hibberdine was told that it was unlikely Swaran Singh would have asked Kumar for any such intervention and that 'it would be totally out of character for Swaran Singh to act in such a way'.

The British soon concluded what they believed must have been the chain of events. They gathered that Singh must have, in the presence of Kumar, spoken about how Teja was close to the Nehru establishment which Kumar thought was tantamount to Singh not wanting the extradition to take place. It is difficult to ascertain whether Kumar acted on his own or indeed had the green signal from someone at the top in the Indian political establishment.

Finally, Teja left the UK for India on 15 April 1971. The travel arrangements were kept secret as it was feared that he might feign illness or create other means of delaying his return. Teja was sentenced to three years, rigorous imprisonment by M.L. Jain, district sessions judge in Delhi and fined Rs 14.3 lakh. The trial lasted for a year from April 1971 when he was extradited to India from the UK. The CBI produced thirty-three witnesses to nail him.

He was released from prison in March 1975 on a writ petition filed on his behalf in an Andhra court which contended that he had completed the substantive sentence of imprisonment. After his release, he settled down in Hyderabad, but agencies kept a close watch over him. The income tax authorities wrote to international airlines to keep Teja on a no-fly list because he still owed the taxman.

While he was in jail, the Lok Sabha was informed that Teja topped the list of individuals with income tax arrears. At Rs 4.65 crore he was ahead of the infamous Calcutta-based stock broker Haridas Mundra, who was then credited with the largest financial scam of independent India of just over Rs 3 crore. He also owed another crore in wealth tax arrears.

In June 1978, news emerged that Teja had left India in July 1977. To add insult to injury, investigations revealed that he had in fact left India in May 1977, but had come back only to embark on the second foreign trip in July 1977.

As per the rules, due to his conviction on charges that entailed a prison term of more than three years and the huge outstanding money he owed to the taxman, he should not have been issued a passport for the period of five years from the date of his conviction, which would have been around October 1977. Teja could have got a passport earlier only at the discretion of the prime minister or the home minister.

Teja returned to Hyderabad in 1982, and by then his income tax and wealth tax due had risen to reach figures of Rs 7 crore and Rs 1.76 crore, respectively. He was in Geneva where his wife was posted as a Costa Rican diplomat with the United Nations. In July 1982, he flew to the US and met Prime Minister Indira Gandhi during her official visit to Washington.

It was a legal quagmire with the international airline Pan Am that brought out lurid details of his vast patronage network. Teja might have been close to Nehru and his family, but that did not stop him from being in the good books of other leaders and political parties other than the Congress. In June 1993, Pan Am sued India in a bankruptcy court in the US, seeking to recover $3.7 million lying with Citibank that was frozen by the Indian tax authorities.

The interim government of Charan Singh had filed a suit against Pan Am for allowing Teja to fly out of India. In July 1977, Teja had taken a flight to New York from Delhi on a valid passport and a ticket endorsed to Pan Am from Air India. In their petition, Pan Am revealed that Teja was seen off at the New Delhi airport by Kanti Desai, the son of the then Prime Minister Morarji Desai, and industries minister Sikander Bakht. This, they asserted, was proof enough that Teja's exit was not only known but aided by the top leadership. The airline told the US court that Teja was given a farewell reception which also included customs officers.

Despite Teja himself returning to India in February 1983, the case against the airline was not withdrawn, as the tax authorities continued to hold the airline responsible for Teja's dues and it was subject to strict clearances that only allowed it to remit funds to its head office in the US. In December 1985, Teja died in New Jersey, but this too did not end Pan Am's woes.

In December 1988, the airline was asked to draw up a payment plan to pay Teja's outstanding dues, amounting to over Rs 10 crore in the next six months. The case lingered, but when Pan Am became bankrupt in 1991, it sought to defreeze the funds frozen in India to ensure creditors and employers were paid. India opposed the airline's suit claiming sovereign immunity. However, an agreement was later made wherein the airline was to receive $2 million with the remaining $1.7 million to be adjusted against Teja's outstanding tax dues. In this bizarre development, a third party airline ended up paying Teja's dues!

India may have won the extradition case in the UK against Teja, but in reality, he emerged the ultimate winner.

12

CHARLATAN IN CASHMERE

Terry Adams, assistant commissioner with the Bombay Police, reached the Santa Cruz airport just twenty minutes before Air India's flight to London was to take off. It was a Saturday (1 March 1952) and it was absolutely crucial for Adams to be on the flight to ensure he was present at London's Bow Street court on Monday. The confirmation of the arrest of Mubarak Ali Ahmed, a Pakistani national, by Scotland Yard had got the Bombay Police's headquarters working overtime. Ahmed, a forty-year-old suave entrepreneur, wealthy and well-connected, always impeccably dressed in cashmere tweed suits irrespective of the scorching Indian summers, had jumped bail—worth a humongous Rs 3 lakh—in July 1950, in a cheating case while it was being heard in the sessions court in Bombay.

Ahmed escaped to Lahore from where he went to London, his favourite city and the seat of the British Empire. Here he always lived lavishly over two flats in the posh and exclusive Dorchester Hotel in central London. He was often seen entertaining senior British army officials. Ahmed had developed a reputation of being a contractor with unparalleled access to senior figures in the British armed forces.

So, it comes as little surprise that it was in London that Ahmed was finally apprehended under the Fugitive Offenders Act. Ahmed had not expected that a former colony would get the opportunity to grab him from the soil of her erstwhile political masters. Caught unaware by the swift machinations of the Indian state, Ahmed found himself face-to-face with officers of Scotland Yard in the lounge of his posh London hotel on 26 February 1952.

Initially, he told the officers that he was suffering from dysentery, and hence, it would not be possible to come with them. But, armed with a warrant, Scotland Yard officers took Ahmed to Bow Street Magistrates' Court where he was ultimately committed to India for trial on charges of cheating and forgery. This meant that the Bombay Police had their task cut out. There was little time to lose and apart from deciding on which officer to dispatch, they also had to get the paperwork in order.

Clutching a sealed packet containing papers of Ahmed's case, Adams was about to board the plane when a police rider rushed to hand him another sealed packet. This was meant for V.K. Krishna Menon, the acerbic high commissioner for India in London, who was already a public figure in Britain due to his activism during his student days and long association with Britain's Labour Party.

In an era predating computers and mobile phones, preparing the Ahmed dossier quickly must have been nothing short of a monumental task. And it would be only after another twenty-four hours that Adams would reach London following stopovers in Cairo and Rome. Ahmed and the Bombay Police had been playing the cat-and-mouse game since 1948, and Adams knew that this was a golden opportunity to lay hands on the smooth-talking Ahmed.

The urgency also stemmed from the fact that Ahmed had acquired a Pakistani passport, after jumping bail in 1950 and escaping to Lahore. So, it was only in jurisdictions like Britain that he could be nabbed. Besides, Ahmed was also suspected of aiding the escape of Mir Laik Ali, the Nizam of Hyderabad's prime minister, among other senior functionaries, so it was an issue of prestige for New Delhi.

The case of Mubarak Ali Ahmed is one of the most high profile cases of extradition in independent India. The arrest and trial in London of Ahmed, also described as a former Hyderabad-based industrialist, generated a substantial amount of attention in the media, not just in India and Pakistan but also in Britain. Much before the media circus over Vijay Mallya and Nirav Modi, Ahmed's case was the first to bring out the potency of extradition in statecraft. Ahmed was no petty criminal, and the strings that the Pakistani high commissioner was pulling in the power corridors of London to have him free, made it clear that Ahmed's case had deeper connotations. It was as if the two newly created modern states were reliving their existential angst in the familiar backdrop of London, the heart of the British Empire.

It is most likely that Ahmed was in London on a short business trip and also perhaps assisting the Pakistani High Commission in the legal battle against India over the Hyderabad funds belonging to the Nizam and deposited in Britain's NatWest Bank. A verdict came in October 2019 in favour of the titular eighth Nizam of Hyderabad and his brother, who had reached an agreement with India. The UK court ruled that Pakistan had no claim over the funds which had grown to Rs 350 crore. The case was fought bitterly in British courts, and was halted when Pakistan claimed sovereign immunity. But in 2013, Pakistan initiated legal proceedings against the bank which brought the case into the ambit of the high court in the UK.

On 26 February 1952, Ahmed was produced at the Bow Street court where the magistrate was informed by A.J.G. Hardwicke, the defence counsel, that Sir Kenneth Morley Loch who was master-general of ordnance (MGO) in India during the Raj, and a factory owner from Newcastle were ready to stand sureties for £1000 each. Ahmed was not a petty criminal, and hence, the stakes were really high. Right from his first appearance in the court, Ahmed accused India of political vendetta.

Detective sergeant James of Scotland Yard recounted to the court what Ahmed had told him in custody: 'I have done nothing wrong. The charges are fabricated. I did appear at the Bombay court, but left because the matter was political. You people don't understand the treachery that exists in India against Pakistan. The Indian government is our enemy; we are enemies of the Indian government. This is a political matter.'

And this was precisely the reason why Terry Adams had made his way to London. The significance of the arrival of a Britisher from India still employed with the Bombay Police four years after the end of British rule in August 1947 when the majority of European officers opted for retirement was difficult to ignore. Besides, Adams had a persona that went much beyond his policing duties. The affable assistant commissioner of police was fondly called India's Mister Boxing due to his pioneering efforts to popularize boxing in Bombay and India. He had single-handedly built Rangers Club and organized bouts and tournaments. In the Bombay of the 1940s and 1950s, the path to take part in a boxing tournament started with his office in the police headquarters where he would deftly sift through crime diaries and applications from amateur boxers with equal ease.

At that period, the Indian High Commission in London was among the largest in Britain. Housed in the palatial India House, around 1200 people manned its twenty-odd departments. It soon became clear to India that Ahmed was trying to take control of the narrative and was seeking to gain sympathy against the might of a 'vindictive' Indian state. But the problem was that Ahmed's assertion of political vendetta was misplaced as the offence for which he was wanted was committed in 1946, much before the happening of events which were to make him act and plead as a political victim.

Hyderabad, guided by an indecisive Nizam, was one of the bigger princely states resisting integration with India after Independence. Members of the Nizam's political elite were arrested, including his premier Mir Laik Ali and the head of the private Razakar Army—Kasim Razvi. In that charged atmosphere, individuals like Ahmed, a resident of Hyderabad with known proclivities to Pakistan, were under intense scrutiny. Ahmed's lawyer Sir Godfrey Vick claimed that he had helped in the escape of several Hyderabad ministers, and hence, India was keen to get even with his client.

During the course of the next hearing on Monday, 17 March 1952, Christmas Humphreys, the counsel for India, upped the ante. 'The Indian government deeply resents this allegation that they are not capable of trying the accused fairly and I must ask, therefore, that he prove it or withdraw it,' Humphreys told the court. Seeking to puncture the claim of political vendetta and the high risk Ahmed posed, Humphreys also submitted that he had jumped bail to frustrate the judicial process.

One of the main reasons for Ahmed to hire Sir Godfrey, apart from preventing his extradition, of course, was to ensure that he could escape jail by securing bail. Arranging any amount of funds would not have been a problem for a person of Ahmed's stature, but the magistrate, it seems, was not inclined to take any chances, and turned down the bail application. The trump card for India was the rather dramatic way in which Ahmed had jumped bail in July 1950.

Four days later, on 21 March 1952, when the case came up in Bow Street Magistrates' Court, Ahmed pleaded not guilty to the strong assertions made by Humphreys, that he had conned three individuals in Bombay into parting with Rs 12–13 lakh in 1946 under the impression that he had a contract with the army (entered into in November 1945) to supply goods. Military contracts and buying/selling goods from the army had thrown up quite a few notable millionaires, and the charge was that the smooth-talking Ahmed had easily impressed people to part with lakhs of rupees in anticipation of large profits. But instead of repudiating the charges of cheating and forgery, Ahmed's lawyer Sir Godfrey Vick stressed upon the alleged political victimization of his client. The magistrate was informed that Ahmed could not get a fair trial in India as he was accused of being a Pakistani spy and in the aftermath of the escape of Mir Laik Ali to Pakistan, he was held in custody by the Indian authorities.

Elaborating on his client's suffering, Sir Godfrey told the magistrate that Ahmed's wife and daughter were asked to leave Hyderabad within forty-eight hours and the family's jewellery was taken away. New Delhi had indeed charged him of possessing an illegal transmitter and receiver, but as Ahmed and the Pakistan High Commission discovered, much to their chagrin, these arguments did not cut much ice at Bow Street Magistrates' Court.

The other technical point raised by Sir Godfrey was that there was no extradition treaty between India and Pakistan, and because India was now a sovereign country, the 'Fugitive Offenders Act did not apply to the Republic of India'. The magistrate Francis Bertram Reece agreed that if the argument put forward by Sir Godfrey was correct, then the extradition proceedings would be 'misconceived'. But much to the consternation of Ahmed, the magistrate eventually did not see much merit in not committing the fugitive to India. Ahmed was left with no option but to approach the high court. However, the circumstances in which he escaped from Bombay in July 1950 went a long way to demolish his contention that he was a victim of political vendetta.

* * *

Ahmed's first brush with the Bombay Police was on Thursday, 3 June 1948, when a chartered plane from Hyderabad bound for Karachi landed at Bombay's Santa Cruz airport for refuelling at around mid-day. Among the seven passengers was Mubarak Ali Ahmed, who was arrested the moment he stepped on to the tarmac. The arrest was undertaken on the basis of a complaint filed against Ahmed in Delhi in 1946. Shapoorji Pallonji Mistry and other financiers had lodged a complaint of cheating against Ahmed with the Delhi Police. The allegation was that Mistry and others had given him Rs 10 lakh to fulfil a military contract for the army in the Middle East. The Delhi Police were on the lookout but Ahmed had escaped to Hyderabad state, after which there was not much that the Delhi cops could do.

His arrest and subsequent release on bail was splashed in the local newspapers of Bombay, especially as he was travelling on a chartered flight and that too from Hyderabad. But his freedom was short-lived. On Tuesday morning, 15 June 1948, he was re-arrested on fresh charges of cheating by the Bombay CID (Criminal Investigation Department). Perhaps buoyed by his first arrest and discovering a similar modus operandi deployed by Ahmed, three Bombay merchants—Priyamitra Nagarshett, D.I. Kania and Mohan Kripalani—lodged a complaint that they were conned into investing Rs 12.5 lakh.

The chief presidency magistrate sent him into custody till 29 June after the prosecution alleged that Ahmed, on the basis of a forged contract implying supply of sports and textile goods to the British Army's South East Asia Command (SEAC), had defrauded the trio. In the meanwhile, he was sent to Delhi where he appeared before the first-class resident magistrate and was given bail for Rs 3 lakh. But the Bombay Police were in no mood to relent. Ahmed's bail application, moved by his counsels F.G.R. Khairaz and C.N. Kanuga on Thursday (1 July 1948), was rejected by Oscar Brown, the chief presidency magistrate at the Esplanade Police Court, Bombay.

It was only by the end of July 1948, and bolstered by the assurance that Ahmed had letters of credit to the tune of Rs 28 lakh in Bombay and Calcutta, that he was granted bail on Rs 3 lakh. Ahmed was now free to travel between Hyderabad (where his family was) and Bombay, while appearing on dates at the Presidency Magistrate Court.

In March 1950, Mir Laik Ali, who was placed under house arrest in Hyderabad, made a daring escape which shocked the Indian establishment. His relatives and government officials suspected of aiding his escape were questioned and arrested. The same month, Ahmed was arrested by the Bombay Police at the request of the Hyderabad Police on suspicion of playing a role in the escape of Laik Ali. Ahmed was flown to Hyderabad and taken to the residence of Laik Ali for interrogation. No further action was taken against Ahmed, but an externment order was served on him, his wife and minor daughter under the Public Safety and Public Interest Regulations of Hyderabad. Ahmed knocked on the

doors of the Supreme Court, but just before the matter came up for
hearing, the externment orders were withdrawn. This was a minor
victory for Ahmed, but it also sent a signal that perhaps Ahmed
wouldn't escape to Pakistan. But the Bombay Police were caught
unawares.

Ahmed's link with Hyderabad was a source of discomfort to
the Bombay Police. At the time of India's independence, the fate
of the princely states hung in the balance. While the smaller ones
reconciled—either by choice or fear of force—to opt for India, the
bigger ones like Kashmir and Hyderabad remained indecisive for
too long. During the colonial rule, they were under the clutches of
British residents and political agents, but could still boast of some
autonomy. But with the British gone, the self-government was
bound to give way to an overarching control by a young republic.
The princely states were also not the site for anti-colonialism
with the same intensity and magnitude as the Presidency towns
and territories directly under British rule, where they continued to
enjoy the pomp and glory.

In the case of Hyderabad, a further complication stemmed
from the fact that a largely Hindu population had a Muslim ruler.
The Nizam, one of the richest rulers, signed a standstill agreement
with India in November 1947, but faced opposition from the
militant Razakars. In September 1948, Indian armed forces poured
into Hyderabad leading to its merger with India. The police action
codenamed 'Operation Polo' left a bitter legacy and there were
large scale communal riots. Much historical work continues to
be done on Operation Polo. A large section of the Muslim elites
and intelligentsia went over to Pakistan, while the Nizam was
appointed the Raj Pramukh of Hyderabad in 1950.

* * *

Since his arrest in June 1948, Ahmed was entangled in a complex
web of court cases. He had spent thousands of rupees in legal
fees paying lawyers to represent him in courts in Delhi, Bombay,

Hyderabad and Punjab. But the noose was now tightening. Around the same time when he got relief from the Supreme Court, the magistrate court in Bombay in April 1950, after prolonged committal proceedings, commended the investigation done by deputy inspector Basil Kane, and ruled that Ahmed should stand trial in the sessions court as a prima facie case had been made against him.

What made the prosecution's case particularly strong was the evidence of Major Donald Salter who was working in the war office in London. Salter was posted in the same army unit—SEAC, based in Singapore—which had allegedly given Ahmed the contract to supply military stores. With a straight face, Salter ripped apart Ahmed's claims one by one. The contract was produced in the court and Salter pointed out that it was signed by the chief of information and civil affairs holding the rank of major-general at the SEAC, whereas at no time was there a major-general in charge of civil affairs. Besides, the headquarters of the SEAC was abolished in May 1944, so there was no chance of drawing a contract with Ahmed in November 1945!

Salter's evidence must have driven home the point that Ahmed would be in for a long haul if the trial ran its normal course. Besides, if Mir Laik Ali could escape, then why couldn't he? As the trial began at the sessions court, Ahmed was staying in a suite at the Cricket Club of India (CCI). Ahmed was regularly attending the sessions court, but the cops got a jolt when he did not turn up for the hearing on Thursday, 6 July 1950. There was a plainclothes cop from the Bombay Police to keep a watch, but clearly, he was no match for Ahmed. Just four months ago, Mir Laik Ali and a few others had escaped from Hyderabad to Pakistan, and now the Bombay Police were faced with the same prospect of having Ahmed give them the slip. For the Bombay Police, it was a double blow as just a day earlier (5 July 1950), five accused arrested for a daring dacoity, where Rs 5.6 lakh were stolen from Central Bank in December 1949, escaped from a police van while being taken to the court from Byculla jail. They sprinkled chilli power on the police escorts and vanished into the crowded by-lanes around the populous Zakariya Masjid where the van had stopped.

Considering that Ahmed was arrested from a chartered plane trying to make his way to Karachi, the police could have been more alert. But in the aftermath of Partition, which brought with it mass-scale rioting, disorder and enforcement of various wartime restrictions, the city police were hard-pressed. Besides, Ahmed was given bail at a high amount of Rs 3 lakh.

Police officers rushed to his suite at the CCI and found three letters left by Ahmed. And just as he would resist officers of Scotland Yard, claiming he had an upset stomach, he tried to throw the Bombay Police off track by saying he was committing suicide by jumping into the sea.

This was a sensational escape and though cops fanned out far and wide, he was not to be found. In a matter of a day, the majority of the Bombay Police personnel was pressed into locating criminals who had escaped under their watch. Ahmed's counsel S. Baptista faced the music before the judge M.B. Honavar. Baptista told the court that he was with Ahmed at CCI till 9.30 p.m. on Wednesday and was supposed to meet him again at 10 a.m. before the hearing.

The judge was quick to issue a non-bailable warrant and directed the forfeiture of the Rs 3 lakh bail bond. Intel reports suggested that Ahmed was spotted in Lahore which confirmed the worst fears of the Bombay Police. It might seem difficult to imagine now, but the Bombay Police had managed to get an accused extradited from Pakistan in November 1949, just four months before Ahmed ran away to Lahore. There was a glimmer of hope.

Sher Dil alias Jimmy alias Joachim was the mastermind of the famous Bruce Street dacoity committed on 10 January 1949. Brandishing firearms, Sher Dil and his accomplices, including Pathans, took away four trunks containing Rs 3.50 lakh just outside Bombay House, the headquarters of the House of Tatas on Bruce Street (now known as Homi Modi Street). The accused knew that on the tenth of each month, trunks of money, meant to be disbursed among the mill workers at Parel, were taken out from Bombay House.

Sher Dil had done his homework well and the car in which they escaped belonged to a judge of the Bombay High Court. John, the judge's chauffeur, keeping his master in the dark, had lent the car to Sher Dil. Once the money was disbursed, Sher Dil, taking a circuitous route, entered Pakistan without a permit, in the belief that he was safe. He was wrong. Pakistan handed over Sher Dil to the Bombay Police after extradition proceedings were launched by the GoI. Sher Dil was ultimately sentenced to ten years' rigorous imprisonment. The Bombay Police had a precedent, but Mubarak Ahmed was neither a dacoit nor was he short of friends in high places.

Stung by the escape, the administration swung into action declaring Ahmed an evacuee, thus facilitating the takeover of his assets. The new states of India and Pakistan would declare a person an evacuee if they crossed the border, and take over their property with the aim to rehabilitate the new arrivals. The custodian of evacuee property seized Ahmed's well-furnished bungalow in Jubilee Hills and other properties in Hyderabad. Another casualty of Ahmed's escape was a merchant from Punjab, Sardar Jagmirsingh, who had stood surety for him. Jagmirsingh flew to Bombay from north India, met the Bombay Police commissioner and announced a reward of Rs 5000 for any information leading to the arrest of Ahmed. After much haggling, the court reduced his surety from Rs 3 lakh to Rs 1 lakh.

There were other players as well in the Ahmed saga. A Bangalore resident, Ishaq, filed a suit in a Hyderabad court seeking a share in the property left behind by Ahmed. Ishaq, who claimed to be a cousin of Ahmed, alleged that he had not received his share of Rs 2 lakh in the contract for supplying jeeps to the government. It was clear that Ahmed was a smooth operator who had spun a large web. After graduating from Panjab University in 1928, he joined government service till he resigned in 1943. He moved to Hyderabad and flourished as a military contractor,

making the most of the contacts he made during his employment
with the government.

* * *

In the journey from Bombay to London, Adams must have gone
through Ahmed's case file. As a senior officer of the CID, he must
have personally felt the insult caused by Ahmed's escape. It was of
utmost importance to present Ahmed's case in its entirety, leaving
no room to make it a political cause. After the success in the Bow
Street court, as expected, Ahmed had moved the high court to stall
his extradition.

At the Bow Street court, Humphreys's argument that Ahmed
ran away as he 'saw the grave possibility of being convicted', was
latched on to by British court reporters. This was a direct assault
on the endeavours by Pakistani High Commissioner M.A.H.
Ispahani, who had taken up the post just a month ago, to put India
in a bad light. Ispahani was drumming up support for Ahmed
which would come in handy once the matter reached the office of
the home secretary. As per the procedure, after the judgment by
courts, it was the home secretary who had the final say.

It was on 21 March 1952 that the Bow Street magistrate
ruled against Ahmed, sending him to Brixton prison pending his
extradition to India. The appeal process did not turn out to be a
long wait for Adams. In less than a fortnight, the high court junked
Ahmed's application for leave to apply. Sir Godfrey had raised two
points in the application. The first was that the Fugitive Offenders
Act, 1881, under which Ahmed was arrested, was no longer in
force between India and Britain; and the second was that his client
was being persecuted as a political offender. It was also brought to
the notice of the court that the press in India had branded him a
spy for Pakistan, and hence, the jury in Bombay would not be fair
and unbiased.

The application came before a two-judge bench comprising
Lord Chief Justice William Goddard and Justice Hubert Parker.

In throwing out the application, the chief justice explained that though India became an independent republic, she remained a member of the Commonwealth, denoting a shared link between both the countries. Besides, the British Parliament framed the India (Consequential Provision) Act, 1949, in contemplation of India becoming a republic with the intention to keep in force all the laws relating to India and Britain. As the Fugitive Offenders Act was in force when India became a republic, by virtue of the India (Consequential Provision) Act, 1949, it continued to remain in full force between India and Britain.

The high court went on to say that it would be 'an insult to the courts of India, just as much as if India refused to hand over a fugitive offender for trial in this country on the ground that he would not have a fair trial'. In saying so, the court noted that Ahmed was on trial for a charge of forgery, which was when he fled to Pakistan, and hence, it would be 'astonishing for them to hold that it would be unjust or oppressive to hand him back'.

'No shelter for Mr Ahmed' screamed the *Daily Mail* headline on Saturday, 19 April 1952. The weekend for the staff at the Pakistani High Commission was ruined as the newspaper reported that the Home Secretary Sir David Maxwell Fyfe would not stop the extradition of Ahmed. The home secretary's decision had removed the last block to Ahmed's extradition to India. The report noted that the Pakistani high commissioner had personally asked (the home secretary) that Mr Ahmed be allowed to stay in England.

While Ispahani, belonging to a successful and famous business family, was new in the diplomatic circles of London, his Indian counterpart V.K. Krishna Menon, a heavyweight, was about to relinquish his post after being in charge since 1947. Nothing must have given Menon more pleasure than the sight of Adams escorting Ahmed back to Bombay.

Just before the decision of the home secretary, *Dawn* newspaper in an editorial commented that 'if a Pakistani citizen armed with a Pakistani passport is so unsafe in the UK there may well be unpleasant repercussions in this country'. It was also difficult for

Pakistan to not view the developments in London on the basis of
Britain's partiality towards India. 'Despite the reported intervention
of our high commissioner in London this Pakistani will be offered
by the British as a sacrificial goat for the appeasement of Bharati
vendetta.' This was indeed a major victory for India.

Adams, along with two officers of Scotland Yard, landed with
Ahmed in Bombay on Sunday, 21 April 1952. In less than two
months since his arrest in London, Ahmed was in Bombay to face
the sessions court. The Air India flight had a total of five passengers,
including Ahmed and the three escorts. To avoid media attention,
the four names were added to the passenger list only a few minutes
before the departure. Ahmed was driven to the tarmac in a car and
only select officials knew of the date of the deportation.

In Bombay, along with a huge contingent of reporters
and photographers, there were members of the public who had
assembled to get a glimpse of what was happening. Notwithstanding
the tough days ahead, Ahmed did not lose his sense of sartorial
elegance. He landed in Bombay in a woollen suit and felt hat,
telling an acquaintance in the crowd: 'I am as I was before. I have
not changed a bit.' Photographers were not allowed in the airport
and, made to sit between two officers in the police van, he was
taken to the Bombay CID lock-up.

Ahmed's extradition meant that assistant commissioners N.J.
Gibbs and D.K. Pednekar, Superintendent N.P. Paranjpe and
Inspector Basil Kane—the team that investigated Ahmed had to get
back to the drawing board to present a tight-knit case. On Monday,
21 July 1952, Ahmed appeared before the sessions court for a fresh
trial pleading not guilty. As he stood in the dock in brown tweeds, he
was ordered to remove his shoes, signifying the shame and suffering
that Ahmed faced while he remained in India till 1958.

* * *

Sher Dil was a small fry whose extradition was obtained with
hardly any diplomatic wrangling. In fact, Sher Dil's return shows

that co-operation between the two states was possible while hostilities were at their height. But in May 1952, when a Delhi magistrate issued a non-bailable arrest warrant against Yusuf Abdullah Haroon, the Pakistani high commissioner in Australia, Karachi couldn't take it anymore. According to the *Bombay Chronicle*, the political establishment was actively toying with the idea of dragging India to the International Court of Justice (ICJ) in The Hague. As if the successful extradition of Ahmed was not enough, the possibility of a diplomat standing before a court in India seemed unbearable to Pakistan.

At the ICJ, Pakistan would argue that as the extradition arrangement was entered upon by the British government of undivided India, it could not be in operation for the new and independent state of India. The immediate fear was that Australia too was in the Commonwealth and should India formally approach her, it was a possibility that the diplomat could face legal proceedings.

The case against Haroon pertained to over-invoicing the army for a contract to supply ghee during the Second World War. Haroon, it was alleged, was one of the two active partners of the Sindh Ghee Purchasing Agency, the firm which had cheated the (undivided) GoI. The investigations began in 1946 but, due to Partition and difficulty in locating witnesses and paperwork, the case got delayed. The warrant against Haroon was issued after the investigations had resumed and investigative officers in India had got case papers which were in Lahore as the accused was a resident of Sindh.

Offences of fraud and cheating in army contracts were rampant as they involved huge amounts and contacts to bag prestigious projects. Supplying sub-standard or poor quality materials, over-charging or charging for goods which were not supplied were not uncommon. In 1949, a year before Ahmed was extradited, Bow Street Magistrates' Court had found no bar to the removal of Colonel Henderson to India to stand trial on charges of fraud. Henderson had passed bills for contractors in excess of what they were entitled to.

Ahmed's trial did not begin as he did not have money to pay his lawyers. The trial was delayed as he sought and was given one month's time by the sessions court to get money from Karachi to pay for his defence. The city civil and sessions court were established in 1947 to ease the burgeoning case list before the Bombay High Court. These courts were to conduct trials in civil and criminal cases, which could be appealed to the high court.

Karl Khandalavala was one of the four judges appointed to the sessions court. A lover of arts and sculpture, he also dabbled in photography and painting. But Khandalavala did not last long as a judge, as he found marshalling arguments, rather than presiding over them, far more alluring. Moving away from the orthodoxy, Khandalavala, all through his remarkable career, never restrained himself to the higher courts. Appearing in the lower courts provided him the opportunity to be engaged at the trial stage. And as a criminal lawyer, he seemed to have a fondness for dealing with witnesses and documents, instead of the limited arena of arguing points of substantive law in the higher courts. Ahmed got sufficient funds wired from Karachi to hire Khandalavala in the sessions court.

Ahmed's case was to be tried in the court of no-nonsense Judge Jaishankar Manilal Shelat. As a lawyer, Shelat had defended several freedom fighters arrested by the British for taking part in the 1942 Quit India movement. In one of the early hearings, the judge took umbrage to Ahmed not conducting himself properly. Shelat turned over to Khandalavala, his former fellow judge, asking him to convey to Ahmed the importance of decorum. In a rather childish way, Ahmed was caught laughing and making mirthful gesticulations. At one point, he was seen winking at the prosecution witness, D.I. Kania, as he was giving evidence.

Kania was recounting how he met Ahmed and became a partner at his insistence. His first meeting with Ahmed was in February 1946 at the house of M.C. Zaveri, a common friend. As was his modus operandi, Ahmed told Kania about the contract from the SEAC and that he was on the lookout for a partner who could invest Rs 15 lakh. After few months, when Ahmed made it known that one of his partners had exited the business as he was unable to bring in the required cash, there was still a possibility for Kania to join him. To discuss the modalities, Kania took his friend Nagarshett to meet Ahmed at the Taj Mahal Hotel where he was staying. Kania told the court that it was in his room at the Taj Mahal Hotel that Ahmed showed them papers relating to the lucrative contract he had got from the SEAC and the various orders he had placed with merchants across India to fulfil his obligations.

The other partner was P.K. Nagarshett who alleged that Ahmed showed them the contract he had signed with the SEAC. Nagarshett told the court that a partnership deed was signed in July 1946 and a bank account for the partnership was opened in the ABC Bank. The new partners directly wrote to the SEAC to inform them of the new partnership formed. They thought it would be better to enter into correspondence with the SEAC as a large sum of money was involved. Despite a few letters and cables, they did not receive any reply.

According to Nagarshett, Ahmed was not happy when he was shown the copies of the letters Nagarshett had written to the SEAC in his absence and also the fact that they had not received any replies. Nagarshett sensed something was amiss and told Kania that he wished to exit the partnership. But Ahmed continued with the farce. After a visit from Hyderabad, he showed them some letters which he claimed were addressed to him by the SEAC at his Hyderabad office to reinforce to them the genuineness of the contract. But by then, they had decided to file a police complaint against Ahmed.

The evidence was all stacking up against Ahmed, reaching a stratospheric height when Judge Shelat heard evidence from Major Donald Salter. Major Salter had also given evidence against Ahmed in 1950, and was summoned a second time. This time he had flown to Bombay from Germany where he was with the Command Secretariat of the British Army in Rhine. Major Salter's evidence was crucial as he had visited Bombay in October 1946 to conduct an investigation following the letters and cables that were sent by Kania, Nagarshett and Kripalani. At that time, he was with the SEAC in Singapore.

Major Salter told the court that he had met Ahmed and Kania during his Bombay visit. Ahmed showed Major Salter the contract and repeated the same story that he had signed the contract with two high ranking army officers at the Taj Mahal Hotel. Major Salter said that there was no way an army contract would be signed in a hotel. Kania had no idea how the contract was entered into, except that it was all done by Ahmed and he had a copy of the contract and a receipt for the Rs 5 lakh deposit paid to the army to get the contract.

Major Salter pointed out some glaring errors that showed that the papers with Ahmed could not have been genuine. Army contracts were in printed form while the one with Ahmed was typewritten. Ahmed maintained that in that case he too was a victim of a fraud played by two men who posed as army officers and took Rs 5 lakh from him. According to him, the duo had told him that they were special representatives of the SEAC and could enter into a contract with him. So it was not just the three partners, but he too was a victim as he had paid Rs 5 lakh deposit!

In the cross-examination, Khandalavala asked Major Salter for more details of his October 1946 visit to Bombay. He asked Major Salter whether he had prepared a report. The court heard that Major Salter had prepared an interim report, which he had submitted to his seniors while he was still in Bombay. This was followed by a final report in 1948. 'Do you have a copy of the report,' asked Khandalavala. Major Salter then produced a letter from the War Office to the effect that the final report was a privileged document and could not be submitted as evidence.

Answering a pointed question, Major Salter accepted that his evidence that Mubarak Ali had used Rs 1000 notes to pay the deposit to the army officers at the Taj Mahal Hotel was not from his notes but recollection. During the cross-examination, it also came out that Major Salter had not filed any complaint with the

Bombay Police or the military police, neither against Mubarak Ali Ahmed nor against M.A.I. Ahmed & Company. All Major Salter did was to discuss the issue informally with an officer of the Bombay Police.

But this was not the only case that Ahmed had to face. His successful extradition to India had alerted Luis Antonio Correa, a director of Goa-based Colonial Trading Company. According to Correa, Ahmed fraudulently extracted Rs 5.47 lakh to supply 2000 tonnes of rice from Karachi. Ahmed, he alleged, did not fulfil the contract neither did he return the money. This happened between July and November 1951, which means just a year after he fled from his CCI suite in Bombay.

Ahmed maintained that this was a civil case with no criminality involved and that it would be wrong to make him stand trial in a case other than for which his extradition was sought. The correct forum for the trial, he told the court, was Goa, a Portuguese territory, which was where Correa resided and not Bombay.

In August 1952, Judge Shelat sentenced Ahmed to three and a half years' imprisonment and a Rs 15,000 fine. He was found guilty of both the charges of cheating and using forged documents as genuine. This was the case for which he was extradited, and in some ways, he was prepared for it. But the real shock came when despite Ahmed's protestations, the Goa cheating case too went on trial in the sessions court in June 1953. Reams of correspondence and records of telephone calls presented before the court show how Correa was induced to part with his money in a very measured and calculated way.

Initially, the agreement was to supply 1200 tonnes of rice from Pakistan to Goa on the condition of payment of 25 per cent advance amounting to Rs 81,000, which was paid in July 1951. Ahmed then reasoned that if the consignment was increased to 2000 tonnes and more money was paid to his agent in Bombay, the consignment would be shipped immediately. This way he got an additional Rs 2,30,000 and Rs 2,36,900 in August 1951. Goa faced an acute scarcity of rice in that period, and Correa was desperate to receive consignments. Correa's desperation ended up in dismay as despite paying Rs 5.47 lakh, no consignment of rice reached him. He then visited Karachi on a three-month visa where he was assured by Ahmed that the consignment of rice was ready to be shipped.

But when Correa demanded papers to show that the consignment was meant to be shipped to Goa, he found himself with a government order to leave Karachi. Correa alleged that he had reason to believe that Ahmed had pulled strings in high places to ensure he left Karachi. Correa continued to follow-up, but all he received were names of vessels carrying the rice consignment, and they never arrived. Ahmed's agent in Bombay and other witnesses too appeared before the court strengthening Correa's case. In September 1953, Judge J.M. Barot found Ahmed guilty and sentenced him to forty-six months of rigorous imprisonment.

Judge Barot could not avoid mentioning Ahmed's 'charlatanry and native bluff' which had blinded Correa. His dishonest correspondence with Correa was taken into consideration as being responsible to induce him to part with such a large sum of money. Ahmed had boasted that he had a line of credit worth Rs 94 lakh with the Malayan government, which the judge said even the most circumspect person might have fallen prey to.

Ahmed appealed against his conviction to the high court saying that the evidence against him was fabricated and that the agents to whom money was given were not his agents and he had not received the money. In January 1954, the Bombay High Court admitted the appeal, giving him some hope. But that was short-lived as in July 1954, Justice Bavdekar and Justice Vyas dismissed Ahmed's appeal and upheld his conviction. The Bombay High Court did not give him permission to appeal to the Supreme Court, following which he directly approached the Supreme Court for permission.

In October 1955, the Supreme Court gave him permission to appeal the high court order. Ahmed sought the permission to appeal under article 136—a special leave petition which gives the Supreme Court the power to grant special leave. His appeal stated that he was in Pakistan when the Goa rice contract was agreed upon, and hence, the courts in India did not have jurisdiction to try him. Besides, he said his extradition from England was allowed in respect of a different case and he was wrongly subject to trial for a new case which was bad in law.

In September 1957, after two years, the Supreme Court finally gave a ruling, dismissing his appeal. Following this, Ahmed had to abide by the sessions court's judgment of undergoing a prison sentence of forty-six months. As Ahmed was extradited under the Fugitive Offenders Act, 1881, there was no bar to put him on trial for a case different to what he was sought to be extradited. This was because the 1881 Act did not have specialty protection. If Ahmed was extradited under the Fugitive Offenders Act, 1967, the successor to the 1881 Act, he wouldn't have to face the new case, and would have gone to Karachi much earlier.

Ahmed remained in India for six years from his arrival in 1952 to 1958. Fortunately for him, there were no additional cases against him in India, but his Atlas Trading Company continued to be the subject of a long-drawn-out legal battle in Karachi, over what else but, rice consignments.

13

IN THE DOCK

The Bow Street Magistrates' Court in Covent Garden was synonymous with extradition cases in Britain. Situated in a Greco–Roman style building, the court had a rather chequered history dating back to 1740 when Thomas de Veil established a magistrate's office on the ground floor while holding his private residence on the upper floors in a house on 4 Bow Street which became the most important magistrates' court in England. A decade later, his successor Henry Fielding expanded the site to establish the first police station in Britain with the first uniformed police unit of eight men, thus giving birth to the famous Bow Street Runners who patrolled the street in scarlet waistcoats and earned the nickname 'Robin Redbreasts'.

Subsequently, it became the court where the senior district judge (for England and Wales), also known as the chief magistrate, would sit and it became the natural home for extradition and other high-profile cases involving public figures. And the Robin Redbreasts were replaced with the London Metropolitan police force with their black and white gear.

For over two centuries, the court and the Royal Opera House were neighbours in the busy Covent Garden. Both were sites of well-rehearsed and well-researched dialogues, which gained much attention. Giacomo Casanova, whose name is synonymous with womanising, author and gay icon Oscar Wilde, pioneering suffragette Emmeline Pankhurst, Chilean dictator Augusto Pinochet, and the millionaire author Lord Jeffrey Archer were some of the famous personalities in the dock at the Bow Street Magistrates' Court. As we discussed in this book, industrialist Dharma Jayanti Teja, smuggler Manu Narang, music director Nadeem and gangster Iqbal Mirchi were presented in the Bow Street Magistrates' Court.

The starting point for extradition between India (along with other parts of the Empire) and Britain is the Fugitive Offenders Act of 1881. An arrest warrant issued in India could be endorsed by the secretary of state or Bow Street Magistrates' Court which would enable the arrest of the requested person to face committal proceedings. Cheating and financial bungling figured prominently even in colonial times. In 1938, Changaram Kumarath Unnittiri, a bank cashier from Calicut, was placed before the court for extradition to India on a provisional extradition warrant issued by Government of Madras. He was charged with cheating to the tune of £50,000.

The earliest case of extradition in independent India was that of Major Thomas Henderson of the Royal Engineers. Henderson, a resident of Cheshire, was charged with conspiring with contractors to cheat the army. The cheating case against him was lodged in 1942 for the sum of Rs 3,98,400 as he had knowingly passed inflated bills by civilian contractors. He had spent four years in Indian prisons, and he came to the UK after jumping bail. Henderson's contention was that he was repatriated by Pakistan with the knowledge of the authorities in India. However, India maintained that his return was due to a misunderstanding with the Pakistani authorities and India had never given a consent to his removal to the UK. In June 1949, the Bow Street Court gave the assent to Henderson's extradition to India. The Court of Appeal ruled that his extradition would not be oppressive.

Before the spectacle of Sikh and Kashmiri separatists going to Britain, Naga leader Angami Z Phizo made his way to London way back in 1960. He was granted asylum, and though

India informed Britain about the cases against Phizo, a formal extradition request was not made. The decision was made right at the top with Prime Minister Jawaharlal Nehru informing the Lok Sabha that extradition would involve a 'petty trial' which would revive interest and make him a martyr. The Indian high commission in London countered his 'baseless' charges but never went to the courts against him.

Perhaps a similar stand was required in the case of Naranjan Singh, who was working for BOAC (previous avatar of British Airways) and unknown to him was being sought on charges of cheating. The thirty-seven-year-old had started a new life in London after arriving from India in 1951. A decade later he was arrested on India's request, and on 9 February 1961, the Bow Street Magistrates' Court sent him to Brixton prison to await extradition. Singh appealed to the high court, where the three-judge bench of Chief Justice Lord Parker, Justice Salmon and Justice Edmund Davies heard the case. The proceedings against Singh, accused of cheating to the tune of a paltry £112, were described as dilatory. His arrest more than ten years after the alleged offence was committed, while he continued to live openly in England, went in his favour. In May 1961, the high court ruled that extraditing Singh would be 'unjust and oppressive', and he was set free.

An independent India hoped to secure a better treaty with its once colonial master to cement a new beginning. But decolonisation necessitated changes for Britain to apprehend foreign criminals, especially from its former colonies and dominions which were now independent republics. The Fugitive Offenders Act 1967, which replaced the 1881 Act, not only did not include offences of political nature, it also provided safeguards to those who could potentially face discrimination based on religion, caste, or nationality. This was not so under the 1881 Act which listed treason as an extraditable offence. By the 1980s, Britain was seen as harbouring, those articulating political positions which could be seen by India as not just undesirable, but dangerous; yet India, with its newfound independence, was in no position to influence Britain to think and do otherwise.

When preliminary talks for UK–India extradition treaty were being conducted in the 1980s, a battle of sorts was playing out in the diplomatic circles. Both the countries wanted to not appear to give out more than what they stood to gain. To begin with, London tried to simply dismiss India's request for an extradition treaty, by claiming that the Fugitive Offenders Act 1967 was good enough to get the desired results. This position was best articulated by Sir Geoffrey Howe, the foreign secretary, who maintained that there was no need for a bilateral treaty with India.

But in the wake of the assassination of Prime Minister Indira Gandhi on 31 October 1984, there was increased pressure from India to rein in 'Sikh extremists' who had entered Britain and claimed asylum. British Prime Minister Margaret Thatcher was a good friend of Indira Gandhi and had flown from London to attend the funeral. Calling her 'a great leader', Thatcher had confessed that she will miss her very much. In October 1985, Rajiv Gandhi visited Britain, the first after the assassination of his mother. Welcoming Indira's son and the new prime minister of India, Thatcher offered to make some changes in the Fugitive Offenders Act and offered to extend to India the provisions of the Suppression of Terrorism Act 1978, under which political offence exception would not apply to acts of murder, kidnapping, terrorism.

The Suppression of Terrorism Act 1978 was principally a European construct, but its provisions were extended to the US in 1986 to ensure that extradition of dangerous individuals, charged with violent activities, should not be debarred under the guise of furthering a political cause. Rajiv Gandhi found this of not much benefit to India and maintained that a separate treaty between India and the UK was imperative. New Delhi also wanted a clause similar to Britain's anti-IRA extradition treaty with the US, which did not allow Irish Republican Army (IRA) soldiers to gain safe haven in the US and facilitate their extradition to Britain. There was a precedence, but Britain was not ready to give similar leeway to India as the US had given to her.

The other contentious point was India's insistence on having a 'grave effect' clause which meant that Britain would recognize India's right to seek extradition for a conduct in Britain which led to crimes being committed in India. This would bring under its ambit those accused of financing and planning criminal activities in India, while stationed in Britain. India, to forward this argument, used the example of the Indo-Canadian treaty which recognized that courts in Canada would consider the extradition of people responsible for supporting or planning crimes which have an effect in India.

The 1980s were trying times for the India–UK relationship. In October 1986, Indian High Commissioner P.C. Alexander was summoned to the Foreign Office in London to show their 'surprise and regret' on Rajiv Gandhi calling British visa controls for Indians 'racist'. London was also peeved with New Delhi's procrastination over the appointment of two drug liaison officers to work in India, which the British complaint was a major source for drugs reaching their shores. It is ironic that Sikh bodies in the UK are now trying to unravel the role of British security agencies in the storming of the Golden Temple, but in the mid-1980s some experts took the view that the Tory party was supporting Sikh extremists as a counter to Labour's popularity with the larger population of Sikh immigrants in Britain.

In January and October 1986, legal experts met in New Delhi and London respectively to discuss the draft of the extradition treaty. Timothy Renon, minister of state in foreign office, visited India in December 1986 and again in 1987 as Home Office minister in charge of immigration. Natwar Singh, India's external affairs minister, raised these two issues in a contentious debate with his UK contemporaries, on his visit to London in April 1987. A draft proposal, made in June 1987, fell short of India's expectation as it did not have retrospective effect, which meant that several of the alleged terrorists who had escaped to Britain could not be covered under it.

Much of India's angst was over the prima facie issue, which it felt was akin to putting on trial in a British court the Indian judicial system. But the determination of a prima facie case was a necessity under the 1967 Act. Douglas Hurd, the British home secretary, in September 1986, was adamant that India would have to resort to normal extradition proceedings, which meant going through the norm of establishing prima facie case in British courts. The treaty was signed in London in September 1992. In November 1993, it was Hurd, as the foreign secretary, who exchanged the instruments of ratification with the minister of external affairs, Dinesh Singh, in Delhi. This put the treaty into force.

When the treaty was signed, India became the first country from the Commonwealth to have a bilateral extradition treaty with Britain. As additional benefits, Britain watered down the political defence barrier to extradition by bringing India under the ambit of the Suppression of Terrorism Act 1978. An agreement was also signed permitting the confiscation of assets of individuals involved in terrorism and drug trafficking. But this did not mean that Britain could not refuse extradition if there were sufficient grounds to believe that it was sought on account of an individual's religion, nationality, race, political opinion.

Following the cancellation of Vijay Mallya's passport, India sought his deportation, which was refused by the UK, and the extradition process was set in motion. The celebrated case of Karamjit Singh Chahal shows why the UK, unlike countries like UAE, is reluctant to deport an accused person. In August 1990, the UK home secretary ordered the deportation of Chahal to India on grounds of national security due to his alleged involvement in terrorism for Sikh separatist groups. Chahal, who was in Britain since 1971, was an Indian national and had an indefinite leave to remain, maintained his innocence.

Chahal remained in detention for more than five years, as successive home secretaries maintained that his deportation was necessary. His application for political asylum was refused and was not given the right of appeal to an independent tribunal due to security concerns. India had provided diplomatic assurances against torture and ill-treatment. But Britain's longest-serving detainee was freed after the ECtHR ruled in November 1996 that the UK would breach human rights provisions if Chahal was deported to India.

Some observers saw the judgment as an intrusion with British efforts to deal with terrorism, while others saw it as the rightful triumph of human rights. The Chahal dilemma has always weighed heavily on the UK, and one of the measures it took was the establishment of an independent judicial tribunal to hear appeals against immigration decisions of the home office. It was achieved by the passage of the Special Immigration Appeals Commission Act 1997, which also allowed for special representation in cases which had non-disclosable security evidence.

* * *

The Bow Street police station closed in 1992, and in July 2006 the Bow Street Magistrates' Court heard its last case. The Royal Opera House, however, continues to regale audiences, and as per the latest planning permission the court premises are to be turned into a hotel and a museum. Covent Garden is now a thriving food and arts district, making it least desirable commercially to have a busy and specialist magistrates' court. The extradition cases were transferred to the Horseferry Road Magistrates' Court for few years, before being taken over by the Westminster Magistrates' Court in 2011.

Today, the extradition between India and the UK is governed by the Extradition Act 2003 and the India–UK Extradition Treaty 1993. India is in the category 2 territory under Part 2 of the 2003 Act. Within the Part 2 category, India is expected to make out a prima facie case (as during the earlier 1967 Act) against a requested person for the extradition to be successful. For India, the process begins with an extradition request to the UK. The Home Office is the central authority for certifying the requests from India.

The Home Office certifies the extradition request after ensuring that some basic criteria are fulfilled. It is then sent to the court for the issuance of an arrest warrant. At this stage the court has to be satisfied of the dual criminality (the alleged offence for which extradition is sought must constitute a crime in Britain) and ensures it has enough information to issue an arrest warrant. If these conditions are not met, extradition proceedings do not move as it happened in the cases of Patrick Bowring, Kartik Venugopal and Rishikesh Kardile.

Bowring, a British national, wanted by the CBI for smuggling of antiques, came to UK while a criminal case was going on against him in the Metropolitan Magistrate Court in Delhi in 2014. Bowring was employed with a prominent auction house, Sotheby's, and operated from India since the 1980s. He was popular with the Page 3 crowd in Mumbai and Delhi and had also opened India's specialist fine art auction house called Bowrings in 2001. The denial to issue a warrant by the UK means that the seventy-year-old cannot risk travelling outside the country for fear of being arrested, but will remain safe as long as he remains in the UK. Similarly, Kardile, facing a matrimonial dispute case, and Venugopal, a case of fraud, will remain stuck in the UK, or go back to India to engage in a long litigation to earn their full-fledged freedom. If they travel to another country from the UK, they risk facing extradition cases based on India's request.

For India, the Home Office requires a 'full evidence file' which means that unlike the European Union, New Delhi has to share a fairly detailed body of investigation against the requested person. Effectively, this can also mean a huge delay between the request being received and the requested person being apprehended. This explains the delay in the commencement of extradition proceedings for Vijay Mallya and Nirav Modi.

It is believed that the UK was not satisfied with the information submitted against Nirav Modi with the request to extradite him.

They requested more details from New Delhi but that went unanswered for months, thus delaying the UK from initiating extradition proceedings against the fugitive diamantaire. No doubt, it was a story in the *Telegraph* that got Nirav Modi in the net, but the long silence from India to respond to further queries could have a role in Modi being free on London streets for a longer time.

Besides, the Metropolitan Police has just about two dozen specialist officers who deal with extradition cases. The bulk of the extradition requests that the UK gets comes from the EU countries which follows a much straight forward process, compared to India. It shouldn't be a surprise then that faced with a poor response and limited manpower, extradition requests from India take more time to get initiated.

There was no such bottleneck in the case of the Anguralas. Jatinder and Asha Rani Angurala were sought by the CBI for cheating Bank of India's Jalandhar branch, where Jatinder was branch manager. The offence was alleged to have taken place between 1990 and 1993, and when the extradition request came, the Anguralas were already living in the UK for more than two decades. The home secretary certified India's request on 1 April 2015 and the couple was arrested on 4 June 2015. The Anguralas won their case in Westminster Magistrates' Court on the grounds of 'passage of time' in October 2017. The couple, who escaped not just from India, but also from the clutches of Indian authorities when the British court refused to order their extradition, now run a busy corner shop in London's bustling Elephant and Castle area.

Billionaires like Nirav Modi and Vijay Mallya hire the best legal minds who as pre-emptive measures liaise with the Metropolitan Police and the CPS in anticipation of action from India. In fact, the CPS and Nirav Modi's legal team had agreed on a surrender date on which he was to be brought to court. Usually, bail is granted then on a surety befitting the crime. Mallya paid a whopping £6,50,000 as surety while bail eluded Nirav Modi right from the beginning. Even with consistently increasing the surety to a mind-boggling £4 million and suggesting very stringent bail conditions, Modi was unable to get out of jail.

In the first hearing before the district judge, the requested person has the option of either consenting or contesting the extradition. Depending on the information flow, number of charges, complexity of the allegations, marshalling of expert witnesses and other factors, the case management hearings work its way towards the finality of (written and oral) submissions of material and can take from a few months to some years. Several defendants from the European Union often consent to return to their country to face trial for minor crimes. This way, they can ensure access to their family in those countries while still keeping the option of returning to the UK when the case is over. Samir Vishnubhai Patel, arrested in UK on charges of rioting and murder, gave his consent to go back. Patel's removal in October 2016 marked the first successful extradition from England to India in recent years. No other individual sought by India consented to the extradition.

If the requested person says, loud and clear to the judge, that they do not consent to the extradition, then the court sets in motion the preliminary hearings. Bail is granted if the requested person is not seen as a flight risk. Pakistani businessman Arif Naqvi was granted bail, after being turned down on a couple of occasions, for a record £15 million security in May 2019. Naqvi, facing extradition to the US, remained in jail for three weeks despite the bail order, as he couldn't immediately deposit the security. Wikileaks's founder Julian Assange's bail was denied even after the district judge gave the order to not extradite him to the US, because the US government sought an appeal against that decision. Assange continues to be looked upon as a flight risk.

Despite the seriousness of the offence and the complexity of the case, bail was not denied to Rajesh Kapoor, whose extradition was sought by India in 2011. Rajesh was wanted by the CBI on allegations that he had helped his sister Seema to abduct the daughter of their elder brother Deepak and flee to the UK in December 2007. Deepak, an inspector with the Central Industrial

Security Force (CISF), approached the high court in London in November 2008, seeking the return of his daughter Aishley.

Aishley and Seema were located in Southall, after which the girl was put into the care of social services. Seema opposed Deepak's plea, but the high court ruled in April 2009 that Aishley should be returned to India where the courts were better placed to decide on whom she should live with. But in an unexpected and reckless move, Seema took away Aishley just after she was dropped at her school by her foster parents, and they have remained untraceable since then.

Rajesh, who had moved to the UK in 2007, was later joined by his wife and children. He was unaware that based on the November 2008 FIR in Punjab, which named him as an accused, the CBI had initiated extradition proceedings against him. Based on India's request (dated 14 October 2011), Rajesh was arrested on 17 May 2012 but managed to get out on bail.

Rajesh Kapoor lost his case in Britain, but he was not removed from England. In 2015, Rajesh filed a petition in the Punjab and Haryana high court, seeking quashing of proceedings against him. His brother, Deepak, the complainant, supported Rajesh's petition and said that he had resolved the dispute and reached a compromise. Deepak told the high court that he realized that Rajesh was not in a position to sponsor the visit and stay of Seema and the child who fled to the UK from India. Deepak, it seems, was also satisfied that it could not be held that Rajesh was the one who had filled the passport application form for his daughter which facilitated the escape. The Punjab and Haryana high court, in February 2018, ordered the quashing of FIR against Rajesh despite the opposition from the CBI. Seema and the child continue to be untraceable, and Rajesh remains a free man.

The judge can bar extradition to India as specified in the 2003 Extradition Act. In the case of India, requested persons usually raise the issues of extraneous considerations, passage of time and specialty. An increasing number of extradition cases cite (unsuccessfully) the example of Abu Salem in invoking specialty. The rule of specialty means that the requesting state will put the requested person on trial or sentence him only for the charges for which the person was extradited and not for any other offence committed before his return to the requesting state.

* * *

The Joint Select Committee of the House of Lords and House of Commons in 2011 agreed that adding a requirement for the requesting country to show a prima facie case before a person is extradited will improve the protection of human rights of those subject to extradition. Thus, Indian agencies need to assess the available evidence before issuing a request for extradition. This works as a safeguard to prevent the UK from extraditing a person based on speculative charges or for an alleged offence which they could not have committed.

This was observed in extradition cases where the CPS was asked specific questions and to provide further details. In the case of Sanjeev Chawla, the judges wanted to know the status of co-accused and where the trial had reached in India. Ravi Shankaran's case was dismissed by the court as the CBI failed to establish that the mysterious Vic Branson was the ex-naval officer as the statement of the witness did not stand the scrutiny of the UK court. In Vijay Mallya's case, the judge asked for further assurances. When Mallya appealed in the high court against the decision of the district judge to extradite him, the only point that the court agreed to re-examine was the prima facie evidence.

The importance of establishing a prima facie case is best explained through the extradition case of Palaniappan Rajarathinam, a disgraced Takeover Tycoon from Coimbatore, and a confidante of Jayalalitha's aide Sasikala. He is accused of taking over Synergy Finance Exchange Private Limited in 1999 and defrauding depositors and shareholders by diverting company's funds worth several crores for his own benefit. Following the heat from investigative agencies in India, he fled to the UK in the early 2000s and has since stayed on with his family.

India first made a bid to get him extradited in 2007 but failed when the UK courts turned down the request citing that the evidence provided was inadmissible. A decade later, India made another bid to extradite Rajarathinam, and he was arrested in November 2017, based on the request. However, in just less than six months, Rajarathinam again managed to frustrate India's attempt to remove him from the UK.

His acquittal in April 2018 has set a new benchmark for India's inefficiency, as the Westminster Magistrates' Court termed the crucial affidavit presented by India as just a 'narrative case summary'. The ruling by Judge Venessa Baraitser on 25 April 2018 was extempore which means the court did not even consider the case worth a detailed written judgment. Baraitser also said that there was nothing in India's submissions that showed that Rajarathinam either diverted the funds or benefitted from them. To add insult to injury, even the CPS barrister, John Hardy, representing India, 'realistically' accepted in court that the papers submitted by India 'do not satisfy' the prima facie sections of the extradition act. In the history of extradition cases in the UK courts, Rajarathinam's discharge will go down as a dark example of shoddy paperwork, unprofessionalism and lack of coordination.

* * *

Human rights is another matter taken extremely seriously in the courts as Britain abides by the ECHR and in almost all extradition cases article 3 (prohibition of torture, or inhuman or degrading treatment) is mostly raised by the defence in terms on jail conditions in India which is an absolute, non-derogable right, and article 8 (right to respect for private and family life) where an accused has been living with his family in this country for many years and has a legitimate aim to evoke this article. Others include article 5 (right to liberty and security), article 6 (right to fair trail) and article 14 (prohibition of discrimination).

Within the European Union, there is a presumption that member states will comply with the ECHR obligations and most decisions favour an extradition even when there is evidence to the contrary, a parliamentary report found. India belongs to category 2 for extradition purposes and is not a signatory to the EU conventions, and therefore there is a presumption within the UK–India extradition treaty that India would respect fundamental rights. This is reinforced by case specific assurances from India to ensure that proper safeguards are in place. It is now being increasingly recognized that it is difficult for Britain to monitor assurances provided by the requesting states.

John Hardy QC, who represented India in Rajarathinam's extradition case, gave evidence to the British parliamentary committee on the Extradition Bill that the prevailing view was that human rights provisions 'constituted some sort of universal panacea against injustice and/or unfairness' in the extradition process but this was not so. He added that 'there is a strong presumption that the requesting judicial authority will honour its Convention rights obligations, and that presumption can only be displaced by cogent and powerful evidence. Any student of the jurisprudence of the courts of the United Kingdom will see this test appropriately applied in the vast majority of cases.' He also noted that 'any extradition scheme will inevitably produce cases which expose its innate imperfections'.

Once a prima facie case has been established, the most likely reason for an extradition to be refused would be if a judge decides it is in breach of human rights as defined in the Human Rights Act (HRA) 1998, which includes these articles of the ECHR. Every lawyer on the defence side makes use of the articles of ECHR and HRA to argue against their client's extradition.

This was a crucial factor that gave Chawla relief in the Westminster Magistrate's Court with Judge Rebecca Crane discharging him on the grounds that overcrowding and violence at New Delhi's Tihar jail infringed upon his human rights. In Mallya's case, too, several days were spent arguing on conditions at Mumbai's Arthur Road jail where similar arguments were invoked

by Mallya's counsel Clare Montgomery to allude to inhuman
conditions in the jail.

A similar argument was seen in Arti Dhir and Kaval Raijada's
case with respect to the Junagardh prison in Gujarat. Even in the
paedophile Raymond Varley's case, Peter Cadwell used article 3
against the prison conditions in Goa to plead the discharge of his
case. In Hanif Patel's case articles 5 and 6 were invoked. Edward
Fritzerland QC argued that Patel's detention in India would not be
for legitimate purposes and he would not receive a fair trial in India.
He also told the court that Patel would be tortured in prison (just
like Abu Salem) after extradition in breach of article 3. However,
none of these arguments seems to hold water in the British courts.
It wasn't easy though.

In almost every extradition case from India, the issue of prison
conditions is raised. There has been an increasing push towards
having an investigation and assessment of what happens with
individuals after their extradition to requesting states. Apart from
counsels representing requested persons, in 2014 the office of the
chief magistrates' office, in a written statement, suggested that there
could be independent investigations especially in cases where there
have been dire predictions of human rights abuses upon return:
'Such an enquiry could disclose whether the courts have been wrong
to order extradition, and it could act as yardstick for future decisions.'

But this is easier said than done. To begin with, extradition
is just one part of the wider ambit of the judiciary, and to have
such a mechanism involves the deployment of overseas diplomatic
resources which are already under immense strain. However, if it
comes to fruition, then it will be a huge concern for India. As of
now it seems that the trial court only have to deal with 'expert
reports' in relation to prisons, which as the written statement from
the chief magistrates' office says are more often based on an expert's
opinion formed through media reports or government reports as
opposed to first-hand knowledge from an actual visit.

Although assurances provided by the requesting state do
seem to pass the muster in countering arguments of human rights

abuses, an increasing number of practitioners do not relish the idea of assurances being taken as the panacea of all ills. Although the case law involving India is still low to assess if there is a defined general attitude from UK courts to assurances given by India, by and large we can see that assurances from India have worked in her favour. There is a clear rider though, that the assurances must come from the appropriate authority, which makes the job easier for the prosecutor as courts do not seem to subject them to intense scrutiny.

In the Raymond Varley case experts visited the prison twice while the latest visit took place in Dhir-Raijada's case where a prison expert visited Junagarh prison for three days in April-May 2018. Since then, India has relied on assurances over prison conditions to counter arguments of possible human rights violations in jails. In the absence of assurances, the trial court has been reluctant to order extraditions to countries like Poland, Italy, South Africa, Turkey, Russia, Lithuania, Greece, Kenya, Romania and few others due to poor prison conditions. India has never been in the category of countries where the UK courts have adopted a general policy of not agreeing to extradition due to inhuman prison conditions.

Bookie Sanjeev Chawla, who was extradited to India, had seen the High Court give priority to India's assurance on prison conditions over his arguments against it. It is not surprising that defence lawyers are keeping a close eye on Chawla's treatment in India. In the case of alleged drug dealer Kishan Singh, which came in the high court just days after Chawla's extradition to India, his lawyer raised the issue of India breaching its assurance by keeping Chawla in the police station instead of Tihar jail. The Westminster Magistrates' Court in May 2019 found no bar to Singh's extradition to face charges of supplying drugs in Delhi and Mumbai to party goers. Unknown to him, Singh's phone was being tapped with the permission of the UK home secretary in January and February 2017 providing incriminating evidence.

The court did not agree with the poor conditions in Tihar and risk of an unfair trial arguments, among others. Singh took the case to the high court, where he unsuccessfully argued that as India's assurance to him was similar to the one made to Chawla, which was not followed, he should be discharged. In July 2020, Justice Andrew Baker did not agree with that but gave Singh three months to provide 'solid evidence' of a real difficulty in relation to prison condition and COVID-19 response which would undermine the assurances given in pre-COVID conditions.

As a financial powerhouse and with a long-standing history of attracting the high and the mighty, young professionals and entrepreneurs, along with provisions to provide refuge to those oppressed, extradition offers unique set of challenges to Britain. The fugitives sought by India belong to all the above categories. But as soon as their cases enter the contested judicial realm, it can bring a surprising convergence at the end. Vijay Mallya just like Hanif Patel has applied for asylum despite court ruling in both their cases that they have a case to answer. Patel's stay is now regularized and he faces no threat of forced return while the home office is still to make a decision on Mallya's application.

Needless to say each case is decided on its own merits and circumstances, but the quality of the legal team, and the funds at disposal can bear heavy on the outcome. Eighty-eight-year old Robert Scott was extradited to Australia in December 2020, to face charges of sexual abuse committed between 1972 and 1978 after UK courts held that his old age, passage of time, and the pandemic were not good enough reasons to stall it. Pakistani national Asif Hafeez, an international drug lord and partner of Bollywood actress Mamta Kulkarni's former husband Vicky Goswami, managed to stall his extradition to the US by approaching the ECtHR. Chawla too had approached the ECtHR but was unsuccessful.

Karachi-born international businessman Jabir Motiwala, an alleged member of Dawood Ibrahim's gang, could not convince the Westminster Magistrates' Court that the prison in New York would breach his human rights due to his precarious mental health and suicidal tendencies. The court however ruled that Julian

Asssange's extradition would be 'unjust and oppressive' for the same reasons. Both the cases are now subject to an appeal. For Britain, it is the extradition requests from US that garners the most attention due to the high volume, contentious nature of cases and also a perception that the extradition arrangement with US works at a disadvantage for Britain.

India however continues to keep the CPS busy with constant requests for extradition. Sanjay Bhandari, alleged defence middleman and aide of Robert Vadra, will be facing the music in the Westminster Magistrates' Court in 2021. His posh flat in central London next to exclusive showrooms for Rolls Royce and Bentley has already been flashed in the media. Also in the pipeline are the extradition requests for the first wife and sons of Iqbal Mirchi. And no less than the Supreme Court has castigated the centre to produce Ritika Avasty before them. Avasty faces a cheating case and was granted permission by the SC on humanitarian grounds to briefly join her family in the UK.

The SC forfeited her security of Rs 86 lakh but that seems to be a small price to pay to enjoy the safe confines of London, especially as the Avastys own several well-known food products, including Neesa Rice, whose brand ambassador was Bollywood superstar Madhuri Dixit. Ritika and husband Virkaran continue to be in London, but many assets belonging to their Bush Foods in India have been seized by agencies.

After a lull period, extradition requests for Sikh separatists have increased. Kuldip Singh, accused of helping to organize terror camps, and plotting the assassination of Punjab chief minister has already appeared before the Westminster Magistrates' Court, and in January 2021 was discharged due to insufficient evidence by Judge Gareth Branston. In December 2020, three further arrests were made in connection with the 2009 murder of Rulda Singh a member of the Rashtriya Swayamsevak Sangh (RSS). Brothers Gurshanvir and Amritvir Singh Wahiwala, and Piara Singh Gill were produced before a magistrate at the Westminster Magistrates' Court where India will seek their extradition, bringing into focus

fault-lines that worked as the catalyst for India-UK extradition
treaty in 1993.

What will be the outcome of an extradition case is uncertain,
but it is no longer surprising, in fact it is now almost expected, that
a person who has reason to escape India will go to London.

SOURCES

King of Bad Debts

1. Nick Hoult, 'Kevin Pieterson suited to IPL franchise owner Vijay Mallya's lavish lifestyle', *The Telegraph*, 06 February 2009, https://www.telegraph.co.uk/sport/cricket/kevinpietersen/4536652/Kevin-Pietersen-suited-to-IPL-franchise-owner-Vijay-Mallyas-lavish-lifestyle.html
2. 'Spotted: Mallya's country house in UK', Times Now, 13 March 2016, https://timesofindia.indiatimes.com/india/spotted-mallyas-country-house-in-uk/articleshow/51377910.cms
3. Danish Khan, 'Mallya had no intention of repaying bank loans', *Mumbai Mirror*, 05 December 2017, p.10, https://mumbaimirror.indiatimes.com/mumbai/crime/mallya-had-no-intention-of-repaying-bank-loans/articleshow/61923244.cms
4. Danish Khan, 'Mallya himself invested in KFA, and not just through bank loans', *Mumbai Mirror*, 06 December 2017, p. 10.
5. Danish Khan, 'Prosecutor cites Mallya's £2 million birthday bash', *Mumbai Mirror*, 08 December 2017, p.10.
6. Danish Khan, 'F1 payment part of KFA sponsorship cost', *Mumbai Mirror*, 12 December 2017, p.10.
7. Danish Khan, 'CBI coerced banks against Mallya; Witness', *Mumbai Mirror*, 13 December 2017, p.10.
8. Danish Khan, 'Cell will have 2 grilles, good ventilation', *Mumbai Mirror*, 15 December 2017, p.8.

9. Danish Khan, 'Final hearing in Mallya extradition starts', *Mumbai Mirror*, 17 March 2018, p.14.

10. Danish Khan, 'UK court wants video of Arthur Road jail cell', *Mumbai Mirror*, 01 August 2018, p.9.

11. Ruhi Khan, 'UK High Court allows Mallya to appeal Extradition order', The Wire, 02 July 2019, https://thewire.in/business/vijay-mallya-extradition-high-court-london.

12. 'Fresh trouble for Vijay Mallya, may lose possession of London home', Times Now, 11 October 2018, https://economictimes.indiatimes.com/news/politics-and-nation/abusing-private-sector-for-votes-no-longer-acceptable-pm-modi-in-lok-sabha/videoshow/80791622.cms

13. Danish Khan, 'UK court asks Vijay Mallya to pay £88,000 to Swiss Bank', *Mumbai Mirror*, 22 November 2018, p.1.

14. 'UK court orders Vijay Mallya to pay 88,000 British pounds to UBS Bank', ET NOW, 21 November 2018, https://economictimes.indiatimes.com/news/politics-and-nation/uk-court-orders-vijay-mallya-to-pay-88000-british-pounds-to-ubs-bank/videoshow/66740819.cms

15. Ruhi Khan, 'As extradition verdict looms, is this the end of the line for Mallya?', The Wire, 23 November 2018, https://thewire.in/business/as-extradition-verdict-looms-is-this-the-line-of-the-game-for-vijay-mallya

16. Danish Khan, 'Mallya may have to cough up Rs 2 crore in legal bills', *Mumbai Mirror*, 14 December 2018, p.6.

17. Danish Khan, 'Banks pursue wealth "hidden by Mallya"', *Mumbai Mirror*, 23 February 2019, p.1.

18. 'Vijay Mallya to sell Switzerland property in order to save plush London home', Times Now, 28 March 2019, https://www.timesnownews.com/videos/times-now/world/vijay-mallya-to-sell-switzerland-property-in-order-to-save-plush-london-home-exclusive/27386

19. Ruhi Khan, 'As lenders move to cut Mallya's access to his bank account, spotlight on his lavish lifestyle', The Wire, 04 April 2019, https://thewire.in/business/as-lenders-move-to-freeze-mallyas-bank-account-spotlight-on-his-lavish-lifestyle

20. Danish Khan, 'Poor little rich Vijay Mallya', *Mumbai Mirror*, 04 April 2019, p.8.

21. Ruhi Khan, 'Mallya's request to appeal against extradition rejected, but legal process to continue', The Wire, 08 April 2019, https://thewire.in/government/vijay-mallya-extradition

22. Danish Khan, 'Mallya on the verge of losing extradition battle', *Mumbai Mirror*, 09 April 2019, p.6.

23. Ruhi Khan, 'UK court orders Vijay Mallya to pay $135 million to Diageo', The Wire, 25 May 2019, https://thewire.in/business/uk-court-orders-vijay-mallya-to-pay-135-million-to-diageo

24. Danish Khan, 'UK court allows Mallya to appeal against extradition', *Mumbai Mirror*, 03 July 2019, p.16.

25. Danish Khan, 'UK court cuts Mallya's expenses by £4000', *Mumbai Mirror*, 14 July 2019, p.3.

26. 'PIL in apex court against Rakesh Asthana's appointment as CBI Special Director', *Indian Express*, https://indianexpress.com/article/india/pil-in-apex-court-against-rakesh-asthanas-appointment-as-cbi-special-director-4920116/

27. Rishi Majumder on Vijay Mallya, 'Indian Envoy Walks Out of Book Launch After Seeing Vijay Mallya', YouTube.

28. Danish Khan, 'Mallya loses appeal in British high court', *Mumbai Mirror*, 21 April 2020, p.10.

29. Danish Khan, 'Mallya one step away from being brought back to India', *Mumbai Mirror*, 15 May 2020, p.1.

30. Danish Khan, 'Vijay Mallya wards off bid to declare him bankrupt', *Mumbai Mirror*, 24 July, 2020, p.8.

31. Danish Khan, 'UK court releases Rs 2.3 cr for Mallya's legal costs', *Mumbai Mirror*, 12 December 2020, p.5.

32. https://www.telegraph.co.uk/sport/cricket/kevinpietersen/4536652/Kevin-Pietersen-suited-to-IPL-franchise-owner-Vijay-Mallyas-lavish-lifestyle.html

Count of Monte Corruption

1. Pavan C. Lall, *Flawed: The Rise and Fall of India's Diamond Mogul Nirav Modi* (Hachette India, August 2019).

2. https://www.bloombergquint.com/business/pnb-nirav-modi-scam-a-year-after-indias-biggest-bank-fraud-the-pain-is-far-from-over

3. Danish Khan, 'London court issues arrest warrant against Nirav Modi', *Mumbai Mirror*, 19 March 2019, p.8, https://punemirror.indiatimes. com/news/india/uk-court-issues-arrest-warrant-against-nirav-modi-to-be-arrested-soon-officials/articleshow/68469741.cms

4. Danish Khan, 'Nirav Modi arrested in London: Here's how the drama unfolded in a local bank', *Mumbai Mirror*, 20 March 2019, https://mumbaimirror.indiatimes.com/mumbai/crime/nirav-modi-arrested-in-london-heres-how-the-drama-unfolded-in-a-local-bank/articleshow/68502520.cms

5. Danish Khan, 'Journalist Mick Brown who tracked down Nirav Modi in London reveals why he did it', *Mumbai Mirror*, 24 March 2019, https://bangaloremirror.indiatimes.com/bangalore/others/finding-nimo-the-journalist-from-the-telegraph-who-tracked-nirav-modi-down-in-london-says-he-never-expected-the-social-media-storm-his-video-has-generated/articleshow/68542020.cms

6. Ruhi Khan, 'Nirav Modi threatened to kill witness and destroy evidence, London court told', The Wire, 30 March 2019, https://thewire.in/political-economy/nirav-modi-threatened-to-kill-witness-and-destroy-evidence-london-court-told

7. 'New name, old fame', *Mumbai Mirror*, https://mumbaimirror. indiatimes.com/opinion/the-informer/new-name-old-fame/articleshow/70441822.cms

8. Ruhi Khan, 'Lack of British ties, witness concerns shut down Nirav Modi's third bail plea', The Wire, 09 May 2019, https://thewire.in/law/witness-concerns-nirav-modi-third-bail-plea

9. Danish Khan, 'UK court denies bail to Nirav Modi for third time', *Mumbai Mirror*, 09 May 2019, p.8, https://punemirror.indiatimes. com/news/india/uk-court-denies-bail-to-nirav-modi-for-third-time/articleshow/69240083.cms

10. Danish Khan, 'Westminster Magistrate Court judge seeks details about jail where Nirav Modi will be kept, if extradited', *Mumbai Mirror*, 31 May 2019, https://mumbaimirror.indiatimes.com/mumbai/crime/indias-clumsy-paperwork-gets-noticed-at-nirav-hearing/articleshow/69589871.cms

11. Ruhi *Khan*, 'London court denies Nirav Modi bail, says he has strong incentive to flee', The Wire, 12 June 2019, https://thewire.in/business/nirav-modi-high-court-bail-plea

12. Danish Khan, 'Court allows further evidence from India', *Mumbai Mirror*, 14 May 2020, p.10.

13. Danish Khan, 'Nirav Modi extradition case: UK court rejects plea seeking partial ban on reporting', *Mumbai Mirror*, 08 September 2020, https://mumbaimirror.indiatimes.com/mumbai/other/nirav-modi-extradition-case-uk-court-rejects-plea-seeking-partial-ban-on-reporting/articleshow/77988050.cms.

14. 'CAM got rubber stamps, letterheads from Nirav Modi's office', *Bar & Bench*, https://www.barandbench.com/news/pnb-scam-role-of-cyril-amarchand-mangaldas-requires-further-investigation-cbi-to-special-court

15. Danish Khan, 'Nirav Modi extradition case: Evidence filed by ED, CBI allowed, says UK court', *Mumbai Mirror*, 04 November 2020, https://mumbaimirror.indiatimes.com/mumbai/other/nirav-modi-extradition-case-evidence-filed-by-ed-cbi-allowed-uk-court/articleshow/79031549.cms

Bowled-Out Bookie

1. Danish Khan, 'Bookie Chawla gets court relief in London', *Mumbai Mirror*, 06 May 2018, p. 4, https://mumbaimirror.indiatimes.com/mumbai/crime/bookie-chawla-gets-court-relief-in-london/articleshow/64046422.cms

2. 'UK Court quashes bookie Sanjeev Chawla's discharge', Times Now, 16 November 2018, Times Now https://twitter.com/TimesNow/status/1063396239582982144?s=20

3. Ruhi Khan, 'UK Court accepts assurances about India prisoners in Sanjeev Chawla extradition case', The Wire, 16 November 2018, https://thewire.in/law/indian-prison-fine-says-british-court-extradition-case-bookie-sanjeev-chawla

4. 'Alleged bookie Sanjeev Chawla loses UK appeal, set to be extradited to India', Times Now, 16 January 2020, https://timesofindia.indiatimes.com/india/alleged-bookie-sanjeev-chawla-loses-uk-appeal-set-to-be-extradited-to-india/articleshow/73303547.cms

5. 'Danish Khan Alleged bookie set to be extradited to India', *Mumbai Mirror*, 17 January 2020, https://mumbaimirror.indiatimes.com/

mumbai/crime/alleged-bookie-in-uk-set-to-be-extradited-to-india/
articleshow/73311588.cms

6. 'Cricket "bookie" Sanjeev Chawla extradited from UK', Times Now,
    13 February 2020, https://economictimes.indiatimes.com/news/
    politics-and-nation/cricket-bookie-sanjeev-chawla-extradited-
    from-uk/videoshow/74113476.cms

7. UK Home Office, 'Country Policy and Information Note | India:
    Prison conditions', November 2016, at https://www.ecoi.net/en/file/
    local/1286068/1226_1478177331_cpin-india-prison-conditions-
    v2-0-november-2016.pdf

8. Commonwealth Human Rights Initiative, 'Rights Behind Bars',
    2009, https://humanrightsinitiative.org/publications/prisons/
    rights_behind_bars.pdf

9. Amnesty International, 'Amnesty International Report 2015/16—
    India', 24 February 2016, https://www.refworld.org/docid/56d05b4c4f.
    html [accessed 12 January 2021]

Gangsta Grandpa

1. Naresh Fernandes, 'Morale among officers badly hit', *Times of India*,
    17 October 1993, p. 7.

2. 'Two Held in huge drug haul', *Times of India*, 07 September 1993,
    p. 3.

3. 'Iqbal Mohammad Memon vs State of Maharashtra', 1996, https://
    indiankanoon.org/doc/1405822/

4. Velly Thevar, 'Rights panel listens to Iqbal Mirchi's plea', *Times of
    India*, 31 January 1995, p. 29.

5. Christopher Thomas, 'Bombing suspect arrested', *The Times*
    (London), 05 April 1995, p.11.

6. Velly Thevar, 'India presses for Mirchi's extradition', *Times of India*,
    19 May 1995, p.1.

7. Joaquim P. Menezes, 'Clinching proof for Mirchi's extradition',
    Times of India, 23 May 1995, p. 3.

8. 'Mirchi's aide sentenced to ten years of RI', *Times of India*, 28
    November 1998, p. 5.

9. Satish Nandgaonkar, 'Mirchi case shows up narc cell', *Times of India*,
    22 September 1995, p. 31.

10. Pankaj Pachauri and Lekha Rattanani, 'Iqbal Mohammad Memon, wanted in India freed by British court citing lack of evidence', *India Today*, 15 October 1995.
11. M. Rahman, 'Drug czar Iqbal Mirchi arrested in UK, faces extradition proceedings to India', *India Today*, 30 April 1995.
12. Ashok Mathur, 'From mirchiwala to drug-lord', *Blitz*, 15 April 1995, p. 6.
13. Ali Haider v Syed, England and Wales High Court (Chancery Division), 19 December 2013.
14. Ministry of home affairs, 'Vohra Committee Report', 9 July 1993, https://adrindia.org/sites/default/files/VOHRA%20COMMITTEE%20REPORT_0.pdf

Musician of Mayhem

1. R. M. Vijayakar, 'Nadeem, As I saw him: A Reporter's Impressions', India West, 12 September 1997.
2. 'Whatever Gulshan touched turned into gold', *Times of India*, 13 August 1997, p. 3.
3. Harinder Baweja, 'Bringing Melody back, Nadeem-Shravan churn out hit after hit', *India Today*, 15 April 1992.
4. 'Nadeem facing the music in Gulshan murder case', *Times of India*, 02 September 1997, p. 1.
5. Smruti Koppikar, 'Desperate for funds, underworld dons extort money from Bollywood', *India Today*, 25 August 1997, https://www.indiatoday.in/magazine/cover-story/story/19970825-desperate-for-funds-underworld-dons-extort-money-from-bollywood-831993-1997-08-25
6. M. Rahman and Arun Katiyar, 'Bollywood falters as Sanjay Dutt's arrest lifts the lid off the muck beneath the tinsel', *India Today*, 15 May 1993, https://www.indiatoday.in/magazine/cover-story/story/19930515-bollywood-falters-as-sanjay-dutts-arrest-lifts-the-lid-off-the-muck-beneath-the-tinsel-811095-1993-05-15
7. Smruti Koppikar, 'Mumbai Police believes Nadeem Saifee arranged murder of music tycoon Gulshan Kumar', *India Today*, 15 September 1997, https://www.indiatoday.in/magazine/crime/story/19970915-mumbai-police-believes-nadeem-saifee-arranged-murder-of-music-tycoon-gulshan-kumar-830573-1997-09-15

8. V. Shankar Aiyar, Sheela Raval, 'Desperate underworld targets Bollywood, muscle their way to larger share of profits', *India Today*, 01 January 2001, https://www.indiatoday.in/magazine/cover-story/story/20010101-desperate-underworld-targets-bollywood-muscle-their-way-to-larger-share-of-profits-776082-2001-01-22

9. Anil Singh, 'Gun for your money', *Times of India*, 17 August 1997, p.19.

10. Devendra Mohan, 'Bollywood Vendetta', *Blitz*, 06 September 1997, pp. 1 and 3.

11. S. Balakrishnan, 'I wasn't the only one who spoke against Gulshan', *Times of India*, 09 September 1997, p.3.

12. Pritish Nandy, 'I have even done a free show for the Mumbai police! Was that also a pay-off?', *Times of India*, 11 September 1997.

13. Tyrone D'Souza, 'Nadeem sets terms for surrender', *Times of India*, 16 September 1997, p.3.

14. Smruti Koppikar, Anupama Chopra, Anita Anand, 'Gulshan Kumar murder: Mumbai Police believe they have enough evidence to nail Nadeem Saifi', *India Today*, 29 September 1997, https://www.indiatoday.in/magazine/defence/story/20140428-war-room-leak-case-cbi-prime-accused-802427-1999-11-30

15. Mahesh Hebbar, 'Nadeem: Bye Bye India', *Blitz*, 1997.

16. Smruti Koppikar, 'Nadeem used as a "tool" in Gulshan Kumar's murder: Bal Thackeray', *India Today*, 29 September 1997, https://www.indiatoday.in/magazine/cover-story/story/19970929-nadeem-used-as-a-tool-in-gulshan-kumars-murder-bal-thackeray-830653-1997-09-29

17. A. K. Dhar, 'Hearing of Nadeem's extradition case will begin from Dec.1', *Times of India*, 25 November 1997, p.18.

18. Tyrone D'Souza, 'Builder's evidence crucial in Nadeem extradition case', *Times of India*, 12 December 1998, p. 3.

19. Swati Deshpande, 'Approver in Gulshan Kumar murder case to be questioned by London lawyers', *Times of India*, 25 July 2000, p.3.

20. Khozem Merchant, 'Bollywood stars gripped by fear of underworld's hold', *Financial Times* (London), 28 December 2000, p.6.

21. Ian Cobain & Stephen Farrell, 'Bollywood murder suspect to stay in UK', *The Times*, 22 December 2000, p.11.

22. Saifi v Brixton Prison & Anor, England and Wales High Court (Administrative Court), 21 December 2000.

Terror Tiger

1. Kamal Saiyed, 'Surat blasts: Eid comes early for the families of five acquitted', *Indian Express*, 19 July 2014, https://indianexpress.com/article/india/india-others/surat-blasts-eid-comes-early-for-the-families-of-five-acquitted/

2. 'Former minister gets 20 years for Surat blasts', *DNA*, 04 October 2008, https://www.dnaindia.com/india/report-former-minister-gets-20-years-for-surat-blasts-1195527

3. '1993 Surat terror blast accused held in UK', *Indian Express*, 04 March 2010, http://archive.indianexpress.com/news/1993-surat-terror-blast-accused-held-in-uk/586551/

4. '93 Surat blasts: Ex-Congress minister gets life imprisonment', *Ahmedabad Mirror*, 05 October 2008, https://ahmedabadmirror.indiatimes.com/ahmedabad/cover-story/93-surat-blasts-ex-congress-minister-gets-life-imprisonment/articleshow/37827659.cms

5. Uday Mahurkar, 'Who will give us back these 12 years? ask Surat blast', *India Today*, 25 August 2014, https://www.indiatoday.in/magazine/special-report/story/20140804-surat-blasts-case-acquittal-804736-2014-07-25

6. 'SC acquits all accused in 1993 Surat bomb blast case', *The Hindu*, 18 July 2014, https://www.thehindu.com/news/national/sc-acquits-all-accused-in-1993-surat-bomb-blast-case/article6224656.ece

7. 'Supreme Court acquits all 11 men in 1993 Surat twin blasts cases', DeshGujarat, https://www.deshgujarat.com/2014/07/18/supreme-court-acquits-all-11-men-in-1993-surat-twin-blasts-cases/

8. Irfan Engineer, 'Backward communities and migrant workers—in Surat riots', *Economic and Political Weekly*, 28 May 1994; https://www.epw.in/journal/1994/22/special-articles/backward-communities-and-migrant-workers-surat-riots.html

9. Kalpana Shah, Smita Shah and Neha Shah, 'The Nightmare of Surat', *Manushi*, 1993, http://manushi-india.org/pdfs_issues/PDF%20ISSUE%2074-75/50.%20The%20Nightmare%20of%20Surat.pdf

10. 'Man arrested in Bolton loses extradition appeal over India attacks', Manchester Evening News, 18 April 2013, https://www.manchestereveningnews.co.uk/news/greater-manchester-news/tiger-hanif-arrested-bolton-over-2768354

11. Patel v India (2013) EWHC 819 (Admin).

12. Hussein Ghadially and others v State of Gujarat (2014) 8 SCC 425.

13. 'UK blast suspect Tiger Hanif "wanted revenge"', BBC, 07 October 2010, https://www.bbc.co.uk/news/uk-11496591

14. 'UK blast suspect Tiger Hanif "faced torture"', BBC, 05 April 2011, https://www.bbc.co.uk/news/uk-12966169

15. Scarlet Howes, 'Theresa May allowed Muslim bomber "wanted for terrorism" and death of schoolgirl to REMAIN in Britain', *The Sun*, 08 September 2016, https://www.thesun.co.uk/news/1568999/theresa-may-allowed-muslim-bomber-wanted-for-terrorism-and-death-of-schoolgirl-to-remain-in-britain/

16. 'Grocer held on terror chares', *The Bolton News*, 02 March 2010, https://www.theboltonnews.co.uk/news/5035352.grocer-held-on-terror-charges/

Pilgrim Paedophile

1. 'Girl breaks up vice ring at vicarage', *Daily Mail*, 15 January 1975, p.3.

2. 'Vicar on vice charges', *Daily Mail*, 16 January 1975, p.3.

3. 'Vicar allowed church to be defiled, judge says', *The Times* (London), 22 March 1975, p.3.

4. 'Teacher and vicar corrupted boys—QC', *The Times* (London), 10 June 1975, p. 11.

5. 'Ex-PC warned teacher of lodger's record', *The Times* (London), 18 June 1975, p.5.

6. Caroline Lees, 'Britons ruin Indian paradise', *Times of India*, 22 February 1995, p.11.

7. Vishwa Mohan, 'Goa child sex racket accused being brought to Mumbai', *Times of India*, 05 August 2005, p.7.

8. Paul Peachey, 'Fury in India as UK judge refuses extradition of convicted British paedophile', *The Independent*, 02 June 2014.

9. 'India appeals against UK refusal to extradite child sex offender', *The Hindu*, 29 May 2014.

Parasite Parents

1. Paul Bracchi, Andrew Pereira, 'Why are this couple walking free in London when they're wanted over the murder of their adopted

son in India? Because Britain is worried about their human rights', *Daily Mail*, 15 February 2020, https://www.dailymail.co.uk/news/article-8005605/Couple-wanted-India-murder-adopted-son-allowed-walk-free-London.html

2. Danish Khan, 'London high court calls India's assurance a waste of time', *Mumbai Mirror*, 29 January 2020, https://mumbaimirror.indiatimes.com/news/world/london-hc-calls-indias-assurance-awaste-of-time/articleshow/73718449.cms

3. Danish Khan, '12-year-old's murder in Gujarat: Case stares at long extradition battles', *Mumbai Mirror*, 13 September 2017, https://mumbaimirror.indiatimes.com/news/india/12-year-olds-murder-in-gujarat-case-stares-at-long-extradition-battle/articleshow/60488440.cms

4. Ruhi Khan, 'UK court refuses to extradite Indian-origin couple accused of murdering adopted son', The Wire, 04 July 2019, https://thewire.in/world/uk-court-refuses-to-extradite-indian-origin-couple-accused-of-murdering-adopted-son

5. Ruhi Khan, 'UK-based couple could be extradited to India, face trial for adopted son's murder', The Wire, 23 January 2019, https://thewire.in/diplomacy/uk-based-couple-could-be-extradited-to-india-face-trial-for-adopted-sons-murder

6. 'Gujarat killer couple let off, India loses extradition case in High Court', Times Now, 06 February 2020, https://www.timesnownews.com/videos/times-now/india/gujarat-killer-couple-let-off-india-loses-extradition-case-in-high-court/52754

7. Ruhi Khan, 'India loses extradition case of UK-based couple accused of murdering adopted son', The Wire, 07 February 2020, https://thewire.in/world/india-loses-extradition-case-couple-double-murder

8. Danish Khan, 'Couple accused of killing adopted child in Gujarat discharged by London high court', *Mumbai Mirror*, 08 February 2020, https://punemirror.indiatimes.com/news/india/couple-accused-of-killing-adopted-child-in-gujarat-discharged-by-london-high-court/articleshow/74014526.cms

War Room Leak Lieutenant

1. Saikat Datta, 'Shadow on the chief', *Outlook*, 16 January 2006, https://magazine.outlookindia.com/story/shadow-on-the-chief/229825

2. Saikat Datta, 'Man out of periscope', *Outlook*, 26 June 2006, https://magazine.outlookindia.com/story/man-out-of-periscope/231684

3. Dipankar De Sarkar, 'Arms dealer Ravi Shankaran's UK trial held in-camera', *Hindustan Times*, 05 May 2011, https://www.hindustantimes.com/world/arms-dealer-ravi-shankaran-s-uk-trial-held-in-camera/story-mMYN0GczBbq7laL03bZsGJ.html

4. Danish Khan, 'CBI's clumsiness costs key accused Shankaran's extradition', *Mumbai Mirror*, 03 April 2014, https://mumbaimirror.indiatimes.com/news/india/cbis-clumsiness-costs-india-key-accused-shankarans-extradition/articleshow/33146179.cms

5. 'War room leak case: UK court refuses to extradite Ravi Shankaran', Times Now, 03 April 2014, https://timesofindia.indiatimes.com/videos/news/war-room-leak-case-uk-court-refuses-to-extradite-ravi-shankaran/videoshow/33159649.cms

Filmy Moorti Chors

1. 'Leading city hotelier held', *Times of India*, 06 October 1974, p. 1.

2. 'Narang's lockers, shop sealed', *Times of India*, 08 October 1974, p. 1.

3. 'Hearing of Ramlal Narang case opens', *Times of India*, 28 October 1974, p. 4.

4. J. D. Singh, 'Proceedings for Narang's extradition on', *Times of India*, 30 May 1976, p. 9.

5. J. D. Singh, 'Narang remanded by London court', *Times of India*, 30 June 1976, p. 9.

6. 'Man remanded for extradition proceedings', *The Times* (London), 09 July 1976, p. 3.

7. 'No extradition for brothers on India smuggling charge', *The Times* (London), 27 November 1976, p. 3.

8. 'Brothers can stay', *The Guardian*, 27 November 1976, p. 5.

9. 'Two brothers are facing extradition', *The Daily Telegraph*, 24 March 1977, p. 3.

10. 'No reprieve for Indians', *The Daily Telegraph*, 26 July 1977, p. 2.

11. 'Indians' attempt to avoid extradition fails', *The Times*, 26 July 1977, p. 4.

12. 'Regina v Governor of Pentonville prison, Ex parte Narang', Union of India v Narang, 1978.

13. A.G. Noorani, Ivan Fera, 'The Plundered Past', *The Illustrated Weekly of India*, 19 May 1985, pp. 28–31;

14. Chander Uday Singh and Bonny Mukherjee, 'Smuggling of art treasures from India and holding of national treasures in western museums', *India Today*, 15 March 1981, https://www.indiatoday. in/magazine/international/story/19810315-smuggling-of-art-treasures-from-india-and-holding-of-national-treasures-in-western-museums-772752-2013-11-25

15. Sunil Sethi, 'Indian antiques continue to be drained drown a bottomless pit', *India Today*, 30 June 1980, https://www.indiatoday. in/magazine/crime/story/19800630-indian-antiques-continue-to-be-drained-down-a-bottomless-pit-821200-2014-01-24

16. 'I don't go for pseudo directors like Satyajit Ray: Neetu Singh', *India Today*, 15 July 1976, https://www.indiatoday.in/magazine/ eyecatchers/story/19760715-i-dont-go-for-pseudo-directors-like-satyajit-ray-neetu-singh-819236-2015-04-09

17. Anil Saari, 'Theft of old art works become an established source of easy money for crooks in India', *India Today*, 30 June 1979, https:// www.indiatoday.in/magazine/society-the-arts/story/19790630-theft-of-old-art-works-become-an-established-source-of-easy-money-for-crooks-in-india-822170-2014-03-04

18. 'Antique smuggler given RI', *Times of India*, 24 December 1986, p. 3.

19. 'Ram Lal Narang etc Vs State of Delhi', 1979 AIR 1791.

20. Rahul Singh, 'Why better laws are needed to preserve our art heritage', *The Tribune*, 10 November 2019, https://www.tribuneindia.com/ news/archive/column/why-better-laws-are-needed-to-preserve-our-art-heritage-858801.

21. Regina v Governor of Pentonville Prison, Ex parte Narang (1977) 2 All E.R. 348.

22. Regina v Governor of Pentonville Prison, Ex parte Narang (1978) A.C. 247.

Political Piper

1. 'Reddy reveals Rs 2.9 crore "swindle" by Teja', *Times of India*, 01 September 1966, p.7.

2. B.M. Kaul, *The Untold Story* (New Delhi: Allied Publishers, 1967).

3. H.R. Vohra, 'Indian envoy to Costa Rica seeks Teja's expulsion', *Times of India*, 02 January 1967, p. 6.

4. 'Costa Rica refuses to arrest Teja', *Times of India*, 30 March 1968, p. 9.

5. 'Costa Rica seeks view of court on Tejas', *Times of India*, 19 April 1968, p. 13.

6. Inder Malhotra, 'Haven for man 'in £10M fraud', *The Guardian*, 16 June 1969, p. 1.

7. 'India seeks "Diplomat" extradition', *The Daily Telegraph*, 27 October 1970, p. 3.

8. J.D. Singh, 'Tashkent figures in Teja case', *Times of India*, 29 October 1970, p. 1.

9. J.D. Singh, 'No fair trial in India: Teja', *Times of India*, 20 November 1970, p. 11.

10. J.D. Singh, 'Younger people persecuted in India, says Teja', *Times of India*, 21 November 1970, p. 13.

11. 'Sir Dingle Foot to represent Teja', *Times of India*, 05 January 1971, p. 9.

12. 'Nehru's friend claims he is 'persecuted', *The Daily Telegraph*, 19 January 1971, p. 3.

13. 'Indian nuclear scientist loses extradition plea', *The Times* (London), 20 January 1971, p. 23.

14. Dharam Yash Dev, 'Jayanti Dharma Teja', *The Illustrated Weekly of India*, 02 May 1971, pp. 30, 31.

15. 'Teja charged with 90-lakh breach of trust', *Times of India*, 15 July 1971, p. 7.

16. 'Rs 14.3 lakh-fine for Dharma Teja', *Times of India*, 20 October 1972, p. 13.

17. Shah Commission Hearings, India–West (California), 15 March 1978, p. 3.

18. 'Probe into Teja escapade begins', *Times of India*, 22 June 1978, p. 9.

19. 'Extradition of Dr Jayanti Dharma Teja from the UK to India', FCO 53/191, FCO 53/254, FCO 53/255, British National Archives, Kew.

20. Sumit Mitra, 'Dharma Teja: An unheralded comeback', *India Today*, 31 March 1983.

21. Nikhil Lakshman, 'The Merchant Adventurer', *The Illustrated Weekly of India*, 22 September 1985, pp. 44–47.

22. 'Pan Am sues India to reclaim $3.7 million', Indiawest, 25 June 1993, p. 27.

23. Regina v Governor of Pentonville Prison, Ex parte Teja [1971] 2 Q.B. 274.

Charlatan in Cashmere

1. 'Army Contractor Arrested', Times of India, 04 June 1948, p. 9.

2. 'Witness gives details of partnership: Mubarak Ali case hearing', Times of India, 23 July 1952, p. 3.

3. 'Hyderabad Merchant Escapes', Bombay Chronicle, 07 July 1950, p. 2.

4. 'Daring Escape of Bank Dacoity Accused', Bombay Chronicle, 06 July 1950, p. 3.

5. 'Extradition by India opposed', The Times (London), 18 March 1952, p. 3.

6. 'Regret at Pakistani's extradition', The Times (London), 18 April 1952, p. 5.

7. 'High Court of Justice—Extradition of fugitive from India', The Times (London), 05 April 1952, p. 9.

8. 'Police fly man to India', Daily Mail, 21 April 1952, p. 3.

9. '3.5 years' jail & fine of Rs 15,000 for Mubarak Ali: Majority verdict by jury on both the charges', Times of India, 12 August 1952, p. 8.

10. 'Cheating charge denied: Mubarak Ali on trial', Times of India, 01 July 1953, p.5.

11. 'Jail and fine for Mubarak Ali in cheating case', Times of India, 24 September 1953, p. 5.

12. Regiva v Brixton Prison Governor, Ex parte Mubarak Ali Ahmed [1952] 1 All E.R. 1060.

In the Dock

1. K.N. Malik, Kanchan K. Malik, India and the United Kingdom: Change and continuity in the 1980s (Sage Publications, 1997).

2. Nicholas Ashford, 'Howe seeks time over extradition', The Times (London), 29 March 1986, p. 7.

3. John Elliott, 'UK offers India Extradition treaty', Financial Times, 19September 1986, p. 3.

4. K. N. Malik, 'India for 'retrospective extradition', *Times of India*, 01 October 1986, p. 1.

5. K. N. Malik, 'Hitch in extradition treaty', *Times of India*, 05 October 1986, p.9.

6. 'UK Sikhs fear extradition pact', *Times of India*, 02 September 1987, p.15.

7. 'Extradition hope with India', *The Daily Telegraph*, 01 May 1987, p.6.

8. Andrew McEwen, 'India-UK extradition deal on extradition near', *The Times* (London), 29 April 1987, p. 9.

9. Max Madden, 'UK-India extradition treaty', *The Times* (London), 29 February 1992, p. 13.

10. Stefan Wagstyl and Ralph Atkins, 'Major hails Investment fruits of his Indian trip', *Financial Times*, 26 January 1993, p. 4.

11. '*UK ratifies extradition treaty with India*', *Times of India*, 16 October 1993, p.15.

12. Extradition Act 2003 (UK); https://www.legislation.gov.uk/ukpga/2003/41/contents.

13. Clive Nicholls, Clare Montgomery, Julian Knowles, Anand Doobay, Mark Summers, *The Law of Extradition and Mutual Assistance* (Oxford University Press), 2013.

14. Sir Scott Baker, David Perry, Anand Doobay, 'A review of the United Kingdom's Extradition Arrangements', September 2011, https://assets.publishing.service.gov.uk/government/uploads/system/uploads/attachment_data/file/117673/extradition-review.pdf

15. 'The Government response to Sir Scott Baker's Review of the United Kingdom's Extradition Arrangements', October 2012, https://assets.publishing.service.gov.uk/government/uploads/system/uploads/attachment_data/file/228566/8458.pdf

16. Regina v Governor of Brixton Prison, Ex parte Naranjan Singh (1962) 1 Q.B. 211.